Fourth Edition

Integrating Computer Technology into the Classroom

SKILLS FOR THE 21ST CENTURY

T0082367

Gary R. Morrison
Old Dominion University

Deborah L. Lowther
University of Memphis

PEARSON

Boston   New York   San Francisco
Mexico City   Montreal   Toronto   London   Madrid   Munich   Paris
Hong Kong   Singapore   Tokyo   Cape Town   Sydney

Acquisitions Editor: Kelly Villella Canton
Editorial Assistant: Annalea Manalili
Senior Development Editor: Mary Kriener
Vice President, Marketing and Sales Strategies: Emily Williams Knight
Vice President, Director of Marketing: Quinn Perkson
Senior Marketing Manager: Darcy Betts
Production Editor: Paula Carroll
Editorial Production Service and Interior Design: Omegatype Typography, Inc.
Composition Buyer: Linda Cox
Manufacturing Manager: Megan Cochran
Electronic Composition: Omegatype Typography, Inc.
Photo Researcher: Annie Pickert
Cover Designer: Elena Sidorova

For related titles and support materials, visit our online catalog at www.pearsonhighered.com.

Between the time website information is gathered and then published, it is not unusual for some sites to have closed. Also, the transcription of URLs can result in typographical errors. The publisher would appreciate notification where these errors occur so that they may be corrected in subsequent editions.

Many of the designations used by manufacturers and sellers to distinguish their products are claimed as trademarks. Where those designations appear in this book, and Allyn and Bacon was aware of a trademark claim, the designations have been printed in initial or all caps.

Library of Congress Cataloging-in-Publication Data

Morrison, Gary R., Ed. D.
 Integrating computer technology into the classroom : skills for the 21st century / Gary R. Morrison, Deborah L. Lowther.—4th ed.
  p. cm.
 Includes bibliographical references and index.
 ISBN-13: 978-0-13-514529-6 (pbk. : alk. paper)
 ISBN-10: 0-13-514529-5 (pbk. : alk. paper)
 1. Computer-assisted instruction. 2. Computer managed instruction. 3. Computers—Study and teaching. 4. Instructional systems—Design. I. Lowther, Deborah L. II. Title.
 LB1028.5.M6374 2010
 371.33'4—dc22

                                                                2009009548

Printed in the United States of America

10 9 8 7 6 5 4 3 2 1   EB   13 12 11 10 09

Credits appear on page 357 which constitutes an extension of the copyright page.

www.pearsonhighered.com

ISBN-10: 0-13-514529-5
ISBN-13: 978-0-13-514529-6

About the Authors

Gary R. Morrison received his doctorate in instructional systems technology from Indiana University. Since then he has worked as instructional designer at the University of Mid-America, Solar Turbines International, General Electric Company's Corporate Consulting Group, and Tenneco Oil Company. As a professor at the University of Memphis, he taught courses in instructional design and served as a faculty associate in the Center of Academic Excellence. Currently he is a professor and graduate program director in the Instructional Design and Technology Program at Old Dominion University, where he teaches courses in instructional design and distance learning. His credits include print projects, multimedia projects, and more than 30 hours of instructional video programs, including a five-part series that was aired nationally on PBS-affiliated stations.

Dr. Morrison has written more than 100 papers on topics related to instructional design and computer-based instruction and has contributed to several books and instructional software packages. He is co-author of *Designing Effective Instruction* with Steven M. Ross and Jerold E. Kemp. He is the editor of the *Journal of Computing in Higher Education* and former president of the Association for Educational Communications and Technology's Research and Theory Division, Design and Development Division, and Distance Learning Division.

Deborah L. Lowther received her doctorate in educational technology from Arizona State University. She was a seventh-grade science teacher before completing her doctoral work. She is currently a professor in the University of Memphis Department of Instruction and Curriculum Leadership. Her area of concentration is Instructional Design and Technology. She teaches courses primarily focused toward preparing preservice and inservice teachers to integrate computer technology into their curriculum. She also teaches courses that lead to state certification in instructional computing applications. Her research is centered on factors influencing the integration of technology into various learning environments. Dr. Lowther is the senior faculty researcher for technology at the University of Memphis Center for Research in Educational Policy. In this role, she has been the lead researcher on numerous studies investigating various aspects of K–12 technology integration. Her scholarly interests span from the international to the local level and include conference presentations, working with multiple grants focused toward technology integration, serving on advisory boards, and providing professional development to K–12 schools across the nation.

Brief Contents

Contents

When the first edition of *Integrating Computer Technology into the Classroom* was published in 1999, Google was a young startup company indexing an Internet of about 4.5 million pages. Since then, we have seen the introduction of such popular sites as YouTube, Facebook, and MySpace, as well as a wide array of Web 2.0 technologies that have permeated all areas of society including schools, government, news, shopping, and politics. As we finish the fourth edition of *Integrating Computer Technology into the Classroom,* some estimate that the Internet has grown to over 1.5 billion websites. The world of technology continues to change at an increasingly rapid pace.

In this rapidly changing world of technology, our goal to prepare students to use computers to solve meaningful problems extends not only to enhancing their 21st-century skills, but also to deepening their understanding of core content. We provide a rationale and model for integrating computer technology into the curriculum by using it as a tool rather than as an instructional delivery device. This book presents an approach to creating an integrated inquiry lesson that increases student engagement, higher-order learning, and, most importantly, preparation for using technology skillfully as a tool in both educational settings and the workplace. Our approach is structured to include the standards or benchmarks of the school district or state. We believe that computers can make a difference in student learning when teachers change the way they guide students to use computer technology in the classroom.

By using computers as a tool for problem solving, teachers provide an instructional environment that allows learners to construct meaning based on their individual experiences. This approach is quite different from the traditional approach of using computers for drill and practice and tutorials to help learners memorize information for a test. Our approach incorporates a variety of cognitive and constructive practices to create a student-centered learning environment that is highly active and motivational, resulting in increased student achievement.

Integrating Computer Technology into the Classroom is written with both preservice and inservice teachers in mind. For the preservice teacher, this book will meet the needs for an introductory instructional technology course, as well as for a methods course focused on problem-based learning. For the inservice teacher, *Integrating Computer Technology into the Classroom* also meets the needs for graduate-level technology courses, including advanced methods courses with a focus on problem-based learning. Additionally, this text can be used to illustrate how to integrate computers as a learning tool.

The primary focus of *Integrating Computer Technology into the Classroom* is not on developing basic computer literacy skills (though skill levels will increase as new functions are introduced and used), but rather to develop new methods for using computers in the classrooms. Our goal is to help teachers learn to determine when computers should be used and how to use them.

New to This Edition

The fourth edition of *Integrating Computer Technology into the Classroom* includes a number of additions that reflect the changes in the field of educational technology.

- **NTeQ Lesson Plans** have been added to Chapters 7–10, describing the key components of an NTeQ lesson in the context of the chapter.
- The fourth edition correlates to the **new ISTE National Educational Technology Standards for Students (NETS-S) and Teachers (NETS-T),** revised in 2007 and 2008, respectively.
- **New emphasis** on 21st-century skills throughout the text.
- **The Teacher's Diary** boxes document teacher experiences with incorporating the NTeQ model in the classroom.
- **New chapters** on hardware, software, Think Sheets, the Internet, multimedia, and graphic organizers provide a comprehensive, problem-based introduction to educational technology.
- **Teacher Technology FAQs** answer teachers' most common technology questions.
- **MyEducationLab** margin callouts in every chapter signal readers to go to the MyEducationLab site for Educational Technology. This rich, assignable online resource offers prospective teachers the opportunity to view live classroom footage, evaluate classroom lessons, access technology tutorials, download valuable assessment resources, and much more.

- **Major reorganization** streamlines the book to 12 manageable chapters and provides a logical approach to teaching technology integration:

  Chapter 1, "Rethinking Computers and Instruction," introduces the NTeQ model and provides a basis for using computer technology as a tool for solving problems.

  Chapter 2, "NTeQ: Designing an Integrated Lesson," focuses on developing an integrated lesson plan using the NTeQ model.

  Chapter 3, "Digital Tools in Today's Classrooms," presents a survey of hardware in today's classrooms ranging from desktop computers to webcams to USB drives.

  Chapter 4, "Computer Software in Today's Classrooms," examines the range of software available to teachers and students in today's classroom.

  Chapter 5, "Think Sheets: Using Technology for Higher-Order Thinking," focuses on the use and development of Think Sheets to encourage student engagement in higher-order thinking and analysis.

  Chapter 6, "Exploring the World Wide Web in the Classroom," explores a wide range of Internet resources and how to integrate them into the classroom.

  Chapters 7, "Word Processing," 8, "Spreadsheets," 9, "Integrating Multimedia as a Tool," and 10, "Graphic Organizers," describe how to integrate student use of word processing, spreadsheets, multimedia, and graphic organizers into inquiry-based lesson plans.

  Chapter 11, "Integrating Problem-Solving and Educational Software," focuses on integrating educational software into an NTeQ lesson.

  Chapter 12, "Teacher, Technology, and the Classroom," examines the characteristics of the technologically competent teacher, how to implement an NTeQ lesson plan, and how to manage a classroom with computers.

Features of This Edition

Integrating Computer Technology into the Classroom, Fourth Edition, includes a number of features that reinforce technology learning and understanding and help teachers learn to integrate technology into their classrooms.

- **The NTeQ Model** continues to be the central focus of the book, providing a research-based problem-solving model for integrating technology into the classroom. This edition includes refined concepts of the 10-step NTeQ model and increased emphasis on the role of *teacher as designer.*

- **Reflecting on What I Know** focus questions at the beginning of each chapter stimulate interest and focus learning.
- **Classroom Snapshot** vignettes begin each chapter by illustrating key concepts in an authentic context. Each example provides ideas and models for effectively integrating technology.
- **NTeQ Lesson Plans** provided at the end of selected chapters illustrate how to use the NTeQ model at different grade levels and in different disciplines.
- **Lesson Bytes** at the ends of Chapters 7–10 provide possible topics for developing integrated lessons using the tool described in the chapter.
- **NTeQ Portfolio Activities** at the end of each chapter offer reflection on the chapter content and various hands-on activities to reinforce learning. Students are challenged to reflect and develop their own perspectives on teaching with technology. Some chapters provide a framework for the students to develop an integrated lesson plan for immediate or future use. Students are encouraged to use these activities to develop a paper or electronic-based portfolio for teaching.
- **Technology Integration Activities** at the end of each chapter describe how to integrate the technology presented in the chapter into educational practices.

Supplements to the Text

- **The Instructor's Manual/Test Bank** offers a variety of chapter-by-chapter resources and ready-to-use classroom activities. The first section provides a sample outline for a 13-week course using *Integrating Computer Technology into the Classroom*. The manual then provides teaching strategies for each of the chapters, including **key chapter topics,** a **Getting Ready** section that provides suggestions on how to prepare and plan for the instruction on each chapter, **Lesson Tips** that offer activities for students that range from sample lesson plans to activities to developing an integrated lesson plan, and **MyEducationLab activities** that integrate valuable online assets that bring the classroom to life. The manual also includes **activity handouts** that can be duplicated or modified and Test Bank questions. This instructor resource is available for download by logging into the Instructor Resource Center from the Pearson Higher Education catalog (www.pearsonhighered .com/educator). Please contact your local Pearson representative if you need assistance downloading this manual.

- **The NTeQ website** (www.nteq.com) includes a variety of resources for preservice and inservice teachers. In particular, the **Lesson Plan Builder** offers students the opportunity to create lesson plans online following the NTeQ Model. Site visitors can also search for lesson plans by grade level, subject area, and topic area.

- **MyEducationLab** is a research-based learning tool that brings teaching to life. Through authentic in-class video footage, technology tutorials, case studies, examples of authentic teacher and student work, and more, MyEducationLab prepares you for your teaching career by showing what quality instruction looks like.

  - Book-specific practice tests help review chapter content.
  - Activities and Applications under each topic offer assignable activities that can be used to extend classroom learning and assess understanding. Authentic classroom videos provide students with immediate access to real classrooms where effective technology integration is happening. Students can watch teachers as they use technology in their classrooms to shape and support learning. Web activities connect readers with resources available to extend important concepts.
  - Building Teaching Skills and Dispositions activities, designed around key concepts in educational technology, help preservice and inservice teachers develop instructional skills important for technology integration.
  - Tutorials offer hands-on learning with software applications that teach basic skills such as using spreadsheets, presentation software, layout programs, classroom management and assessment, and much more.
  - Rubrics and Checklists provide valuable resources that can be incorporated into daily lesson planning.

  To start using MyEducationLab, activate the access code packaged with your book. If your instructor did not make MyEducationLab a required part of your course or if you are purchasing a used book without an access code, **go to www.myeducation lab.com to purchase access to this wonderful resource!**

Acknowledgments

For the fourth edition, we would like to thank Jennifer Maddrell and Julie Moustafa of Old Dominion University, who provided help with ideas for several chapters. Of course, we are still indebted to colleagues and students who have made contributions through the years.

Most of the ideas for the lesson plans in this book were conceived or suggested by our colleagues and classroom teachers, whom we want to thank for sharing. For ideas presented in the first edition we would like to offer a special thanks to the Project SMART teachers and to Dr. Richard Petersen, who gave us ideas and helped us develop some of the materials.

Several people deserve a special thank you. First, we want to thank Dr. Katherine Abraham, the Project SMART director, who was always willing to provide us with ideas related to the math curriculum and help with our spreadsheet and database problems. For the third edition, we would like to acknowledge ideas from the Anytime Anywhere Learning teachers in the Walled Lake Consolidated Schools and from many of our colleagues, including Steve M. Ross, Gary J. Anglin, J. Dan Strahl, Michael M. Grant, Lee E. Allen, Clif Mims, Julie Forbess, Amy Leggett-Overby, Yuki McNeil, Riley Bogema, and others.

Second, we want to thank Fran Clark, who not only helped us refine but also tested the NTeQ model in her third-grade classroom. She documented her experiences in many of The Teacher's Diary sections that appear throughout the book.

Finally, no project like this is possible without the assistance of reviewers who provided valuable feedback for this edition. These individuals include Sherry Allen, University of Southern Indiana; J. Michael Blocher, Northern Arizona University; Carol Brown, East Carolina University; Kathleen Conway, Hofstra University; Ana Cruz, St. Louis Community College at Meramec; A. Keith Dils, King's College; Ellen Dobson, East Carolina University; Linda Moss, Northeastern State University; Heidi Schnackenberg, SUNY Plattsburgh; Michael Spaulding, University of Tennessee at Martin; David Stoloff, Eastern Connecticut University; and Anastasia Trekles, Purdue University Calumet.

Gary R. Morrison
Deborah L. Lowther

Dear Teacher

As this country strives for positive change that will improve future opportunities as well as current situations, the impact of technology is a central and critical component. It is a clear and evident fact that students in today's classrooms need to emerge from high school with knowledge and skills that not only equal the education received by their parents, but also expand student capability to succeed in the 21st century. For these goals to be reached, today's teachers need to know how to create learning environments that equip students with basic subject-matter content and skills and how to think critically and solve real-world problems.

However, after numerous years of substantial funding for technology initiatives, integration of computer technology into classroom instruction has been a slow process. For example, education was ranked as the least technology-intensive enterprise among 55 U.S. industries (ESA, 2003). In addition, newly employed high school students at 400 U.S. businesses were deficient in most of the 21st-century knowledge and skills needed to achieve successful careers (Casner-Lotto & Barrington, 2006). These concerns may be related to general conceptions of how K–12 technology should be used versus how it is actually used. When observing nearly 10,000 K–12 classrooms, we found that direct instruction and student completion of worksheets were the most frequently used instructional practices and that computers were infrequently used or used for low-level activities such as drill and practice or word processing (Ross, Smith, Alberg, & Lowther, 2004). Though these findings sound dismal, the trend can be changed by implementing a student-centered approach in which students use computers to solve meaningful problems that are engaging, fun, and require use of 21st-century skills.

In this book we explore these ideas and present a clear and practical approach to enable you as a K–12 teacher to better prepare students for the 21st century. We guide you through the process by presenting you with the 10-step iNtegrating Technology for inQuiry (NTeQ) model for designing lessons. We provide detailed descriptions of the types of hardware and software used in today's classrooms and give you numerous ideas for integrating these resources into your lessons. We also present strategies for implementing computer integration lessons and managing students during computer use. In other words, this book provides the information, examples, and resources to help you become a 21st-century teacher.

Enjoy the transition!

Gary R. Morrison
Deborah L. Lowther

Rethinking Computers and Instruction

Getting Started

The United States has a history of introducing technology into the schools to solve educational problems (see Figure 1.1). Shortly after the launch of Sputnik in 1957, Congress passed the National Defense Education Act to improve science and math achievement in public schools. One aspect of this plan was to place an overhead projector in most if not all K–12 classrooms. In the 1960s, we saw the introduction of both programmed instruction and educational television in the classroom. In the early 1980s, microcomputers were introduced into the classroom. During the 1990s, we saw federal and state initiatives enacted to place more computer technology in K–12 classrooms in the hope that technology would again solve our educational problems. At the start of the 21st century, we saw schools adding wireless connections, laptops, and a variety of digital tools to the classroom.

Although Bork (1987) predicted that microcomputers would revolutionize our schools, after numerous years of substantial federal and state funding for technology initiatives, we have yet to see any large-scale gains attributed to the infusion of this latest technology into the classroom. For example, a study by the U.S. Department of Commerce examining 55 U.S. industries revealed that education is ranked as the least technology-intensive enterprise (ESA, 2003). In addition, students graduating from U.S. high schools were rated by 400 U.S. employers as being deficient in most of the 21st-century

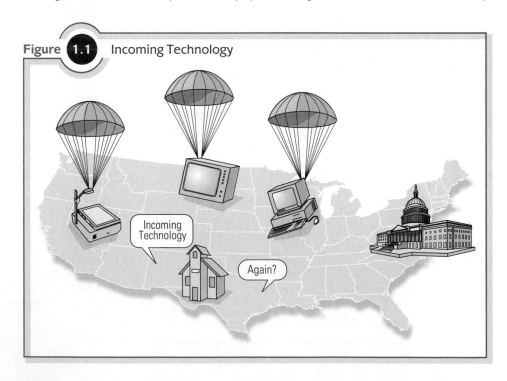

Figure 1.1   Incoming Technology

knowledge and skills needed to achieve successful careers (Casner-Lotto & Barrington, 2006). One reason the revolution has yet to start may be due to the discrepancy between general conceptions of how we should use technology in our schools versus how it is actually used. This chapter explores these ideas and discusses how to prepare students for the 21st century; it explores the link between educational reform and technology and ends by presenting the iNtegrating Technology for inQuiry (NTeQ) model. The NTeQ model provides step-by-step guidance for creating lessons that engage students in the use of 21st-century knowledge and skills while improving learning in core content areas.

Reflecting on What I Know

1 Must I use a inquiry-based learning approach in my classroom to use computers as a tool?

2 Can I still use tutorials and drill-and-practice software?

3 Won't I have to spend a great deal of time to develop these units of instruction?

4 Won't every student need a computer to use it as a tool?

Classroom SNAPSHOT

Ms. Londhe and Mr. Drake are high school teachers in a school that is well equipped with technology. However, the two teachers use computers very differently. Ms. Londhe has students use laptops for real-world investigations to learn social studies while Mr. Drake uses computers to deliver biology instruction. Which method do you think will result in greater student learning? Let's examine a technology lesson from each classroom.

As Ms. Londhe's ninth-grade social studies students entered the classroom, each took a laptop computer from the cart before sitting down. Our first hint that this class would be quite different from any other was the way the students were seated. Some were clustered in spots on the furniture and floor around the perimeter of the room. Others were moving desks together to accommodate groups of four or five students. Rather than beginning with a lecture, Ms. Londhe simply said, "Class, let's get started in continuing to solve this week's problem: How is our state dependent on other states and which states depend on our state?" Immediately, the students started to work as Ms. Londhe walked around the room to ask questions, listen to student thoughts, and provide guidance.

The students actively discussed ways to determine how the economy of one state depends on that of another. They were researching industries in each state, mapping the major roads and rails from manufacturing centers, finding information on employment and income, and determining what each state manufactured, as well as the source of natural resources and raw materials needed for the products. Some groups of students were working together on one computer while other teams appeared to have divided the work among individual team members. URLs, tables, and charts were all emailed to other members of the team when a piece of information that could solve the problem was found.

In Mr. Drake's ninth-grade biology class, students were studying the human skeleton. The students were sitting two at a computer and working through a computer lesson to help them memorize the name of major bones. In the tutorial software, a student could move the cursor over a bone, so the name appeared and the student could hear the correct pronunciation. There was little dialoging between the students other than who would control the mouse or which bone to do next. Mr. Drake's room was very orderly and quiet compared to Ms. Londhe's class.

Preparing Students for the 21st Century

A clear distinction is evident between student use of computers in Ms. Londhe's class as compared to Mr. Drake's class. Although both would probably receive high marks for technology integration on the principal's yearly evaluation, the inherent benefit to students in the two settings is remarkably different. When students use computers to *retrieve, evaluate, and manipulate* real-world information to solve a meaningful problem, they not only increase their 21st-century skills, but also gain a deeper understanding of core content. On the other hand, when technology is used to *deliver* instruction, 21st-century skills are not required and the context is less authentic and focused more on retention of facts or procedural knowledge. Although one can agree with the general consensus that students need to use technology during the school day in order to prepare them for future careers, actual classroom practices often fall short of this ideal use. So was Bork (1987) correct in predicting that computers would "revolutionize" education? Yes—with a caveat. Technology does have the potential to transform education if teachers reform their instructional practices to engage students in meaningful learning and use of 21st-century knowledge and skills. However, for the most part today's schools have not yet experienced Bork's "revolution."

21st-Century Knowledge and Skills

Concerns over these issues have led to the creation of partnerships and alliances of key businesses, associations, and institutions to identify and achieve solutions. A 2007 report released by the International Society for Technology in Education

Together, students
use a computer to
solve problems.

(ISTE), the Partnership for 21st Century Skills, and the State Educational Technology Directors Association (21st Century Education System Task Force, 2007) addressed these concerns:

> How will we create the schools America needs to remain competitive? For more than a generation, the nation has engaged in a monumental effort to improve student achievement. We've made progress, but we're not even close to where we need to be. It's time to focus on what students need to learn—and on how to create a 21st century education system that delivers results. In a digital world, no organization can achieve results without incorporating technology into every aspect of its everyday practices. It's time for schools to maximize the impact of technology as well. (p. 2)

The Partnership for 21st Century Skills (2008) indicates that all students, regardless of their desired career path (college, trade school, or entry-level job), require 21st-century skills to succeed in work, school, and life. These skills, grouped under five general headings, include the following:

- **Knowledge of Core Subjects:** English, reading or language arts, world languages, arts, mathematics, economics, science, geography, history, government and civics
- **21st Century Themes:** global awareness, financial, economic, business and entrepreneurial literacy, civic literacy, and health literacy
- **Learning and Innovation Skills:** creativity and innovation skills, critical thinking and problem-solving skills, communication and collaboration skills.
- **Information, Media, and Technology Skills:** information literacy, media literacy, and ICT (information and communication technology) literacy
- **Life and Career Skills:** flexibility and adaptability, initiative and self-direction, social and cross-cultural skills, productivity and accountability, and leadership and responsibility (p. 13)

Most educators would agree that students in today's schools should emerge from high school with the ability to apply this list of 21st-century knowledge and skills. Yet the concern over "how" to integrate this new curriculum approach into classroom instruction can be somewhat daunting to new and often even more so to experienced teachers. ISTE has addressed this concern through the creation of National Educational Technology Standards for Students (ISTE, 2007).

National Educational Technology Standards for Students

ISTE has extended their full support to meet the critical need for students to emerge from high school with the requisite 21st-century knowledge and skills evidenced in their National Educational Technology Standards for Students (NETS-S). As shown in Figure 1.2 and Table 1.1, the NETS-S (ISTE, 2007) assist teachers in defining and integrating 21st-century knowledge and skills into their everyday teaching practices. ISTE supplements the NETS-S by providing teachers with Profiles for Technology (ICT) Literate Students for grades PK–2, 3–5, 6–8, and 9–12. The profiles provide example learning activities to help teachers better understand what effective technology integration "looks like" when implemented in the classroom. ISTE emphasizes the importance of students regularly using a variety of digital tools

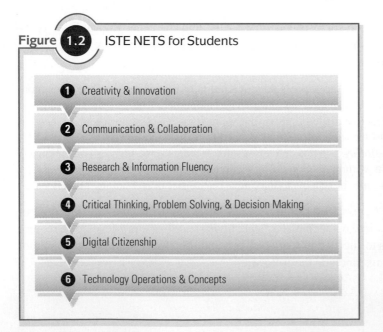

Figure 1.2   ISTE NETS for Students

1. Creativity & Innovation
2. Communication & Collaboration
3. Research & Information Fluency
4. Critical Thinking, Problem Solving, & Decision Making
5. Digital Citizenship
6. Technology Operations & Concepts

Table 1.1	ISTE National Educational Technology Standards for Students (NETS-S)

1. Creativity and Innovation	Students demonstrate creative thinking, construct knowledge, and develop innovative products and processes using technology.	Students: a) apply existing knowledge to generate new ideas, products, or processes. b) create original works as a means of personal or group expression. c) use models and simulations to explore complex systems and issues. d) identify trends and forecast possibilities.
2. Communication and Collaboration	Students use digital media and environments to communicate and work collaboratively, including at a distance, to support individual learning and contribute to the learning of others.	Students: a) interact, collaborate, and publish with peers, experts, or others employing a variety of digital environments and media. b) communicate information and ideas effectively to multiple audiences using a variety of media and formats. c) develop cultural understanding and global awareness by engaging with learners of other cultures. d) contribute to project teams to produce original works or solve problems.
3. Research and Information Fluency	Students apply digital tools to gather, evaluate, and use information.	Students: a) plan strategies to guide inquiry. b) locate, organize, analyze, evaluate, synthesize, and ethically use information from a variety of sources and media. c) evaluate and select information sources and digital tools based on the appropriateness to specific tasks. d) process data and report results.
4. Critical Thinking, Problem Solving, and Decision Making	Students use critical-thinking skills to plan and conduct research, manage projects, solve problems, and make informed decisions using appropriate digital tools and resources.	Students: a) identify and define authentic problems and significant questions for investigation. b) plan and manage activities to develop a solution or complete a project. c) collect and analyze data to identify solutions and/or make informed decisions. d) use multiple processes and diverse perspectives to explore alternative solutions.
5. Digital Citizenship	Students understand human, cultural, and societal issues related to technology and practice legal and ethical behavior.	Students: a) advocate and practice safe, legal, and responsible use of information and technology. b) exhibit a positive attitude toward using technology that supports collaboration, learning, and productivity. c) demonstrate personal responsibility for lifelong learning. d) exhibit leadership for digital citizenship.
6. Technology Operations and Concepts	Students demonstrate a sound understanding of technology concepts, systems, and operations.	Students: a) understand and use technology systems. b) select and use applications effectively and productively. c) troubleshoot systems and applications. d) transfer current knowledge to learning of new technologies.

Source: From the International Society for Technology in Education (ISTE), *National Education Technology Standards for Students,* Second Edition. © 2007. www.iste.org. All rights reserved. Reprinted by permission.

from the time they enter school through graduation. It is this continuous involvement that results in student mastery of 21st-century skills.

If you reexamine the Classroom Snapshot presented earlier, you will discover that Ms. Londhe's lesson fulfilled many of the recommended 21st-century knowledge and skills addressed in the NETS-S. For example, the lesson developed knowledge of core content by focusing on the social studies aspect of state economics, while embedding 21st-century content by having students research and analyze the financial and business aspects of employment, income, and natural resources. Students' learning and thinking skills were developed through examining a real-world problem that had contextual importance because students studied the state in which they lived. The lesson also built on students' information and communication technology literacy through the requirement to locate and evaluate online data about their state and other states that had an economic connection with their state. And finally, students strengthened their life skills by working together in collaborative groups to investigate and "solve" the posed problem.

The goals and direction for use of computers in today's schools is clear. Yet reaching these goals is challenging for several reasons. Our schools are still quite traditional in their approach to teaching. Some of this is the result of federal initiatives such as No Child Left Behind (U.S. Department of Education, 2001) that require improved achievement on standardized tests. Other factors include use of outdated "industrial" models as well as the persistence of initial beliefs that a key role of technology is to "teach" students rather than to use technology as a tool to help them discover new knowledge. Educational reform is viewed as a start in the right direction.

Linking Educational Reform and Technology

Since the beginning of the 20th century, schools in the United States have operated on a factory model. Their aim was to create obedient and competent workers for the many factories and industries that were a part of the industrial revolution. Thus, like factory workers, students sat individually in rows, completing their individual tasks, memorizing their work, and learning not to question but rather to obey authority. As the century progressed, industry changed. Specialized workers with communication skills who could work as part of a team, think independently, and question the status quo were needed.

Schools, however, have remained essentially unchanged since the early 1900s. Soon after the publication of *A Nation at Risk* (National Commission on Excellence in Education, 1983), educators, politicians, parents, and citizens began to look critically at the educational process, which resulted in the current educational reform movement. These various reforms have taken many paths, but a consistent theme was to break from the traditional factory models of education. An early criticism of past reform movements was the lack of a relationship between educational reform and educational technology (Means, 1994). One reason for the lack of technology integration into the restructured schools may be attributed to both the way technology is used and the types of technology available.

Technology has typically been used to *deliver* instruction, practice, and feedback. The most common types of software used in the classroom are drill-and-practice/educational games, which are based on a behavioral approach to teaching and emphasize rote memorization (Ross, Smith, Alberg, & Lowther, 2004). This approach to using technology and software is inconsistent with current reform initiatives, which focus on preparing students for the 21st century. Specifically, the newer educational models encourage teachers to implement a student-centered approach in open-ended environments that engage collaborative groups of students in using technology to solve meaningful problems.

Achieving educational reform involves multiple facets ranging from administrative support to parent and community involvement, as well as integrating 21st-century knowledge and skills into the instruction. The following section discusses some basic themes of educational reform and technology: student-centered learning, open-ended learning, and collaborative learning.

Moving from Teacher-Centered to Student-Centered Instruction

The emphasis on increasing student achievement within a context of school reform has resulted in an increased use of standardized achievement tests, such as the Iowa Tests of Basic Skills, to assess student progress. Teachers must focus on how they can improve student achievement as measured on a specific test. There seems to be a clear dichotomy of approaches teachers take in addressing the benchmarks and standards assessed by these tests (Newmann, Bryk, & Nagaoka, 2001). One approach is teacher centered, with a focus on memorization of facts, formulas, dates, names, and so on. The student is then expected to recall the exact information for the test. The second approach focuses on authentic intellectual work in a student-centered environment. This approach requires students to formulate problems, collect information and data, organize and manipulate the information and data, and then formulate an answer. The debate between these two approaches has been fueled by the increased demand for accountability required by the No Child Left Behind Act, which often translates into increased use of standardized tests. However, research also shows that use of technology in student-centered learning environments can result in improved achievement as a result of innovative teaching strategies.

A study by Newmann and colleagues (2001) found that the authentic learning approach in a student-centered environment produced substantially more achievement gains than the teacher-centered memorization approach. Newmann and his associates studied 400 classrooms in 19 different elementary schools. They analyzed over 2000 classroom assignments and standardized scores for almost 5000 students. When they analyzed the results of classrooms using high-quality assignments (i.e., those involving authentic intellectual activities), they found that the learning gains were 20 percent greater than the national average. Students who were in classrooms that focused primarily on a memorization approach scored 25 percent *less* in reading and 22 percent *less* in mathematics than the national average. Newmann and his colleagues also found that high-quality assignments in mathematics tended to help the low-achieving students even more than their high-achieving classmates. The low-achieving students showed a 29 percent gain in achievement over similar students in classes that focused on a more direct instructional approach. Overall, the results indicate that both high- and low-achieving students in a classroom that stresses high-quality intellectual assignments benefit with resulting increases in achievement.

These results suggest that combining the use of computer technology as a tool with an emphasis on problem solving and reflection will result in increased student achievement. The key component for achieving this combination is the use of student-centered instructional practices. In the following paragraphs, we will describe the theoretical basis for using a student-centered learning environment and examine three components of this environment that serve as the structural foundation for effective technology integration: open-ended learning environments, learning context, and collaborative learning.

Theoretical Basis for Student-Centered Learning.   There are three basic premises of a student-centered learning environment. First, student-centered learning emphasizes understanding one's world rather than mimicking (i.e., rote memorization of) the content. Understanding is a result of the learner reshaping and transforming information (Gardner, 1991). Understanding one's world requires the student to actively process and manipulate information. Second, students will strive to reduce discrepancies between what they know and what they observe. Savery and Duffy (1995) refer to this phenomenon as *puzzlement*. This cognitive dissonance (Festinger,

1957) between what the student knows and what is observed is a motivating factor for seeking resolution of the difference by developing a new understanding (Brooks & Brooks, 1993). Third, one's knowledge is refined through negotiations with others and evaluation of individual understanding (Savery & Duffy, 1995). Students use other students to test their understanding and examine the understanding of others. This collection of understanding provides a means for an individual to evaluate and understand propositions, which when grouped together are called *knowledge*. Collaborative groups allow a student to learn the views of others in order to challenge and test the viability of his or her own views. The teacher's responsibility is to understand what and how students think.

Creating Open-Ended Learning Environments

One characteristic of a student-centered teaching approach is the use of open-ended learning environments. These environments often require students to solve a problem, which exposes them to new information. As a result, students gain new understanding by reshaping and transforming their knowledge. This section focuses on the features of an open-ended learning environment and discusses three open-ended approaches: inquiry-based learning, problem-based learning, and project-based learning.

Open-ended learning environments focus on the learner by allowing the learner to make decisions about what information is needed and what approach should be taken to solve a problem. These environments stand in contrast to traditional instruction, in which content is selected and transmitted through lectures and assigned readings in textbooks. Open-ended methods can also vary in the amount of structure and direction the teacher provides (Albanese & Mitchell, 1993; Land & Hannafin, 1997). Direction from the teacher can range from providing specific tutoring or resources to coaching individual students on how to identify needed information.

Open-ended learning environments also require the teacher to adopt new approaches. The primary mode of teaching switches from one of lecturing to one of facilitating student investigation. Teachers work as facilitators and tutors to help students understand the material and to provide the necessary scaffolding. The emphasis is on the student developing an understanding of the material through direct contact with information, data collection, and data manipulation. Students then generate and test hypotheses and determine the best solution.

Selecting content for an open-ended learning unit is a process of negotiation involving input from students and knowledge of curriculum frameworks. Teachers must consider standards imposed by their school district or state and those recommended by national associations (e.g., National Council of Teachers of Mathematics) when designing the units. Similarly, students should have input based on their interests. The final objectives for the unit evolve from discussions between the teacher and students on how to address the problem as identified by expressed societal needs and the interests of the students, while meeting curriculum standards. Guidelines for achieving this combination are discussed below.

The terms *problem-based, inquiry-based,* and *project-based learning* are often used interchangeably by educators. While all three are examples of open-ended learning environment strategies, there are subtle differences. All three approaches have a problem as the central focus of the strategy. The teacher's role, however, varies in each. Within each strategy it is critical to ensure that the learning context is meaningful to the students. For example, traditional textbooks and instruction separate learning from the context. The effectiveness and appropriateness of this practice has long been questioned by researchers (Brown, Collins, & Duguid, 1989; Bruner, 1960). For example, a common time–distance math problem might appear as "It is 932 miles between Philadelphia and St. Louis. A car leaves Philadelphia at 8:00 A.M. headed west and traveling 65 miles per hour. A second car leaves St. Louis at 8:00 A.M. headed east traveling at 57 miles per hour. What time will they meet?" A logical answer is "Never," because the car from Philadelphia is headed to Chicago and the car from St. Louis is headed to Nashville! The author of this fictional problem (and others like it) intended both cars to take the same route and for the student to calculate when they would meet. Consider, however, a student who lives in Memphis and has never traveled from St. Louis to Philadelphia or visited the two cities. The instruction failed to provide a meaningful context for the learner. Imagine the same problem being posed in the city or town where the students live. It involves two cars traveling from different directions along a well-known road at different speeds to reach a popular park (both within the speed limit). The solution requires the same math skills, but the context is meaningful and will result in more student engagement (Jonassen, Howland, Marra, & Crismond, 2008).

Inquiry-Based Learning.   Inquiry learning, which has been widely used in K–12 education for many years, is based on the writings of John Dewey (1916). Inquiry strategies start with a question and then engage students in problem-solving activities. As the students explore, gather data, and analyze their data, they create new knowledge. The teacher's role in inquiry learning is one of a facilitator and provider of information (Savery, 2006). Ill-structured problems that have multiple solutions and multiple paths to a solution (Jonassen, 1997) are favored over well-structured problems that have one correct answer.

Problem-Based Learning. Problem-based learning (PBL) was first used in medical education (Barrows, 1985) and then adopted by K–12 educators. Ill-structured problems are also typical of problem-based learning instruction, providing the learner with a broad area of exploration. Like inquiry learning, PBL encourages the development of understanding and skills through exploration and experimentation. The teacher's role in PBL differs from the role in inquiry learning. In PBL, the teacher acts as a facilitator, but does not provide information to the learner. Instead, the learners are expected to seek out the necessary information needed to solve the problem (Savery, 2006).

Project-Based Learning. Like inquiry learning and PBL, project-based learning is also an active learning strategy that often focuses on a problem. The problem in project-based learning is well structured such that the learners are provided with the specifications for the end project (Savery, 2006), such as determining the percentage of people voting in a district, creating a bird-friendly area in the school yard, or charting the growth of the federal deficit. Student learning is focused on following a process described by the teacher, whether a series of steps for doing a calculation or reading specific teacher-provided materials. In contrast to the first two methods, the teacher's role in project-based learning is more likely to be as a coach who provides feedback and guidance (Savery, 2006).

It is easy to see why these terms are often used interchangeably, as they all focus on solving a problem, and the teacher's role in each approach is quite different than that of a lecturer in a teacher-centered classroom. These three strategies provide a means to integrate computer technology into the classroom through the use of authentic problems that are of interest to your students. The remainder of this book will focus on how to develop lesson plans to use all three of these approaches to integrate technology. You will need to select either inquiry learning, problem-based learning, or project-based learning as the strategy that best fits your teaching style and the needs of your students.

PEARSON
myeducationlab
The Power of Classroom Practice

Go to MyEducationLab, select the topic "Diverse Populations," and go to the Activities and Applications section. Access the video "Using Technology to Meet Objectives" and consider how technology can be incorporated into classroom instruction. Complete the activity that follows.

Achieving Collaborative Learning

Teachers and students today are required now more than ever to collaborate in their work. Reform movements push teachers toward site-based management, team planning, peer coaching, and community partnerships; thus we can no longer accept the notion of the teacher as an isolated decision maker. Our evolving society requires citizens to have specialized skills. Employees must be able to work as part of a team, support a larger vision, and communicate and work effectively with others. Therefore teachers are not only modeling collaboration in their own work, but they are also required to use instructional processes that facilitate collaboration and the development of social skills among their students.

The Social Nature of Learning.   The social impact on learning has been discussed for centuries by scholars such as Aristotle, Dewey (1916), and Vygotsky (1978). As people attempt to find meaning in an experience or encounter, they reflect on their beliefs, values, and concepts, which all arise from a common and shared understanding within their culture. Although a collaborative environment involving several learners can be advantageous, students also often benefit from the opportunity to "articulate, reflect, and scaffold" (Herrington & Oliver, 2000) with one partner. Collaborative learning also aligns with a constructivist approach that supports the notion of the self-construction of meaning within a *social* context. Although constructivists emphasize the self-construction of meaning, it would be a misconception to believe that whatever an individual thinks is in fact "the truth."

Collaborative versus Traditional Group Learning.   How can teachers effectively capitalize on the social nature of learning? Many educators are now taught to integrate small-group learning into their pedagogy. However, as more teachers move toward the use of group learning arrangements such as dyads, triads, and collaborative learning, it is important to distinguish features of teaching that promote cooperation and the development of social skills from features of traditional group work (see Table 1.2).

The development of group social skills is necessary when integrating technology as a tool. A collaborative group is doomed to failure when given a task without appropriate teacher support to develop the necessary social and technical skills needed to complete the assignment. Often group members passively sit while others work at the computer or on different aspects of the assignment. To avoid this problem it is important for a teacher to require groups to use a system to decide and record how the tasks will be divided and how students will accept responsibility for their assigned tasks. The use of technology in group work also provides the opportunity for students to educate one another. For example, if a student is unfamiliar with a web browser, the teacher might decide to assign that student the responsibility for locating websites on a given topic with the support of a knowledgeable student sitting alongside as they work. The learners are empowered as they acquire new skills, and the students serving as coaches become empowered through the opportunity to educate others.

In reading what it takes to create a "reformed" classroom in which the instruction is student centered and problem based, engaging students in meaningful col-

Table 1.2	Collaborative versus Traditional Groups

Collaborative Groups	**Traditional Learning Groups**
Heterogeneous	Homogeneous
Social skills emphasized	Social skills assumed
Task and group performance emphasized	Only task emphasized
Teacher observes and facilitates	Teacher ignores group functioning
Shared leadership and responsibility	One leader and self-responsibility
Interdependent	No interdependence

Source: Adapted from D. W. Johnson, R. T. Johnson, & K. A. Smith, *Active Learning: Cooperation in the College Classroom.* Edina, MN: Interaction Book Company, 1991.

laborative group work, you may think that achieving Bork's "revolution" is a distant dream. The good news is that the strategies described in this chapter are achievable when you begin with and follow a step-by-step model designed for creating 21st-century classrooms, called the iNtegrating Technology for inQuiry, or the NTeQ model (pronounced "in-tech").

The NTeQ Model

The NTeQ model uses an easy-to-follow ten-step lesson plan as the basis for achieving computer integration lessons (see Figure 1.3). However, even if you develop a "super" lesson plan, it probably won't be successful unless it is implemented in an environment that is student centered, uses a form of inquiry instruction, and engages students in meaningful collaborative group work. In other words, the philosophical approach for creating this "reformed" environment needs to be different from a traditional approach. The philosophy of the NTeQ model provides the foundation needed to create reformed classrooms in which students gain requisite 21st-century knowledge and skills.

NTeQ Philosophy

The five basic components of the NTeQ philosophy are the teacher, the student, the computer, the lesson, and the learning environment (see Figure 1.4). The NTeQ model, when successfully implemented, will have the following characteristics:

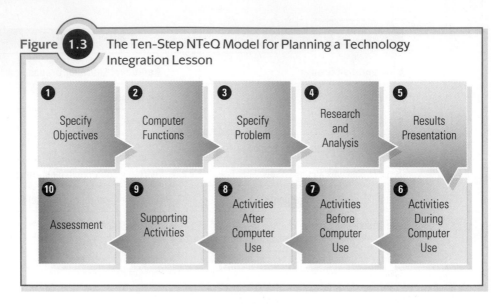

Figure 1.3 The Ten-Step NTeQ Model for Planning a Technology Integration Lesson

1. The teacher is technologically competent and assumes the roles of designer, manager, and facilitator.
2. The student actively engages in the learning process, assuming the role of researcher and gaining technological competence.
3. The computer is used as a tool, as it is in the workplace, to enhance learning through the use of real-world data to solve problems.
4. The lesson is student centered, problem based, and authentic, and technology is an integral component.
5. The environment incorporates multiple resource-rich activities.

NTeQ and the Teacher

It is assumed that if teachers learn how to use word processing, a browser, and a spreadsheet or are computer literate, they will be able to integrate technology into their lessons. Yet many teachers who have basic computer skills often let the computers sit idly at the back of the classroom or have students use them for simple drill-and-practice or educational games (Lowther, Inan, Strahl, & Ross, 2008). For classrooms to be reformed, teachers need to go beyond computer literacy to become technologically competent, as shown in the following three-step process:

1. Teachers need to personally experience using the computer as a tool to learn new information.

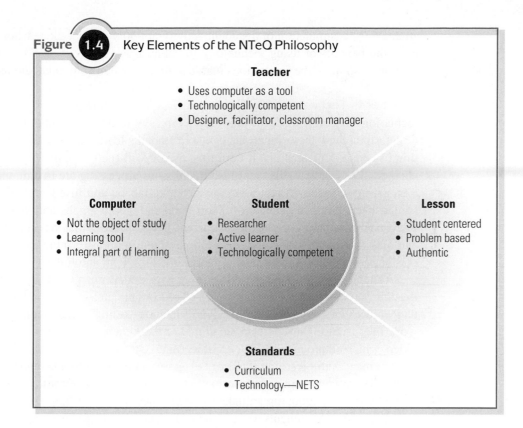

Figure **1.4** Key Elements of the NTeQ Philosophy

Teacher
- Uses computer as a tool
- Technologically competent
- Designer, facilitator, classroom manager

Computer
- Not the object of study
- Learning tool
- Integral part of learning

Student
- Researcher
- Active learner
- Technologically competent

Lesson
- Student centered
- Problem based
- Authentic

Standards
- Curriculum
- Technology—NETS

2. Teachers need to understand the relationship between basic computer functions and student learning.
3. Teachers need to use their knowledge of student learning and technology to design, manage, and facilitate a student-centered learning environment.

Teacher Uses Computer as a Learning Tool. Most of us have spent the majority of our academic lives in a traditional classroom in which the teacher typically lectured while the students listened and sometimes took notes. Classroom activities included answering questions at the back of the book or on a worksheet, copying diagrams from books, drawing pictures, writing stories, doing science activities, and taking quizzes. So when we ask teachers to assume the new role of a facilitator and to create lessons that integrate the use of technology as a tool, they have little if any prior experience or models to draw on. Therefore it is imperative for teachers to experience learning activities similar to those they are expected to use with their students. This simulation of a student activity not only will let the teachers experience the benefits of using technology to enhance learning but also will let them encounter some of the frustrations that tend to arise when computers are used.

Teacher Is Technologically Competent. With the NTeQ model, teachers gain technological competence in that they learn how to analyze computer functions to determine how these functions can help students learn. Each computer application has basic functions that it performs, as you will see throughout the remaining chapters. For example, the key functions of word processing are to edit and format text, create outlines, format columns, generate tables, and insert graphs, whereas spreadsheets perform calculations, sort data, and create graphs and charts. If you examine the functions of graphic organizers, you'll discover that they insert graphics and audio/video files, add text, create links, capture brainstorming ideas, generate outlines from concept maps, and organize graphics, text, and links.

The next logical step is to determine how students can use these capabilities to achieve one or more lesson objectives. For example, in a traditional lesson on endangered species, typical student activities include reading the textbook, completing worksheets, writing a report on an animal of their choice, and perhaps watching a video, which all produce a low level of learning. On the other hand, students can engage in meaningful learning if use of the appropriate digital tool is integrated into a lesson. The students can enter information into a graphic organizer to discover common elements by grouping animals by where they live, what they eat, or why they are endangered. As students work with the data, patterns begin to emerge, giving rise to new questions and new ways to look at and learn the information. For example, are carnivores or omnivores more likely to become extinct? Which continent has the most endangered species? Which group of animals is the most threatened? By having the students use computers to examine information and solve problems, they emerge with a deeper level of understanding.

Teacher Is Designer, Facilitator, and Classroom Manager. Once teachers understand how to integrate student use of basic computer functions into lessons, they can combine this understanding with what they know about how students learn to create an environment that integrates technology to enhance learning. Generating the *design* is the first step (see Chapter 2). When the teacher assumes the role of a designer, each aspect of the NTeQ lesson must be considered and carefully arranged to support and foster meaningful student learning.

The next step in creating the learning environment involves the teacher assuming the role of a *facilitator*. In a traditional classroom, the teacher provides the students with what they are to learn, typically with a lecture or by assigning a chapter of the textbook. In a reformed classroom, the teacher as facilitator does not tell the students information they need to learn but rather provides a resource-rich environment through which the students are guided into learning. In this environment, the students work collaboratively to learn or solve a problem. The teacher as facilitator keeps a close watch on the progress of each group and asks directed questions to stimulate student thinking and decision making. Facilitation also involves teachers modeling various processes for the students. This modeling can include both physical processes, such as how to create spreadsheet charts, and cognitive processes, such as describing each step the teacher might take to solve a problem. Facilitation has long been known to ensure students receive the necessary scaffolding or remediation to proceed with the learning (Vygotsky, 1978).

The last step to create the environment, *classroom management,* involves not only planning but also the actual management of a classroom that now has computers. The NTeQ lesson plan depicts what the students do before they use the computer, their activities at the computer, and activities after using the computer. One way to plan for managing a technology-based lesson is for the teacher to actually use the software to create a product similar to what the students will produce during the lesson. This activity not only gives the teacher the expertise to handle student problems as they arise but also ensures that the lesson can be completed. The management plan also should include procedures for addressing two technology-related issues: lack of student computer skills and technical problems. The use of job aids (simple instruction sheets posted in the computer area) can help, and teachers can employ the assistance of the students who are "computer experts."

NTeQ and the Student

When examining the role of students in relation to the NTeQ model, we find that students are affected in the following three important ways:

1. The student is actively engaged in the learning process.
2. The student assumes the role of a researcher.
3. The student gains technological competence.

Student Is Active Learner. Students involved in a lesson based on the NTeQ model spend very little time, if any at all, sitting quietly at their desks while they take notes on the teacher's lecture. They also very rarely, if ever, answer the chapter questions in their history or science books. Instead, the students are involved in a learning environment that has small groups of students collaboratively solving problems using real-life resources. This approach is seen in the scenario of Ms. Londhe's class presented in the Classroom Snapshot. In this learning environment, the students were actively and collaboratively engaged in collecting and analyzing actual data that affect each state's economy. This type of active engagement and discussion with peers reinforces what is being learned by giving students the opportunity to apply their knowledge.

Student Is a Researcher.   The inquiry approach taken with the NTeQ model places the students into the role of researchers. The students are not merely given the information they must learn; rather, they are given situations they must investigate. During the investigation, or problem-solving process, the students work collaboratively to solve the problem, which leads to learning the appropriate concepts and principles. For the students to solve the situation or problem, they must use the techniques of a researcher, or the scientific method: identify the problem, formulate a hypothesis, collect and analyze data, and draw conclusions. Implementing the NTeQ Problem-Solving Process in Chapter 5 helps guide students through the steps needed to successfully conduct an inquiry.

Student Gains Technological Competence.   When students are given the opportunity to learn in an environment that is based on the NTeQ model, they will begin to become technologically competent. Technological competence means the student has achieved the following:

- Capably uses basic computer applications often found in the workplace, such as word processing, database, spreadsheet, graphics, Internet browser, email, and presentation applications
- Understands the capabilities of each type of computer application and when and where it is appropriate to use each one

This technological competence will enable students to gain more from their K–12 and postsecondary education and benefit them throughout their future careers.

NTeQ and the Computer

Computer Is Not the Object of Study.   The role of the computer in the NTeQ model is based on two ideas. First, the computer is not the point of emphasis, yet it is a critical component. In other words, there is no emphasis on learning the history of computers or the electronic functions of a computer. Most people in the business world know very little about how computers operate, yet, for example, they use computers all day long to solve complex financial problems for major corporations.

Computer Is a Learning Tool.   Second, we view the computer as a learning tool, similar to a calculator. When calculators were introduced into the classroom, students were not expected to learn the history of calculators or how the electronic circuitry enabled the calculator to function. Instead, students were shown the basics of how a calculator could assist them in solving math problems. The computer should be viewed in the same manner. It is a tool that can help students look at information in new and different ways. In other words, the computer is used as an extension of what students are able to do for themselves because computer functions closely align with students' abilities. The computer, however, is more efficient in performing these functions (see the Appendix for a list of computer functions aligned to learning tasks). Thus, students can place a greater emphasis on discovering new ideas rather than on sorting and classifying data. For example, students in Ms. Londhe's class could have compared states without a computer, but it would have taken a tremendous amount of time for the students to experiment with the different economic factors. With the use of a spreadsheet, the students can quickly and accurately experiment with the information to reach the best solution. Both the spreadsheet and the state information sheets are artifacts we use to make us smarter (Norman, 1993). The computer, however, is more efficient and allows the students more time to attend to higher-order thinking tasks. Students are then free to focus on the "why, what, and where" questions that can help them discover relevant principles. If we use the computer as a tool for solving problems, it can enhance interest and motivation by providing access to information outside the classroom and allowing students to manipulate data in a variety of ways (Blumenfeld et al., 1991).

Computer Is an Integral Part of Learning.   Because the NTeQ model closely aligns what the students are learning to the functions of a computer, the computer becomes an integral part of the lesson. The students must use a computer to answer the questions in an efficient and effective manner. After students have used computers in this manner, *they* begin to ask to use the computer. They start to realize that learning information becomes more meaningful when they can examine the information from multiple viewpoints. Students may ask to compose reports with word processing software that can import bar graphs to support their results or add clip art to enhance the meaning of their writing. In other words, each student begins to recognize that the computer is an integral part of his or her learning process.

NTeQ and the Lesson

The NTeQ lesson is composed of 10 major components. The components fit together to create lessons that are student centered, problem based, authentic, and integrated with technology. The lesson activities keep the students actively involved in the learning process. With the students playing a greater role in the classroom, the teacher assumes the role of facilitator and guide. The central lesson focus is a problem embedded in meaningful and authentic contexts for the students. For example, problems may involve finding the shortest route to a favorite place, examining local water quality or voting behaviors, tracking global warming trends, or comparing prices for clothing, pizza, or a movie. Students can relate to the material because they decide what to collect and how to find and determine the relevant information and activities they need to solve the problem: in other words, the activity is student centered, problem based, and authentic. And, as the name iNtegrating Technology for inQuiry implies, the NTeQ model also focuses on the integration of technology, such that the lessons are dependent on technology.

NTeQ and the Standards

Today's teachers must address two types of standards in their planning and teaching: curriculum and technology standards. First, they must address the national, state, and local district's curriculum standards, which focus primarily on content such as writing a coherent paragraph or explaining the reasons for animal migration. Second, as mentioned previously, teachers must address the ISTE NETS-S. The following paragraphs describe how to ensure NTeQ lessons are standards based.

Curriculum Standards. National curriculum standards are prepared by professional organizations such as the National Council of Teachers of Mathematics (www.nctm.org), National Council for the Social Studies (www.ncss.org), National Science Teachers Association (www.nsta.org), and National Council of Teachers of English (www.ncte.org). State and local school districts may also develop standards that meet their specific needs, yet are based on the national standards (see www.educationworld.com/standards for a listing of state standards). These standards prescribe the skills and knowledge students must master in each subject area at each grade level. Teachers then use these standards to plan the individual class curriculum.

Technology Standards. In contrast to the curriculum standards, the technology standards called NETS for Students (http://cnets.iste.org) focus on technology skills and knowledge in six broad categories: creativity and innovation; communication and collaboration; research and information fluency; critical thinking, problem solving and decision making; digital citizenship; and technology operations and concepts.

How Do Teachers Create Standards-Based NTeQ Lessons?

The standards are primarily guidelines that teachers must translate into instructional objectives that provide a meaningful context to achieve targeted learning goals. Once you have translated your standards into an objective, you can use the NTeQ model to determine if there is a match with a computer function; then you can begin to develop an integrated lesson. Similarly, you can purposely translate a standard into an objective that has a match with a computer function. An integrated lesson developed with the NTeQ model can address a variety of objectives.

Summary

The evidence is clear that today's schools need to better prepare students to enter the 21st-century workforce. To do so students need to experience reformed learning environments that engage them in meaningful activities in which they use computers as tools to solve real-world problems, which in turn deepen and enrich their understanding of requisite core content and skills. The NTeQ model is an inquiry-based approach that teachers use to create a student-centered learning environment. This approach requires teachers to design or adapt lessons, assume the role of facilitator, and plan the management of the classroom. Students take on the active role of a researcher rather than that of a passive listener. The result is a student-centered classroom in which students are actively engaged in learning while acquiring 21st-century knowledge and skills.

Teacher Technology FAQ

Must I use a inquiry-based learning approach in my classroom to use computers as a tool?

No, you do not need to use an inquiry-based learning approach. We have found that integrating computers as a tool works best in an open-ended environment. The most common approaches to creating this type of learning environment are problem-based learning, inquiry learning, or project-based learning. The approach presented in this text is flexible and will allow teachers to adapt it to their own teaching styles.

Can I still use tutorials and drill-and-practice software?

Yes, there is a place for computer-based instruction (CBI) if it is used appropriately. CBI is most useful when it supports the scaffolding the students need to solve a problem. Thus, you need to carefully select applications that support your objectives for the unit. Chapter 11, Integrating Problem-Solving and Educational Software, provides more detail on effectively using educational software.

Won't I have to spend a great deal of time to develop these units of instruction?

It does take some time and effort to develop an integrated computer lesson. Many times you can adapt a unit you are currently using, or you might work with a group of teachers in the same grade level or closely grouped grades. The payback in developing one of these units comes from using it more than one time. It will take less effort to implement the unit each time you use it. Starting with the second use, you should be able to focus on minor modifications to strengthen the lesson. You can also find a wide variety of lesson plans developed by others on the NTeQ website (www.nteq.com).

Won't every student need a computer to use it as a tool?

Ideally, every student would have a computer, just like every student has a pen and notepad. The NTeQ model works well when each student has a computer (see Lowther, Ross, & Morrison, 2003). However, the NTeQ model was designed to work in classrooms that have four to six computers, with students working in groups. This book focuses on this type of classroom and includes a variety of strategies and management plans for implementation.

Technology Integration Activities

There are multiple viewpoints and approaches for integrating technology into the classroom. Compare the NTeQ philosophy with Bernie Poole's ideas in the article "What Every Teacher Should Know about Technology," located at the following site: www.education-world.com/a_tech/columnists/poole/poole015.shtml.

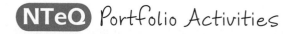

NTeQ Portfolio Activities

The following activities are designed to help you build your NTeQ Portfolio for teaching.

Reflections

The Getting Started portion of this chapter posed four Reflecting on What I Know questions that teachers might commonly ask. In this portion of your journal, reflection activities have been added to help you reflect on each question. Please use information from this chapter to answer the questions.

❶ Must I use a inquiry-based learning approach in my classroom to use computers as a tool?

Reflection Activity: As part of your education program, you have studied a number of instructional approaches. Make a list of three to five of these approaches and then describe how you might use computers with each approach or why it would not be practical.

❷ Can I still use tutorials and drill-and-practice software?

Reflection Activity: Answer this question in the broader scope of your teaching style—what are the benchmarks you will address, and what is the topic you will teach?

❸ Won't I have to spend a great deal of time to develop these units of instruction?

Reflection Activity: Identify three to five lessons that you might teach each year and would only need to do minor updates in order to teach them again.

❹ Won't every student need a computer to use it as a tool?

Reflection Activity: Consider a classroom with only 1 computer and classroom with 10 computers. How would you utilize the computer(s) with a class of 25 students? What is your definition of technology integration—that is, what does technology integration mean to you?

NTeQ: Designing an Integrated Lesson

Getting Started

A wide variety of curriculum guides and materials are available for classroom use. Some guides are very thorough and include lecture notes, handouts, PowerPoint presentations, tests, and worksheets. A teacher or substitute teacher can easily pick up a package and teach a class in a matter of a few minutes. Planning to achieve successful learning, however, can take a good deal of time. In this chapter, we guide you through the process of planning and developing your own integrated lesson by following steps of the NTeQ model introduced in Chapter 1. We use the term *integrated lesson* because the NTeQ model integrates the technology as a tool for learning with the content.

Reflecting on What I Know

1. How do I plan an integrated lesson that will work with my students?
2. Why do I need objectives to help with my planning and lesson development?
3. How can I encourage my students to engage in the processing of information?
4. Do I have to use a different lesson plan when I want my students to use computers?
5. What is the relationship between objectives and computer functions?
6. Can you use a computer for every objective or lesson?

Classroom SNAPSHOT

As Mr. Anista was driving to school on this crisp morning, he noted one of the first signs of fall. The appearance of mayoral and city council campaign signs and billboards dotting the landscape was a sure sign of fall. This year's election promised to be controversial, especially for the district around his school. The local newspaper, TV stations, and radio stations were full of stories, editorials, and advertisements. The incumbent mayor and council had fought a bitter battle regarding the creation of a development near the school that resulted in the construction of a new golf course. The developers had used fly ash from coal plants to create rolling hills that were capped with dirt in landscaping the course. When chemicals from the fly ash started leaching into the water supply, there was great concern about the quality of the drinking water. Mr. Anista wondered how he could spark his eighth-grade class's interest in the election process. He was particularly concerned with how they would obtain information and use the information to make informed decisions.

Arriving at school, he noticed bottled water dispensers located next to each water fountain and a supply of bottled water in the teacher's lounge. There were signs above the water fountains and sinks warning not to drink the water. Mr. Anista's first period social studies class was alive with questions. Several students wanted to know why they had to drink bottled water, while others had questions about their health. As he was explaining the problem, one student living in the new development loudly proclaimed it was the mayor's fault. When asked how he knew that, the student responded that he heard his dad tell a neighbor. Two other students mentioned signs they had seen. Mr. Anista decided to start the unit on elections two weeks early to capture their attention. He started by asking students how they had heard about the water problem. Most indicated they had heard their parents talking or they had seen a television advertisement. When asked if anyone had read a newspaper story or watched the news, the class fell silent.

After a short discussion, the students all agreed that the election was important and that they would hold their own election on Election Day. When asked how they would decide to vote, the class again fell silent. With some prompting, the students began to identify sources of information and learned that some, like advertisements, are frequently biased. With growing concern and excitement the students began to develop an interest in the election. The next day, they agreed to bring in different advertisements, editorials, and political cartoons from last week's newspapers. One student suggested that the goal was to find the truth.

Designing an Integrated Lesson with the NTeQ Model

The amount of time devoted to lesson planning can vary depending on available resources and objectives. For example, it will not take as long to adapt an existing lesson plan to an integrated computer unit as it does to design such a plan from scratch. One approach is to follow a process that will guide you through each step of developing the lesson plan. You might think of this process as similar to cooking. Beginning cooks need very specific directions to create a culinary delight, following every step of the instructions to a T just to create something edible. Experienced chefs probably started their early careers in much the same manner. However, as they gained experience, they began to modify the recipe and directions in an attempt to create a slightly different dish. Yet even these chefs always follow basic rules.

In Chapter 1, we identified five components of the NTeQ philosophy. Considering the five elements of teacher, student, computer, lesson, and learning environment will help you develop an integrated lesson plan that is inquiry based and student centered, in which computers are used as a tool and the teacher facilitates student learning.

An integrated computer lesson can vary in length from an hour or whole day to one period a day for a week or several weeks. The length of the lesson depends on the complexity of the problem the students investigate, the specified instructional objectives, the content you intend to cover during the lesson, and the capabilities of your students. As you design a lesson that integrates the use of computers, you need to consider two additional factors. The first is the attention span of your students. How long, in minutes, hours, or days, can your students stay focused and interested in solving a problem? For example, a lesson for third-grade students might last two to five days, whereas a high school geography lesson might last two or three weeks or longer. Longer lessons, however, are not required just because students have a longer attention span. You should plan a lesson that is appropriate for your students and your objectives or intentions.

Second, you should not expect to teach all of your objectives with a computer. Students should use other resources (books, newspapers, magazines, and possibly journals) and other instructional activities (group and individual work). Historically, educators have viewed computers as an all-inclusive teaching machine that a student could learn from throughout the school day. The NTeQ approach views the computer as a tool rather than as a teacher. It is used by the students to *solve* problems rather than to *deliver* instruction. For example, a pencil and paper are tools that are used extensively in almost every class. However, we would not expect a student in a language arts class to write all period every day. Rather, we would expect the student to use other activities such as reading, conducting research, and discussing ideas in addition to writing. Thus each individual student does not need full-time access to a computer, as in the computer-as-teacher model. We have observed several classrooms in which each student has a laptop computer. Often, we have seen a group of four or five students divide the tasks and each work independently on an aspect of the problem, whereas another group will all gather around a single laptop and work on a single task. It is nice when every student has a computer, but it is not necessary.

When students use a computer to help solve a problem, their motivation and engagement can increase. Even though many students use computers at home or perhaps in a computer lab at school, using a computer in class may be something new or novel and result in increased student motivation to learn. This "novelty" effect has occurred since the early introduction of computers into the classroom (Clark, 1983). With time, however, the motivation stems from the computer being a useful tool. Students are motivated to use computers because the job gets done more easily and quickly than without it, just as we use a microwave oven because it is more efficient and quicker than a traditional oven. Or, to put it in a more realistic context, computers are not used in the workplace because they are fun and something new. Rather,

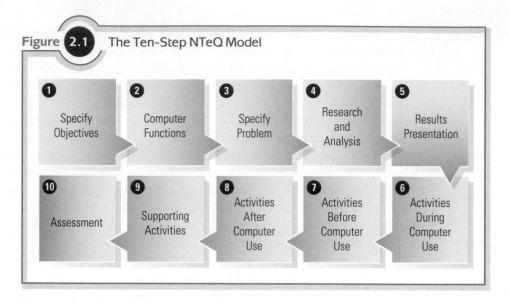

Figure 2.1   The Ten-Step NTeQ Model

1 Specify Objectives

2 Computer Functions

3 Specify Problem

4 Research and Analysis

5 Results Presentation

10 Assessment

9 Supporting Activities

8 Activities After Computer Use

7 Activities Before Computer Use

6 Activities During Computer Use

the technology has become an integral component of everyday operations because of its efficiency and accuracy. The NTeQ model is structured to engage students in the use of computers as a tool to increase learning.

The NTeQ model consists of ten steps (Figure 2.1) for *designing* an integrated computer lesson. Although you can complete the steps in any sequence, we have found that starting with objectives and working in a clockwise sequence is the most efficient. As you gain experience and expertise in developing integrated lessons, you will find that you may complete the steps in various sequences based on your ideas. This model is for designing your lessons. The sequence in which the lesson is implemented in your classroom will be much different. Let's examine the process for designing an integrated lesson that uses the computer as a tool.

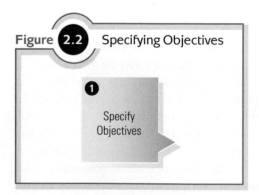

Figure 2.2   Specifying Objectives

1 Specify Objectives

Specifying Objectives

The lesson design starts with specifying your objectives (Figure 2.2). These objectives should cover *all* the instruction for the unit or lesson, not just the information related to the computer component. A lesson can also cross disciplines, either in your own classroom or as part of a team teaching project. For example, you might collect the data in a geography or a science class, analyze the data in a math class, and prepare the report or presentation in an English class. The objectives for the lesson should be inclusive of all the content.

Source of Objectives.   One question teachers often ask is whether they are responsible for generating the objectives. In recent years, most districts have created objectives or standards for each content area and grade level. These objectives are typically derived from state curriculum standards, which are aligned to national standards developed by organizations such as the National Council of Teachers of Mathematics (www.nctm.org). Most teacher editions of textbooks include objectives relevant to the book's content. While the objectives are often provided in one form or another, we advocate that teachers refine the objectives for classroom application of knowledge and skills.

You can write your objectives in one of two formats. Many teachers prefer to use a traditional behavioral objective that includes the conditions, criteria, and behavior. For example, "*Given* a right triangle, the student will *correctly calculate* the length of the hypotenuse." This style of objective works very well when you can easily identify the student outcomes. Student behaviors like *recall, identify, calculate,* and *select* are easily specified in a behavioral objective. As an alternative approach to behavioral objectives, cognitive objectives (Gronlund, 1985, 1995, 2004) are used to describe student learning goals that are not easily specified in a single sentence. Objectives for tasks such as interpreting a graph, searching the Internet for information, working effectively in a group, or writing an essay or report are not easily reduced to a few words or captured in a single behavioral objective. Cognitive objectives provide a means to specify a number of behaviors that can describe the achievement of the objective. Cognitive objectives consist of two parts; the first part is a general instructional objective stated in broad terms (Gronlund, 2004), as in the following examples:

- Selects information using Google Kids and Teens
- Interprets a chart of classroom cookie sales
- Explains the meaning of a story

The second part of the cognitive objective includes one or more statements describing specific performances that indicate mastery of the objective, as the following examples illustrate:

- Selects information using Google Kids and Teens
  - Finds a specific article related to the problem
  - Compiles a list of websites related to the problem
  - Identifies productive search terms

- Interprets a chart of classroom cookie sales
  - Identifies the student with the most sales
  - Compares this year's sales with sales during the previous 3 years
  - Identifies the students who sold more than the class average
- Explains the meaning of a story
  - Summarizes the plot
  - Identifies the characters
  - Explains the meanings of the characters' actions

A teacher can adapt existing objectives or write new objectives. Regardless of their source, the objectives should support the goals, standards, or objectives of the district. Often, it is both easier and more efficient to adapt existing objectives than create new objectives from scratch.

Example Unit

Let's examine a sample lesson as we work through the NTeQ model to develop an integrated lesson plan. Our sample lesson is for eighth-grade students in a social studies class and addresses two benchmarks. The first focuses on responsible citizenship, of which one component is voting knowledgeably. The second benchmark focuses on critical reading strategies to determine points of view, understand nuances, and draw inferences.

Three objectives were developed for the lesson discussed in the above Example Unit based on the benchmarks.

1. Students in working groups will determine the primary sources of information voters use to make decisions about a presidential election and a local election such as mayor or city council.
2. Students will analyze an election campaign advertisement.
   a. identify general message of advertisement
   b. identify who or what are in the pictures
   c. identify the action(s) taking place in the advertisement
   d. describe ideas the writers and authors are trying to convey
3. The student will analyze a political cartoon.
   a. identify the main focus of the picture
   b. identify who is speaking
   c. identify the target audience of the cartoon
   d. identify recognizable symbols in the cartoon
   e. identify the humor in the cartoon

We have developed three objectives for this lesson. Objectives 2 and 3 are written as cognitive objectives as it was difficult to express the outcomes in a single behavioral objective.

Matching Objectives to Computer Functions

To create a successful integrated lesson, you must find a match between your objective(s) and one or more computer functions (Figure 2.3). Computer functions are tasks that computer software can assist with or perform. For example, spreadsheet programs can *calculate* the area of a rectangle when the student enters the length and width. Draw and paint programs are used to *create* maps and manipulate images and photographs, and word processing is used to *create tables* and *sort* a list of information in alphabetical order. A table of learning tasks (i.e., objectives) and related computer functions is presented in the Appendix.

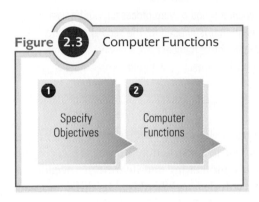

Figure 2.3   Computer Functions

1 Specify Objectives

2 Computer Functions

Now that you have defined your objectives, you need to determine if there is a match between an objective and a computer function. Some objectives, such as *calculate, draw, graph,* and *sort* are easy to match with a spreadsheet, drawing, or word processing application. Objectives describing such behaviors as *plan, discriminate, evaluate, combine, infer, predict, interpret,* and *judge* require careful planning and thinking to match the *process* with a computer function. For example, an objective requiring the student to evaluate a story or data might use a spreadsheet or database to aid the analysis, a chart to evaluate the data, and a word processor to generate the report that explains the evaluation.

One approach to finding an appropriate match between your objectives and computer functions is to analyze how you would achieve the objective if you were the student. What processes would you need to perform to master the objective? For example, would you need to collect data, perform a calculation, and then graph it? Once you have identified the process or processes required to master the objective, you can select one or more computer functions for the student to use as part of the learning process. For example, to evaluate the best store to purchase a week's groceries, you might use a spreadsheet or database to help collect or organize the data, a spreadsheet to calculate the means and highest and lowest values, and a spreadsheet chart function to display the results. An objective might require only one computer function, such as *calculate, draw,* or *sort;* or it might involve several functions to arrive at the solution. The tool chapters for word processing (Chapter 7), spreadsheets (Chapter 8), multimedia (Chapter 9), and graphic organizers (Chapter 10) provide specific details about the functions of each tool and how the functions can be used to enhance student learning.

Example Unit

The verbs in the objectives are *determine* and *analyze.* Just glancing at the verbs, we might suggest that a spreadsheet is the only tool we need. Closer examination of the objectives, however, suggests that a spreadsheet and a word processor will be used for the first objective. A word processor is all that is needed for the second and third objectives as they do not require any manipulation of numbers. Thus, we have a match between computer functions and learning tasks for each of our objectives.

Specifying a Problem

The next step in the design of the integrated lesson is specifying a problem the students will investigate and solve as part of the instructional process (see Figure 2.4). It is critical that this problem is highly motivating and interesting, because as students strive to solve the problem they will develop the thinking skills and gain the knowledge specified in the objectives.

Problems in an integrated lesson are based on real-world events, issues, or phenomena. The problems need to come from the students' world so the students can relate to them in a meaningful manner. By using a realistic problem, the students can more readily manipulate the data needed to solve the problem and interpret the results in terms of the original situation (Deming & Cracolice, 2004; Hancock, Kaput, & Goldsmith, 1992; Wolf & Fraser, 2008). As you develop the problem, it is important to make it as relevant as possible to the students by keeping the problem "real world" (Bransford, Brown, & Cocking, 1999; Bransford, Sherwood, Hasselbring, Kinzer, & Williams, 1990; Bruner, 1996; Deal & Sterling, 1997; Jonassen, Howland, Marra, & Crismond, 2008; McCain, 2005; Merrill, 2007; Petraglia, 1998). For example, imagine yourself as a student in the fifth grade in Bedford,

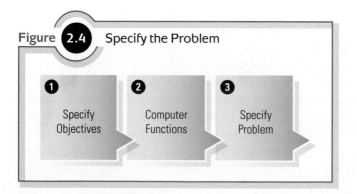

Figure 2.4 Specify the Problem

1. Specify Objectives
2. Computer Functions
3. Specify Problem

Indiana. Your textbook presents the classic time–distance problem of one car leaving New York and one leaving Los Angeles, asking you to determine when they will meet. This problem has little relevance to the student's world. The same problem could be written in a context the student could relate to using locations from the local area. While the distance might not be as great as a cross-country trip, the problem-solving approach is the same.

Using realistic problems requires you, the teacher, to take an additional step in the lesson design process. For example, consider the teaching of frequency distributions in an advanced high school math class. The problem was presented without any context or concrete data—it was simply a calculation students were supposed to complete with no purpose. Little did they realize then that this calculation is a central part of doing research! Today if we were to teach this topic, we could easily present it as a problem in a realistic context for our students. We could construct a problem in which they survey how much their fellow students make an hour or week at work, the number and types of songs on their iPods, the number of hours of television they watch during the week, the length of their text messages, or the number of times their favorite Facebook application or YouTube video is viewed. They could also survey their neighbors on a topic such as how far they drive to work, their recycling practices, or the carbon footprint for each household. They could then construct a frequency distribution to determine the mean, the mode, and the median. Presenting a realistic problem to which the students can relate increases both their chances of comprehending the content and their motivation.

When you define your problem, it is important to address the following four questions (Moursund, 2007):

- Do the students clearly understand the given problem?
- Do they know what the goal is?
- Do they know what resources are available to solve the problem?
- Do they have ownership of the problem?

There are several ways to ensure that students have a clear understanding of the problem they are solving. One way is to collaboratively develop the problem statement as a whole-class activity by writing it on a whiteboard or a SMART Board. The teacher can also create a Think Sheet that lists the problem at the top and includes additional components that engage students in defining and solving the problem, such as identifying the "Given," "Goals," and "Resources."

When working through a problem, the computer can become a valuable tool for research or for creating an image, document, or interactive presentation.

You can establish one or more goals in several ways—for example, by leading the whole class in a discussion that identifies the goal, by assigning cooperative groups to define the goals, or by providing goals as a separate part of the handout. If students define the goals of the problem they are solving, it will more than likely *not* be a statement of the objectives. Yet as they achieve the goals of the problem, they are also achieving the objectives. Through teacher facilitation skills, the students are able to "discover" the content or skills defined in the objective through an inquiry approach (Bruner, 1960; Collins & Stevens, 1983; Grambs & Starr, 1976; Mayer, 1987; Wolf & Fraser, 2008).

When possible, involve students in identifying the resources needed to solve the problem. Provide multiple sources for flexibility in reaching solutions. For example, students might use CD-ROM encyclopedias, the Internet, books, magazines, field trips, visits from experts, surveys, or experimental data collected by students.

Another starting approach is to have students identify what they already know about the problem. Then ask them to identify what they want to know to solve the problem. Finally, after they have solved the problem, ask them what they have learned.

Student ownership of the problem is very important and is easier to achieve in a student-centered learning environment than a traditional setting. The more involved students are in various aspects of solving the problem, such as identifying the goal, determining the resources needed, and deciding how to configure the database, the more ownership they will feel. "We have known for years that if you treat people, young kids included, as responsible, contributing parties to the group, as having a job to do, they will grow into it—some better than others, obviously, but all benefit" (Bruner, 1996, p. 77). Ownership is also increased if the problem is relevant to the students. This relevancy is enhanced by having students generate their own data when possible or finding real data from a survey, an experiment, the Internet, newspapers, or television. Another means of achieving ownership is by letting students define the initial problem. Present a rough idea of what you want to accomplish; then let them develop a clear problem. For example, you might tell the students, "Our school is doing a schoolwide thematic unit on Native Americans. One of our objectives for this year is for you to identify different kinds of Native American art from the 1800s. If we have to create a display of this artwork, how can we approach this project?" The teacher can facilitate the discussion to guide the students in identifying a problem based on the artwork project. However, because the students defined this problem, they will have more ownership and more involvement in reaching a solution.

Specifying a problem for the students typically begins by translating a problem or topic in the textbook or curriculum into a realistic problem, as illustrated with the frequency distribution problem. You might also let your students participate in the development of the problem by asking them to suggest ideas or problems. They can provide rich contexts you can use to embed the problem.

Once you have identified the problem, you need to check that the problem-solving process will support the achievement of your objectives. For example, your objective for a unit might focus on the effect of climate on the types of plants grown. Your problem, however, might have the students determine how to convert a Celsius reading to Fahrenheit and to identify those countries that use the two forms of measurement. If the problem does not support the achievement of your objective, then it needs to be revised.

Example Unit

Because students will participate in presidential elections for most of their lives, we want them to have input in developing the problem. We start with some questions that will stimulate the students to think about presidential elections and help them focus on the problem. In general terms, our problem will focus on how they, the students, would make a decision for their candidate of choice. More specifically, we want to determine which information sources adults use to make voting decisions. We could then focus on the meaning and effect of political cartoons.

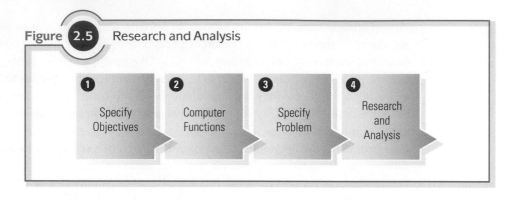

Figure 2.5   Research and Analysis

Research and Analysis

The fourth step in designing an integrated lesson is to consider the research and analysis activities students must complete to solve the problem (Figure 2.5). This decision is directly related to the computer functions and your objectives. How will students gather data? Once the data is saved in a spreadsheet or database, what will they do with it? Similarly, how much instruction or guidance must you provide the students concerning their use of data? The following paragraphs discuss research and analysis.

Problem Data.   To solve a problem, the students must have access to appropriate data or information. There are three sources of data you can use for the lesson.

1. *You can provide students with the data.* This approach is used when the instructional time is limited, the students have no feasible way of obtaining the data, or students lack the necessary skills (e.g., Internet search, interviewing others). Or consider a geography unit focusing on the types of crops grown in various countries. The students need to discover relationships between the weather and crops. Searching for the raw data is not a focus of this unit. You might provide the students with the necessary information so they can concentrate on manipulating the data and discovering relationships.

2. *Students can generate their own data through experiments or observations.* There are many ways students can gather data—laboratory experiment (e.g., chemistry, physics, biology, or social studies), survey, interviews, or by observation, such as the number of students wearing seat belts as they arrive at school. A sixth-grade class, for example, could measure the height of a sampling of boys and girls in several grade levels as they study the relationships among physical growth, age, and gender. Similarly, a language arts class might count the number of times a particular grammatical structure or theme is used.

3. *Students can search for data in a library, on CD-ROMs, or on the Internet.* (See Chapter 6, Exploring the World Wide Web in the Classroom.) Although computers create many opportunities for finding both useful and not so useful data, student data searches should not be limited only to computers but should also include printed materials and other resources from the library, as appropriate. For example, an economics class studying organized labor might search the Internet for historical events in the labor movement and then search the local newspaper for information on strikes or other organized labor activity in their community.

As you design the lesson, you will need to decide if students should gather the data or if you should provide them with it. If the process of gathering the data is part of the instruction, such as in a lab experiment or a survey, then the students need to collect the data. However, when the emphasis of the lesson is primarily on manipulating the data (e.g., calculations or probing the database), you may decide that it is a more efficient use of classroom time to provide the students with a template and the data, or even a spreadsheet with the data. You will need to determine the importance and value of either option. The tradeoff is one of instructional time and how it is used.

PEARSON
myeducationlab
The Power of Classroom Practice

Go to MyEducationLab, select the topic "Internet," and go to the Building Teaching Skills and Dispositions section. Open "Exploring and Implementing WebQuests" and complete the activity.

Collecting Data.   If the students will collect the data, you will need to determine the type and amount. If the students are conducting a survey or an interview, how many individuals must each student survey? If they are collecting data from an experiment, how many observations does each student or group need to complete? You can also involve the students in this decision as part of the problem-solving process. If you need consistency in the data among students or groups, the class can create a data collection form to record results.

Using Existing Data.   When students will use a data set created by you or by others, you need to consider the following. First, are the data in a format (either paper or digital) that the students can use? If the data are not in appropriate formats, can you modify the format so the data are useful to the student? Second, are students allowed to modify, delete, or add data? Third, if the students are entering the data, must each one enter all the data or can they divide the work among groups and then merge the files? Fourth, where will the students save their data? Will they use their own disk(s), the hard drive, or the server? Careful consideration is needed to protect students from losing their data and becoming frustrated with the process.

Test the Data.   We encourage teachers to try a test run of the data at this stage of the planning cycle. You can conduct this test with actual or random data to make sure your recording form and file template (e.g., database or spreadsheet) are designed correctly. This simple test run can save time and frustration if there is a problem. Also, consider the data you are using and make sure that it will help in solving the problem and achieving the objectives.

Providing Instructions.   If your students are advanced in the use of word processing, spreadsheets, or databases, they may be quite capable of entering the data. Less advanced students may need step-by-step instructions on entering data in tables or forms, entering formulas, or matching and searching criteria (see Figure 2.6). Another alternative is to teach all the students how to do the data manipulation and then provide assistance on an individual basis. We have observed good and bad examples of both approaches. In one excellent approach, a teacher modeled the steps on a large monitor as students created their own lists of steps. At the other extreme, another teacher let four students at a time complete the process as she and the other students observed and commented. The students sitting at their desks could not see the individual monitors, and there was little if any motivation to focus their attention on what the teacher was doing.

Think Sheet.   Simply entering a formula, sorting data, making a graph, or creating a drawing is rather mechanical. Students can complete the steps to solve the problem but fail to process or reflect on the results. A Think Sheet provides guidance to help students organize their thinking and probe the implications of the data manipulations. It helps them determine what to do once they have created a graphic organizer, sorted the data, edited a video, or created a chart. Generic Think Sheets that can be used for a variety of lessons can include guiding questions, such as which is the largest, which is the smallest, what is the most common, and what is the least common. Specific lesson Think Sheets can include probing questions asking the student about implications, interpretations, generalizations, and predictions using the data. Figure 2.7 illustrates a sample Think Sheet. More detailed information on creating a Think Sheet, as well as a step-by-step guide for implementing the problem-solving process discussed in this section, can be found in Chapter 5, Think Sheets: Using Technology for Higher-Order Learning.

Example Unit

The students will collect their own data for the voting question. Working in small groups, they will conduct research using materials in the library and on the Internet to identify various sources of information a voter can use to make a decision. Once

Figure 2.6   Sample Spreadsheet Calculation

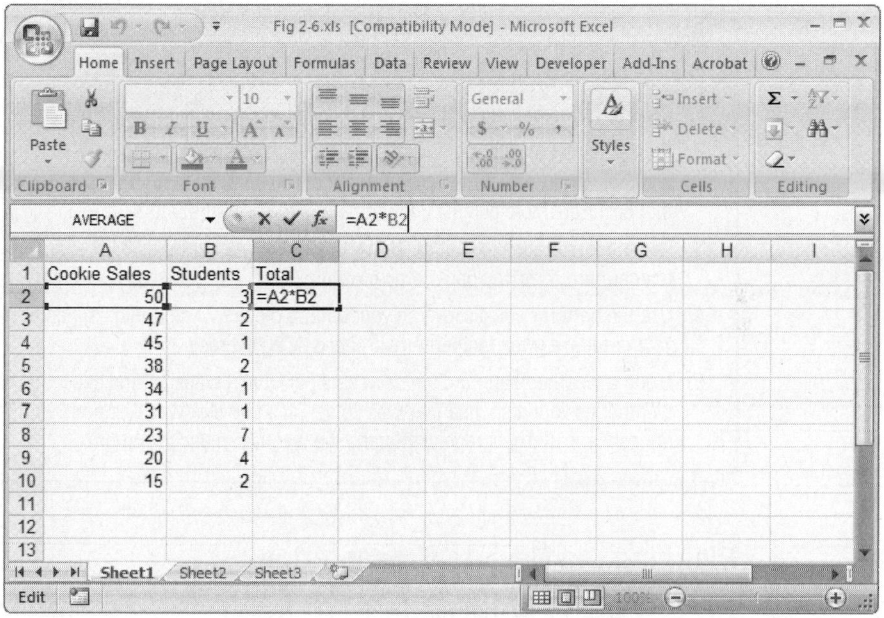

Calculating the number of packages sold

1. Click in cell C2
2. Enter the folowing into the formula field = A2*B2
3. Press Enter and you will see the results of your calculation

the groups are finished, they will develop one survey. Each student will ask five adults to complete the survey. They will then enter the data into a spreadsheet where each group will determine the primary source of information used for presidential and local elections. Students will use both teacher-provided and student-collected advertisements and political cartoons to answer questions.

The teacher will provide information about how to collect the survey data (approval was received from the principal before starting the unit) and a job aid for calculating averages for the survey responses and for creating a bar chart of the results. A Think Sheet will be developed for analyzing the voting data. Additional Think Sheets will be developed to guide the students' analyses of the advertisements and political cartoons.

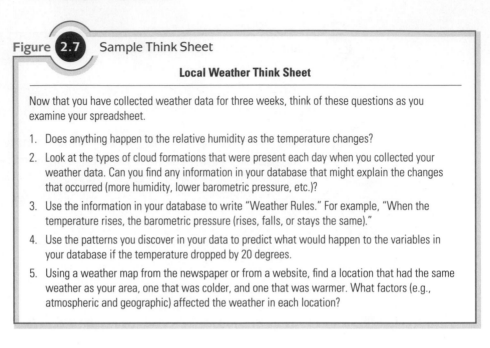

Figure 2.7 Sample Think Sheet

Local Weather Think Sheet

Now that you have collected weather data for three weeks, think of these questions as you examine your spreadsheet.

1. Does anything happen to the relative humidity as the temperature changes?

2. Look at the types of cloud formations that were present each day when you collected your weather data. Can you find any information in your database that might explain the changes that occurred (more humidity, lower barometric pressure, etc.)?

3. Use the information in your database to write "Weather Rules." For example, "When the temperature rises, the barometric pressure (rises, falls, or stays the same)."

4. Use the patterns you discover in your data to predict what would happen to the variables in your database if the temperature dropped by 20 degrees.

5. Using a weather map from the newspaper or from a website, find a location that had the same weather as your area, one that was colder, and one that was warmer. What factors (e.g., atmospheric and geographic) affected the weather in each location?

Planning the Results Presentation

The next step of designing the NTeQ lesson is presentation of the results (Figure 2.8). What type of product will the students produce to demonstrate they have achieved the objectives? These products can take a variety of formats (see Chapters 7, 8, 9, and 10), as seen in the examples provided below.

1. Each student or group of students can prepare a written report using either a word processor or paper and pencil. Using desktop publishing techniques, the students can prepare books, magazines, or newsletters and distribute their products to classmates, students in lower grades, parents, or possibly a government agency such as the city council. If the students have worked on a problem

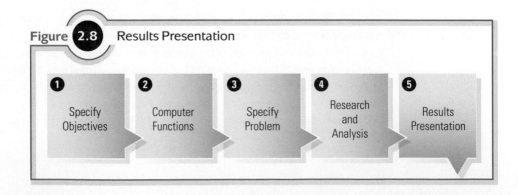

Figure 2.8 Results Presentation

1. Specify Objectives
2. Computer Functions
3. Specify Problem
4. Research and Analysis
5. Results Presentation

of community interest, they might submit their story to a local newspaper for publication. For example, one third-grade class created a history of downtown buildings for children their age. When they finished the project, a realtor worked with the teacher to have the finished booklet printed by a local printer and included in materials the community provided to individuals considering moving to the community.

2. Students can create a digital audio and/or video presentation that demonstrates the problem solution as well as student achievement of the learning objectives. The products can include student-generated narration, artwork, and video clips, as well as other copyright-free materials.

3. Students can prepare a poster or bulletin board display of their results. This type of presentation can take a variety of formats, from interactive displays to timelines, and can include both computer-generated and other student products.

4. Students can publish their results to a teacher-approved wiki or blog.

5. Students can make a presentation to other students or parents. Students can present their findings in a scientific format using an electronic slide show. Or the presentation might take the format of a lesson using printed materials or multimedia to teach other students. Other possibilities include a radio or television news show format, poster sessions, and web pages.

Publishing the results encourages students to analyze their findings in a critical manner and draw appropriate conclusions, because their work will be viewed by others. This analysis was started with Think Sheets as students analyzed their data. The presentation component allows students to interpret their results and apply their findings to a solution.

As you plan the results presentation, you need to develop criteria for what students should include. For example, you might include a basic outline for a report similar to that used in scientific journals. A report on a survey the students have conducted might use the outline in Figure 2.9. You can create similar outlines and criteria for web pages, graphic organizers, and presentations. The criteria will help you assess the results presentation as well as let students know your expectations.

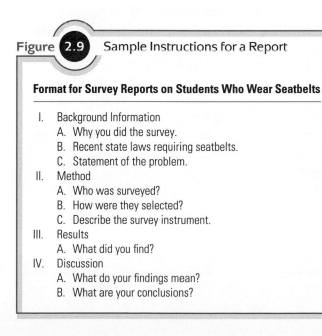

Figure 2.9   Sample Instructions for a Report

Format for Survey Reports on Students Who Wear Seatbelts

I.   Background Information
   A. Why you did the survey.
   B. Recent state laws requiring seatbelts.
   C. Statement of the problem.

II. Method
   A. Who was surveyed?
   B. How were they selected?
   C. Describe the survey instrument.

III. Results
   A. What did you find?

IV. Discussion
   A. What do your findings mean?
   B. What are your conclusions?

The Teacher's Diary

When I plan a literature-based thematic unit, I always look through my district's curriculum frameworks, classroom literature, and language textbooks. I use these frameworks to help define my instructional goals for the unit and review textbooks for ideas in the content areas. For example, after reviewing the resources, I decided that my third-grade students needed to learn how to use an index and table of contents to find information, read for specific information, and summarize in writing what they had read. With these instructional goals in mind, I went to our school library and looked for books related to owls that would be of high interest and age appropriate to my students. I checked out a variety of books on owls and chose two as the basis for the unit. As I read these books, I began to formulate how I would use them to meet my instructional goals, and I made a list of activities.

The next day I asked my students to create knowledge charts about owls. On one side of their paper, they listed everything that they already knew about owls and on the other side those things that they would like to learn. The class then discussed what they wanted to learn about owls, and we made a list of questions they would like to have answered. We ended up with 34 excellent questions!

I recorded their questions and took them home with me that night. I used my list of instructional goals and activities and the students' questions to help me write the instructional objectives for this unit. After I had written the objectives, I checked my objectives against the list of state-mandated objectives to ensure alignment with as many as possible.

Then I used the activity list and the students' questions to help me create a thematic activity web for this unit. I tried to include a variety of activities that would cross all curriculum areas and include the use of the computer in as many of the activities as possible. I wanted the students to use the computer in real-life situations and as a tool to help them accomplish their instructional goals.

I searched the Internet and found some excellent owl resources and brought in several different CD-ROM encyclopedias. The students used both the computer materials and books checked out from the school and public libraries to obtain information about owls. They then used this information about owls to create a database, write informative paragraphs, and create a multimedia report.

The final assessment for this unit was a group multimedia report about a topic related to owls. Considering student interest expressed in the questions, the topics for these reports were (1) unusual owls, (2) feathers and flight, (3) special owl features, (4) owl habitats, (5) owl diet, and (6) owl babies. Each group was responsible for a topic. They searched for information on that topic using printed materials, the Internet, and the CD-ROM encyclopedias. The students kept individual notes and combined this information with that of other group members to create a group HyperStudio multimedia report. These reports were shared with other students in the classroom.

Fran Clark
Third-Grade Teacher

This step of the planning process requires careful thought to avoid problems such as computer access if all the students are required to prepare a written report. Students are easily frustrated if they have completed all the steps except the final one because of the limited number of computers in the classroom. Thus a paper-and-pencil report supplemented with database reports, a spreadsheet chart, or graphic organizer may be a more efficient use of instructional time than requiring each individual to use word processing for the report.

The next steps focus on designing the specific activities you will use in the classroom. There are two reasons for these activities. First, not all objectives are best taught with a computer. Second, many classrooms have only a limited number of computers; therefore, several activities are used to achieve the objectives. We can hardly expect each student in a class of 27 to have extensive computer time when there are only 4 computers in the classroom. Moreover, management and planning concerns even affect classrooms where all students have laptops at their disposal. To address these issues, the NTeQ lesson uses a variety of instructional activities. Activities are grouped into four timeframes: before computer use, during computer use, after computer use, and supporting activities used anytime. Notice, however, that designing activities *during* computer use is done before designing the activities *before* computer use. You must know what your students will do while they are using the computer *before* you can determine what they must do before using the computer. Many research and analysis activities, such as data collection, data manipulation, and results presentation, are included in these multidimensional activities. The following sections describe each type of activity.

Example Unit

The students will create a report and presentation showing and explaining their survey data. Our Think Sheet will help them ask appropriate questions about their data and help them draw conclusions. For the advertising analysis, each student will create a poster with a print advertisement in the center. They will use callouts with string or ink to explain their analysis of the various components of the advertisement. Students will write an essay of their analysis of the political cartoon.

Activities during Computer Use

Now that you have identified your objective(s) and the problem the students will be solving and know how the students will use a computer to analyze the information and data, the next step is to determine what the students will do while they are working with computers (see Figure 2.10). There are two factors to consider when planning computer activities. First, identify the activities the students will engage in while using

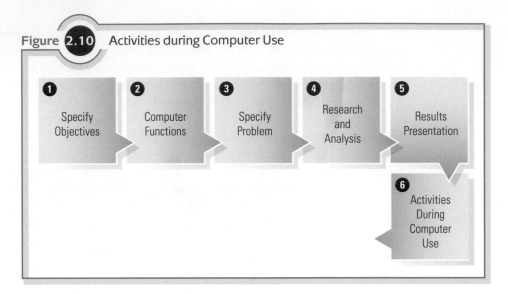

Figure 2.10   Activities during Computer Use

a computer. How will the students obtain information to find an answer or to solve the problem? If students are searching for information, will they search a CD, the Internet, a database on the hard drive, or all three? If students are using a database or spreadsheet, will they use a template you have created or make their own? Depending on your objectives, you might want the students to use your template and concentrate on entering and manipulating the data to find an answer. For other lessons, the emphasis might be on finding the correct solution by creating the correct formula. If students are preparing a report, drawing, or graphic organizer, can they use clip art or must they do original artwork or incorporate digital photos that they have taken? Similarly, do they need to show a graph of the results in their report? Students will need clear and precise instructions of what they are to do while working at the computer.

Second, will the students work individually or in groups? If they are working in groups at a computer, assist students with identifying and assigning different roles, ensuring that students have the opportunity to rotate through the different roles. When working in a group, one student can read the data, another can enter the data, and a third can check the accuracy of the entry. Defining roles before using a computer can help you develop a rotation schedule so that students have a variety of experiences.

Example Unit

Students will use computers for the following activities:

- Searching for sources of information for making voting decisions
- Creating a survey

- Entering survey data into a spreadsheet
- Analyzing the survey data and creating a bar chart
- Writing a report of the survey findings
- Creating a PowerPoint presentation of the findings
- Creating callouts for an advertisement poster
- Searching for political cartoons at selected sites
- Writing an essay analyzing a political cartoon

Activities before Computer Use

Once you have determined the activities the students will engage in while working at a computer and whether the students will work individually or in groups, then you can focus on the activities they complete before using a computer. If your students have limited access to computers because of time limitations or lack of computers in your classroom, it is essential to design activities the students need to complete before using a computer (see Figure 2.11). For example, if the students are entering data from an experiment or survey into a spreadsheet, they can collect the data and organize it before they use a computer. Similarly, if they are writing a report, they can create their outline and gather materials before their computer time. Students who are searching a CD-ROM encyclopedia or the Internet need to plan their search by identifying key words before they start searching. With proper design, students can have efficient and productive use of their computer time.

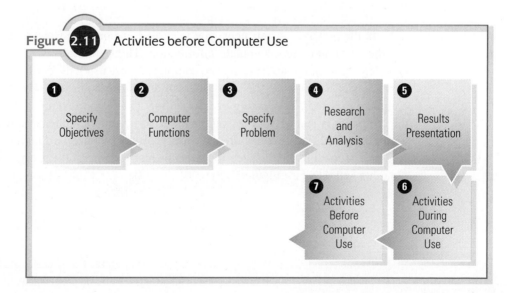

Figure 2.11   Activities before Computer Use

Figure 2.12   Checklist for Work before Using the Computer

Getting Ready to Do a Search on the Internet

What is your topic? _____

List at least three terms you can use to search for information on this topic:

_____

_____

_____

_____

_____

List at least two other terms that mean the same as some of the above:

_____

_____

_____

What are you searching for?

❑ Articles   ❑ Sound

❑ Pictures   ❑ Software

❑ Movies   ❑ Other: _____

In the previous design steps, you identified one or more ways students would use the computer and manipulate information. Think through each of these steps and identify what the student needs to complete *before* using the computer. You may find it easier to complete the steps yourself and make notes as to what you did to complete the steps. This listing of information and steps to complete before using the computer is part of your lesson plan that you can communicate to the students with a handout, through a lecture, or with a poster or whiteboard listing. For some students, a checklist with space for notes or blanks is helpful for organizing their thoughts and data (see Figure 2.12).

Example Unit

Students will be provided with information voters use to make decisions, including YouTube advertisements, recordings of debates, newspaper articles, magazine articles, and political campaign information on the Internet and available locally. Students will use this information to complete the following activities before computer use.

- Students will use pencil and paper to draft survey items on note cards. After editing the items they will sequence them and write the instructions with paper and pencil.
- Students will use pencil and paper to outline the report of their findings.
- Students will create paper and pencil storyboards of their PowerPoint presentation.
- Students will create a mock-up of their advertising analysis poster and write out their analysis.
- Students will generate a list of search terms for political cartoons.
- Students will write an outline of their analysis of a political cartoon using paper and pencil.

Activities after Computer Use

If students are using a computer to solve problems, their learning and work do not end with their computer time (see Figure 2.13). While working at a computer, they have produced some results. Activities after using the computer should focus on exploring the results of the computer activity. If the students have created a concept map of brainstormed ideas or analyzed the data of an experiment or study, they should focus on interpreting or explaining the results. Students who have searched for information can read, paraphrase, compare and contrast, and interpret the information in a written report.

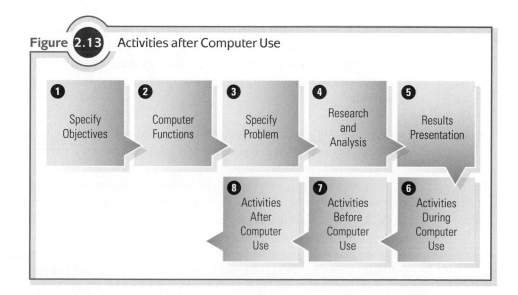

Figure 2.13 Activities after Computer Use

The purpose of this activity is to use the information generated from using the computer as a tool. You might find a Think Sheet (see Chapter 5) helpful for guiding the students' analysis and interpretation. Once again, the handout can include either generic questions such as "What is the writer's perspective in this news story?" or specific questions such as "Using the graph you created, what happened to humidity as temperature increased?" Think Sheets can also include directions for how the students should read an article or story, including steps for what they should do (e.g., paraphrase or summarize the content) after they finish reading the material.

Example Unit

Example generic Think Sheets that could be used with this unit are listed below:

- Creating a survey
- Entering survey data into a spreadsheet
- Analyzing the survey data and creating a bar chart
- Writing a report of the survey findings
- Creating a PowerPoint presentation of the findings
- Creating callouts for an advertisement poster
- Searching for political cartoons at selected sites
- Writing an essay analyzing a political cartoon

Supporting Activities

An NTeQ lesson incorporates a variety of instructional activities. Some require the use of a computer, and others rely on other forms of instruction (Figure 2.14). After you have designed the activities that are directly related to the computer activities, you will need to focus on supporting activities that also help students achieve the objectives.

Lesson-Related Supporting Activities.   The objectives for the lesson should cover a variety of skills and topics. Some require the use of a computer, whereas others require different student engagement activities such as experimentation, practice, and gathering information via multiple resources (reading, videotapes, teachers, and other content experts). Students engage in these activities as part of the instruction for the *total* lesson. It is often helpful to have a variety of activities that are not dependent on completing the computer activities, so that students can work on them at any time. For example, if the students are using computers to research a topic and build a graphic organizer, the supporting activities could include researching

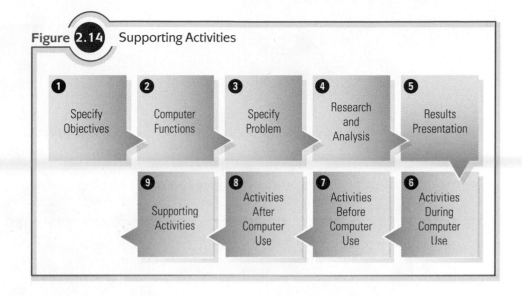

Figure 2.14 Supporting Activities

and reading in several books, creating a poster, developing a presentation, and generating debate questions. Students engage in these activities as they wait their turn to do additional research on the Internet and create their graphic organizer. Similar strategies are often used when students must share limited resources such as a microscope or manipulatives. You must consider the broader context and objectives rather than just focusing on the computer aspect, regardless of the students' access to computers. Interesting lessons include a variety of instructional activities to achieve the objectives.

Multiple Lesson Supporting Activities.   Another approach to designing supporting activities is to provide multiple units for the students. If you teach only one subject, such as math, science, language arts, or social studies, you may want to develop several units students can work on at one time. You do not, however, need to use a computer for each of the units. If you are teaching a geography class, for example, you might have the students working on units on reading maps, weather, and influences of technology on people and towns. Similarly, a math teacher might have students working on addition of fractions, comparing fractions with fraction strips, converting fractions to decimals, and doing fraction additions with a calculator. These units are independent and are not sequential; thus students can work on them at any time. All of the units provide instruction leading to the achievement of the objectives, although the objectives may be for different units of instruction.

When NTeQ is implemented, students are engaged in a variety of activities.

Interdisciplinary Supporting Activities. An NTeQ lesson is an excellent approach to use across content areas. Such activities require a team-teaching approach if the students are not in a self-contained classroom. For example, students might collect data in science class or social studies class, make the calculations in a math class, and prepare the results presentation in a language arts class. Using this approach, students can work on various tasks related to the project in the different classes, with the goal of completing the project in a timely manner.

The supporting activities are often the most difficult to design. These activities should provide instruction related to objectives as opposed to "busy" work. If you are having difficulty identifying supporting activities, reconsider your objectives. You may need to broaden their scope or add additional objectives.

Example Unit

There are two supporting activities to engage students in related content. First, students will create a collection of recent newspaper articles that focus on local public issues and then analyze the different perspectives presented. Second, students will study the judicial system and prepare for a mock court trial that is a joint project with the social studies and language arts class.

Assessment

The final step of the NTeQ model is the design of your assessment strategies (see Figure 2.15). In recent years, educators have moved away from traditional forms of assessment, such as multiple-choice tests, and toward more authentic forms of

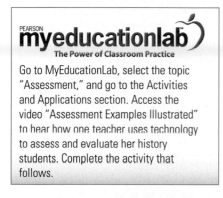

assessment, such as portfolios, performance assessment, presentations, and experiments (Campbell, 2000; DiMartino & Castaneda, 2007; Latourelle & Elwess, 2006; Marcoulides & Heck, 1994; Sharma, 2007). Assessment of an integrated computer lesson will typically require more than a paper-and-pencil test. During lesson implementation, students can use a task list to guide productivity and assist with self-reflection on the quality of work being accomplished. At the conclusion of a lesson, we might use a traditional multiple-choice and short-answer test to assess the students' understanding of the concepts and principles. Then we might develop a rubric to assess student portfolios

documenting their searches, the completion of the Think Sheets, and their presentations (Christensen, Overall, & Knezek, 2006; Spandel, 2006; Yoshina & Harada, 2007). We might also include an assessment of the group and individual work behaviors based on both a journal we kept and the students' personal journals.

Rubrics provide a means of rating student productivity on content standards according to predetermined performance standards (Danielson, 1997). Content

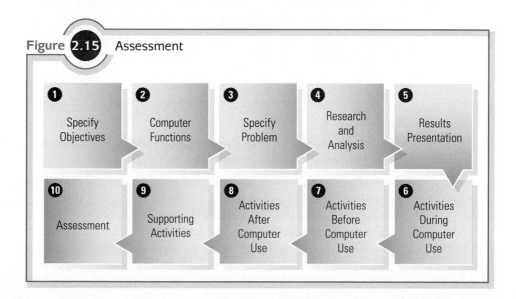

Figure 2.15   Assessment

1. Specify Objectives
2. Computer Functions
3. Specify Problem
4. Research and Analysis
5. Results Presentation
10. Assessment
9. Supporting Activities
8. Activities After Computer Use
7. Activities Before Computer Use
6. Activities During Computer Use

standards define the subject knowledge and skills students should reflect. Performance standards indicate to what level a student presentation meets the content standard (Gandal, 1995).

Example Unit

At the beginning of the unit students will be provided with a checklist of key components that need to be addressed in each product. They will also be provided with a rubric that will be used to assess the overall quality and achievement of the unit objectives as demonstrated in the written and presentation products.

Effective use of computers in your classroom requires careful planning to integrate their use into a lesson. The NTeQ model provides ten steps to help you complete this lesson planning. The first five steps involve the planning of the content: specifying the objectives, identifying a match with the computer functions, specifying the problem the learners will seek to answer, planning how students will conduct research and analyze the information and data, and finally, planning how they will present the results of their research. The next three steps require you to plan how your students will use the computer(s) in the classroom. These three steps involve classroom management and planning for Think Sheets and job aids. The ninth step is the planning of supporting activities that can include support for objectives in the same unit or another unit that do not require the use of a computer. Last is the planning of assessment. The assessment of student learning when using an authentic task often requires more than a traditional paper-and-pencil test. This step will guide your planning of a rubric or other strategy to accurately assess student achievement.

Why should I create an integrated computer lesson rather than use some of the existing computer-based instructional (CBI) software?

We do not see the use of integrated computer lessons and CBI as an either/or question. Decide instead which approach will best help your students achieve the objectives. You may decide that the CBI can help provide the scaffolding necessary to solve the problem you present in the integrated lesson. The integrated lesson allows you to create unique, inquiry-based units that are highly relevant for your students. You can custom tailor problems to meet your curriculum standards while providing a local context to which the students can relate. Providing this type of real-world, local context increases the meaningfulness of the instruction. Students see a problem that is concrete and easily understandable. The integrated lesson also helps construct an exciting learning environment incorporating a variety of instructional strategies rather than just focusing on the computer. As a result, "book" learning has as much importance as "computer" learning in the minds of the students.

I will never be able to create enough units for next year. Is there any reason to adopt this approach?

The first year of any new approach is the most difficult. We would not expect a teacher to develop enough materials in a year to cover every lesson of instruction for every class. Teachers that we have observed start with a few units or lessons the first year and add additional new ones each year. Units and lessons that you can adapt and modify are available from other teachers on the Internet (www.nteq.com). Teachers also are able to adapt many of their existing units to an integrated lesson by adding or rethinking the problem and objectives.

One of the best sources of ideas for lessons is your old lesson plans and textbooks. It is often easier to adapt an existing idea to an integrated lesson plan than to generate a new lesson plan from scratch. Consider your objectives, standards, or benchmarks; then compare the behavior in those to the various computer functions. Teachers are often surprised at the number of possibilities they can generate for existing materials.

ⓣechnology Integration Activities

The following activities provide an opportunity for you to explore the options for using the NTeQ model described in this chapter.

1. Locate online lesson plans appropriate for your curriculum and compare components of those lessons with the NTeQ components. Which components are most frequently the same and which are most frequently different?
2. Generate a list of lesson ideas for using the NTeQ model.

NTeQ Portfolio Activities

Please complete the following activities as part of your NTeQ Portfolio on educational software.

Reflections

The Getting Started portion of this chapter posed six Reflecting on What I Know questions that teachers might commonly ask. In this portion of your journal, reflection activities have been added to help you reflect on each question. Please use information from this chapter and from the MyEducationLab resources to answer the questions.

❶ How do I plan an integrated lesson that will work with my students?

Reflection Activity: Make a list of key components of an integration lesson that better ensure it will be effective with your students.

❷ Why do I need objectives to help with my planning and lesson development?

Reflection Activity: Describe the benefits of objectives.

❸ How can I encourage my students to engage in the processing of information?

Reflection Activity: Review chapter suggestions and MyEducationLab resources to create a list of interesting lesson topics for the subject area(s) that you teach and ideas for creative activities to engage student interest.

❹ Do I have to use a different lesson plan when I want my students to use computers?

Reflection Activity: Describe why it is important to use an NTeQ lesson plan when integrating student use of technology into a lesson.

❺ What is the relationship between objectives and computer functions?

Reflection Activity: Cut and paste the district standards/objectives for a week and list the computer functions that your students could use to achieve each one.

❻ Can you use a computer for every objective or lesson?

Reflection Activity: This chapter presents a wide variety of digital tools that are used in today's classrooms. To help you understand relationships between the tools, create a chart that shows key basic functions of each category of digital tools discussed in the chapter.

The second task is to create an NTeQ job aid in which you describe what is needed to complete each of the steps in the NTeQ model (see Figure 2.1). For example, for Specifying the Problem, you might list the various ways you could find a problem that is of interest to your students. You might also list the criteria for a good problem. This job aid can then serve as a guide when you develop an integrated lesson because it will have guidelines and criteria that you have created.

The third task is to create an integrated lesson plan using the NTeQ model. You may want to take one of your favorite and most successful lesson plans and adapt it to the NTeQ model. This will involve identifying computer functions that can be used to help students achieve the objectives, identifying a problem students will solve, determining the specific research and analysis the students will conduct and the student products that will demonstrate student results, and then planning the during, before, after, and supporting activities as well as how to assess learning.

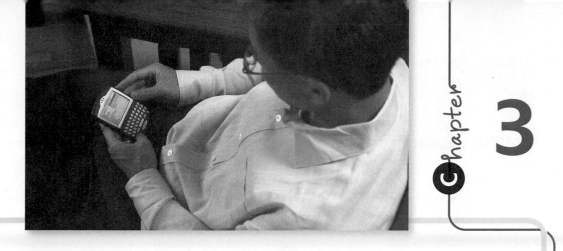

Digital Tools in Today's Classrooms

Getting Started

Digital devices are everywhere! We use them in our homes and cars, take them with us on vacations, and increasingly use them to communicate with others and locate information. These same trends are in today's classrooms as more and more schools go digital. The variety and options for technology tools is seemingly limitless—which is exciting as well as challenging for classroom teachers. This chapter provides a general overview of some of the most common digital tools used in today's classrooms and how the devices can be used to help students learn core content as well as 21st-century skills.

Reflecting on What I Know

1. Why is it important to learn about different technology tools when they are constantly changing?

2. Most desktop computers do the same things as mobile devices, so why do teachers need to use both?

3. How can the cost of digital devices be justified when the functions they perform are often limited in number and scope?

Classroom

SNAPSHOT

Mrs. Washington begins her day as principal of Meade Elementary by visiting the classrooms from one grade level. Today she goes to the fourth-grade hall and begins in Mr. Lee's class, where she discovers student pairs listening to podcasts of today's news stories downloaded to mp3 players. Next, she visits Ms. Lawrence's class during language arts. The class is using the electronic whiteboard to create a book report concept map that depicts the main components of *Because of Winn-Dixie* (DiCamillo, 2000). One student is at the whiteboard and calling on students as they suggest additions or modifications to the map. A second student is entering information into the laptop that is projecting to the whiteboard. Students at the whiteboard and laptop rotate to depict various aspects of the story. Mrs. Washington then visits Mr. Moore's math class where student groups are creating digital video tutorials for measuring the perimeters of triangles, quadrilaterals, and polygons. Student groups view each other's tutorials to offer editing suggestions and to reinforce math skills. In the last fourth-grade classroom students are working individually at laptop computers to create a presentation that compares their lives with same-age students in colonial times. Students save their work to a personal USB flash drive so they can work on it at home. As Mrs. Washington walks back to her office, she feels renewed confidence that the bake sales, grant proposals, and presentations to the county commissioners to raise funding for the school to "go digital" was definitely the right decision.

Using Digital Tools in the Classroom

As technology becomes more ubiquitous and mobile, it is critical for teachers and students to take full advantage of the enhanced learning opportunities provided by digital tools. The International Society for Technology Education (ISTE) supports this approach in the National Educational Technology Standards for Students (NETS-S). Specifically, use of digital tools and new technologies are recommended in three of the six NETS-S (ISTE, 2007) as seen below:

3. *Research and Information Fluency:* Students apply **digital tools** to gather, evaluate, and use information. Students:
   a. plan strategies to guide inquiry.
   b. locate, organize, analyze, evaluate, synthesize, and ethically use information from a variety of sources and media.
   c. evaluate and select information sources and digital tools based on the appropriateness to specific tasks.
   d. process data and report results.
4. *Critical Thinking, Problem Solving and Decision Making:* Students use critical thinking skills to plan and conduct research, manage projects, solve problems and make informed decisions using appropriate **digital tools** and resources. Students:
   a. identify and define authentic problems and significant questions for investigation.
   b. plan and manage activities to develop a solution or complete a project.
   c. collect and analyze data to identify solutions and/or make informed decisions.
   d. use multiple processes and diverse perspectives to explore alternative solutions.
6. *Technology Operations and Concepts:* Students demonstrate a sound understanding of technology concepts, systems and operations. Students:
   a. understand and use technology systems.
   b. select and use applications effectively and productively.
   c. troubleshoot systems and applications.
   d. transfer current knowledge to learning of new **technologies.** (ISTE, 2007, p. 1)

Four Digital Tool Categories

We begin by grouping digital tools into four categories: computers, mobile devices, peripherals, and data storage. Within each category, we discuss the tools most commonly used in today's classrooms (see Figure 3.1). These tools can be classified by the factors that influence their use: (1) platform (PC or Mac), (2) connectivity (wired vs. wireless), (3) networking, (4) device software, and (5) file format.

Figure 3.1   Four Categories of Digital Tools Used in Today's Classrooms

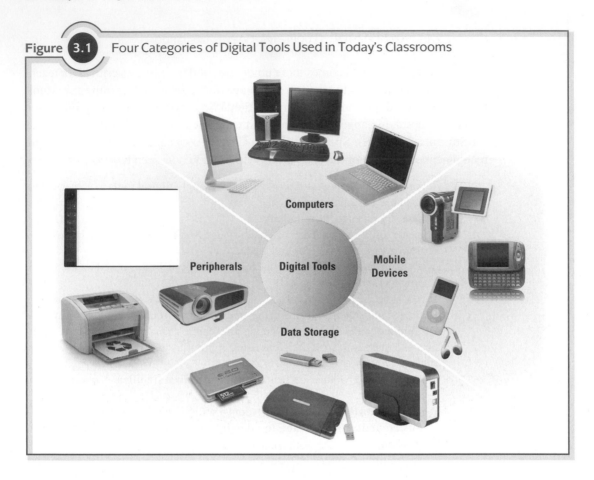

Platform

PC versus Mac.   PC, or personal computer, is a term that is generally applied to computers running the Windows operating system, while Mac refers to Apple, Inc., computers running a Macintosh operating system (OS). Another option is Linux, which offers more affordable operating systems. A computer includes an operating system and other related hardware and software that allow the computer to run in a specific way. Think of the operating system as the language and infrastructure of a country. While both Peru and the United States are considered democratic nations, there are language and infrastructure differences between the countries. In Peru, you would expect to bargain for your groceries in Spanish, Quechua, or Aymara in small markets while in the United States, you would expect to speak English and pay the marked price in a supermarket. The results are the same, you buy groceries, but the particulars vary by country. Both are democratic countries, just as both a PC and Mac are computers that will do word processing, spreadsheets, presentations, and so on—but the particulars vary by platform.

Before Apple changed to Intel processors, the differences between Windows-based PCs and Mac OS–based Apples were significant. Now, thanks to virtual desktops, the Windows operating system can run on Macs. The virtual desktop allows users to switch among multiple desktops that are running different operating systems (Natsu, 2008), as shown in Figure 3.2. The Mac OS (Leopard) uses a system called Spaces to accomplish this and Windows uses Microsoft's Virtual Desktop. Often, a school's choice between PC and Mac is based on the type of support the school district chooses to offer.

Figure 3.2 Four Screens Available on the Monitor when Using a Virtual Desktop

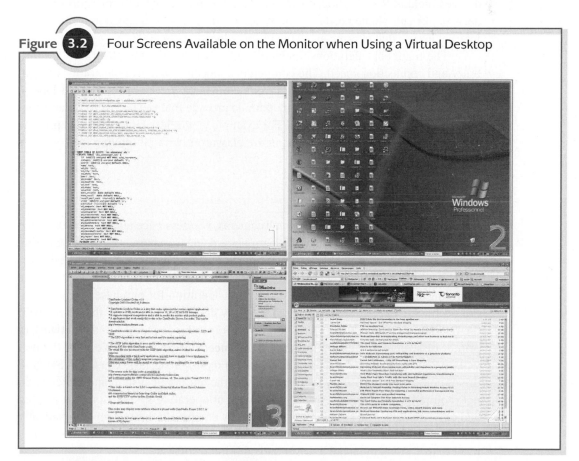

Source: Screenshot reprinted with permission from Apple, Inc.

Connectivity

Wired versus Wireless. Wired computers, such as most desktop computers, are connected to the Internet through physical devices like cables, routers, switches, and so on. Wireless computers, such as PDAs and most laptops, are connected using radio waves much like a cell phone or radio connects. The term WiFi refers to a wireless connection to a network. There are numerous protocols that can take data around a network. These protocols are like vehicles that take a motorist on a trip. Some vehicles are slow (802.11a protocol) and some are fast (802.11g protocol) while some are the Ferraris of protocols (802.11n). These protocol numbers come from the Institute of Electrical and Electronic Engineers (IEEE) and fortunately, most are backwards compatible with the older, slower protocols. Other familiar protocols for wireless devices include WPAN (802.15), otherwise known as Bluetooth for short distance devices like cell phone headsets, and WiMax (802.16), a high-speed longer distance Internet access that became available in some locations in 2008.

The main considerations for wired versus wireless in the classroom are mobility and connection speed. The computers connected by wires cannot move from classroom to classroom or even be moved within a classroom like a wireless laptop. Wireless computers are an excellent option to provide Internet access to a classroom that normally does not have access. For example, a wireless laptop cart can provide computers and Internet access to an entire classroom without moving the class to a separate computer lab.

Device Software

Devices such as printers, scanners, web cameras, wireless mice and keyboards, some computer storage devices, and other peripheral devices may require the installation of "driver" software to enable the operating system to communicate with the device. Specifically, the software acts as a translator between the peripheral device and the operating system. When a device is under consideration for purchase, the information technology department will need to verify the compatibility of the device with the operating system of the computer, and if it is to be connected to the network (a printer or scanner for example), then it also needs to be compatible with the networking system. Some devices such as headset microphones, speakers, or USB flash drives come with the ability to interface with the operating system and typically do not require installation of a driver. Most current operating systems include a "plug and play" feature. You simply plug in your new device and the system automatically installs the driver. For some equipment, such as web cameras (webcams), you may need to use a disk to install a driver and additional software.

File Format

Due to the varied nature of technology use, multiple types of digital formats are needed for the computer to distinguish the unique purpose of each. The file format for PCs is designated by an extension to the file name that consists of a period and specific letters added to the end of each digital record. For example, some common file formats are .doc for word processing files, .ppt for PowerPoint files, and .html for web files. The Macintosh does not use file extensions to identify different file types; rather, the information is stored in a manner that only the computer can detect. Thus, when opening a Macintosh file on a PC, the user must rename the file to add the extension. A summary of file formats that your students will frequently encounter is found in Table 3.1 (p. 64). Both PCs and Macintoshes can read many of these file formats.

Computers

Although computers come in a myriad of types and sizes, schools most frequently use desktops and/or laptop computers. Desktop computers are intended for use in a single location and can be in the form of separate components placed on or around a desk or combined into a single all-in-one unit. On the other hand, laptops are portable units that offer flexibility in when and where students use them.

Technology can level the learning environment so that the needs of all students can be met.

Table 3.1		File Formats Frequently Used in Schools

File Type	Extension	Description
Text	.doc .docx	Microsoft (MS) Word file MS Word 2007 file
	.txt	Text file—does not include formatting, e.g., bold, spacing, bullets. Use with Mac and PC.
	.rtf	Rich text format—retains most formatting when opened in different programs. Use with Mac and PC.
Graphics	.gif	Graphical interface format—compressed file used for web icons and animations. Size is smaller because only 256 colors are used. Not appropriate for photos. Use with Mac and PC.
	.jpg .jpeg	Compressed file not limited in number of colors; best for photos, but resolution can be lost with greater degrees of compression. Use with Mac and PC.
	.tif	Adobe tagged image file format (TIFF) used for storing images and data in a single file
	.psd	Adobe Photoshop document
Audio	.mp3	Compressed digital files used with digital audio players
	.midi .mid	Musical instrument digital interface used to transmit digital data produced by electronic musical instruments and synthesizers
	.wav	Waveform audio format primarily used with Windows for uncompressed audio
	.wma	MS Windows Media audio file comparable to .mp3 and RealAudio
Video	.mov	Apple Quicktime movie file that contains different types of data, e.g., audio, video, text
	.mp4	MPEG-4 compressed media files
	.swf	Macromedia Flash movie
	.wmv	Windows Media video file
Other	.pdf	Adobe portable document format allows documents from multiple applications to be viewed using free Adobe Reader software on PC and Mac platforms
	.xls .xlsx	MS Excel spreadsheet documents MS Excel 2007 file
	.ppt .pptx	MS PowerPoint presentation documents MS PowerPoint 2007 file
	.pub .pubx	MS Publisher document MS Publisher 2007 file
	.isf	Inspiration flowchart
	.kid	Kidspiration
	.html .htm	Hypertext markup language used for web-based files
	.zip	Zipped or compressed files that maintain fidelity during the compression and opening process; Windows uses WinZip and Mac uses Quick Zip

Desktop Components

The desktop computer in most schools consists of separate components connected to create a working unit. At minimum, the components will typically include a computer case containing the central processing unit (CPU) drives, network connector, and connectors for devices. Connected to the case you will find a monitor, keyboard, and mouse or touchpad. While most computers have a very simple speaker built in, most users prefer to connect external speakers for better sound quality.

All-in-One Desktops

Newer all-in-one computers consist of a flat screen monitor, central processing unit, speakers, and often a digital webcam combined into one case. The all-in-one desktop units need input devices such as a keyboard and mouse. Since 1983, Apple has been the leader in producing all-in-one computers (Wichary, 2004); however, all-in-one desktops are available for both the PC and Macintosh platform (see Figure 3.3).

Figure 3.3   Mac and PC All-In-One Desktop Computers

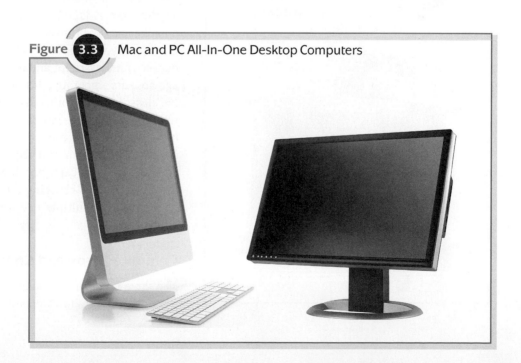

Laptops

Laptop computers are portable versions of desktop computers that are capable of most of the same functions. Laptops can include both wired and wireless connections, a hard drive for storage, CD/DVD readers and/or burners, as well as connections for an external monitor/display, USB and Firewire, and audio and video inputs and outputs. Newer laptops may have a built-in microphone and camera. Laptops are smaller than desktops, lighter in weight (three up to twelve pounds), and completely portable, which makes them excellent tools for moving between classrooms. Some laptops are equipped with a writing tablet that allows the user to write with a magnetic pen on the screen. The scripted information is stored in the computer in a digital format (see Figure 3.4).

Some disadvantages to laptop computers are the degradation of battery life over time and the theft issue due to its smaller size. A laptop will fit easily into a backpack, so an inventory system that is diligently used before and after distribution in a classroom and a secure storage area are imperative for laptop use in the classroom. The other disadvantage to the mobility of the laptop is the likelihood that it will be dropped by a student during transport to and from the storage area. Laptop carts provide a convenient storage and charging area that can be utilized in multiple classrooms (see Figure 3.5).

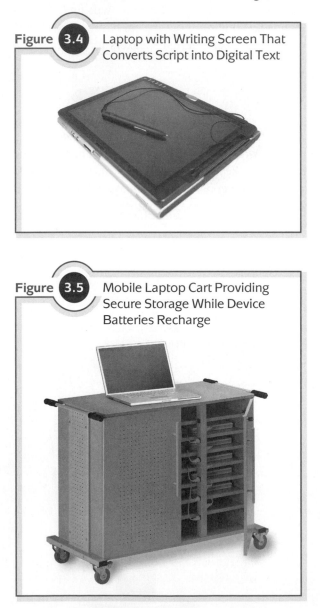

Figure 3.4 Laptop with Writing Screen That Converts Script into Digital Text

Figure 3.5 Mobile Laptop Cart Providing Secure Storage While Device Batteries Recharge

Computer Pros and Cons

The three types of computers most commonly used in today's classrooms have

Table 3.2	Pros and Cons of Types of Computers	
Digital Tool	**Pros**	**Cons**
Desktop components	• Individual components are easily replaced or upgraded by school personnel • Monitors are often large enough for easy group sharing	• Desk workspace reduced • Heavy • Immobile
All-in-one desktop	• Compact size provides additional space for individual or group work • Drives (e.g., USB, CD, DVD) may be more accessible if CPU is not stored on desktop	• Higher cost • Entire unit must go for repairs • Immobile
Laptop	• Portable—can be used in multiple locations • Compact size • Many schools keep extra laptops for use when others are sent for repair	• Requires access to power outlets • Easily damaged from dropping • Short battery life • Smaller screen limits usability for small-group learning

advantages and disadvantages that should be considered when making purchasing decisions. Table 3.2 provides a brief list of pros and cons for desktop components, all-in-ones, and laptops.

Mobile Devices

There are numerous types of handheld mobile devices that provide a wide variety of digital tools. Teachers and students often use mobile devices for playing or recording audio and video files, taking photos, reading e-books, navigating to designated locations, graphing mathematical information, scheduling and organizing a project, and entering personal responses to questions that are displayed to the class. Descriptions of these tools are in the following sections.

Digital Media Players/Recorders

Sales of the increasingly popular iPod, SanDisc's Sansa Fuse, and Microsoft's Zune are in the millions (Apple, 2008; Electronista, 2008). As a result, many schools are taking advantage of these easy-to-use devices that play specially compressed audio

(.mp3) and video files (.m4v, .mov) (see Figure 3.6). The players store media on flash memory cards or hard drives; some use a touchscreen and others are screenless (e.g., iPod shuffle).

Numerous educational audio and video files are available for mobile media players, as described in Chapter 6, Exploring the World Wide Web in the Classroom. Locations where such files are available include:

- NASA (http://nasa.ibiblio.org/vod cast.php)
- Smithsonian (www.si.edu/podcasts)
- National Geographic (www.national geographic.com/podcasts)
- National Gallery of Art (www.nga .gov/podcasts/index.shtm)
- National Public Radio (www.npr .org/rss/podcast/podcast_directory .php)

The market for audio recorders has made a dramatic shift from tapes to digital format. Digital voice recorders (DVR) are used to capture any type of audio, such as interviews, podcasts, class discussions or lectures, reflection notes, nature sounds, and music. They are small enough to fit in the palm of your hand and available in mono and/or stereo formats (see Figure 3.7). As compared to older tape recorders, digital versions use very little power and can record substantially more audio. For example, two AA batteries provide sufficient energy for four hours of recording time, while a 16 gigabyte (GB) memory card stores up to 24 hours of .wav file recording in CD-quality format or over 280 hours in .mp3. Some digital recorders offer CD-quality multitrack recording and high-impedance phone inputs to record with external microphones or from electronic instruments. Recorders include

Figure 3.6 A Mobile Media Player

Figure 3.7 A Small Yet Powerful Digital Voice Recorder for Recording Different Audio Input

USB interfaces for easy transfer of files to your computer. Recorded material can be distributed through an online interface like iTunes, uploaded to a learning management system, or distributed like any other file. The students may play the audio or video files back on a regular computer or on a handheld device.

Through the use of digital voice recorders, students can record the step-by-step processes of a science experiment, solution steps for a math problem, or reflections on writing decisions taken when drafting a persuasive argument. They can also be used to capture living history interviews, oral histories, the calls of birds, or students reading a play. Each use provides easy-to-use tools that engage students in critically analyzing the captured audio files.

Digital Cameras

The switch from film to digital cameras has also been widespread, both for still and video formats. Key features that have inspired this trend include instant viewing and ability to delete unwanted photos, large storage capacity via memory cards, ease of sharing photos and videos via email or the Web, and ability to edit photos by adding text or backgrounds or fixing defects such as "red eye" or cropping off unnecessary images. All cameras have a measurement of output in megapixels. While most monitors and printers lack the ability to display or print the picture in the same resolution, special photographic printers can take advantage of the higher resolutions. Therefore, spending the extra money for the maximum megapixel output may not be worth the expenditure for images that will only be used in a digital format (e.g., Web) or printed on a typical laser or inkjet printer.

Digital still cameras can be divided into two categories, point-and-shoot and single lens reflex digital cameras. The point-and-shoot or all-in-one cameras are small, inexpensive, and very effective. A good all-in-one camera with some zoom function will fit in the palm of your hand and is thinner than a deck of cards. Most of these cameras store images and some will store short 10- to 30-second videos on a flash memory card, which are continually getting smaller, cheaper, and greater in data storage capacity (see Data Storage Devices later in this chapter). Single lens reflex (SLR) digital cameras are similar to 35-mm SLR film cameras with interchangeable lenses. SLR cameras are more costly than the all-in-one versions but provide a greater range of photo quality, shooting options, and range that may be needed for some student projects. They allow the photographer to directly view the photo through the viewfinder and have a greater range of lenses for use from wide angle (large buildings) to macro (tiny bugs) to telephoto (wild life).

Digital video recorders are often called *camcorders* because they contain a video camera and mechanisms for recording video and sound. In earlier equipment,

Figure 3.8   Varieties of Digital Cameras (Waterproof Camera for Capturing Underwater Images and a Camera Small Enough to Fit in Pocket)

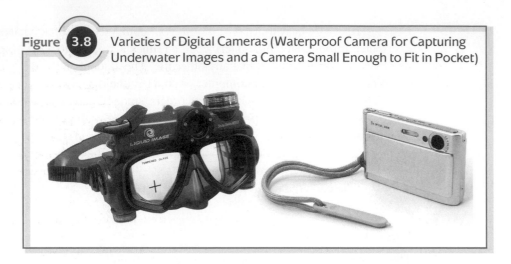

two separate components were needed to create video with sound. Most digital camcorders also include features to take still photos. Transfer of video files to a computer for editing and sharing is typically done with a USB connection or from the media storage card. As with other mobile devices, digital cameras are available in a wide range of handheld sizes. The cameras also come as an added feature embedded into a variety of other tools, such as cell phones, PDAs, and diving masks (see Figure 3.8).

Figure 3.9   e-Book Reader

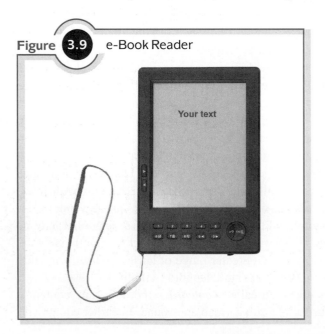

Your text

Advantages of student use of digital cameras are similar to those of audio recorders, with the further enhancement of imagery. Students can review each step of a science experiment to identify areas of needed improvement or to verify why their results are valid. They can see the facial expressions of the World War II veteran as he recalls his overseas duty. Video captured during a museum visit can be explored to identify details of a sculpture that students found interesting.

e-Book Readers

As the name implies, e-book readers present electronic books in a reader-friendly format that resembles the features of a book. For example, the display screen is about the same size as a book page. Pages "turn" when prompted, and readers can highlight text, add comments, and bookmark pages (see Figure 3.9). Most readers use E-Ink technology that provides a display screen presenting text in a crisp, easy-to-read format that is viewable in bright light yet requires minimal power usage. An advantage of e-books is the adjustability of the print size to meet visibility needs and the capacity to download and store over 200 books. However, they lack the aesthetic appeal and feel of books, loved by so many.

GPS Navigation Receivers

The Global Positioning System technology was developed by the United States Department of Defense in 1978 and at the time of this writing consists of 24 strategically located NAVSTAR satellites that are equipped with atomic clocks and transmit microwave signals (Pellerin, 2006). When a GPS device receives triangulated information from at least three satellites, it can determine location, speed, direction, time, and altitude, whereas latitude and longitude can be pinpointed with signals from two satellites. The most common use for GPS receivers (see Figure 3.10) is providing real-time driving directions on street maps. However, handheld GPS devices are used by those who trek through nature via cycling, hiking, canoeing, and so on, because the receivers (1) precisely define your *location* (and elevation), (2) provide a *route* for getting from one point to another, and (3) indicate *waypoints* along the route (Moss, 2006)

Teachers use these features to plan outdoor activities in which students follow a designated route to investigate natural, historical, or community locations. Teachers and/or students can conduct research prior to the trek to identify key waypoints to examine while on the journey or locate "hidden" geocache treasures, such as historical landmarks, unusual rock formations, or architectural styles used on school buildings. Another use is to document the location of local sites such as cemeteries or places of historic significance.

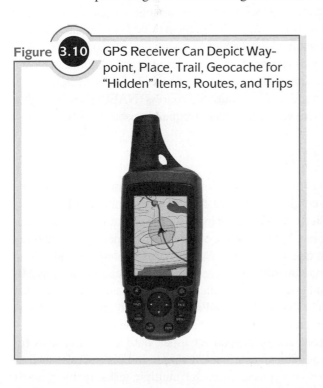

Figure 3.10 GPS Receiver Can Depict Waypoint, Place, Trail, Geocache for "Hidden" Items, Routes, and Trips

Figure **3.11**   Graphing Calculator

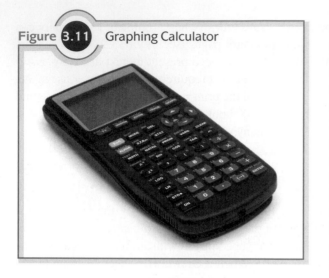

Graphing Calculators

Programmable calculators capable of plotting graphs (often in color and/or 3-D) or solving simultaneous equations are classified as graphing calculators (see Figure 3.11). The calculators allow students to generate tables of data and solve algebraic equations and geometric constructions and perform numerous other tasks involving variables. Student work can be saved, modified, or shared with others. Specialized software that emulates a graphing calculator, such as gCalc from gWhiz, can be installed on PDAs, thus reducing the need for an additional device.

Graphing calculators enable students to go beyond the basic skills of math worksheets because they require students to become actively engaged in mathematical thinking in a format that communicates results and solutions, allowing discussion and reflection on the learning process. For this and other reasons, the use of technology-produced graphing is recommended in the national mathematics curriculum standards (National Council of Teachers of Mathematics, 2000). Two research studies that used a meta-analysis approach revealed graphing calculators can have a positive effect on student learning (Ellington, 2003; Khoju, Jaciw, & Miller, 2005). Data from the National Assessment of Educational Progress (NAEP) showed higher student achievement when these calculators were frequently used (NCES, 2001).

PDAs (Personal Data Assistants)

Personal data assistants (PDAs) are palm-sized multifunctional minicomputers (see Figure 3.12). The two most common platforms for PDAs are Palm and Pocket PC (Thornton, 2008). Basic applications include an interactive appointment calendar that sounds an alert for upcoming meetings, address book, calculator, memo pad that often converts handwritten notes into text, and a task list. Additional features include photo albums, digital media players, cameras, and basic software applications such as Microsoft (MS) Word, Excel, and PowerPoint Mobile. Smartphones are cell phones that provide access to email, web browsing, radio and/or web TV, and other digital tools. PDAs can also connect to the Internet via WiFi to browse websites and check email.

PDAs have a touchscreen and/or keypad for input, hard drive, and slots for memory cards, and they accommodate external keyboards and peripherals, such as printers or science probes. When PDAs are used for multiple tasks, memory cards

Figure **3.12** Pocket PC

can be used for specific purposes (e.g., e-books, music, or photos). Data from PDAs are transferred to digital devices by direct USB, infrared signals (IrDA), Bluetooth, or wireless (WiFi) connectivity.

Many schools have chosen handheld devices rather than laptops because of the cost difference. This decision works out well because, as seen, PDAs offer many of the same basic functions as full-sized computers, yet offer full mobility. Students can take notes, write papers, keep track of assignments, create presentations, search the Internet, listen to podcasts, and exchange documents through infrared file sharing. In recognition of this trend, software developers have started producing PDA software for the K–12 market including encyclopedias, content-specific learning programs, and other software for students, as well as teacher tools for classroom management and testing. There are numerous online resources available for teachers. For example, one popular site, Kathy Schrock's (2007) "Power in the Palm of Your Hand" (http://kathyshrock.net/power) provides over 100 online resources comprising websites, information about hardware and software, related books, and presentations.

Personal Response Systems

Personal response system (PRS) technology is probably best known for its use to obtain audience opinions on popular TV programs. However, the polling tools are also frequently used by teachers to collect and graphically display real-time student responses to questions. Also known as classroom response systems (CRS), student response systems (SRS), or "clickers," most systems comprise PRS software, student transmitters, and a wireless receiver attached to a computer and digital projector. However, low-cost "computerless" response systems are also available.

The PRS software provides an interface for teachers to create a variety of questions (multiple choice, yes/no, ordering, numeric, etc.) in a PowerPoint or KeyNote format or format provided by the software. Typical classroom use begins with students picking up their

PEARSON
myeducationlab
The Power of Classroom Practice

Go to MyEducationLab, select the topic "Emerging Trends," and go to the Activities and Applications section. Access the video "Using Handhelds in the Classroom" and consider what advantages can be gained by incorporating handheld technologies in instruction. Complete the activity that follows.

Figure **3.13**   Three Student PRS Remote Control Transmitters

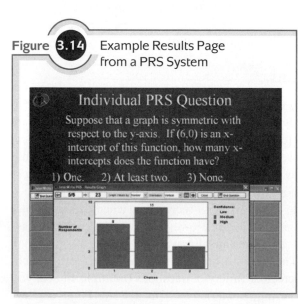

Figure **3.14**   Example Results Page from a PRS System

designated PRS remote control transmitter as they enter the room. The device includes some type of alphanumeric keypad that relays responses via infrared or radio frequency transmission (see Figure 3.13). The teacher then displays one of the questions previously entered into the system or orally asks a question. Students respond by using the keypad to enter their answers. The results can be displayed as frequencies, tables, or graphs (see Figure 3.14) with or without the correct answer and student names.

These devices can transform a presentation from a passive to an active environment by collecting student opinions and assessment during the presentation. PRS systems transmit instant feedback regarding student understanding of the content being addressed. The data can also be used to spark student interest through competitive answering and to stimulate discussions when responses are not as expected. Teachers can download the responses into a spreadsheet to follow class trends and for student assessment if data are collected in a non-anonymous format.

Mobile Device Pros and Cons

Many of the advantages and disadvantages of mobile devices are similar, yet each device has specific features to consider before adding them to your school's technology collection. Table 3.3 provides a brief list of pros and cons for the mobile devices discussed in this section.

Table 3.3   Pros and Cons of Mobile Devices

Digital Tool	Pros	Cons
Digital media players/ recorders	• Portable for field use • Review at home • Stores more data than a tape • Fewer moving parts than a tape recorder • Digital format produces higher-quality recordings that are easy to edit • Files easily transfer to other digital devices • Files can be copied indefinitely without degradation	• Higher cost than some tape recorders • Video display models more costly • Typically replaced rather than repaired • Theft
Digital cameras	• Inexpensive all-in-one models • Easy to use • Instant viewing of images • Digital editing and deletion of unwanted photos • Large storage capacity	• May break when dropped • Theft
e-Books	• Stores multiple books that can easily be exchanged or deleted • Enables digital manipulation of contents, e.g., searching, highlighting, bookmarking, audible reading, increasing font size • Enables digital enhancements, e.g., links to video or related information	• Initial cost • Devices become outdated • Lacks esthetic feel of a book • Management software for tracking e-book downloads and returns • Management plan for scheduling downloads of student reading materials • Security system to keep students from downloading unassigned books or sharing school-purchased books
GPS navigation receivers	• Provides a variety of real-time information • Small portable size	• Cost for frequency of use • Speed and location accuracy varies by type of device • Small screen reduces readability • Some are difficult to read in sunlight
Graphing calculators	• Graphical display of mathematical information • Durable device	• Can be used to play distracting games
Personal data assistants	• Low cost compared to laptops • Light weight—easy to carry • Multifunction • Uses less power than a laptop	• Some applications will not run • Small screen and keypad make completion of student work difficult. Use of a keyboard with the PDA is helpful
Personal response systems	• Increases teacher–student interactivity • Collects responses for display or storage for assessment	• Mixed research results on effectiveness • Small and easy to lose

Peripherals

The definition of peripherals varies based on the source of information. For this discussion, peripherals refer to any external input and output (I/O) device that is an optional attachment to a computer. Thus, a monitor, keyboard, and mouse are not considered peripherals because they are necessary components of a computer, whereas a printer and webcam are optional devices. Specifically, this section discusses audio devices, interactive whiteboards, printers, projectors, scanners, science probes, and webcams.

Audio Devices

Listening and speaking are integral components of learning. By hearing an explanation, story, bird call, music, or our own reflections, we gain new knowledge. This section discusses tools for digital input (microphones) and output (headphones, speakers).

Microphones.   As of 2007 over two billion microphones were produced annually with the market being split between high-end devices for mobile phones, video cameras, and headsets and low-end microphones for toys, greeting cards, and so on. (Nielsen & Furst, 2007). All digital microphones convert sound into a digital format, but the high-end, expensive microphones are better able to produce more precise sound in crisp, clear recordings than the low-end microphones.

The microphones of interest to teachers are those attached as peripherals to digital devices to enable students to create original recordings for products such as podcasts, videos, narrations, and live chats with students and experts from around the globe. When purchasing microphones, teachers may be tempted to go with the least expensive (under $10) models due to budget restraints. However, these low-end models tend to break down more frequently and produce audio that is difficult to understand. For most instances a midrange (i.e., voice frequencies) device will provide sufficient recording quality for student projects. Microphones for classroom use should include the following features to increase sound clarity: noise canceling filters to reduce background noise, distortion filters, and integrated circuits. It is also important to ensure that microphone connectivity aligns with the input device that will be used, whether audio jacks, USB ports, or wireless interfaces. Desktop microphones should have weighted bases, mute buttons, adjustable arms, and long cords for ease of placement on desks or tables. Omidirectional pickup pattern is best for groups of students while a cardioids pattern is best for recording one or two students. A handheld microphone should have an on/off switch, internal shock mount for reduced handling noise, durable construction, a long cord (if wired), and a stand.

Headphones/Headsets.   The popularity of headphones, or earphones/earbuds, has increased as mp3 players such as iPods have become standard equipment for young people. The audio devices consist of small speakers mounted in headgear that holds them on or in the ear, while headsets also include a microphone mounted on an arm that places it by the user's mouth. Most digital devices accept a 3.5-mm headphone plug that is inserted into a jack typically marked with a headphone icon.

Speakers.   As mentioned earlier, external speakers are required to listen to quality audio output from a computer. When transmitting sound to a classroom, external speakers are recommended. Most computer speakers come in pairs. One speaker typically has the balance and volume controls for the pair and is connected to the computer, a power source, and the second speaker. Higher-quality speaker sets can also include a woofer to enhance the bass sounds. Speakers can generally be used with any digital device that has audio output jacks.

Interactive Whiteboards

Interactive whiteboards look like almost any whiteboard, yet they emulate the touch-screen of a computer. Teaching with whiteboards requires a computer with whiteboard driver software connected to both the whiteboard and a digital projector via a wired or wireless connection. When the system is operational, the whiteboard becomes a human input device controlled by a teacher or student using specialized "pens" or even a finger to operate computer applications, replacing the mouse or keyboard. In addition, the whiteboard software captures handwritten notes and diagrams added to the computer display—for example, circling the nouns in a sentence, adding arrows to a water-cycle diagram, or highlighting World War II invasion locations on a map (see Figure 3.15). The software also allows the handwritten information to be saved and shared with students. Most provide options for using multiple screens during a lesson so earlier work can be referenced and perhaps modified based on newly learned content. Since the computer is controlled at the whiteboard, student presenters or the teacher remain at the front of the classroom rather than at the computer station typically at the back of a class. Interactive whiteboards are available as front projection models, as described above, rear projection models, and portable units that use a roll-up screen that attaches to a whiteboard. The costs range from just under $1000 to around $5000 for school-quality models.

Figure **3.15** An Interactive Whiteboard

Another option for those of you who are fairly tech savvy is to use a Wii remote control (Wiimote) with Bluetooth, an infrared LED pen, and free multi-point interactive whiteboard software developed by Johnny Chung Lee, an alumnus of Carnegie Mellon's Human-Computer Interaction Institute (Flavelle, 2008). The Wiimote is pointed at the projection screen in a position that tracks movement of the LED pen, while interacting with the computer software as if a mouse were used. With the price of a Wiimote being under $50, this approach provides a very low-cost interactive whiteboard option. However, it is important to note that the software provided by Mr. Lee, which is primarily created for developers, is to be used at your own risk and does not include support or guarantees. Further information may be found at WiimoteProject.com.

Some disadvantages of interactive whiteboards include the size and resolution of display for text manipulation and visibility in large classrooms. The electronic pens are easy to lose and use of a permanent marker or even an erasable marker on the whiteboard may ruin the surface. When using wired connectivity, be prepared to deal with a lot of exposed wiring and the need for recalibration if the system is used as a portable unit that is moved to different classrooms. If it is not necessary for this device to be portable, then an optimal arrangement is mounting the whiteboard to a wall, the projector to the ceiling, and the computer to a stationary desk.

Printers

Printers in schools are usually either stand-alone units or all-in-one units including printer, copier, scanner, and sometimes a fax machine. The all-in-one units are usually larger but offer the convenience of one device. However, in a classroom where the printer and scanner must be used at the same time during high-volume project jobs, it may be advisable to purchase separate devices and ergonomically arrange them in the classroom according to demand. Inkjet and laser printers are the two most common types of printers used.

Inkjet Printers. Inkjet printers imprint paper with extremely small dots, small enough to fit over one million in a square inch, or 1440×720 dots per inch (dpi) to print computer-generated products. This high level of resolution results in a very precise image that achieves the quality of a photograph. Inkjets can print black-only or full-color images. Most also offer the choice to print draft copies of documents, using less ink. The draft copies are excellent for work that is primarily text and in the formative stage. There are also inkjet printers designed exclusively for printing digital photographs that should only be considered when the primary classroom printing is photographs.

The overall cost of an inkjet printer is reasonably low; however, under heavy use they will not last as long as laser printers. The printers use ink cartridges that must be replaced or refilled when empty. Due to the high cost of new cartridges, many schools are opting to have ink cartridges refilled by a reputable company.

Laser Printers. A laser printer uses similar technology as a photocopy machine. Specifically, the printers use a laser beam to transfer digital information (text or graphics) from your computer onto a photosensitive rotating drum or belt. This creates a static electricity mirror image of the computer file that attracts particles of the dry toner, which are then transferred and fused to a sheet of paper using a heat process. Laser printers are available in models that print black-only or full-color toners. Compared to inkjet printers, they are faster and more durable but cost more to purchase and maintain as there are costly operating supplies needed. A color laser printer can cost hundreds of dollars to replace toner (frequent) and even more to replace the drum (infrequent). Take care to avoid highly heated parts in a laser printer when replacing toner cartridges.

Projectors

Digital or data projectors display what is seen on a computer monitor and, if configured correctly, can also project video from a VCR, DVD, or cable TV/HDTV. The display can be projected on an interactive whiteboard, a screen, or even a wall;

New developments in technology integrated into instruction can help motivate students for learning.

however, the clarity is diminished greatly on a wall. Projectors have different display resolutions and light output (lumens) capabilities that determine the quality of the projected image. When using an older projector having lower resolution than a newer computer, the projected display will look distorted and "squished" compared with the display's look on the computer screen. Changing your computer display resolution to match that of the projector will alleviate this effect. When considering light output, a large classroom with no lighting control would need an output of at least 3000 lumens to produce a visible display while a 1500 lumen output may work for a low ambient or controlled-light environment. Most projectors work with PCs, Macs, and some mobile devices, such as PDAs. This section focuses on the two most commonly used projectors in schools, the liquid crystal display (LCD) and digital light processing (DLP) devices.

LCD.   Early data projectors used in schools were typically liquid crystal display (LCD) panels that were connected to a computer and sat on top of overhead projectors. These older devices use a prism to divide the light from the overhead projector into red, green, and blue (RGB) before it passes through three translucent LCD panels (one for each RGB color). Each panel contains a multitude of tiny pixels that transmit light if signaled by data from the computer. The number of pixels determines the resolution—more pixels result in a higher resolution. Light from the three panels is passed through a dichroic prism, which recombines the colors to create a full color image. Current LCD projectors use a more refined and improved process compared to the one just described in that they include a much brighter and purer light source (3000+ lumens) inside the projector rather than depending on light from an overhead projector. The new projectors display very accurate colors but don't produce an absolute black (due to the use of three LCD panels), resulting in images lacking contrast.

DLP.   Schools also use digital light processing (DLP) projectors with Texas Instruments' digital micromirror devices (DMD) or memory chips rather than liquid crystals. The DMDs are covered with microscopic hinged mirrors that tilt 10 degrees in two directions to reflect light based on computer data input, with one mirror for each pixel. Thus, a projector with a resolution of 1280×1024 would contain over a million mirrors. The output from DMDs is only in black and white. Color is added through the use of a high-speed spinning color wheel (with three to six colors) through which the reflected light passes before it is focused and projected. The DLP projectors offer a three-mirror option to rival the color clarity of an LCD projector. An advantage of DLP over LCD is that mirrors produce less pixelation than the liquid crystal panels; however, the color wheel adds a disadvantage because it is a mechanical device that periodically needs to be replaced.

Scanners

Scanners work very similarly to printers and photocopiers. An image is scanned by an optical device, in this instance a charge-coupled device (CCD) that detects variations in light from the image to be scanned. This information is translated into a digital form that can be used by a computer. The images can be scanned in black and white or color. If the computer is equipped with optical character recognition (OCR) software, then scanned pages of text are translated into American Standard Code for Information Interchange (ASCII—pronounced "ask-ee") characters that can then be edited with word processing software. A key consideration is the resolution output of the scanner. Scanner resolution is measured in pixels per inch (ppi), which typically ranges from a low of around 1600 ppi to 5000+ ppi. Most scanners include some type of software that lets you modify the scanned images by resizing, rotating, or cropping unwanted portions; alternatively, you can use a graphic software package. Scanners typically connect to the computer through a USB port. The three most common types of scanners in classrooms are flatbeds, sheet-fed, and handheld.

Flatbed Scanners. Schools and classrooms typically use flatbed scanners because of their ability to not only scan individual sheets of paper, but also pages from books and magazines or even aspects of a three-dimensional object that has a fairly flat surface, such as a coin, leaf, or etching on an antique box. The object to be scanned is placed face-down on a glass plate. The CCD array moves along a track beneath the glass to record an image of the page or object that is converted to a digital file and output to a computer.

Sheet-Fed Scanners. These devices work similarly to a printer in that document pages are scanned as they move across the CCD, which is immobile. Sheet-fed scanners are less frequently seen in classrooms because their use is restricted to digitizing single sheets rather than book pages or objects.

Handheld Scanners. These smaller devices are popular for individual scanning of small images, such as photos, or short sections of text, such as web addresses, quotes from newspapers, article references, or data tables. The handheld scanners use the same technology as the flatbed and sheet-fed scanners, but depend on the user to move the device (equipped with a small roller ball) across the page at a steady pace and along a straight path (see Figure 3.16). Thus, the input quality can vary. Handheld scanners are also used to read or translate lines of text to different languages through audio output in a variety of voices.

Figure 3.16 Handheld Scanner Able to Copy and Provide Audio Translation of Three Lines of Text

Science Probes

Scientific probes or "probeware" are digital tools used to collect data for use in scientific studies. The information collected can involve motion, light, heat, temperature, pH, pressure, and similar data (see Table 3.4). Probes often display the data in real-time graphs as well as in numerical format (see Figure 3.17). The data from the probes are transferred to a computer or graphing calculator for examination and analysis. Some devices provide software specifically programmed for the probeware and/or in formats compatible with spreadsheet, database, or word processing software.

Table 3.4	Science Probe Examples

Accelerometers	Ammonium ISE	Barometer
Blood pressure sensor	Calcium ISE	Charge sensor
Chloride ISE*	CO_2 gas sensor	Colorimeter
Conductivity probe	Current probe	Differential voltage probe
Digital control unit	Dual-range force sensor	Dissolved oxygen probe
Drop counter	Garmin® GPS units	EKG sensor
Electrode amplifier	Heart rate monitor	Flow rate sensor
Force plate	Light sensor	Gas pressure sensor
Hand dynamometer	Microphone	Infrared thermometer
Ion-selective electrodes	O_2 gas sensor	Low-g accelerometer
Magnetic field sensor	pH sensor	Motion detector
Nitrate ISE	Radiation monitors	Ohaus balances
Soil moisture sensor	Respiration monitor belt	Relative humidity sensor
Sound level meter	Rotary motion sensor	Salinity sensor
Temperature probes	Spectrometers	Surface temperature sensor
Turbidity sensor	UV sensor	Voltage probe

*Ion-selective electrode (ISE)

Classroom use of scientific probes is steadily increasing. One factor influencing this growth is a national focus on the "STEM" fields of science, technology, engineering, and mathematics. This renewed interest is backed by funding for professional development as well as new technologies that have a proven track record for improving student performance (Leath, 2007). An additional factor is that probeware, as with most technology, produces higher-quality data with easier-to-use interfaces, while costing less.

PEARSON
myeducationlab
The Power of Classroom Practice

Go to MyEducationLab, select the topic "Science Integration," and go to the Activities and Applications section. Access the video "Hands-On Science" and consider how digital tools can be used to collect data. Complete the activity that follows.

Webcams

A webcam is a small digital video camera connected to or built into a computer that sends real-time streamed video via a live connection to a designated Internet location (see

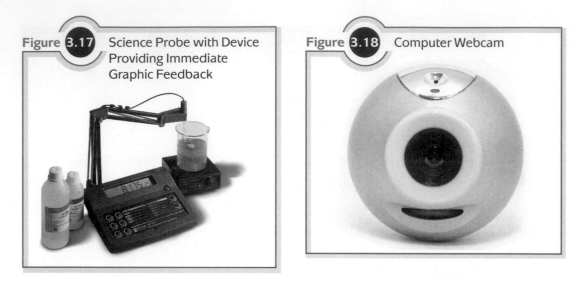

Figure 3.17 Science Probe with Device Providing Immediate Graphic Feedback

Figure 3.18 Computer Webcam

Figure 3.18). Real-time uses of webcams include video conferencing and instant messaging for which users from different locations can see and hear each other during the online sessions. Students can also view video from real-time webcams stationed at zoos, botanical gardens, historical landmarks, and famous geologic locations (see Table 3.5). Webcams are also used to capture video or photographs to be posted to websites.

Table 3.5	Live Webcams around the Globe
CapitalCam: Washington, DC	www.earthcam.com/usa/dc/metrosquare
Panama Canal Cam	www.pancanal.com/eng/photo/camera-java.html
Paris-Live	www.paris-live.com
PyramidCam	www.pyramidcam.com
RailCam: Switzerland	www.railserve.com/jump/jump.cgi?ID=22444
Times Square Cam	www.earthcam.com/usa/newyork/timessquare/index.php?cam=tsone
VolcanoCam: Mt. Saint Helens	www.fs.fed.us/gpnf/volcanocams/msh
WildCam: Africa	http://video.nationalgeographic.com/video/wildcamafrica

Table 3.6	Pros and Cons of Peripheral Devices	

Digital Tool	Pros	Cons
Projectors	• Large display • Easy to see • Mobile or mounted option	• Replacement bulbs are expensive • Cost is higher for high ambient light room
Interactive whiteboards	• Interacts with computer • Stores annotations in computer • Places teacher or presenter in front of students	• Often too small for large classroom • Resolution depends on projector and may not be suitable for detailed displays • Low height of floor models makes it difficult for some students to see entire whiteboard
Printers	• Inkjet—inexpensive • Laser—excellent quality prints	• Refreshing laser printers is costly • Needs special supplies for printing labels, photos, etc.
Scanners	• Inexpensive • Easy to use	• Requires driver installation
Science probes	• Inexpensive • Portable • Connect to desktop, laptop, PDA	• Delicate
Webcams	• Inexpensive models available • Broadcast live video	• Typically requires a driver installation

Peripherals Pros and Cons

As seen in this section, computer peripherals provide a wide range of functions in different types of devices. Some general overall pros and cons of peripheral devices are provided in Table 3.6.

Data Storage Devices

In this age of data collection, manipulation, and distribution, data storage devices are convenient and in some cases necessary. Some school systems have network storage drives for student and faculty use at school and at home, but often the space offered is limited and will fill up very quickly when working with high-resolution digital images or video. External hard drives, flash drives, and storage cards are common solutions for data storage.

Figure 3.19   An External Hard Drive Small Enough to Easily Be Transported with a Laptop

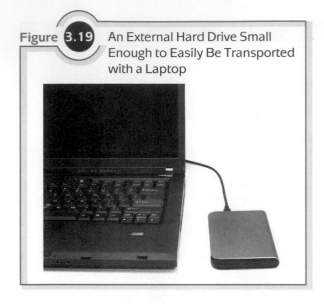

External Hard Drives

External hard drives are basically the same as an internal hard drive that is placed in a case and equipped with ports to connect to a computer via high-speed interface cables such as universal serial bus (USB) and Firewire (IEEE 1394) (see Figure 3.19). As with other technology, the capacity of external hard drives is increasing as the size and price decrease. Lower-end devices cost less than $50 and hold up to 100 GB of data, while high-end units costing around $400 have the capacity to store a terabyte (TB) of data. A terabyte is one trillion bytes or 1000 gigabytes. You can compare the costs of drives by dividing the capacity by the price to determine the price per gigabyte.

Most external hard drives are plug-and-play devices that are typically compatible with both PCs and Macs. They are becoming an increasingly popular way to back up data on a computer's hard drive, which is always susceptible to loss from drive failure or compromise due to Internet viruses and spyware. They are also a great solution for storing multimedia files (e.g., music or DVD videos) that require a large amount of hard drive space.

Students often choose to purchase an external hard drive rather than a flash drive to obtain greater storage capacity in a device that is larger, more durable, and less likely to be misplaced. The drives allow students to keep schoolwork from all classes for multiple years in one location. Students have access to their documents when working at any computer in the school as well as at a home computer or one at a friend's house.

Along with the positive aspects of external drives are some concerns. The drives can be infected with data-corrupting viruses, like any other storage device. They are also susceptible to the same environmental hazards as other technologies, such as heat, sunlight, liquids, and dust, as well as damage from exposure to electromagnetic fields from monitors, speakers, and so on. Plus there is the added risk of being owned by a student, which means the device may end up in the washing machine, left in the backseat of a hot car, or left behind on a sidewalk while skateboarding.

Flash Drives

These portable storage devices usually come with a USB connection and are referred to by many different names, such as jump drive, thumb drive, flash drive, or USB

Figure **3.20** Four Types of Data Storage Cards

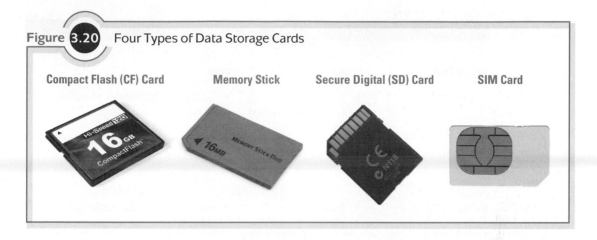

Compact Flash (CF) Card	Memory Stick	Secure Digital (SD) Card	SIM Card

drive. These convenient drives offer portable storage in a small device. Sizes can be up to 32 gigabytes for average usage although sizes are increasing and prices are decreasing steadily. Because the flash drives easily disconnect or get lost, some models come on "around-the-neck" lanyards to help users keep track of the small devices. Most will not withstand a beating at the bottom of a backpack, briefcase, or purse.

Storage Cards

Storage cards fit inside a device such as a digital camera, music player, or game console. The four major types of storage cards are compact flash (CF), memory stick, secure digital (SD), and SIM (see Figure 3.20). Information is transferred from a card to a computer with a portable or built-in reader (see Figure 3.21). The transferred data can then be manipulated with software.

Figure **3.21** Portable Reader That Transfers Data from Several Types of Storage Cards to a Computer

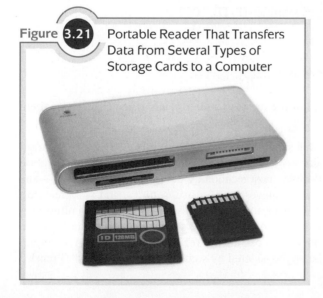

Digital Storage Pros and Cons

As with any digital tool, data storage devices have advantages and disadvantages to consider. Table 3.7 on page 88 provides a brief list of common pros and cons. Please note that devices should be regularly backed up to prevent loss of data.

Table 3.7	Pros and Cons of Digital Storage Devices	
Digital Tool	**Pros**	**Cons**
External hard drives	• Small • Large capacity storage • Easy to use	• Susceptible to damage from multiple sources • Can spread viruses
Flash drives	• Small • Easy to use	• Easy to lose • Susceptible to damage from multiple sources
Storage cards	• Small • Fits directly in device	• Needs an adapter to transfer data to computer

Summary

This chapter presented an overview of four types of digital tools that are commonly used in today's classrooms: computers, mobile devices, peripherals, and data storage devices. The platform (PC or Mac), connectivity (wired or wireless), device software, and file formats need to be considered when planning technology purchases and classroom use. The NETS for Students indicate the importance of students using appropriate digital devices to build research and information fluency, to gain a sound understanding of technology operations and concepts, and to develop critical thinking, problem-solving, and decision-making capabilities (ISTE, 2007).

Teacher Technology FAQ

How will I know how to use all of the new technology tools when I integrate them into a lesson?

There are a couple of things that should make you feel more comfortable. First, most technology devices use similar ways to access information about the tool and to use the device functions. For example, most technology devices are menu driven—and have a Menu button that displays suggestions for use, settings, and Help features. This common interface is typically pretty user-friendly. The Internet also offers several user guides for tools and blogs of current users who are more than happy to answer questions. And of course, you can always read the instructions. Another approach is to let students, who are considered by some as "digital natives" (Prensky,

2008), figure out how to use the devices and then teach you and others how to use the key features.

With new technology being released every day, I feel like my technology purchases are outdated by the time I open the package, yet my school's budget is limited. What can be done?

Digital tools tend to be designed to work with a range of technologies that span several years, typically a five- to seven-year spread. To use a new device with an older machine, it may be necessary to download the appropriate software driver. Caution needs to be taken before purchasing any digital tools to ensure the devices will be compatible with your laptop or desktop computer, your digital projectors, or other key technology owned by your school.

Technology Integration Activities

The following activities provide an opportunity for you to explore the options for using digital tools described in this chapter.

1. Describe a management plan that you can implement to help prevent the loss of your digital files or your students' data from portable drives.
2. Select a peripheral or mobile device and generate a list of ways you could integrate the technology into a lesson by using the technology as a tool.

NTeQ Portfolio Activities

Please complete the following activities as part of your NTeQ Portfolio on digital tools in the classroom.

Reflections

The Getting Started portion of this chapter posed three Reflecting on What I Know questions that teachers might commonly ask. In this portion of your journal, reflection activities have been added to help you reflect on each question. Please use information from this chapter and from the *MyEducationLab* resources to answer the questions.

❶ Why is it important to learn about different technology tools when they are constantly changing?

Reflection Activity: This chapter presents a wide variety of digital tools that are used in today's classrooms. To help you understand relationships among the tools, create a chart that shows key basic functions of each category of digital tools discussed in the chapter.

❷ **Most desktop computers do the same things as mobile devices, so why do teachers need to use both?**

Reflection Activity: Review the "Pro" section for mobile devices and computers. Write a summary of the benefits that mobile devices have over nonmobile technology tools.

❸ **How can the cost of digital devices be justified when the functions they perform are often limited in number and scope?**

Reflection Activity: Review the MyEducationLab videos for this chapter and write a statement that supports the purchase of digital devices and proposes a plan that maximizes student exposure to the tools.

Imagine that you received a large technology grant to equip your classroom with each type of technology tool described in this chapter. Write a brief description of how you would use each tool for the grade level and subject(s) you teach or plan to teach.

Computer Software in Today's Classrooms

Getting Started

At the heart of every digital device is the software that enables the user to complete a myriad of tasks. For example, software can be programmed to check spelling, generate a graph, draw a cube, play virtual drums, create 3-D blueprints, drive a simulated racecar, change handwriting to text, demonstrate division of a fraction, or collect golden keys to open the "magic treasure chest" by solving math problems.

This chapter provides a general overview of software used in today's classrooms, divided into five categories derived from the major functions of each type of software. All of the categories are represented in ISTE's (2007) National Educational Technology Standards for Students (NETS-S), either directly or indirectly (see Table 1.1). By following a well-thought-out integration plan, such as the NTeQ lesson plan, a variety of software applications can become an integral component of a lesson. This chapter provides an overview of the five types of software and their basic functions and provides lots of ideas for classroom use. More detailed information regarding specific software functions and classroom applications using the NTeQ model are found in later chapters.

Reflecting on What I Know

1 There are so many types of software; how do I know which ones to include in my lessons?

2 I understand why students should use educational software and the Internet, but why should my fourth-grade students learn to use spreadsheet, database, or video editing software?

3 How can student use of different types of software help improve scores on state tests?

Classroom
SNAPSHOT

Mrs. Jamison's sixth-grade class is equipped with wireless laptop computers for each student. In an effort to strengthen content knowledge and skills while also building 21st-century technology abilities, she integrates multiple software applications into her students' daily activities. Regular activities include using AppleWorks to write sentences from the "Just Vocabulary 2 Words a Day" podcast. Students use iMovie and PowerPoint to add work artifacts and digital video reflections to their electronic portfolios. Inspiration is used to plan research papers, students add ideas to a global warming blog, and emails are exchanged with Alaskan students to compare daily life activities. Geometer's Sketchpad is used to practice math skills, while language arts skills are reinforced with Plato Learning. Technology is seamlessly integrated as a tool into teaching and learning activities to enhance and expand student understanding and experiences beyond the textbook and classroom walls.

Software Categories

As seen in the previous chapter, technology hardware is continuously becoming more versatile and powerful, while decreasing in size and cost, enabling more classroom teachers to integrate the use of new multifunction digital devices into a variety of lesson plans. Teachers who are less experienced with technology may fully appreciate the technology integration efforts of teachers like Mrs. Jamison, although it also can seem somewhat daunting to teachers as they are now faced with even more options to consider when planning for classroom use of technology. One way to begin this adventure is to gain familiarity with five common categories of software and examine specific examples of each to understand key functions and how they can be used in the classroom (see Figure 4.1). The following sections describe each of these five categories of software and the functions of each.

Productivity Software

As the name implies, productivity software is used to produce or create a variety of artifacts or products. The eight key types of productivity software used in today's classrooms are word processing, spreadsheet, presentation, database,

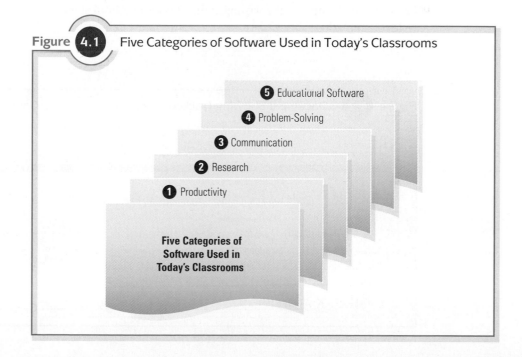

Figure 4.1 Five Categories of Software Used in Today's Classrooms

5 Educational Software
4 Problem-Solving
3 Communication
2 Research
1 Productivity

Five Categories of Software Used in Today's Classrooms

mapping/planning, drawing/painting, audio/video editing, and authoring. A general description of each type of software and how it is used in the classroom is provided below.

Word Processing

Commonly used word processing software in today's classrooms includes Microsoft (MS) Word, MS Works, and AppleWorks, which all come as parts of suites of applications. Word processing easily fits into any style of teaching, because its primary function is to enhance the writing process by automating many of the tedious tasks associated with using paper and pencil. For example, with a few clicks of the mouse, students can check spelling and grammar, change the line spacing, cut and paste text to different locations, change the font style or color, add a table, or insert a photo, Internet hyperlink, or bar graph. The Track Changes, Insert Comment, and Highlight tools provide detailed information to help students when editing a document. For example, Figure 4.2 shows deletions, inserted comments, and highlighted text to provide specific feedback for a particular section of text.

Classroom uses of word processing are limitless; the software can be used any time students are required to write. The automated features of word processing make writing, editing, and enhancing documents easier, which in turn encourages students to write more frequently. Use of word processing on a regular basis has been shown to improve the writing skills of middle school students (Lowther, Ross, & Morrison, 2003).

Figure 4.2 Document Showing Tracked Changes and Inserted Comments

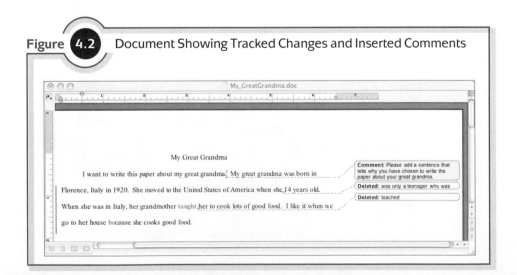

Spreadsheets

MS Excel is probably the most recognized spreadsheet software available on PC computers; schools equipped with Macs often use AppleWorks, which includes an easy-to-use spreadsheet application. InspireData is another popular application that combines spreadsheet functions with databases and concept mapping. The automated features of spreadsheets enable elementary through high school students to carry out two primary functions when working with numeric information: performing calculations and creating graphs. To perform calculations, it is important to understand that spreadsheets consist of a series of lettered columns and numbered rows that create "cells" designated by their associated column and row—for example, B3 or D7. Users enter numbers into the cells and then write a formula or use one of the many built-in functions for performing common calculations such as *sum, average, count,* and *multiply.*

The second primary function of spreadsheets is the creation of graphs or charts. This user-friendly feature is also automated. You begin by using the mouse to select the data you want to graph. Next, click the *chart* icon to open a dialog box that directs you to several options for creating your chart—selecting the type of chart, adding labels and a legend, and determining the scale range. Chart types include *bar, column, pie, area, line, scatter,* and others (see Figure 4.3).

There is a clear connection between mathematics and the use of spreadsheets. An added value is their ability to display patterns and trends in information, a useful function across subject areas and grade levels. For example, third-grade students can better understand their eating habits by examining a pie chart that shows daily servings in each food category. Seventh-grade students from two states can compare presidential voting patterns in the two states by age, gender, and ethnicity. High school students in an English literature class can compare the writing styles of female versus male authors by examining a spreadsheet chart displaying composition features of the authors' last novels. The composition features can be generated with word processing tools that identify reading level scores, average number of words per sentence, and number of sentences per paragraph. These combined features make spreadsheet software an excellent tool for enhancing students' analytical abilities.

Presentation Software

PowerPoint is another commonly used productivity application in today's schools. Presentation software provides a user-friendly interface that lets students create colorful and informative displays in any subject area. The software includes pre-programmed backgrounds, animations, sounds, and functions that can be formatted to create a limitless variety of slides either presented by the student or set to automatically show according to a preset schedule. Presentations can include hyperlinks

Figure 4.3 Insert Chart Dialog Box with Options for Chart Types

to designated slides in the presentation, to other documents, or to Internet sites. Students can insert a pie graph that is displayed one section at a time and includes a student-created narration that explains the content of each slide. These unique features support and encourage student creativity.

Young students can create simple presentations that involve adding only one or two words and images per slide. For example, when studying the seasons, the teacher can create a template that has a title slide and an appropriate background for each season (e.g., winter snow). Students then add clip art to each slide that represents the four seasons and a narration to explain why they chose each graphic. Older students can create more sophisticated presentations, such as a Civil War presentation that includes digital copies of photos, letters, music, and other archived materials from that time period. For social studies, middle school students can create a presentation that demonstrates similarities and differences in their current city council membership. Students can incorporate hyperlinks to create virtual field trips, drill-and-practice, and Jeopardy-style games. As seen, presentation software provides students and teachers with an easy-to-use interface that quickly enables users to create dynamic, interactive multimedia presentations that can demonstrate a deeper level of knowledge than traditional nondigital formats.

Databases

Popular application suites such as MS Office, MS Works, and AppleWorks include database applications, which are used to store sets of related information in data files. When information is stored in a database, it can efficiently and effectively be retrieved in a variety of formats—from one single record to a report of all data in specified fields—which makes them very useful learning tools in K–12 classrooms. For example, if students created a data file for the 50 states, the fields for each record might include state name, flower, bird, population, and average yearly rainfall. Students can use the database to answer a variety of questions. Are states that have the same state bird or flower located in the same region? Which three states could you live in if you wanted very low humidity and a small population? Or high school students can download a database of census data from their county and examine population trends by different categories, such as median income, number of households with a college degree, or type of housing. Each example uses the database sorting features to quickly examine information from multiple perspectives.

Spreadsheet applications can perform sorting functions similar to a database. This sorting task can be accomplished by selecting the entire data set and then sorting by a designated column. For example, when working with a data set of endangered species, students could sort the data by type of animal (e.g., mammal, bird, reptile) to examine frequency trends by animal types. Similarly, you could also filter the data so that only mammals appear in the list. These types of activities traditionally involved student creation of note cards with handwritten information. Yet, answering deep-level questions from a set of note cards can be extremely time-consuming and lead to lack of motivation. On the other hand, when students enter information in a database, students can conduct limitless inquires with the click of a mouse, which rewards and supports the inquisitive nature of student learning.

Graphic Organizers

Students working individually or in cooperative groups can now use graphic organizer software, such as Inspiration or Kidspiration, to visualize and expand on their learning by creating models and concept maps. The software provides tools that let the students represent ideas with graphic shapes, images, and text; students can

Figure **4.4** Concept Map of Geography

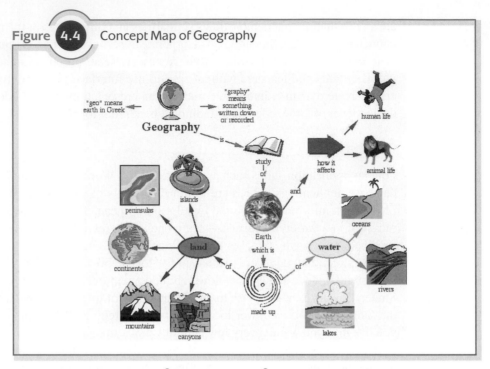

Source: Example created in Inspiration® by Inspiration Software®, Inc. Reprinted with permission.

create and describe links between ideas and arrange the components in meaningful layouts that represent their thinking (Figure 4.4). With the click of a mouse, student ideas are transformed from a concept map to an outline that can be opened in a word processing document, or the concept map can be inserted into a presentation, report, or web page. The main advantage of using digital graphic organizers over paper-based approaches is the ease with which students can make adjustments and changes to reflect ideas as learning occurs.

Graphics Software

There is a wide range of graphics software. Some software provides searchable access to large databases of images, such as clip art, photos, animations, and videos. Other graphics software applications provide tools to create or modify digital images that are formatted as a raster or vector graphic. Raster graphics are stored as tiny square pixels that create a grid-based bitmap of an image. The raster graphics appear with jagged edges if the image is enlarged beyond its original size. Common formats for raster images are .gif, .jpg, .tiff, and .bmp. On the other hand,

Preparing graphics as part of research can help enhance presentations.

vector graphics are stored mathematically as a series of coordinates that generate geometric objects, such as curves and polygons. As a result, vector images can easily be enlarged, reshaped, rotated, and ungrouped into individual components that can each be modified by changing color, size, or shape or even deleted from the overall image. The most common format for vector graphics is .eps (Encapsulated PostScript).

Graphics applications are often embedded in word processing, presentation, and spreadsheet software as "drawing" tools. The MS drawing toolbar provides AutoShapes (e.g., circles, stars, arrows) that can be modified by changing the size, shape, and color and by grouping them with other shapes to create new graphics. It also has freestyle drawing tools that allow users to draw their own art. Each drawing or painting application has advantages and disadvantages. Images created with applications based on raster graphics are not easily changed by deleting individual pieces, whereas vector images are easily modified. More sophisticated graphics applications allow users to manipulate digital photos (Adobe Photoshop, Lightroom, and Corel PaintShop Pro), create and manipulate digital images (Adobe Illustrator), and use interactive animations (Flash).

Students can become fascinated and engrossed in creating "awesome" graphics and animations for their school assignments. However, the key to integrating meaningful use of graphics software is to require students to include graphics that better demonstrate their knowledge and understanding of the learning objectives.

Digital Audio Editing

As seen in Chapter 3, digital recording devices are affordable and offer teachers many different options for integrating the use of audio into their instruction. Teachers and students can use audio recording and editing software to cut, copy, paste, and enhance an original recording and save it as a personalized digital file. Audacity (available for Windows and Macintosh) and Garage Band (Macintosh only) are software applications used for recording and editing audio. There are many other audio recording/editing software applications that are very reasonable in price. When choosing audio software for classroom use, it important to ensure that it includes easy-to-use features such as pulldown menus, preset effects, and built-ins that automatically find the audio files. It is also important to have a user-friendly help menu and FAQ.

An example of classroom use of audio is for middle school students to digitally record each other reading poems they've written about world peace. Students edit the recordings to remove mistakes and to add background music and special effects sounds. Another illustration is elementary student use of mobile devices to record the songs of a variety of local birds. The students add narrative descriptions of the unique features of each bird and include the audio files in a PowerPoint presentation. Similarly, middle and high school students might create an oral history library of recollections of World War II, the Vietnam conflict, the first manned space flight, or some local historical event. The newer digital recording devices and editing software open numerous opportunities for using audio to support and enhance student learning. For example, students could create a weekly podcast that could be made available on the school or classroom website for parents and members of the community.

Digital Video Editing

Digital video cameras are increasing in popularity as a tool in many schools, partly because of the ease with which video can be edited with software included in most computer application packages—iMovie for Macs and Windows Movie Maker for PC computers. The digital video editing software uses nonlinear editing that allows students to edit a video in a way that is similar to how other digital files are edited. In other words, you can copy and paste segments of the video to rearrange the sequence and add titles, music, fun transitions such as fades, or video credits using a *Star Wars* approach.

After a brief training session, even elementary school students can easily use a digital camera and then edit their video. Videos are excellent tools for capturing different stages of student work while creating 3-D models of an ancient artifact, student reenactments of a classical play, or student reporters collecting opinions on current events. They are also excellent tools to record student performance or personal reflections on learning for an electronic journal. Teachers can create digital video demonstrations of skills, such as titration of a chemical, finding the volume of a cylinder, or checking a paragraph for correct structure. The demonstration videos can be placed on the class website for use when students need remediation in the selected areas.

Multimedia Authoring Software

We live in a multimedia, interactive world, and as a result our students have grown up with multidimensional thinking. Through the use of multimedia authoring software such as eZedia and HyperStudio, pre-K through high school students can create interactive products combining audio, video, animation, and graphics to demonstrate multiple levels of their knowledge and skills. The products are created by using preprogrammed (e.g., *hide, show, move, play*) and drag-and-drop functions to add digital media and images that the students have created or that are downloaded from another source. The programs also include full text editing and drawing tools to enable further personalizing of the products, which can be exported as HTML to a web page.

Students can use authoring software to create an interactive timeline of events (e.g., metamorphosis, history of airplanes, steps to divide a fraction), to demonstrate a concept (e.g., freedom, symmetry, colors), or to tell a story (e.g., My Family Traditions, Life before Credit Cards, The Influence of Harriet Tubman). Teachers can also have students create multimedia products that reinforce basic skills. For example, students can be asked to produce interactive tutorials to teach the parts of speech, how to calculate mean scores, or how to interpret a graph. The authoring software enables students to concentrate on the key information to be learned by utilizing multiple types of media to demonstrate their knowledge and skills.

Research Software

The Internet contains a wide variety of resources formatted for use on the Web. When students conduct online research for information about a topic they are studying, they need to use browsers, search engines, and a series of small downloadable software applications called plug-ins to access these resources. A brief overview of these research applications follows.

Browsers

Initial access to the Web begins with a browser, such as Safari, Netscape Navigator, Opera, or Internet Explorer. Users can program the home page of a browser to open with a specified site or they can create a personalized home page to suit their own interests (e.g., adding continuously updated RSS feeds to news broadcasts, bookmarks of frequently used websites, or changing the page layout and background). These features are great for teachers because they can personalize the browsers on classroom computers to highlight subject areas being taught while providing direct links to "kid-friendly" sites and tools. An example from Ms. Ford's English and American history classroom is seen in Figure 4.5. The browser provides common

Figure 4.5   Ms. Ford's Classroom Website

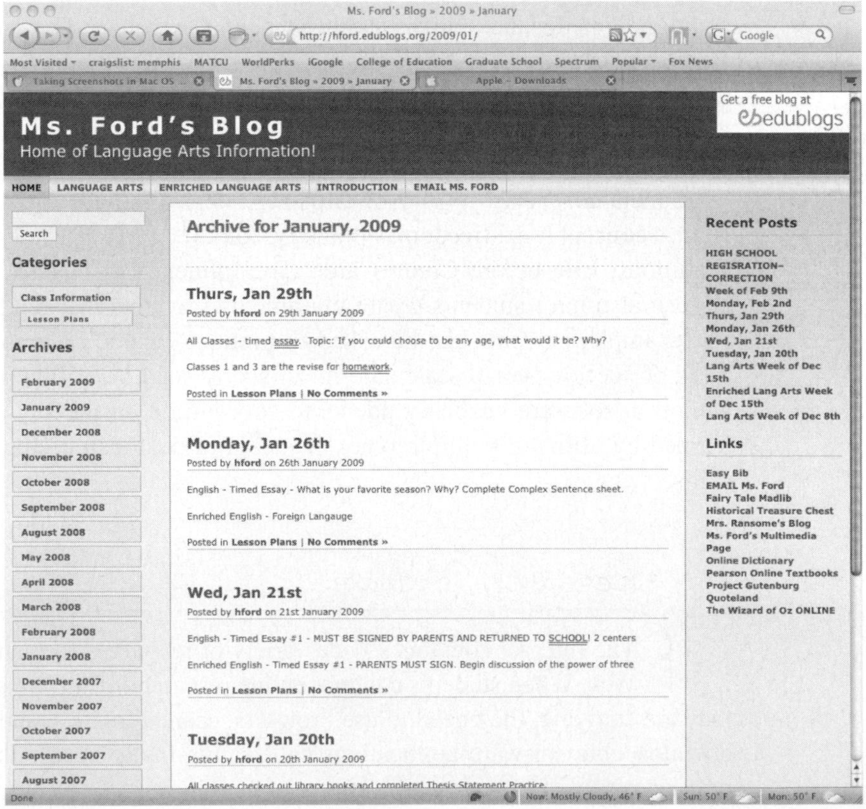

tools that allow students to explore the World Wide Web without feeling lost because they can use the Back or Forward buttons to return to previously visited sites, or they can use the Home button to return to the main page.

Search Engines

Search engines are the primary type of software tools used within a browser. Popular search engines include Google, Ask, and Yahoo! The search engines operate by using keyword searches that instantaneously generate lists of Internet-based resources containing some or all of the key search terms. Options can be selected to provide a specific type of resource (e.g., text, photos, videos, audio). You can also use advanced searches to narrow the scope of results. The advanced searches allow you to more clearly define the search by specifically indicating key words or a phrase that must be included and those that are not to be included. As will be seen in later chapters, it is useful to have students identify key search terms and the types of resources that are needed prior to using search engine software.

Plug-Ins

Plug-in software, which is typically free and easily downloaded and installed, may be needed to access some files located during your Internet search. Common *plug-ins* in the classroom include Acrobat Reader software used to open a document saved as a portable document file (pdf), QuickTime to view digital video, and RealAudio to listen to digital audio files. These applications allow students to listen to audio files of past presidential speeches, to view documentaries of soil erosion, and to examine copies of archived government documents. If your computer does not have the plug-in to access an online resource, you will typically receive an alert message that includes a link to a site where the needed plug-in is available for download.

Communication Software

As mobile and home computing devices become increasingly popular, digital communication is becoming the norm. Digital communication occurs in two forms—asynchronous and synchronous or real-time. Common forms of asynchronous communication include email, discussion boards, blogs, wikis, and podcasts. Blogs, wikis, and podcasts are Web 2.0 tools/platforms because they support the creation and editing of web-based content by any user. Prevalent synchronous communication formats include chats and instant messaging. Key features of communication software include the ability to exchange digital files, such as audio and video, word-processed documents, PowerPoint presentations, and spreadsheets.

| Table 4.1 | Communication Software Features | | | | | |

Software Type	Asynchronous	Synchronous	File Exchange	Multimedia	Hyperlinks	Web 2.0
Email	X		X	X	X	
Lists	X		X	X	X	
Discussion boards	X		X		X	
Blogs	X		X	X	X	X
Wikis	X		X	X	X	X
RSS	X*			X	X	X
Podcasts	X			X	X	X
Chats		X	X	X	X	
Instant messaging		X	X	X	X	

*One-way feed

Other features include embedded multimedia that can play a streamed sound clip or show a presentation and hyperlinks to Internet resources. A summary of these features is presented in Table 4.1.

Before your students engage in any digital communication with people outside of your district, it is critical that you follow your district's acceptable use policy and have all communication projects approved by your information technology department. All communication must occur under extremely careful supervision with rigorous editing of student messages to ensure the safety of you and your students. When these guidelines are followed, communication software opens the door to many rich interactions that enhance and expand student learning, as discussed below.

Asynchronous Digital Communication Software

The term *asynchronous* has Greek roots, with *asyn* meaning "not with" and *chronos* meaning "time;" thus, it can be defined as "not at the same time." The most popular asynchronous digital communication software includes email, discussion boards, blogs, wikis, and podcasts.

Electronic Mail.   Electronic mail (abbreviated as *e-mail* or *email*) has become the communication method of choice at work and is frequently used for family and personal correspondence. Email is often used instead of a phone call because it can be read at the convenience of the receiver and avoids the possibility of calling at the wrong time. Email also has the advantage of providing documentation of interactions. As a teacher, this is useful for archiving messages to and from parents or students in email folders that you have designated for parent or student communications. Other email folders can be created as needed to support your professional correspondence.

Many teachers use school-provided email systems as a means of sending and receiving digital documents. Students can email the teacher a draft report to receive feedback prior to writing the next version. Teachers can email student work to parents for their review rather than relying on students to make it home without the "dog eating" their work before their parents can sign it.

Email can also be used to support the instructional process by allowing your students to interact with and learn from people beyond their classroom walls. Students can send questions or opinions to their mayor, senator, or local newspaper. They can discuss solutions to global warming with a science professor, exchange emails about recent tornados with students living in a neighboring state, send encouraging notes to children diagnosed with a serious illness, communicate with archeologists excavating ruins in Egypt, or improve their French writing skills by exchanging emails with students living in France.

Lists.   Mailing lists, often mistakenly called *listservs,* are another use of email. These lists send the same information to subscribers to the list or to people added by the teacher or originator. For example, teachers can originate a mailing list of all the parents in a class to keep them informed of classroom activities. The teacher can also subscribe to specialized lists to meet and exchange ideas and resources on topics of interest with educators around the world. You can use sites such as TileNet (http://tile.net/lists) or Catalist (www.lsoft.com/catalist.html) to locate lists with easy-to-use search tools. Lists are available in broad topics such as "technology integration" as well as topics aligned to specific grade levels and subject areas. You can easily "unsubscribe" to a list that is not aligned to your needs by following directions provided by the list—typically at the end of each message.

Discussion Boards.   Discussion board software is used to create an environment that permits users to read and/or post comments and questions regarding a designated discussion topic, which often expands into multiple *threads* or subtopics. Discussion boards are also known as message boards, Internet forums, discussion groups, and bulletin boards. Use of the discussion boards can be limited to a specific group of users or open to the general public. Many course management systems, such as Blackboard, provide discussion board and chat options for use by students enrolled in the class. Some discussion boards are programmed to allow users to upload and download documents.

Discussion boards provide teachers the opportunity to exchange ideas and resources with educators from around the globe, using the vast array of free discussion boards tailored to the specific needs of educators. There are subject-specific discussions such as the Math Forum (mathforum.org) and the RTEACHER listserv, which targets reading instruction for children aged 3 to 12 (www.reading .org/resources/community/discussions_rt_about.html). In addition, there are general education websites that host or link to a variety of Internet forums. Education World offers a forum section at their site (http://forums.educationworld.com) that offers moderated discussions under the following headings: General Education, Subject Areas, Grade Level, Special Interest (e.g., special education, gifted education, new teachers), and Miscellaneous (e.g., classroom management, Ask a Teacher). Another general education site that offers secure online interactions for a nominal yearly fee is ePals, which hosts global discussions and email for teachers, parents, and students (www.epals.com/tools/forum).

Blogs. The primary purpose of a blog is to share personal commentaries on the Web. Popular topics include news, politics, religion, hobbies, and health. As of April 2007, there were more than 75 million blogs (Technorati, 2007). The term comes from "we**b log**," reflecting that the blogs are written in a journal format. Most blog software enables the addition of media files and weblinks with the text entry. Blogs also support interaction from readers, who can add comments and reactions regarding the blog entries.

Teachers have the option of integrating existing blogs into the course material to allow students to read and comment on the content or to have students create their own blogs as a way to reflect on what they have learned and to track learning and opinions over time (see Figure 4.5).

Wiki. Wikis are collaborative websites created with "open editing" software that allows users to easily create, add, edit or remove web page content without using complicated programming language. *Wiki* is from a Hawaiian term *wiki wiki* that means "quick," reflecting the ease and speed with which a wiki can be created. Some wiki sites have limited access that requires use of an assigned password, while others are open to the public. Wikipedia, one of the most popular Web 2.0 tools, is an online encyclopedia comprising entries that can be edited by any web user (www.wikipedia.org). Students can create their own wiki on a topic of interest such as a referendum affecting their local area or a historical topic such as the settlement of Jamestown in 1607.

Figure **4.6**   RSS Icon Denoting an RSS Feed

RSS. "Really Simple Syndication" or RSS is used to "feed" updated web-based information such as news headlines, podcasts, or blogs to websites that have added the designated RSS feed. These sites designate this feature with the RSS icon seen in Figure 4.6. The advantage of adding RSS feeds to your class website is that it automatically keeps students informed of current information related to topics that are being studied. The RSS feeds can easily be added or deleted as topics and interests change. Teachers interested in technology can receive news from TechnoKids (www .technokids.com/news.shtml). Science teachers can include NASA podcasts of experts demonstrating science concepts (http://brainbites.nasa.gov). RSS feeds from local or national news sites are excellent resources for social studies. English teachers can include "2 Words a Day" to introduce new vocabulary (www.justvocabulary.libsyn .com), while music teachers can integrate podcasts of famous musicians sharing tips for playing a particular instrument—for instance, an interview with alto saxophonist Eric Person (www.saxtipspodcast.com/2007/04/saxtips-podcast-27-interview-w.html).

Podcasts.   Podcasts are a popular means of sharing digital multimedia files (audio, video, images, PDF, and text) over the Internet. The name is derived from combining Apple's i**Pod** with broad**cast.** Podcasts are .mp3 or .m4v audio files that be distributed to others. A finished podcast can be uploaded to a server for easy downloading or linked to an RSS file as a news feed. Podcasts can be played on most Mac and PC computers as well as on portable devices such as iPods, mp3 players, or PDAs with appropriate software.

There are multiple online collections of podcasts, with most providing search tools that let you target podcasts in your subject area or education in general. For instance, Apple's iTunes (www.apple.com/itunes/store/podcasts.html), the Internet Archives (www.archive.org), and Podcast.net (www.podcast.net) have a wide variety of free educational podcasts. Other podcast collections are designed specifically for teachers, such as Podcasts for Teachers (www.podcastforteachers.org) and Podcasts for Educators (http://recap.ltd.uk/podcasting/index.php).

Synchronous Digital Communication Software

The term *synchronous* also has Greek roots, with *syn* meaning "with" and *chronos* meaning "time"; thus, it can be defined as "at the same time." The most popular synchronous communication tools are chat and instant messaging, which are both being used by innovative teachers to enhance student learning.

Chat.   Online chat software allows users to engage in synchronous text-based "chat room" conversations in which the participants are online at the same time and using the same chat software application to send and receive messages. This real-time setting is what makes online chats different from email. Chat screens show the past few comments to assist users in following along with the conversation. Also notice that messages tend to be brief due to software limitations and from not wanting to keep other users waiting too long before they can read a response. Since discussions are limited to text, it is common to include "emoticons" such as smiley faces to express feelings within the message and to abbreviate frequently used words—for example, "lol" represents "laugh out loud." Many Internet service providers and key services such as Yahoo! and Google provide free access to chat rooms as a service.

Another option is provided with course management systems (CMS), such as Blackboard, which is becoming popular in K–12 environments. A CMS provides teachers a digital environment for each course they teach, allowing teachers and students to exchange digital documents, send and receive secure emails, and use chat and discussion boards.

Instant Messaging.   Instant messaging (IM) is a very popular way for teens to communicate with each other in real time. It is also referred to as "text messaging." Many mobile wireless devices as well as desk and laptop computers include IM options for text, video, or voice communication. The main difference between IM and chats is the number of people who are involved and that the users must be a "member" or on a "buddy list" of the same IM system. Chats can typically involve a larger group of people than IM communication, which normally occurs between two to five people. Several versions of IM software have been developed by different groups, such as America Online (AOL), MSN Messenger, and Yahoo! Messenger, each using their own formatting system. In other words, a standard format for IM does not exist, meaning that IM can only occur if people use the same IM system. As a result, educational uses of IM are somewhat restricted, except for classes that have a one-to-one computing environment.

When each student has access to a laptop, PDA, or other wireless mobile device, use of IM allows students to communicate with the teacher and other students without getting out of their seats or raising their hand to ask a question during class. This "silent" method of communication encourages shy or quiet students to ask questions that they may not feel comfortable asking when other students can hear their questions. IM also provides students with speaking disabilities an equitable means of communicating with others. Use of IM must be carefully monitored because students could also exchange answers during a test.

Schools can subscribe to services, such as Tapped In, that provide options for online communications specifically designed to meet the needs of teachers. Tapped In (www.tappedin.org) is widely used by an international community of education professionals. They provide secure student accounts and Web space for discussions, chats, and IM limited to those registered with the Tapped In system. The teachers can send IM notes to students to provide individual feedback. They also can generate transcripts of all student conversations and Web activity to facilitate learning and to monitor online interactions.

Problem-Solving Software

As computer games increase in popularity among children and adults, there is an increasing trend for educational software to use gameplay in an effort to increase the appeal of learning for today's tech-savvy students. This trend is seen in the use of problem-solving educational software that presents students with fun and intriguing situations requiring the use of higher-order thinking skills to achieve the intended outcome. Many problem-solving programs are game-like, while others involve real-world simulations. Several scholars (Federation of American Scientists, 2006; Prensky, 2007) have suggested that games and, more specifically, serious games can enhance student learning; however, these suggestions are not based on

Basic computer skills are a must in today's world, which is why the "One Laptop per Child" program is dedicated to making sure all students have a level playing field for developing these skills.

empirical research. Game advocates suggest that the following features of games can enhance learning and problem solving:

- Ability to cooperate, collaborate, and work in teams
- Need to make effective decisions under stress
- Conditions allowing prudent risks in pursuit of objectives
- Frameworks for ethical and moral decisions
- Formats requiring scientific deduction
- Ways to quickly master and apply new skills and information
- Situations requiring lateral and strategic thinking
- Difficult problems that demand persistence
- Interactions with foreign environments and cultures
- Scenarios involving managing businesses and people (Prensky, 2007, p. 39)

Games

Games can provide ways for learners to gain new knowledge or skills. Most learning games accomplish this by providing drill and practice of previously learned material, although some teach new information. The difference between computer games and other forms of drill and practice is the competitive and motivational nature of the software. Students can compete against a computer character or the clock or compete to win points or special privileges. Within the game environment, learners control different variables in an effort to win the game, earn the most points, or solve the mystery. To increase the competitive nature of the learning games, many are designed to involve more than one player. A well-known example of a learning game that has been available for over 20 years is Math Blasters. The newest version engages students in solving math problems to "save the world" (see Figure 4.7). A newer example is Immune Attack, sponsored by the Federation of American Scientists (http://fas.org/immuneattack).

Go to MyEducationLab, select the topic "Science Integration," and go to the Activities and Applications section. Access the video "Science Applications" and consider how technology can be used in the science classroom. Complete the activity that follows.

Simulations

Digital simulations enable students to investigate objects, systems, ideas, and concepts that are often difficult or impossible to explore in real life. Simulations also provide "earth-friendly" approaches to conducting science experiments. Simulations are based on the manipulation of realistic images or the use of icons and a mathematical approach to simulate a variety of systems.

Through the use of highly sophisticated video recordings and digital imaging, students can explore the

Figure **4.7**   Scene from Math Blasters:
Master the Basics Software

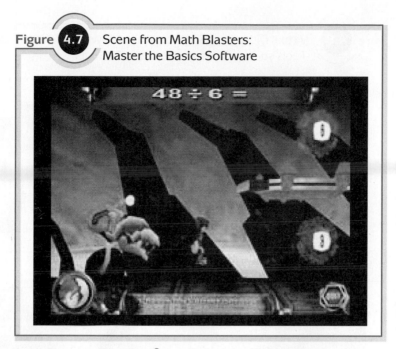

Source: Screenshot of Math Blaster® used with permission of Knowledge Adventure, Inc.

surface of Mars, the intricacy of cell division, or the population growth of a virus. However, the unique feature of a computer simulation not present in a video is the ability for students to manipulate variables. In other words, the students can control a computer character as they explore the Egyptian pyramids, zoom in for a macro view of a virus, turn a butterfly upside down to examine the body structure, or dissect a virtual frog (see Figure 4.8). Similarly, students can manipulate variables such as temperature and pressure in incremental steps to discover the gas laws. This level of control increases student involvement and builds on their natural curiosity by enabling the investigation of higher-level questions.

Most systems modeling software, such as STELLA and Model-It, use diagrams, meters, graphs, and animation to depict and examine interactive relationships in a system. In other words, the students enter basic information for the system variables and the software uses mathematical programming to calculate the resulting impact as these variables are manipulated. Students can easily change the variables to examine "what if?" questions and "see" the effect of change. Models can be tested for voting patterns, population growth, erosion, global warming, or other current trends. The example seen in Figure 4.9 (p. 113) shows a model created by Maryland Virtual High School students that depicts the consequences of tailgating in traffic.

Figure 4.8 Virtual Dissection Software That Allows Students to "Use" Tools such as Scissors, Pins, and Scalpels

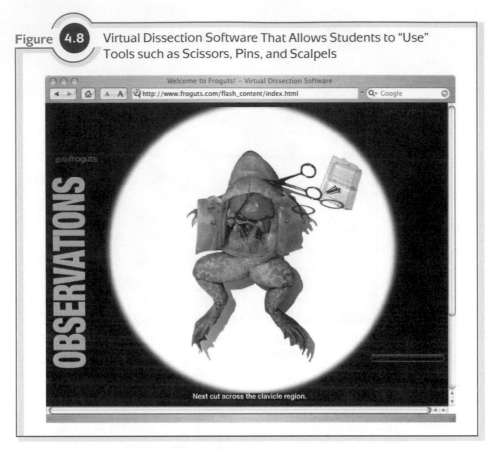

Source: Screenshot courtesy of Froguts Inc. (www.froguts.com).

Educational Software

As the name implies, educational software is designed to educate or teach users. Features of educational software include providing new content, practice, feedback, performance-based tracking over time, and data input beyond answering questions. The degree of teaching depends on the type of software that is used (see Table 4.2). Drill-and-practice software provides the lowest level of teaching, in which the primary purpose is to provide practice and feedback of previously taught content and skills. Next are tutorials that introduce or teach new content or skills and provide drill and practice of the newly presented information. Learners using drill-and-practice or tutorial software will receive the same content and practice, with most programs using a progressive approach that works from simple to more complex learning activities. Most programs allow students to "skip" a section if they can pass a pretest or indicate they know the content; however, this feature can also permit students to skip a section because it is too difficult.

Figure **4.9** Systems Model for Tailgating Created by Maryland Virtual High School Students

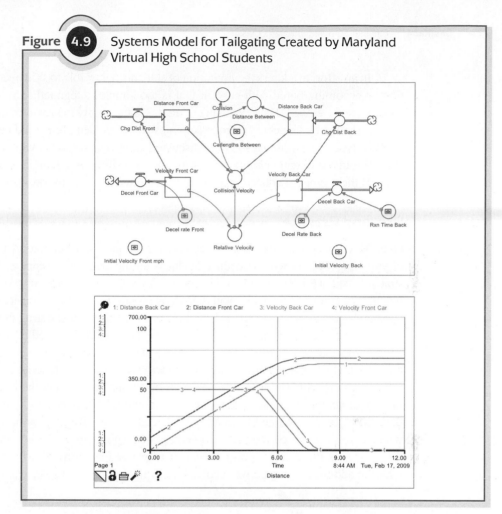

Source: Used with permission of mvhs.shodor.org.

Table 4.2   Levels of Educational Software Components

Software Type	Provides Content	Provides Practice	Provides Feedback	Tracks Progress over Time	Allows Data Input beyond Answer Entry
Drill and Practice		X	X		
Tutorials	X	X	X		
Integrated learning systems (ILS)	X	X	X	X	
Process tools	X	X	X*		X

*Optional

In an effort to address the limitation of students being able to skip needed instruction or becoming bored with content that is too simple, integrated learning systems (ILS) were developed. The key feature of an ILS is the ability to provide students adaptive instruction by branching them to activities based on their ability and performance. The last type of educational software discussed is process software, which guides students through different learning processes such as writing or solving a math problem. Each of these types of educational software is discussed in the following sections.

Drill and Practice

Over 30 years ago, computers first gained entrance into K–12 classrooms as a means of providing students with immediate feedback during drill-and-practice activities. This strategy is still a primary use of computers in today's classrooms, although the software is much more colorful, interactive, and fun. Many programs have lively music, sounds, and animations and often provide narration of the onscreen text to assist struggling readers.

As the name suggests, drill-and-practice software is designed to reinforce student learning of basic skills with applications and uses found most often in language arts and mathematics. Although the context will vary, drill-and-practice software provides students with a series of problems or questions (e.g., select the correct definition; put five apples in the basket; click on the word that rhymes with "time"). After the student responds, one of three types of feedback is given: (1) simple indication whether response is correct; (2) correctness of response plus correct answer if the response was incorrect; (3) correctness of response plus correct answer, if needed, with the addition of instructive feedback to explain why the answer was incorrect.

The Teacher's

Diary

My students use a drill-and-practice software program called Speedway Math. I put a speedway track on the bulletin board. Each student designs a racecar. At the beginning of the week, the students put their racecars on the starting line. The students compete individually as I set the number and difficulty of the problems for each student, based on ability. They use this program as many times as they want during the week and move their car one space for each time they use the program. Their short-term goal is to get to the finish line by the end of the week. Their ultimate goal is to make it to the Hall of Fame, which shows that they have mastered all of the multiplication facts. This is a great motivator to get the students to practice the facts.

Fran Clark
Third-Grade Teacher

Tutorials

As seen in Table 4.2, tutorials present learners with new content and provide practice and feedback on the content. The tutorial content is typically divided into discrete sections or modules that are completed in a structured linear approach or as a branched approach. Many of the newer tutorials incorporate a multimedia format that combines text, narration, video, and images to teach targeted information or skills.

Within each module, the learners are guided through the content and then provided activities that engage them in reviewing and reinforcing the knowledge and skills. These activities typically involve some form of practice requiring the learner to answer questions for which feedback is provided. The feedback can once again consist of any or all of the three levels discussed for drill and practice. When using a linear tutorial, the learners will be automatically transitioned to the next planned module after completing the previous one. When using a branched tutorial, the learners are presented with the option to complete any of the modules or repeat the one just completed.

Integrated Learning Systems

An integrated learning system (ILS) provides a comprehensive learning environment that includes instructional content, practice and feedback, and assessments for students, plus management and instructional tools (e.g., lesson plans) for teachers. Most ILS products align the activities to the state standards of the purchaser and use a mastery-type approach combined with research-based learning strategies that yield a "personalized" instructional plan based on student ILS performance. If a student does not achieve an objective, he or she is branched to a new set of activities that reintroduce the content for repeated practice. A student who achieves an objective is guided to activities at the next level. The ILS curriculum spans multiple grade levels and normally focuses on basic content that is tested on state standardized tests, such as language arts, mathematics, and science. The management system supports generation of progress reports by school, grade, class, and student, with the results being displayed by subgroups (e.g., gender, ethnicity) on request. Teachers can also override the system by assigning students to designated lessons based on class or ILS performance.

Due to the comprehensive nature of an ILS, the most prevalent systems are produced and managed by large educational corporations. For example, Pearson Digital Learning offers SuccessMaker (see Figure 4.10), Waterford Early Learning, and NovaNet, while Plato Learning (www.plato.com) and CompassLearning Odyssey (www.childu.com/solutions.html) primarily offer one pre-K–12 ILS that incorporates the company name in the software title.

Figure **4.10**   Screenshot of SuccessMaker Introductory Page

Process Tools

Process tools go beyond basic software applications such as word processing be-cause they provide questions and prompting to guide students through specific steps required to complete a process. For example, the Book Report software takes stu-dents through each step of writing a book report on a chapter-by-chapter basis or for the entire book (www.ducksoftware.com). When students use Paragraph Punch they are guided through the various stages of writing a paragraph (see Figure 4.11). Algebrator software helps students work through algebra problems that the student

Figure **4.11**   The Paragraph Punch Examples for Prewriting (top)
and Writing the Body of a Paragraph (bottom)

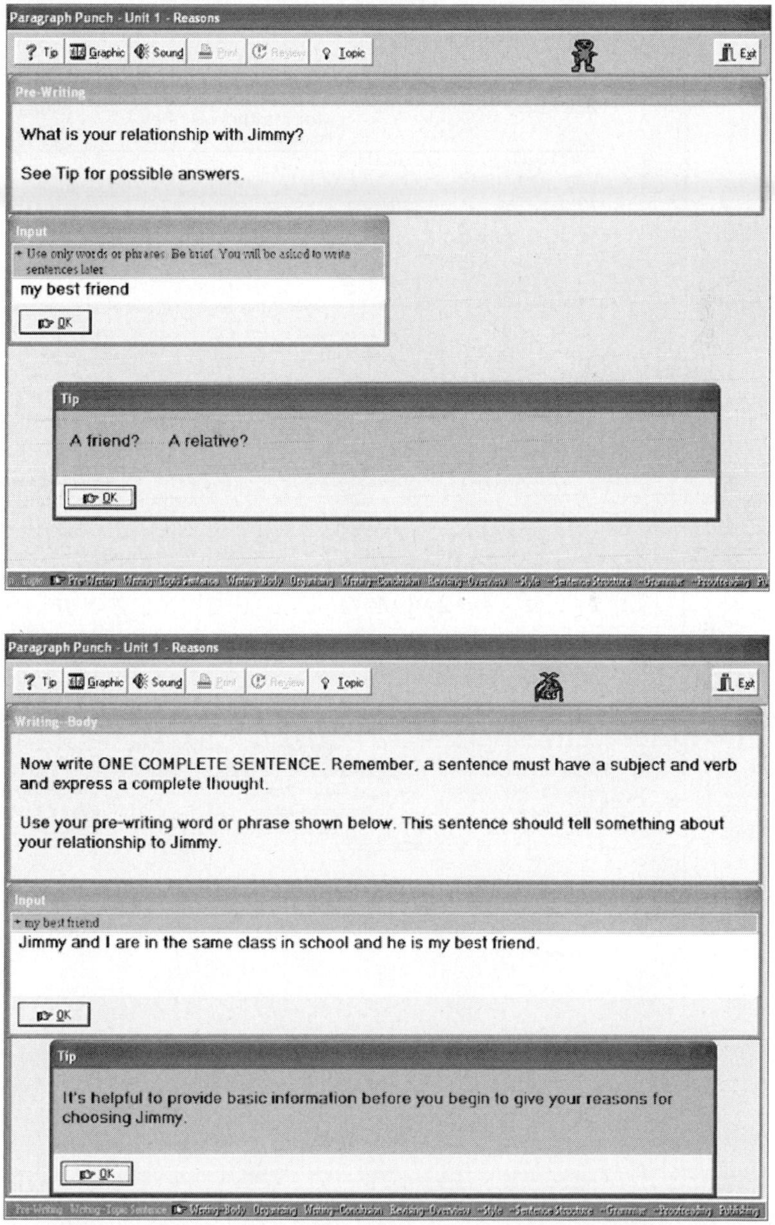

Source: Reprinted by permission of Merit Software.

Figure 4.12   Sample Student AR Report

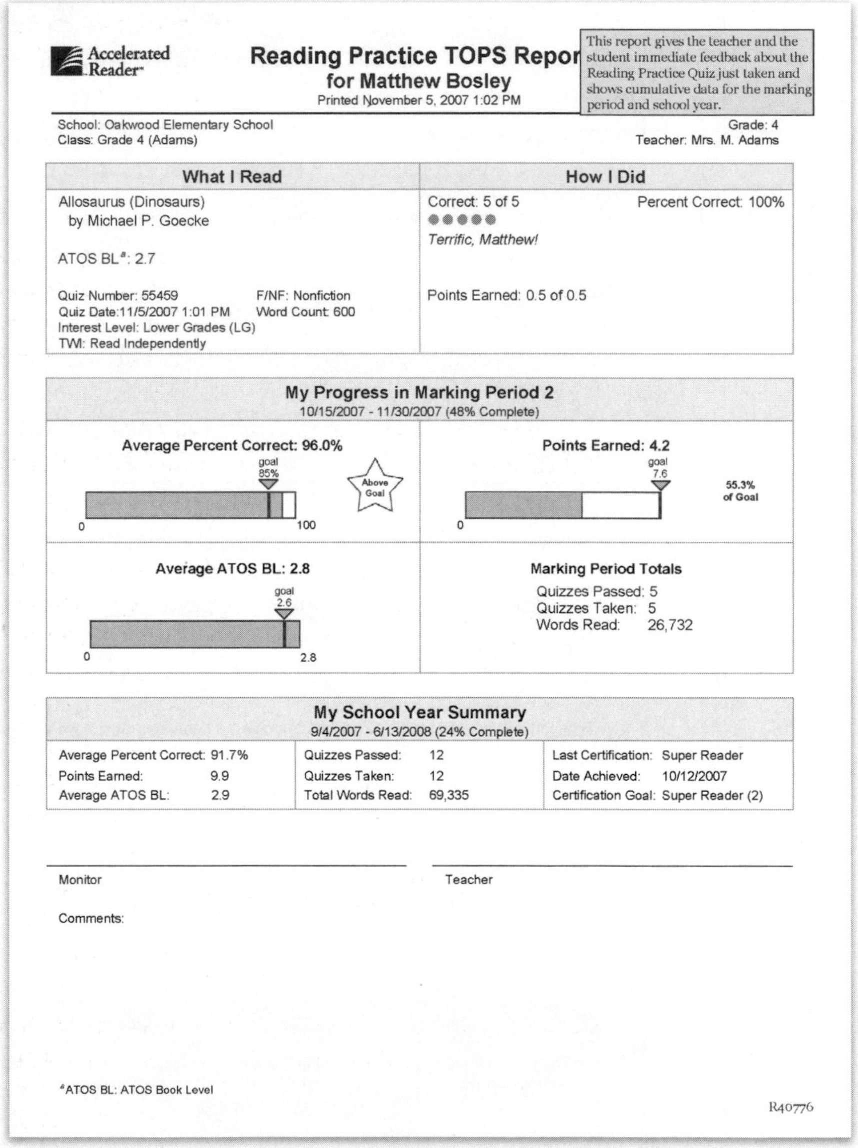

Accelerated Reader™

Reading Practice TOPS Report
for Matthew Bosley
Printed November 5, 2007 1:02 PM

This report gives the teacher and the student immediate feedback about the Reading Practice Quiz just taken and shows cumulative data for the marking period and school year.

School: Oakwood Elementary School
Class: Grade 4 (Adams)

Grade: 4
Teacher: Mrs. M. Adams

What I Read	How I Did
Allosaurus (Dinosaurs) by Michael P. Goecke ATOS BL[a]: 2.7 Quiz Number: 55459 F/NF: Nonfiction Quiz Date:11/5/2007 1:01 PM Word Count: 600 Interest Level: Lower Grades (LG) TWI: Read Independently	Correct: 5 of 5 Percent Correct: 100% ● ● ● ● ● *Terrific, Matthew!* Points Earned: 0.5 of 0.5

My Progress in Marking Period 2
10/15/2007 - 11/30/2007 (48% Complete)

Average Percent Correct: 96.0%
goal 85%
Above Goal
0   100

Points Earned: 4.2
goal 7.6
55.3% of Goal
0

Average ATOS BL: 2.8
goal 2.6
0   2.8

Marking Period Totals
Quizzes Passed: 5
Quizzes Taken: 5
Words Read: 26,732

My School Year Summary
9/4/2007 - 6/13/2008 (24% Complete)

Average Percent Correct: 91.7%	Quizzes Passed: 12	Last Certification: Super Reader
Points Earned: 9.9	Quizzes Taken: 12	Date Achieved: 10/12/2007
Average ATOS BL: 2.9	Total Words Read: 69,335	Certification Goal: Super Reader (2)

Monitor   Teacher

Comments:

[a]ATOS BL: ATOS Book Level

R40776

Source: Reprinted with permission from Renaissance Learning, Inc.

myeducationlab

PEARSON

The Power of Classroom Practice

Go to MyEducationLab, select the topic "Instructional Strategies," and go to the Activities and Applications section. Access the video "Geometer's Sketchpad for Inductive Reasoning" and consider how technology can help motivate student learning. Complete the activity that follows.

enters into the program (www.softmath.com/index.html). Geometer's Sketchpad provides tools for students to solve geometry problems.

Testing Software

Testing software is increasing in popularity in schools due to the high accountability required by the No Child Left Behind mandate (US DOE, 2001). The software ranges from targeting very specific content to grade-level subject areas. Renaissance Learning's Accelerated Reader (AR) is testing software that targets very specific content and skills (see Figure 4.12). According to What Works Clearinghouse (IES, 2008), "Accelerated Reader relies on independent reading practice as a way of managing student performance by providing students and teachers feedback from quizzes based on the books the students read. The program gives students the opportunity to practice reading books at their level, provides feedback on student comprehension of books, and helps students establish goals for their reading" (p. 1). On the other hand, Riverdeep's Destination Success provides tools to produce individualized, ongoing standards-based assessments targeted to improve student performance on high-stakes tests. There are also a wide variety of online and CD-based software testing packages intended to increase student performance on state standardized assessments. Many of these programs are targeted toward teachers and parents and promise outstanding results but frequently do not include reliable reviews of their effectiveness.

Summary

This chapter presented an overview of the five primary types of software applications used in today's classrooms: productivity, research, communication, problem-solving, and educational software. The software is divided into categories based on major application functions. The key focus for teachers is to select software that supports student achievement of content knowledge and skills as well as ISTE's NETS for Students.

Teacher Technology FAQ

Our school uses Macs, yet at home I use a PC. How will this affect my ability to use my home computer to plan for software use on my classroom computers?

The files you save from various applications, such as Word documents from Microsoft, can be opened by both Mac and PC computers that have MS Word installed. Similarly, some applications can save files in various formats such as RTF for word processing and CSV and Sylk for spreadsheets that can be opened by similar applications. Check the product descriptions before purchasing or downloading free software to ensure that it works on both platforms. You will want to check the digital products created on your home computer on your class computers before class to make formatting adjustments that may occur due to switching from PC to Mac.

There seem to be new software applications released every day! How do I stay up to date with what is happening?

There are several options. Subscribe to free technology journals and newsletters. Teacher favorites include *T.H.E. Journal* and *eSchool News*. You can also participate in teacher blogs, discussion boards, and chats. Tapped In sponsors multiple formats to keep teachers informed of the latest technology programs. And finally, talk with your students to get their ideas for using new software in the classroom.

Technology Integration Activities

The following activities provide an opportunity for you to explore the options for using the software described in this chapter.

1. Examine your curriculum for one grading period and identify areas in which each of the five types of software can be integrated into your lessons.
2. Meet with your library media specialist to review the types of software available for classroom use and discuss ways to integrate the various programs into your instruction.

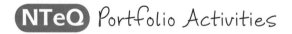 NTeQ Portfolio Activities

Please complete the following activities as part of your NTeQ Portfolio on educational software.

Reflections

The Getting Started portion of this chapter posed three Reflecting on What I Know questions that teachers might commonly ask. In this portion of your journal, reflection activities have been added to help you reflect on each question. Please use information from this chapter to answer the questions.

❶ There are so many types of software; how do I know which ones to include in my lessons?

Reflection Activity: Review the chapter and choose one software application from each of the five categories, and write a description of how you could use that software in your classroom.

❷ I understand why students should use educational software and the Internet, but why should my fourth-grade students learn to use spreadsheet, database, or video editing software?

Reflection Activity: Carefully examine the ISTE NETS for Students for your grade level and make a list of software that is recommended for student use.

❸ How can student use of different types of software help improve scores on state tests?

Reflection Activity: Locate your state curriculum standards for the grade level you teach or plan to teach and select an area in which students perform below expectations. Review the chapter to identify the types of software, beyond educational software, that can be used to support student achievement of the identified standards.

Select a previously developed lesson you have taught or one from the Internet. Modify the lesson by integrating at least two different types of software into the lesson.

Chapter 5

Think Sheets: Using Technology for Higher-Order Learning

Getting Started

The NTeQ model is based on an inquiry approach to learning that uses different strategies than a traditional approach to instruction. A traditional approach typically focuses on having students read a chapter or parts of a chapter in a textbook to gain an understanding of the content so they can pass a state-mandated achievement test. A well-written textbook will guide the student through the material and it might even prompt the learner by special treatments of key ideas and important points. The inquiry approach as used in the NTeQ model does not focus exclusively on a textbook for learning. Rather, students learn from various sources as they conduct research to solve a problem related to the lesson objectives. Both the traditional and inquiry approaches require the students to use self-regulation and learning strategies to achieve the lesson objectives. In the traditional approach, a textbook author often includes these strategies in the text and the teacher supplements the strategies. Students involved in an inquiry unit work independently and may use a variety of informational sources ranging from web pages to graphs created using data they have collected. Since these materials lack the strategies we would find in a textbook, it is important that the teacher create guides that will help the learners develop and use self-regulation and critical-thinking strategies. Recent literature has found that instruction that presents both self-regulation and learning strategies has a positive effect on student achievement (Berthold, Nückles, & Renkl, 2007; Darling-Hammond et al., 2008). In this chapter, we will examine how to use these strategies to engage students in the problem-solving process and improve their comprehension of instruction.

Reflecting on What I Know

1 How can I get my students to ask questions about the research they are conducting?

2 How can I teach my students to solve problems?

3 I've never used an inquiry-based approach, much less computers—so how is a teacher supposed to do both of these at one time?

Classroom
SNAPSHOT

Jeffrey Kott's mother became concerned when Jeffrey kept telling her after school each day that Ms. Francis was a "mean teacher." When Jeffrey's weekly folder included an invitation for parents to observe various classes at the school, Jeffrey's mother decided to sign up for Ms. Francis's science class so she could make her own judgment. Ms. Kott was told to arrive five minutes after class began and was surprised at the classroom. She had expected students to be sitting in nice neat rows with notepads and pencils in hand much like her school experience. Instead, the students were seated around the room in a haphazard manner with laptops. Ms. Francis explained that they were conducting a number of experiments today on simple machines. She had found a website created by a physics professor that used animations to simulate a number of experiments. The only modification she needed was to point out the data the students needed to collect. Ms. Francis invited her to walk around the room, observe, and ask her or any of the students questions.

As Ms. Kott walked around the room, she felt invisible because the students were so intently engaged in the experiments and working together to find a solution. If Ms. Francis was a mean teacher it had to be because she may have made some of the students sit on the floor! As she was observing one small group, a student raised his hand. Ms. Francis came to the group and sat on the floor with them. The students were trying different approaches to interpret the graph they had created and wanted help. Ms. Kott was gratified that she knew the answer since she often created graphs using a spreadsheet for her consulting work. To her surprise, Ms. Francis did not commandeer one of the laptops and show the students how to solve the problem. Rather, she started asking questions. They were tough questions requiring the students to think before answering. And when they were done with the exchange, they still did not have the answer; however, they knew how to solve the problem. As Ms. Francis left the group, the students picked up on her line of questioning and asked more questions of one another until they solved the problem.

That evening, Ms. Kott asked Jeffrey why he thought Ms. Francis was a mean teacher. Was it because some student had to sit on the floor? "Oh no, we prefer to sit there because it is close to the electrical outlets for our laptops." When pressed to explain why she was a mean teacher, Jeffrey finally explained it was because she did not answer their questions. She always asked them other questions that they had to think about before answering. Ms. Kott decided that she liked "mean" teachers for her Jeffrey!

The Self-Regulated Learner

The Classroom Snapshot provided us with a glimpse of Ms. Francis demonstrating self-regulation skills while teaching a lesson based on the NTeQ model. An inquiry approach to teaching encourages the students to use self-regulation skills (Schraw, Crippen, & Hartley, 2006). Using authentic problems that are of interest to the student increases motivation. Self-regulation is also encouraged through the use of metacognitive strategies that require students to think about how they learn, as demonstrated by Ms. Francis when she asked the students questions rather than giving them the answer. By developing and using metacognitive strategies, students not only generate new conceptions and understandings of the content that typically goes beyond rote memorization, but are able to transfer these skills to other learning situations.

What Is Self-Regulation?

Self-regulation is a proactive learning activity that students initiate to gain understanding (Zimmerman, 1998, 2008). Students who demonstrate self-regulation show motivation to complete a task using both behavioral and metacognitive strategies. That is, students use strategies either on their own or at the prompting of the teacher or the instructional materials to complete the learning task. These strategies can include the creation or use of visual images, reading or listening, or determining what is important and where to direct their attention (Zimmerman & Tsikalas, 2005).

Self-regulation is a cyclical process; that is, a student will go through a three-step process to develop and understand the material (Zimmerman, 1998) and then repeat these processes as needed (see Figure 5.1). When a student from Ms. Francis's class begins a learning task, or the "forethought" phase, of understanding how a simple machine works, he or she first develops a plan of action. Techniques such as strategic planning and goal setting are used to enhance the learning effort. The student begins by setting goals that define the expected outcomes and then selects the specific strategies to achieve the goals. For example, if the problem is to understand how a simple machine makes a task easier, then the learner might set a goal

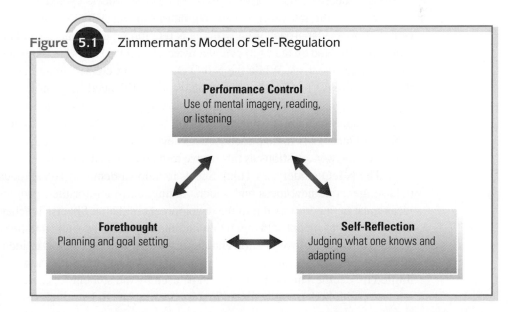

Figure **5.1**   Zimmerman's Model of Self-Regulation

Performance Control
Use of mental imagery, reading, or listening

Forethought
Planning and goal setting

Self-Reflection
Judging what one knows and adapting

of understanding the purpose of the experiment and the procedure (goal setting) by underlining (strategy) the key points in the instructions provided by Ms. Francis. An inquiry unit, such as the simple machine lesson, encourages students to set learning goals as opposed to competitive achievement goals, resulting in more effective learning efforts (Ames, 1992).

A student engaging with the content then enters the "performance control" phase where self-regulation strategies help the learner focus on the task (Zimmerman, 1998). Students must learn to remain focused on the task and not become distracted by other phenomena in the environment. As the student works through the material he or she may use self-instructional strategies that help in solving the simple machine problem. That is, strategies guide the student through the process. Similarly, a student might use mental images to improve recall of specific information or to help paraphrase what was read. Last, a student must engage in self-monitoring that provides feedback on his or her understanding.

The final phase of the process is "self-reflection" or self-evaluation. Students who engage in self-reflection may compare their progress to a standard or to solutions derived by other students (Zimmerman, 1998). During this phase, the student can identify learning errors and adapt his or her performance by selecting another strategy that will be more successful—for example, switching from underlining key ideas to creating an outline or checklist of the steps needed to complete the experiment. This self-reflection phase affects the next "forethought" process and can increase or decrease the motivation to continue the process cycle again.

What is the relevance of self-regulation to the NTeQ model? The student-centered inquiry approach used with the NTeQ model encourages students to work independently and on teams to conduct research and find answers. They are learning to think like scientists. While the NTeQ environment creates an authentic problem that can increase motivation, the students may still need help in developing and refining their reading, research, and questioning skills. Self-regulation provides us with a means for helping students develop these skills within the context of their problem. Our goal is to help each student develop the ability to read, develop questions, and answer questions as they strive to gain understanding.

The NTeQ model uses Think Sheets to help students set goals, focus their attention, generate new ideas and understanding, and monitor their progress. These ideas must be incorporated into the development of Think Sheets. Teachers can use Think Sheets to model self-regulation and inquiry skills as well as to help students develop effective self-regulation and inquiry skills. Our first step is to identify strategies we can incorporate into the Think Sheet. These strategies, however, are not limited to just the Think Sheet, but can be used by the student for a variety of learning tasks with both traditional and inquiry approaches to learning.

Strategies for Self-Regulation

Our goal with the Think Sheets is to help the learner understand the content by using appropriate inquiry skills. This process includes reading and exploring content and data as well as manipulating the data the students have collected or are using to answer the problem. One approach is the use of generative strategies proposed by Wittrock (1974, 1990, 1991, 1992). When students use a generative strategy such as underlining or paraphrasing, they construct new ideas. Generative learning also requires the learners to compare their preconceptions to new observations and then make adjustments. Students who use generative strategies are active learners who seek to relate new and unfamiliar information to what they already know by generating new ideas, concepts, and principles (Wittrock, 1992). Generative strategies encourage students to take control of their learning through the active processing of new information, resulting in increased motivation.

There are four information processing strategies (Jonassen, 1988) that we will use to organize generative strategies. These four categories are recall, integration, organization, and elaboration (see Figure 5.2). Recall strategies are used primarily for remembering information such as learning a list of items or facts. Examples include overt and covert rehearsal such as writing the information multiple times (e.g., "Indianapolis is the capital of Indiana"), reviewing and rereading the material, and mnemonics. Recall strategies typically do not encourage the learner to construct new ideas and will not be our focus in this chapter. Integration strategies help the learner transform information into a form that is more easily remembered. Examples include paraphrasing what they have read, using or generating metaphors, and finding new examples. These three strategies are helpful for integrating

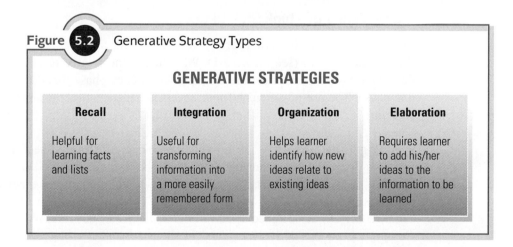

Figure 5.2 Generative Strategy Types

GENERATIVE STRATEGIES

Recall	Integration	Organization	Elaboration
Helpful for learning facts and lists	Useful for transforming information into a more easily remembered form	Helps learner identify how new ideas relate to existing ideas	Requires learner to add his/her ideas to the information to be learned

the new information with existing information the learner knows. The third category, organization strategies, is used to structure new information or restructure existing information and new information to facilitate learning. Organizational strategies can help the learner reconsider what they already know and then analyze relationships with new ideas. Strategies that we can employ to help the learner organize information include the analysis of key ideas, categorizing information, cognitive mapping, and outlining. Our earlier example of a student underlining the steps to conduct an experiment is an example of two strategies—underlining and analysis of key ideas. A language arts teacher might have her students group books or stories as fiction or nonfiction, which is an example of categorization. The final category of generative strategies is elaboration, which encourages the student to add information to make the new material meaningful. Example elaboration strategies include the use or generation of mental images or drawings and sentence elaboration through writing.

Using Think Sheets for Higher-Order Learning

By combining our knowledge of self-regulation and generative strategies, we can create a variety of Think Sheets that will help our students develop an understanding of the information they discover through their inquiries. The Think Sheets will model appropriate behaviors so that they become independent learners.

Three Types of Think Sheets

Let's return to our discussion of self-regulation and the three steps outlined by Zimmerman (1998) (see Figure 5.1). We will use these three phases to structure our Think Sheets. You might use examples from each phase for your unit or only one phase. The use of different Think Sheets is dependent on the abilities of your students.

Planning Think Sheets.   The first place to integrate a Think Sheet in an NTeQ lesson is during student planning. Once students have either identified or read the problem, they are ready to start planning how they will solve the problem. Planning activities can include goal setting and strategic planning (Zimmerman, 1998). A Think Sheet can be designed as part of the Specify Problem and Activities Before Computer Use steps of the NTeQ model to help the students set goals.

Figure 5.3   Investigating Great Depression Photographs: Our KWL Chart

K What I **Know**	W What I **Want** to Know	L What I **Learned**
The photographs have people, buildings, pets, and objects. The pictures are only in black and white.	Who were the people? What type of work did they do? Where was the picture taken? How old were the people? How do their clothes and hair styles differ from today?	

One common strategy we can use for planning is a KWL chart (Ogle, 1986) (see Figure 5.3). A planning Think Sheet will focus on the K, what I know, and W, what I want to know, columns of the chart. The KWL chart can be completed by the whole class, by groups of students, or by individual students. You will need to determine the best approach for your class. If you have groups or individuals complete the chart, then you might want to review the results as a class so that everyone starts from the same point.

During the planning time, students are setting the goals that will enable them to solve the problem. The example in Figure 5.3 is for a history unit on the Great Depression. Photographs from the time period are analyzed by the students to determine how the world of those individuals differs from the students' world today. The students have completed the first two columns and listed their goals, or the information they want to know, for analyzing the photographs. A science teacher might use a different format to help the students plan their goals for conducting an experiment. The format used in a social studies or health class might more closely resemble the planning for the science class. When listing the goals for the social studies, health, or science experiment or data collection, the planning might also include a listing of the steps the students will complete to gather the data or conduct the experiment.

Performance Think Sheets.   The second place we might use a Think Sheet is during the "performance control" phase (Zimmerman, 1998) or what we might call the learning activities. Performance Think Sheets are primarily created for the Activities During Computer Use, Activities After Computer Use, and Supporting Activities

The Power of Classroom Practice

Go to MyEducationLab, select the topic "Internet," and go to the Activities and Applications section. Access the video "Curiosity and Interest" and consider how the teacher uses questioning to engage his students. Complete the activity that follows.

steps of the NTeQ model. Our goal is to help students focus their attention on important information, analyze the information, create connections, and transform the new information into a form that allows for future recall. Let's examine two different Performance Think Sheets.

Focusing Attention. Once our students have collected their data and organized it in some fashion, such as with a spreadsheet or table, we may need to help guide their analysis and interpretation of the data. When scientists conduct research, they engage in four activities (Dunbar, 2000). First, scientists consider unusual results. These findings might be due to the methods used or simply a real deviation from what was expected. Thus, one or more questions can direct students' attention to look for these differences. Second, scientists engage in analogical reasoning to solve problems. For example, a scientist might explain a finding by using a distant analogy (i.e., comparing seemingly unrelated factors). We can encourage students to think of an analogy that explains what they have found. Third, scientists engage in distributed reasoning. Today, scientists are more likely to collaborate and engage in research with other scientists than they

Students can engage in distributed reasoning by working as a group.

were 50 years ago. This collaboration or distributed reasoning can yield new explanations and questions. Students in a classroom can engage in distributed reasoning by working as a group or collaborating with another classroom in another school or even in another country. Fourth, scientists constantly evaluate their goals to make sure the goals are not limiting their thinking. This self-reflection may require students to revise their original goals to solve the problem.

We can also help the students focus their attention on the analysis and interpretation of their data by providing questions. An example of questions to focus student attention and help them identify what caused the differences is illustrated in Figure 5.4. Question 3 asks about the size of the paper towels to encourage the students to check for unusual differences. When a finding is different than expected, the students can ask additional questions to determine if there was an error or if they need to change their way of thinking. A Think Sheet might include questions to direct student attention toward anomalies or unexpected findings. We could also ask the students to draw an analogy with other materials, such as cloth towels or sponges for a close analogy, and maybe add an example of using sawdust, kitty litter, or sand to absorb oil. Finally, we could encourage the different groups to compare their results to see if everyone reached the same conclusions.

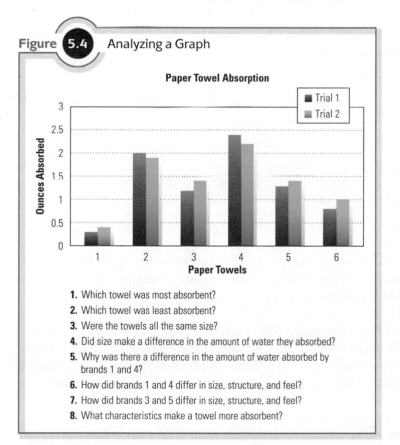

Figure 5.4   Analyzing a Graph

1. Which towel was most absorbent?
2. Which towel was least absorbent?
3. Were the towels all the same size?
4. Did size make a difference in the amount of water they absorbed?
5. Why was there a difference in the amount of water absorbed by brands 1 and 4?
6. How did brands 1 and 4 differ in size, structure, and feel?
7. How did brands 3 and 5 differ in size, structure, and feel?
8. What characteristics make a towel more absorbent?

Generative Think Sheets. One of our goals is to help learners make connections and develop an understanding of the material they read and the data they analyzed. Generative strategies provide a range of approaches we can use to guide students' processing of information to

Table 5.1	Generative Strategy Examples
Strategy	**Use**
Paraphrasing	Students write one or more paragraphs that paraphrase a section of material
Outlining	Students outline written material or prepare an outline of steps to collect data
Imagery	Students generate images or use teacher-provided images
Examples	Students identify new examples of a concept (e.g., other objects that are rectangles)
Underlining or highlighting	Students underline or highlight written material (can use paper or a PDF file)
Tables	Teacher provides or students create a table to organize information (first column lists geometric figures, student enters number of sides in second column)
Graphs and charts	Students create and/or interpret graphs and charts
Questions	Students create questions or answer higher-level questions provided by teacher
Concept maps	Students create a concept map
Predictions	Students predict the outcome of an experiment or event
Photographs	Students interpret a photograph and differentiate between what is known, what is inferred, and what is not known
Analogy and metaphor	Students generate or explain an analogy or metaphor
Notetaking	Students take notes as reading, observing, or listening

help them gain this understanding. Table 5.1 provides a summary of generative strategies that can be incorporated into a Think Sheet.

Think Sheets can incorporate one or more generative strategies. For example, there may be times when you combine strategies such as interpreting a graph and then making additional predictions.

Self-Reflection Think Sheets.   Self-reflection is the final phase of the learning cycle (Zimmerman, 1998). This final step in the cycle allows the learner to self-evaluate and determine his or her understanding of the material. Students can compare what they understand to a standard or to others when no standard exists (Zimmerman, 1998). Self-Reflection Think Sheets are *not* tests. Rather, they encourage the learner to do a self-evaluation such as asking whether they have met their goals or achieved the standard (or benchmark). If they have not achieved the goal, then they should be encouraged to determine the next strategy they should use to help successfully achieve the goal.

Components of Think Sheets

All Think Sheets have two basic components even though their appearance will greatly vary. The first component is an orientation to the task and the second is learner capabilities (Rigney, 1978). Orienting strategies are similar to instructions; that is, their purpose is to engage the learner to use a specific strategy. For example, if we want our students to outline the steps they will use to collect photographs from the Internet, then we might provide an orienting strategy like, "Create an outline of the steps and keywords you will use to find photographs about the Great Depression on the Internet." When we ask students to use a specific strategy, such as a generative strategy like paraphrasing, we must make sure they have the capability to paraphrase materials as opposed to summarizing the material. An awareness of student capabilities is important so that you select an appropriate generative strategy. If you ask students to use a strategy that they have not yet developed, they will not be able to complete the learning task.

A Think Sheet will have an orienting strategy followed by an instructional strategy that the student is capable of completing. Figure 5.5 illustrates a Think Sheet to focus the student's attention on key information in a graph similar to Figure 5.4 that they created with their data. Note the addition of the orienting strategy in Figure 5.5 for the completed Think Sheet.

In the next section, we will examine how to use the NTeQ model for higher-order learning. The section will describe different ways of using Think Sheets as the students work to solve a problem.

Implementing the NTeQ Problem-Solving Process

The NTeQ problem-solving process is used by students to solve a problem as part of an NTeQ lesson. These steps, as seen in Table 5.2 (p. 135), are heuristics that we expect you and the students to modify as you gain experience. Students should be involved in each step of the process, which is adapted to each problem rather than followed as strict rules. As illustrated in the chart, when students apply the problem-solving process, they are required to engage in a great deal of higher-order thinking. A brief description of each component of the NTeQ problem-solving process is presented in the following section.

Figure 5.5 Sample Think Sheet

PAPER TOWEL TEST
Think Sheet

Directions

Using the graph you created with the data collected from the paper towels test, please complete the following items.

1. Which towel was most absorbent?

....

2. Which towel was least absorbent?

....

3. Describe any relationships between size of the paper towel and the amount of water absorbed.

....

4. Compare and contrast difference in the amount absorbed by brands.

....

5. Why do you think they absorbed different amounts?

....

6. For brands that absorbed different amounts, how do they differ in size, structure, and feel?

....

7. In summary, what characteristics make a towel more absorbent?

....

Define the Problem

Let's assume that your lesson is developed and you have followed the guidelines in Chapter 2 to create a very interesting problem. Now you have to arouse your students' interest in the problem, and the key is your initial introduction of the prob-

Table 5.2	The NTeQ Problem-Solving Process Aligned with Bloom's Taxonomy	

Component	Bloom's Level	Student Action
Define the problem	Comprehension Analysis	Write a statement that clearly defines the problem.
Identify what is known about the problem	Analysis	Ideas are stated as "known" information.
Identify what needs to be known to solve the problem	Analysis	List as questions.
Identify data that need to be collected to solve the problem	Analysis	Write as action statements and indicate how to collect.
Determine how the data needs to be manipulated to solve the problem	Application Synthesis Analysis	Describe how the data will be manipulated to develop a solution.
Generate possible solutions	Synthesis	Base solutions on results of the data manipulation.
Determine how to evaluate each solution	Evaluation	Identify criteria that will be used to select the best solution.
Select the best solution	Analysis Evaluation	Consider each alternative and identify the implications of each.
Present findings	Synthesis	Publish the results.

Source: Adapted from B. S. Bloom, M. D. Englehart, E. J. Furst, W. H. Hill, & D. R. Krathwohl (Eds.), *Taxonomy of educational objectives: The classification of educational goals. Handbook I: Cognitive domain.* New York: David McKay, 1956.

lem. This introduction can include, for example, using props to stimulate curiosity, dropping "curiosity builders" before the lesson, asking rhetorical questions to get them thinking, or presenting data that cause puzzlement or dissonance. Curiosity props can include photos, artifacts, books, software, magazines, or newspapers with targeted headlines—the list is endless. The key thing, of course, is that the props are related in some way to the problem to solve in the upcoming lesson.

You may want to use "curiosity builders" that make it easier to introduce the problem to the students on the first day of the lesson. Hints that you could drop before the lesson could include the following:

- I wonder if states tend to get bigger as you move west.
- Our family is planning to visit Nebraska next month, and I'm not sure what kind of clothes to pack.
- I wonder if all Native Americans use feathers in their ceremonial dress.

- My earlobes are attached and I can curl my tongue. I wonder if these two traits always go together.

As you introduce the problem to the students, make sure that you seem interested and curious to find the solution, even when dealing with young children and the answer is quite obvious to you. After you have verbally introduced the problem, it is critical to make sure the students have a clear understanding, or that they *define the problem*. This can be done in two ways: (1) small groups of students define the problem in their own words and then the large group reaches a common definition or (2) problem definition can be done as a large group by printing it on the board or displaying it with a computer. The end product should be a clearly written statement of the problem.

Identify What Is Known about the Problem

After the problem has been defined, students then need to identify what is known about the problem. Just as in the first step, defining the problem, student groups can create a list of what they know about the problem and then a common class list can be compiled. You may need to model how to identify what is known when students are first learning the problem-solving process. You can do this by modeling for the class or you can create a Planning Think Sheet students can use individually or in groups. You can identify one or two items and then ask students to identify the remaining items. For example, let's examine the following problem: Do states get larger as you move west? The "known" items include a map showing the states and our comparisons of the states going from east to west. You also can add an item that does not really fit (e.g., population statistics for the states) to show students the importance of distinguishing between "known" items related to the problem and those that are not.

The Teacher's
Diary

One of the biggest challenges in science education is providing preservice teachers with the skills, understanding, and confidence to effectively and appropriately engage their students in authentic scientific inquiry. Most of the preservice elementary teachers that I have worked with over the years indicated on surveys provided at the beginning of the semester that science was not their favorite subject. Through further probing during course activities they often shared that they don't think of themselves as scientists. They also said that they don't feel confident doing science, and that makes them worry that they won't be able to teach students science—particularly through inquiry-based approaches.

In an effort to successfully meet these challenges I developed the Science Fair Extraordinaire project. This project allows preservice teachers to engage in authentic scientific inquiry in a supportive environment that requires: (a) considerable student reflection and self-regulation; (b) application of inquiry skills and deep critical thinking; (c) construction of more appropriate understandings of how science operates; and (d) the development of more appropriate mental models related to scientific phenomena and pedagogy. By working through this project, the teachers experience inquiry learning from the student's perspective and learn firsthand how to implement an inquiry-based lesson in any discipline.

Throughout the semester, preservice teachers learn about specific elements of science content and pedagogy. This project provides them with the opportunity to develop a complete scientific study from scratch. There are no research topics or data sets provided by the instructor as in other activities completed earlier in the semester. Now they have to do it all—from developing a viable research question to disseminating their findings They call the shots and determine the context of their own learning. Scary stuff, right? That's usually the reaction I receive from the preservice teachers, until they take a closer look at the questions in the project packet I provide. While the packet contains very open-ended types of prompts, I have scaffolded student experiences to the point where students are ready to take additional ownership of their learning. I have done this by conducting activities throughout the semester that require students to ask for tools that are not initially provided, confront their own alternative conceptions, provide rationales for their thinking, think critically about topics using informed skepticism, and work with others to solve problems. The result is that by the time they begin the Science Fair Extraordinaire project, they have developed the skills necessary to effectively deal with initial ambiguity and

avoid cognitive paralysis by developing a plan to answer student-generated questions (aided by the packet prompts) and work together effectively.

The preservice teachers begin by selecting a topic that they find interesting—any topic, not just a science one. This opportunity builds relevance and increases student interest. Then they attempt to develop their research question. Some are viable, but most are not. The prompts aid them in thinking about what constitutes a viable research question. Package prompts also ask the preservice teachers to articulate what sources informed their thinking regarding their research question. Next they are asked to enumerate the tools they used to obtain this information to focus their attention on the issue of credibility. Based on the new information they find, they often revise their research question. The prompts allow for and even promote this nonlinear and often recursive process—an element denoting more authentic scientific inquiry versus the more artificial, idealized version of scientific method that is usually taught. When developing their methods they are asked to first consider their research question, then what types of data they need to answer the question, then what other researchers have done, and finally what they will do. Their research question, logistical concerns, and alternative perspectives are considered when addressing the data collection and analysis prompts. Students often recognize the benefit of multiple perspectives afforded by group work during this time. During data analysis students are also asked to consider what tools they will need and what are the best ways to organize their data. Last, preservice teachers are again required to consider all their responses in light of their research question and are asked to summarize their findings, develop conclusions, and provide explicit links between their results and conclusions. Students are then asked to describe where they can disseminate their results and explain how they benefit from their study's findings. Explaining the implications of their work, for themselves and others, is an important piece that often develops into additional conversations about the project with classmates, friends, and family. It helps the students to better understand that what they did was more than just a project to get a grade to pass a class, but instead it was learning and applying a new way to think about the world, and what they thought and created has meaning for them and others. This is an extremely empowering element that dramatically increases self-efficacy—not only changing the way that the students think about the world, but also the way they think about themselves. When I ask them again to describe a scientist, they now say, "I am and I'm ready to help my kids be real scientists too."

Daniel Dickerson
Assistant Professor
of Science Education,
Old Dominion University

Identify What Needs to Be Known to Solve the Problem

When a common list of what is known has been generated, students then need to determine what is needed to solve the problem. During this process, they will continually need to refer to the defined problem. This component will require students to think creatively, to make predictions and speculations, and to write questions about what they want to know. Again, you may want to create a Planning Think Sheet to help them identify what they need to know. For example, do all states get bigger as you move west? Does the year of entry make a difference? Do resources matter? Or for other lessons, sample questions could include: Are presidents more likely to be Republican or Democrat? Are carnivores more likely to become extinct than herbivores? How are the works of Vincent van Gogh and Claude Monet similar? As students begin to generate a list of questions, other questions will come to mind. It is best to brainstorm and record all ideas before evaluating each one to determine if it is really needed to solve the problem.

Identify Data to Collect to Solve the Problem

The next step requires careful examination of the questions listed in the previous step and the generation of action statements indicating what data to collect and how to collect it. During this segment, you assist students with their thinking to help clarify what is needed to solve the problem, as opposed to what is "nice" to know. These discrimination skills will transfer into future workplace settings where key decisions are made. You can use another Planning Think Sheet (or have an integrated sheet for the entire process) to help students answer these questions. Types of data and how to collect it are shown in the following examples:

The 12 States in Our Region

- *What to collect.* Area in square miles, major cities, total population, major products, key attractions, highest point of elevation, lowest point of elevation, average yearly rainfall, average summer temperature, average winter temperature
- *How to collect.* Data from www.50states.com

Genetic Trait Information from Each Group Member's Family

- *What to collect.* Hair color, hair curl, eye color, earlobe attached, tongue curling, and angle of thumb joint
- *How to collect.* Data from the following, if available: parents, brothers, sisters, aunts, uncles, and grandparents

Determine How to Analyze the Data to Solve the Problem

After students determine the specific data to collect, they next decide how to analyze the data to solve the problem. This will again require that students reexamine the problem statement to keep the data analysis focused toward finding the answers or solutions. When students are just beginning to use basic computer applications, you will need to assist them in understanding the available functions. For example, students may want to use both a database and spreadsheet when examining the data from states. In the database, students could sort by elevation, population, rainfall, temperature, square miles, and products to find similarities and differences among the regional states. They could also use a spreadsheet to determine population density, state with the greatest range in average temperatures, and greatest difference between high and low elevation points.

Generate Possible Solutions

This portion of the process is often where the greatest degree of higher-order thinking occurs because students are examining the results of their data analysis. For inquiry-based learning to be successful, the problems need to be ill structured to the degree that they do not have one right answer but can have multiple solutions. Therefore, as students come to this portion of the problem-solving process, they generate several ways that the problem can be solved. A Performance Think Sheet with generative strategies can help the students with this step. For example, if students were investigating whether genetic traits were grouped by combinations of traits (e.g., if people who could roll their tongues tended to also have attached earlobes), the students could probably generate data to support more than one argument.

Determine How to Evaluate Each Solution

When students have a list of multiple solutions, they then need to determine a consistent way to examine each one by generating a list of evaluation criteria. These criteria could involve meeting specific numeric ratings ("must have five or more"), containing specific content ("must address setting and characters"), or other guidelines needed to solve the problem.

Select the Best Solution

At this point, using the criteria they have determined, students examine each solution and choose the "best" one. They should keep track of the reasons why the solution was chosen and describe possible implications for choosing other solutions. There may be times when more than one solution could be considered as the "best" solution. In this case, students can use both or choose one based on other criteria; for instance, one may be more fun, more current, or more relevant to the school's context. When the lesson involves different groups of students reaching solutions to a common problem, as each group shares their findings, students expand what they have learned by realizing that the problem had many possible solutions.

Present Findings

The findings can be published in a variety of ways. The most appropriate method is determined when designing the lesson. The key consideration for this portion of the problem-solving process is not *how* to present the findings, but rather *what* to present. Students need to determine which information is critical to understanding the problem and the resulting solution. If, in their data set, students found that people who could roll their tongues had attached earlobes, what supporting information needs to be included to ensure understanding? Does their PowerPoint presentation need to include descriptions of different genetic traits, how they collected the data, what other findings were recorded, and the final results? This topic will be discussed further in Chapter 9.

Summary

In this chapter we introduced the concepts of self-regulation and generative strategies and demonstrated how these two ideas can help in creating three different types of Think Sheets for problem solving. Planning Think Sheets are used to help students plan their strategy, typically when students are identifying the problem and determining how to proceed. Performance Think Sheets are used to help the student develop an understanding of the materials by generating new ideas. We typically use this approach as the students are analyzing their data and during both direct and indirect instruction. Finally, students use the Self-Reflection Think Sheet to determine if they understand the material and to select a different approach if they were not successful.

To further expand on implementing an NTeQ lesson, this chapter discussed how to guide students through the problem-solving process. The steps include defining the problem, identifying what is known about the problem and what needs to be known, describing data that needs to be collected and how the data needs to be manipulated to solve the problem, and then generating possible solutions and determining how to evaluate each solution to select the best one. It ends with presenting the findings.

Teacher Technology FAQ

The NTeQ approach seems great, and I think kids will learn more if it is used. But this is a totally new way of teaching for me and I feel very overwhelmed. What do I do?

It can be overwhelming to think about changing the way you teach—especially when you have not seen this method implemented or modeled. You have, though, already overcome one of the greatest obstacles—skepticism that the NTeQ approach will benefit student learning. This is the first and most critical step. Having accomplished that, begin slowly, and adopt what you can handle. Please note that we did not say what you are comfortable with, because change is typically a little uncomfortable at first. Begin with one lesson that is fairly simple or even a portion of a lesson. If your students are not used to working together in groups, this too needs to be approached slowly and with very careful planning and execution. Also, make sure the first attempts involve tasks that will result in positive outcomes, such as a very simple database or spreadsheet with just a few entries. A problem that has several solutions will spark conversation among your students. Choose a topic that you feel is one of your best, so you feel comfortable assuming the role of facilitator. Once you see the lights of learning in your students' eyes and hear them actually discussing a historical event, asking thoughtful questions, and bringing in additional resources, you will begin to increase the implementation of NTeQ because you are reminded of why you became a teacher.

Do I need to create a Think Sheet for every step?

You should only create a Think Sheet when you anticipate that students need either guidance or help. If you are working with elementary students, you may need to provide several different Think Sheets in a lesson. As the students mature and develop self-regulation skills, you may find they can work more independently and require fewer Think Sheets.

Technology Integration Activities

The following activities provide an opportunity for you to explore the options for using Think Sheets described in this chapter.

1. Select a problem that you might use in your classroom and develop a Planning Think Sheet based on the KWL chart.
2. Select a reading from a textbook or other material in your class. Create a Performance Think Sheet that uses one more generative strategies.
3. Select a standard or benchmark that you might address in your class and develop a Self-Reflection Think Sheet for it.

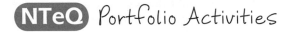

NTeQ Portfolio Activities

Please complete the following activities as part of your NTeQ Portfolio on classroom implementation.

Reflections

The Getting Started portion of this chapter posed three Reflecting on What I Know questions that teachers might commonly ask. In this portion of your journal, reflection activities have been added to help you reflect on each question. Please use information from this chapter to answer the questions.

❶ How can I get my students to ask questions about the research they are conducting?

Reflection Activity: Select an idea you have for a lesson plan and then create a Think Sheet to focus the students' attention on questions they can ask about their data.

❷ How can I teach my students to solve problems?

Reflection Activity: Identify a problem that your students might solve as part of a lesson. Now, develop a planning Think Sheet to help them identify a problem and to plan how they will solve the problem.

❸ I've never used an inquiry-based approach, much less computers—so how is a teacher supposed to do both of these at one time?

Reflection Activity: Write a description that shows how technology supports a problem-based learning approach.

NTeQ Problem-Solving Process

Select an NTeQ lesson that you have developed and generate a sample table similar to Table 5.2 that represents how each component of the NTeQ Problem-Solving Process would be addressed by filling in the Student Action cells.

 **NTeQ** Lesson Plan

Rather than showing a lesson plan in this chapter, we will focus on three Think Sheets based on the example lesson in Chapter 2. The lesson plan described the following objectives:

1. Divided into working groups, students will determine the primary source of information voters use to make decisions about both a presidential election and a local election such as mayor or city council.
2. The student will analyze an election campaign advertisement:
   a. identifying the general message of the advertisement
   b. identifying who or what are in the pictures
   c. identifying the action(s) taking place in the advertisement
   d. describing ideas the writers and authors were trying to convey
3. The student will analyze a political cartoon:
   a. identifying the main focus of the picture
   b. identifying who is speaking
   c. identifying the target audience of the cartoon
   d. identifying recognizable symbols in the cartoon
   e. identifying the humor in the cartoon

The first example is of a Planning Think Sheet for Objective 1 (see Figure 5.6 on page 144).

The second example is a Performance Think Sheet for Objective 3 (since we used a cognitive objective, we can use performance examples to create our Think Sheet; see Figure 5.7 on page 144).

The third example is a Self-Reflection Think Sheet for Objective 2 (see Figure 5.8 on page 144).

Figure 5.6 Planning Think Sheet

K What I **Know**	W What I **Want** to Know	L What I **Learned**
There was a large turnout in our community for the last mayoral election. We have four television stations, one newspaper, and multiple radio stations.	What sources did voters use to determine their candidate of choice? Did voters select the mayoral candidate endorsed by the paper? How much money did each candidate spend on radio, television, and newspaper advertisements? Which local news programs do voters view or listen to?	

Figure 5.7 Performance Think Sheet Questions

Using your political cartoon, answer the following questions:

1. What is the primary focus of the cartoon?
2. Who is "speaking" in the cartoon?
3. To whom is the cartoon directed?
4. What symbols are pictured in the cartoon?
5. What is the humor, if any, in the cartoon?

Figure 5.8 Self-Reflection Think Sheet Questions

Now that you have completed the materials on campaign advertisements, check yourself on the following:

1. Can you identify the general message of the advertisement?
2. Can you identify who or what was in the advertisement?
3. Can you identify the action(s) taking place in the advertisement?
4. Can you describe the ideas the writers and authors were trying to convey?
5. If you could not do each of the above, what would you do differently to help you analyze a campaign advertisement?

Exploring the World Wide Web in the Classroom

Getting Started

The Internet and World Wide Web provide educators and students with a tool for communication, research, and collaboration. What started as a mechanism for a group of university researchers to send messages back and forth has now become perhaps the greatest innovation in communication and information technology since Johannes Gutenberg's moveable type for the printing press. How big is the Internet? A July 25, 2008, posting on the Official Google Blog reports that the first Google index in 1998 listed 26 million pages. By 2000, the Google index had reached one billion entries. In July 2008, the bloggers reported that the Google index hit a new milestone—1 trillion unique URLs (Alpert & Hajaj, 2008).

Opponents and proponents are still debating the issues of access, rights, and security, but the benefits and uses of the Internet for education continue to grow. In 1993, only 3 percent of U.S. classrooms had an Internet connection. By 2003, 100 percent of schools had access to the Internet (Parsad & Jones, 2005). Similarly, the number of computers in the schools has also increased. The ratio of students to computers with Internet access has fallen from 1 computer for every 12.1 students in 1998 to 1 computer for every 4.4 students in 2003 (Parsad & Jones). While we might like to see a ratio of 1:1, the 1 to 4.4 ratio is workable for teachers. We have also seen an increase in the number of public schools that have established a presence on the Web. Between 2001 and 2003, Parsad and Jones found a 75 percent increase in the number of schools with websites to reach a total of 88 percent of public schools with their own websites in 2003.

However, gaining access to the Internet is just the first step. We need to consider how we can use this access to tools and information effectively in our classroom. It is easy to engage in mindless activities as we surf, but we need to give careful thought to how we can use the Internet as a productive tool for learning. Through one lens, we might view the Internet as a *very large* database of information that varies in accuracy and timeliness from immediate to outdated. With a different lens, we might view the Internet as an inexpensive communication tool that offers our students and ourselves a way to interact with the world.

Ten years ago, a classroom was defined by four walls, a textbook, and the teacher's knowledge. With access to the Internet, there are no walls to the classroom, there are alternative sources of information besides the textbook, and the teacher is only one source of information available to the class. This chapter provides some of the basics necessary to begin integrating the Internet into your curriculum.

Reflecting on What I Know

1 Now that I have access to the Web, how can I use it effectively?

2 How do I manage students' use of the Web in my class?

3 Which features of the Web do I use?

Classroom

SNAPSHOT

Students in Mr. Marken's class were working in small groups in various places in the classroom. Some groups were using one or two laptops while two groups were using desktop computers. At one of the desktop computers was heard a rather unusual accent, at least one not native to central Kentucky, where these students lived. The four students were conversing with a scientist at NASA's Jet Propulsion Lab in California. She was answering questions about some newly discovered asteroids the students were researching. The conversation was taking place in real time using video conferencing, allowing the students and the scientist to see and hear each other. Suddenly, cheering came from another group of students using a laptop. It seemed their collaborative team in Dublin, Ireland, had just found some recent pictures of Saturn that they promised to post on their school's website so the virtual team could complete their paper.

A third group of students was staring intently at the screen of their computer. They were using Google Docs to edit their project with students in Calgary, Alberta, Canada. Members from each group would take turns typing a comment in a chat field, which someone else would use to make a change in the document. A fourth group appeared distracted because one of the students was downloading a music file, but closer examination indicated they were using it for their presentation.

After observing Mr. Marken's class it became clear that neither he nor the students were bound by four walls and the textbook. Their Internet connection allowed them to interact with other students around the world while accessing up-to-date information.

The Internet

Today, the Internet is ubiquitous. We can find it everywhere from smartphones to our refrigerator. We can conduct a search for a recipe, send and receive email, chat with someone, or watch a video presentation for personal growth or entertainment. When referring to the Internet, the terms Internet, World Wide Web, and Web are often used interchangeably. However, Internet and World Wide Web (or simply Web) are two different things.

The Internet is a network consisting of cables and radio signals used to connect millions of computers to other computers to form the Internet. Think of the Internet as the cables linking the computers together so that they can exchange information. The Web is a type of language computers use to exchange information by using the Internet connections and cables. If you have ever entered a URL such as

Students gather information for their Internet search.

www.google.com into a browser, then you may have noticed that the browser displayed the website with **http**://www.google.com. The *http* is the protocol or set of standards computers use to communicate. This protocol is used to request a story from www.cnn.com or a picture from a search. Fortunately, we do not need to understand the specifics of the http protocol to use the Internet to retrieve web pages. As each generation of computer applications improves, we as users see fewer and fewer of the lower-level interactions on the Internet. For example, search engines now suggest a correct spelling when we mistype a word. Well-designed websites no longer give us a "Page Not Found" error but direct us instead to a site map or even suggest alternative pages. The result is a much more user-friendly experience for both the novice and the experienced user.

In the following sections, we will examine how students and teachers can use the World Wide Web as a tool with an NTeQ lesson plan. First, we will examine how students can use this tool. Second, we will examine how teachers can use this tool both for instruction and professional development. Third, we will examine appropriate practices for using the Web, and finally, we will explore use of the Internet with NTeQ lessons.

Using the Web to Achieve ISTE NETS for Students

NETS

1. Creativity and Innovation: Students demonstrate creative thinking, construct knowledge, and develop innovative products and processes using technology. The Web is a vast repository of information. When students use data from the Web in an appropriate fashion, they will construct new knowledge and generate products based on research and credible information.

3. Research and Information Fluency: Students apply digital tools to gather, evaluate, and use information. Data from the Internet can range from factual information to opinions to incorrect information. As students do research using various web-based tools, they will learn to evaluate and select information from reliable sources while weeding out information that lacks credibility.

4. Critical Thinking, Problem Solving, and Decision Making: Students use critical thinking skills to plan and conduct research, manage projects, solve problems, and make informed decisions using appropriate digital tools and resources. When the Web is used as a tool with the NTeQ student problem-solving model from Chapter 5, students will use the resources to define problems, determine what is known and not known, manipulate the data, generate and test solutions, and present their findings. They can use communication tools to work collaboratively and refine their critical-thinking skills through discussion.

6. Technology Operations and Concepts: Students demonstrate a sound understanding of technology concepts, systems, and operations. When using the Web, students will develop a variety of skills using different applications, including Web 2.0 applications for communication and searching. Students will learn to post and respond with text information, audio files, and video files. When working with files created by others, students will apply appropriate copyright restrictions to their use.

Students Using the Web as a Tool

Since its inception, the Web has grown from a repository of information to a complex set of tools students can use for searching, collaborating, and communicating. In this section, we examine how students can use the Web to help them solve problems.

The Web as an Information Source

One way of viewing the World Wide Web is to consider it as a massive database of information. You can find almost any information on the Internet, from modifying

The Power of Classroom Practice

Go to MyEducationLab, select the topic "Music and Art Integration," and go to the Activities and Applications section. Access the video "Website and Photoshop in Photography" and consider how the teacher uses a website to expand his lesson. Complete the activity that follows.

your car to use "brown gas" to baking a cake to locating people who have similar interests as you. The problem is finding the information needed to solve your specific questions and problems. In this section will examine how to search the Web for information to answer our questions.

Searching.   The trillion pages composing the Web contain a wide range of information. Our first task is to sort through more than one trillion pages to find the three or four pages that have the information we are seeking. Using a web browser like Internet Explorer, Safari, or Firefox, we can access a search engine. Search engines are web applications that can rapidly search through web pages that have been indexed to find pages relevant to our key words. Google and Yahoo! are two of the most popular search engines and account for over 80 percent of all web searches (comScore, 2008).

Starting a Search.   Each search begins with one or more keywords. With today's search engines, actually typing a question like "How much sunlight does a tomato plant need?" will return a number of pages with information about tomatoes and sunlight. Entering the keywords "tomato plant light" produces similar results; however, we find more direct answers than with the question. There are many variations for entering search terms, often using Boolean terms such as AND and OR. Most search engines assume that when we enter "tomato plant light" we want to search for pages that have all three terms. Thus, the search engine adds the AND to our keywords and actually searches with the phrase "tomato AND plant AND light."

Google provides eight basic search strategies to help you narrow down those trillion pages (Google Guide, 2008). These basic strategies are described in Table 6.1.

Specialized Searching.   While Google and Yahoo! are used for the majority of searches, what if you wanted to search for some very specific information? The website www.altsearchengines.com provides a monthly list of the top 100 alternative search engines. Specialized search engines allow you to search for abbreviations, facts, timelines, health issues, music, images, and photos, to name a few. For example, we could use www.pixsy.com to search for photographs, such as the integration of Central High School in Arkansas, or videotape of Richard Nixon's resignation. We can use a site such as www.songza.com to search for a specific recording such as Mozart's horn concerto or "She Loves You" by the Beatles. Another type of specialized search engine is the meta-search engine that will search several other search

Table 6.1	Basic Search Strategies from Google

Search Terms	Finds Pages with the Following
achondrite meteorite	The words *achondrite* and *meteorite*
welding iron or brass	Pages with *welding iron* or *welding brass*
"ground water"	Will only find pages that have the phrase *ground water*. If the quotation marks were not used, pages that had water and ground in any order and separated by other words would be listed. For example, the search without quotation marks around the phrase would return a page with the following: "There was *water* available in bottles. The *ground* was very dusty."
oil -engine	Finds web pages that mention oil, but not those mentioning engine oil. The minus sign is used to find web pages without a specific term.
cooking +oil	Finds web pages with the term cooking and oil, but not pages with engine oil. The plus sign tells Google to match the terms exactly, thus, the results will not include pages with mineral oil.
educational ~media	Searches for media and the word's synonyms. This search would find web pages with the words educational media as well as multimedia, audio, film, television, and so on.
U.S. trade deficit 1992..1998	Searches for web pages with the terms U.S. trade deficit in the years 1992 through 1998. The two periods are used to search through a range of numbers including dates.
Robert* Kennedy	Returns pages that include Robert Kennedy, Robert F. Kennedy, and Robert Tom Kennedy. The * is a wild card and will find any word between (or lack of) between Robert and Kennedy. It can also be used with Oct* to find Oct. and October.

engines such as Google and Yahoo! at the same time and display the results in an organized fashion. Two examples of meta-search engines are http://clusty.com and www.dogpile.com. Other specialized search engines can be found at www.search engineguide.com/searchengines.html, which lists search engines for topics areas such as architecture, transportation, flags, maps, and so on.

There are also specialized kid-safe search engines that filter information considered inappropriate for students. Popular safe search engines include Google's SafeSearch (www.safesearchweb.com/google.html), Yahoo's Yahooligans (www.yahooligans.com), Ask Jeeves for Kids (www.ajkids.com), and Looksmart's Kid Directory (www.net-nanny-software.com). Additional information on other search tools as well as how to use content filters can be found at SearchEngineWatch (http://searchenginewatch.com/2156191).

Another option is to provide students with a list of URLs that you have pre-screened. Although providing students with a list of websites or start pages does not develop their searching skills, it can focus their efforts on specific sites that are highly relevant. There are several options you can use to create your own start page, such as a Word or PDF document you distribute to the class electronically. If you have your own website, you can create a web page with links. You can also create a Google Doc that has links for students to access online. Another option is the use of free online bookmarks such as Diigo (www.diigo.com) and Delicious (http://delicious.com). While searching the Web, you can use Diigo tools to collect and annotate sites and then share the collection with your students to direct them to specific websites (see Figure 6.1).

Regardless of the search engine students are using, they need to give careful thought to the information they are seeking. Given the trillion or more web pages, a search usually produces hundreds or thousands of pages. A carefully constructed set of search terms may produce a large number of pages, but the most relevant pages will be in the first 10 to 20. Your students become more productive researchers when you help them learn to carefully construct their search terms *before* they use a trial-and-error method.

The Web as a Collaboration Tool

You may recall from the Classroom Snapshot of Dr. Marken's classroom that his students were collaborating with other groups of students on their project. Students work together to solve a problem, typically producing a joint creation such as a report. In this section, we will examine a tool students can use to work collaboratively on a project.

Sharing Documents.   Google Docs is a free set of web-based applications students can use to create and share documents. Students can use Google Docs (see Figure 6.2, p. 154) to create word processing, spreadsheets, and presentations that can be exported as Microsoft Word, Excel, or PowerPoint files. Importantly, Google Docs provides the tools for students to collaboratively create and edit documents in an online environment. For example, Aaron might add a picture to the slide of a presentation, and Melanie can see the change immediately on her computer. An advantage to an online tool such as Google Docs is that you do not need to worry about compatibility of software issues that might occur if team members in different schools use different versions of the soft-

Figure 6.1   Online Bookmarks Created with Diigo

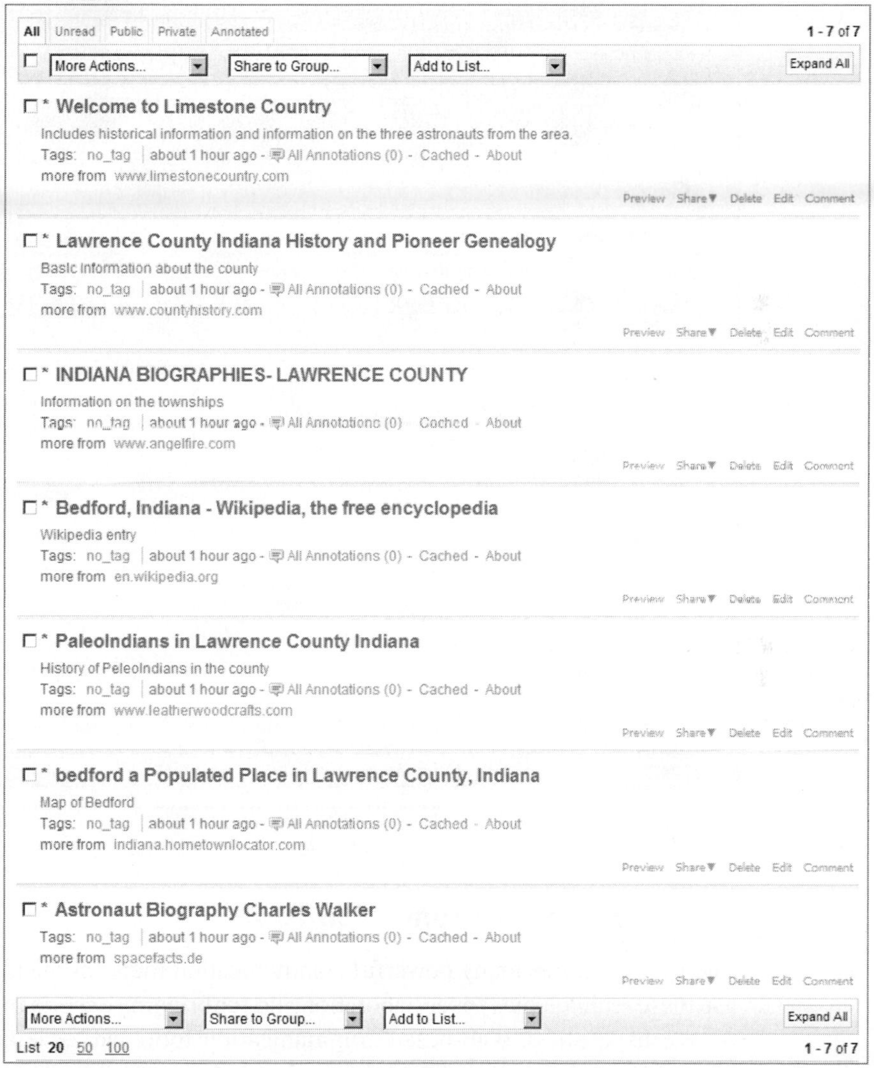

ware. Moreover, since the documents are stored online in one location, work on the project is not delayed due to a lost disk or someone leaving a disk at home.

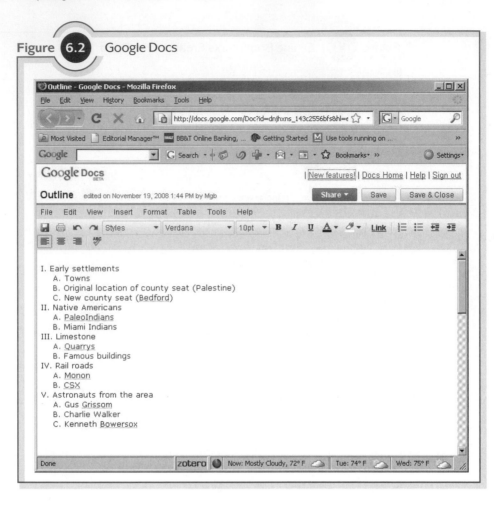

Figure 6.2 Google Docs

The Web as a Communication Tool

The Internet offers many powerful communication tools for the classroom. We can use these technologies for collaboration and for bringing experts into our classroom. As we have noted, web-based communication tools can be either synchronous, which means occurring in real time, or asynchronous, which means communication flows in sequential steps, such as email. You send an email to someone and they read it only after they have checked their inbox for new messages. Then they respond to your email. This process might happen in just minutes, or it might take up to a day or longer depending on individual schedules. Rather than email, you might use an asynchronous tool like a discussion board, blog, or wiki. On the other hand, you might use *synchronous* communication that happens in real time, much like a telephone call or face-to-face conversation. The Internet supports both types of communication—web-based phone calls and video conferencing.

Email.   Email is one of the earliest forms of Internet communication. Students can use email to send messages to government officials and researchers to obtain information related to their school work. They can also communicate with other students and send project files as attachments. However, there are also concerns with email, including students being engaged by adults who have not been approved by the school or students sending inappropriate messages. Two websites offer filtered, kid-safe email accounts. ePals (www.epals.com) offers kid-safe email to students as well as tools for finding other classrooms with similar interests for collaborative projects. Gaggle.net also offers a safe and filtered email service for students. School district policies concerning student email range from prohibiting any type of email account to allowing filtered accounts. Teachers should consult with appropriate administrative personnel before creating integrated lesson plans that depend on students using email.

Connecting with an expert requires some initial work for the teacher. If your students want to submit questions to a government official, you may be able to find an email address on an agency website. For example, you or your students can find the email address of their U.S. representative at https://writerep.house.gov/writerep/welcome.shtml and their U.S. senators at www.senate.gov/general/contact_information/senators_cfm.cfm. Similar web pages are available for state representatives and senators. Many local governments maintain websites, but a phone call may be required to obtain an email address. Finding emails of researchers varies depending on their place of work. If you know that an individual works for a university, then you can probably find the email address in a directory search on the university's home page. Finding researchers in business and government agencies is sometimes more difficult and may require you to email a general address on the website. If your students want to ask an astronaut a question, they can submit it at www.discoverspace.org.

Writing an email to an expert is much like writing a business letter. Students need to carefully craft their request. Their questions should be unambiguous, clearly stated, and directed to the appropriate individual. Rather than having each student in the class email their representative, send one email with all the questions.

Web-Based Phone Calls.   An old technology brought to the Internet is the web-based phone call. One system, Skype (www.skype.com), offers free phone calls between Skype users. Students can use Skype phone calls to talk with experts and with other student groups. Although the calls work best between single individuals using headsets with microphones, a group of students or even a whole class could participate in the call with some minor adjustments. The primary issue is noise or feedback from the microphone in the classroom. One solution is to mute the microphone when the students are not talking or use a noise-canceling microphone. Another solution is to let Skype automatically adjust the microphone and speaker settings by checking the appropriate box.

Web-Based Video Conferencing. AT&T described a videophone in the 1960s (Molnar, 1969); however, widespread access to videophones did not occur until almost 40 years later. Today, there are several options for video conferencing that only require a webcam, microphone, speakers, computer, and high-speed Internet connection. Web-based phone calls allow us to speak to one another while web-based video allows us to see the other individuals involved in the call. For one-on-one or very small groups, students can use the video feature on a Skype phone call. Using a video conference call allows the callers to see one another rather than just hear voices. Another option is to use web-based conferencing.

Web-based conferencing goes beyond just a conversation; it allows users increased interactivity in three important ways. First, multiple individuals from different locations can connect to one another using audio (some offer video). Second, a presenter can show a presentation or other multimedia while talking. Third, callers can interactively edit a document and converse about their changes. There are several options for conferencing software including Adobe Connect, Elluminate, and Flash Meeting. All require a fee to purchase or use although some services offer a free version for very small groups. Web conferencing products allow two-way audio for discussions. For example, your class might contact an expert for a video conference (see Figure 6.3). The teacher or student could email the expert a URL for the meeting, which could include students connecting with multiple computers from a single or multiple schools. Using software such as Adobe Connect, all participants can share a video connection. The expert could show graphics or a PowerPoint presentation. Similarly, the students might show the expert a document or drawing they have created to receive feedback.

There are a variety of web-based tools for students to connect with other students as well as with experts. Communication ranges from text to audio to full video conferencing capabilities. The speed of Internet communication makes it more feasible to do collaborative projects with students at other schools, whether across town or in another part of the world. Collaborating learning using Internet tools allows our students to share ideas with others and gain different perspectives.

Figure 6.3 Video Conference

Teachers Using the Web as a Tool

In today's connected world, it is possible for teachers to throw out their file cabinets and empty the proverbial "teacher's closet" that may have collections contributed by teachers from several generations. Connected teachers can now store most of their materials, including their gradebooks, online. In this section we will examine ways of managing the content used in the classroom, connecting with parents and the community electronically, and accessing the Web for professional development.

Content Management

How many times as a teacher have you had a student ask for another copy of a handout, or as a student how many times have you asked a teacher or instructor for another copy of a handout? In either case, someone must search through a file cabinet and find the correct handout. Content management systems can solve this problem by making materials available to students electronically. Blackboard and Drupal are two types of content management applications available to teachers. Complex content management systems such as Blackboard, WebCT, and Moodle are quite robust in their features. A description of typical features in a content management system is described in Table 6.2. In addition to content management systems, a creative teacher can also adapt a wiki such as www.publicpbwikis.com to function as a content management system. Wikis are a special type of web page that allow one or more users to edit and make changes to the pages.

While the management of documents is very appealing, content management systems and wikis also offer instructional tools. Of particular interest are two broad applications of discussion threads or students posting in wikis. The first is a discussion where the instructor or a student posts a question and then other students respond. Initiating a web-based discussion is similar to the same task in the classroom. The question needs to be open-ended to generate numerous responses. Maintaining the discussion requires the teacher or a student facilitator to ask other questions to direct, redirect, or raise new points. The second application is posting of student reflections or interpretations, which can range from explaining an answer to a math problem to interpreting a poem or picture to reflecting on a project or paper. Other

Table 6.2	Common Content Management Features
Feature	**Function**
Web portal	Provides students a starting point for access to your course
Discussions	A managed threaded discussion (threaded discussions are linear with students and teacher replying to responses)
Materials	Course handouts, syllabus, assignments, and other documents can be posted for easy access; multimedia units can also be uploaded and accessed
Personal web page	Student can create a personal web page with access limited to class members
Collaborative work space	Chat rooms and file sharing can be created for individual groups
Announcements and calendar	Announcements about due dates or changes can be posted as well as a calendar of course activities and due dates
Gradebook	Students can view grades online and submit assignments for grading
Tests and surveys	Tests and surveys can be created and managed

students can then respond and generate a discussion. Online discussions and postings are living documents that change and evolve over time.

Connecting with Parents and the Community

Traditionally, teachers have communicated with parents by notes and parent meetings. As our lives become more complex and living and work patterns change, it is often difficult for parents to attend parent–teacher conferences or special occasions during the day when their son or daughter may be making a presentation. The following section describes options for communicating with parents and the community. Before using these approaches, a teacher should check district and school policies to determine whether such forms of communication are acceptable.

Email.   With the increasing number of individuals having access, email is an excellent tool for communicating with parents about your classroom. These messages about classroom events can take the place of the weekly note sent home in a student's folder. You can create a mailing list or group to which you send these announcements. For example, you can create a contact group in Gmail to which you can add email addresses of parents. In Outlook, you can create a distribution list that includes parents' email addresses. By selecting the group or distribution list, you can compose a single email that will be sent to everyone in the group without entering individual email addresses. Districts may have a policy allowing general emails but prohibiting emails that provide progress or grade information, because it is difficult to verify the confidential information is actually going to the parent.

School and Classroom Websites.   Another means of communicating with parents and the community is through a website. Districts vary in their policies about giving access to a classroom website on the school's server. If you are not allowed to manage a classroom website on a district server, you can instead use a hosted source. Websites for your classroom can be created at www.schoolrack.com, www.teacher web.com, and www.teacherwebsite.com. Different options are available, and you may require visitors to the site to use a password before providing access. Another choice for communicating is a public wiki (www.publicpbwikis.com) that you can use to publish information about your classroom. A third option is to create a blog that you or your students can contribute to using edublogs.org.

Wikis, blogs, and websites are useful for communicating information to parents and others about the events in your classroom. A private website accessible to only parents and students can include homework assignments, descriptions of events in the classroom, reminders about permission slips and fees, and postings of student

Classroom websites are a great way for parents to see what their children are doing in school, and an equally great way for teachers to reach out and communicate with parents and the community.

projects. You might also want to create a website for the community where your students can post the results of their research. For example, if your students have completed a project on the history, businesses, or other aspect of the local community, then having the product(s) posted on a website would be of interest to those in the local community. Any time you post student products on a publicly accessible website, you need to be sure to protect student identities and contact information. You also need to follow school policy for posting student materials. If you want to publish a student video project or video presentation then a different website is needed. One free service is offered by www.teachertube.com, which is considered a kid-friendly website. This website accepts video productions that are relevant to students and teachers.

Making the Classroom Accessible to Parents.   When students have completed an NTeQ-designed lesson plan, they produce a product, whether it is a paper, newsletter, or presentation. Papers and other documents are easily posted on a website or wiki. But what do you do with a live presentation or debate? Parents might want to attend, but work or other commitments can prevent them. Tech-savvy teachers can stream the presentations via the Web so that parents can view the presentations. Streaming or webcasting involves connecting a video camera and microphone to a computer with appropriate software. Generally, a video camera will provide a better image than a web camera. The sound and image are digitized and then streamed to the viewer. For, example, you could use Adobe Connect or Flash Meeting if available in your school. An Internet search for video streaming and webcasting can help you identify various sites that offer free or low-cost services. Before using one of these options, you need to determine if the site can limit access to only parents and guests. If you cannot limit access, then anyone with an Internet connection can view and record the presentation.

Professional Development

There are rich sources of information on the Web for professional development ranging from informal information to well-produced video presentations. Teachers can search education related blogs (edublogs.org) for information on a wide range of topics. Video productions are available from www.tcachertube.com. Classroom 2.0 (www.classroom20.com) includes blogs, wikis, photographs, and video on topics of interest to teachers. You can find topics ranging from social studies to webcasting to creating quizzes online. EdTechTalk.com is a global collaborative platform where educators come together to share experiences, knowledge, and resources related to education and technology. The site offers regularly scheduled interactive webcasts on topics related to the classroom.

Appropriate Practices for the Web

The Internet creates many interesting and exciting possibilities for class-room instruction, but it also provides opportunities for new problems. One type of problem received a great deal of publicity when Fortune 500 companies started dismissing individuals for abusing company email systems by sending in-appropriate materials (sexually oriented, violent, etc.) or using sexually explicit, profane, or other unacceptable language in emails. School districts are not immune from these abuses or problems. The focus of this section is on how to address these problems.

District Policies

Many states suggest or require each school district to develop an acceptable use policy concerning the Internet. This policy outlines conditions for use of the Internet by faculty, staff, and students, and establishes guidelines for appropriate online prac-tices. There are several websites devoted to information on what to include in such a policy. The Virginia Department of Education provides a detailed handbook on de-veloping an acceptable use policy, including templates and several informative links (www.doe.virginia.gov/VDOE/Technology/AUP/home.shtml). The U.S. Department of Justice provides a model acceptable use policy on their website (www.usdoj.gov/criminal/cybercrime/rules/acceptableUsePolicy.htm) as well as information on Internet safety and crime (www.usdoj.gov/criminal/cybercrime/cyberethics.htm).

Acceptable Use Policy.　What should an acceptable use policy include? A review of several policies and guidelines produced the following list of items. This list should not be considered complete, but rather a starting point.

- *Uses of the Internet.* The policy should describe the educational value of the Internet and how it will be used for instructional purposes. For example, the policy might describe how it can be used for communication via email and for gathering information to support instruction or research.
- *Responsibilities.* The policy should explain the responsibilities of administrators, faculty, staff, and students when using the Internet. This section might include reference to user accounts, privileges, and system security. One common theme is that Internet access is a privilege, not a right, and this privilege can be revoked if abused.
- *Acceptable and unacceptable behavior.* It is very important that the policy explain in simple language what is acceptable and what is not acceptable Internet use for all. Many policies explicitly state that it is a violation of the policy to download or send sexually oriented materials or to use sexually explicit language. Other unacceptable behaviors include using the Internet to access another individual's account or files or distributing copyrighted material.
- *Consequences.* The policy should provide guidelines for dealing with violations of the policy. For example, what action is taken against a student who distributes copyrighted material or accesses another student's account?
- *Parent notification.* Some states or districts require parents be notified that their children will have access to the Internet. The policy should address this issue and provide an alternative to students whose parents do not want them to have Internet access.
- *Access.* The policy should describe the procedures for students to access the Internet and school resources. For example, this policy statement might describe how one obtains an individual account or password if needed.

One of the primary concerns about student Internet access is the availability of sexual, racist, violent, and other unacceptable websites. As mentioned earlier, many districts use filtering software, but it is not always effective in preventing or limiting access. The acceptable use policy should clearly define what types of sites are unacceptable and the consequences of accessing unacceptable sites. A clearly defined policy *and* filtering software can provide an initial strategy to help students learn appropriate behaviors.

Classroom Policies

The school's acceptable use policy will define appropriate uses of the Internet and each individual's responsibility. It is the teacher, however, who must implement the policy in the classroom. As a teacher, how can you help your students find appropriate websites and use email responsibly? This section will present strategies for appropriate Web access and use of email in your classroom.

Having access to the Internet in a classroom can enlighten any conversation. We observed a classroom in which a student asked a question about the gestation period of a mammal they were studying. No one knew the length of time. Immediately, three or four students connected to the school's wireless network using their laptops and did a search. Almost immediately, one of them had an answer! However, that same day we saw a few students visiting websites that discussed their favorite idols while they listened to the latest hit songs with earphones and stayed off task as they searched for new music files.

First, let's consider classroom management. How do you manage a classroom or lab in which each student has a computer? If you are using an NTeQ lesson plan, your students are probably working in small groups or individually and are spread about the room, if not in more places. This problem is more pronounced when each student has a laptop that allows him or her to sit almost anywhere. One strategy we have observed is to place the teacher's desk at the back of the room. This vantage point allows you to easily view the computer screens so that you can recognize students who are off task. Another strategy is to place the chairs or tables in a U shape. When the students are working on their laptops, they sit on the inside of the U. The teacher can then easily move around the room in an open area of the U and view each student's computer screen.

Before computers, it was said that teachers had eyes in the back of their heads (we swear it was true of our fifth-grade teachers). Today, you have to be able to read minds and intercept packets of information as they flow from the Internet to a student's computer and from student computer to student computer. If you have created a student-centered learning environment, you are probably working with individual students or groups located around the room, which makes it more difficult to find students who are off task. If your students are using PCs, you can glance at the task bar at the bottom of the screen to see which applications they have open. Similarly, you can check the Mac's application menu on the far right of the menu bar to determine the applications the student is running. If you find something suspicious, you can ask the student to explain how they are using the application or information to solve the problem.

When students are doing Internet searches, "accidents" happen. They may type in the wrong URL or click the wrong link, resulting in accessing a site that is inappropriate. It is not a matter of *if* it will happen, but *when* it will happen. You need to develop a strategy that you can explain to your students *before* they start using the Internet. One effective strategy we have observed is to have the student either turn off the monitor or close the laptop when they arrive at an inappropriate site. The student then goes to the teacher and explains what happened. The teacher can then deal with the problem. You might want to determine how the student got to the site by clicking the back button. A student should not be punished for accidentally arriving at an inappropriate site. For example, simply mistyping common or popular URLs can direct your browser to an inappropriate site.

How can you determine if a student has been accessing inappropriate websites? Internet browsers keep a history of sites visited. You can display a list of all sites visited by reviewing the history file. The sites can be listed in chronological order and the history may include multiple days of information.

Copyright Issues

As with any medium that is in the public sphere, copyright of Internet material is an issue. Copyright protects an author's work from being stolen by someone else or used in a way that the author is uncomfortable with, such as using a graphic in commercial curriculum materials. All information published on the Internet is technically copyrighted, even though the copyright notice may not be visible with the work. So, what can be copied off the Internet freely? When do you need to obtain permission from the author?

The law allows for "fair use" of copyrighted material (Crawford, 1993), which usually includes educational and newsworthy uses. Factors considered in determining fair use include the following:

1. The purpose and character of the use, including profit.
2. The character of the copyrighted work.
3. How much of the work is used: not more than one copy per student; 250 words or less of a poem; a complete article or 2,500 words or less; excerpts of 500 to 1,000 words; one illustration per publication.
4. The effect of the use on the market value of the work.

The following guidelines also apply to classroom use:

1. The copies may be used for only one course in the school.

2. Same author copies may not exceed more than one article or two excerpts, or more than three from a collection of works.
3. Multiple copying for one course is limited to a maximum of nine instances during the term.
4. Copying may not be used to substitute for collections of works.
5. You may not copy "consumable" materials such as workbooks.
6. Students may not be charged for the copied material, other than photocopying costs.

More recently, the Creative Commons movement (http://creativecommons.org) seeks to expand the range of works available for others to use, while maintaining ownership with the original creator. The organization is working to provide a means for copyright holders to offer their work to the public for fair use. In a K–12 classroom you may find a creative commons license for artwork, photographs, music, and even clip art. There are six types of licenses (Creative Commons, n.d.):

Attribution Noncommerical No Derivatives. This license allows others to use the material without alteration as long as a link is provided back to the creator. Thus, a student could use a piece of music with this license in a PowerPoint presentation as long as a link was provided on the page back to the original source.

Attribution Noncommercial Share Alike. This license allows each user to modify and then redistribute items such as music or clip art as long as they assign the same license. For example, a student who adds a piece of music to a clip art animation that both have this type of license can distribute them under an attribution noncommercial share-alike license.

Attribution Noncommercial. Products with this license allow users to modify the piece and redistribute for noncommercial use as long as they provide credit for the original piece.

Attribution No Derivatives. Users are free to distribute the piece for commercial and noncommercial purposes as long as it includes credit for the original piece and is not modified.

Attribution Share Alike. Users can modify the original piece and distribute for commercial and noncommercial purposes as long as others can do the same.

Attribution. Users can modify the original and distribute commercially as long as credit is given to the original creator.

The issue of copyright and the Internet is often confusing. If you want to use something from a website, put yourself in the author's place. How would you feel if someone used your materials? In most cases, you should email either the owner of the materials or the webmaster and ask permission to use the materials. You should also consider the following guidelines when using shareware, icons, and graphics.

Shareware is software that individuals and companies market on the Internet. You are often allowed to use the software on a trial basis. However, if you continue to use it, you are obligated to pay the cost of registration or purchase. Examples of shareware are compression and graphics utilities and games. Some icons and graphics are specifically offered for downloading. Several sites offer free clip art that you can download and use.

The following would be examples of copyright infringement:

- Placing another person's graphic or photograph on your web page.
- Copying text and including it in curriculum materials from which you or others gain profit.
- Copying icons not specifically created to be shared publicly.

To obtain permission to reproduce copyrighted material, contact the author (easy to do because most authors give email addresses on their web pages), indicating how the material will be used and asking what credit they would like to be given and what payment they would like, if any. Getting a signature should avoid problems with future legal actions (see Crawford, 1993, for further guidance). The following websites also offer guidance related to copyright issues:

- Myths about copyright: www.templetons.com/brad/copymyths.html
- U.S. Copyright Office: www.copyright.gov
- PBS guidelines for fair use: www.pbs.org/teachers/copyright
- Media Literacy, copyright and fair use: www.mediaeducationlab.com/index .php?page=265

Using the Internet with an NTeQ Lesson

There are a wide variety of Internet tools students can use for solving problems. We should not plan to use the tools just because they exist or are fun to use. However, having students instant message one another from one desk away just for the sake of using instant messaging makes no more sense than having students in a fifth-grade class type in the Gettysburg address as a part of social studies lesson. However, having students talk to one another helps develop their interpersonal skills while paraphrasing the Gettysburg address provides a strategy to help make it meaningful.

We can divide Internet use for instructional purposes into two broad categories. The first and maybe the most common purpose is searching for information. The second is posting information for others to read and review. Let's examine these two ideas further.

Finding information on the Web is almost second nature to anyone under the age of 18; they have not known a world without the Internet. As educators, however, we have a responsibility to teach our students how to evaluate and select credible information on the Web. We recently heard a story of a middle school teacher who gave his students an assignment to "write a paper on an octopus that lives in trees." The teacher created some websites on the topic and then provided the links to the students, who dutifully wrote their papers. Not a single student questioned the credibility of the information (Bauerlein, 2008). As part of the NTeQ problem-solving process, we need to help students critically evaluate the information they find. They need to know the difference between an article on tigers in a magazine such as *National Geographic* versus a blog entry by Joe the Hunter.

Using the Internet for posting information can be a successful instructional strategy. With appropriate planning, student use of the Web can encourage the development of new information and skills. For example, rather than allowing students to copy and paste information from a website, encourage them to paraphrase the information. When students paraphrase information, they must actively interpret the materials and express ideas in their own words rather than copying or plagiarizing the work of others (Barry, 2006). As an option to a traditional paper-and-pencil (or keyboard and paper) approach, students can post their paraphrases or reflections to a blog or wiki so that other students can respond. This strategy can provide models for other students and stimulate discussion resulting in even more processing of the content. Think Sheets (see Chapter 5) can provide questions and other guidance for these activities.

It is amazing to step back and realize that a computer connected with a common looking cord can access over one trillion web pages and contact friends, experts, and even strangers anyplace in the world. With careful planning you can integrate the use of the Internet into an NTeQ lesson plan that can help a student develop new knowledge and skills.

Teacher Technology FAQ

I'm totally unfamiliar with the Internet and feel intimidated about using it with my students. Where should I start?

Start slowly. Skip the online projects for now. Rather, begin by browsing the Web. Locate information that can help inform lessons you are currently teaching. Keep a record of the sites you visit by creating bookmarks. Or get involved by reading some of the postings on K–12 newsgroups. You don't have to respond until you feel comfortable. Finally, you may be inspired by checking websites specifically developed for teachers (some were mentioned in this chapter). There are a variety of lesson plans available for using the Internet in a classroom setting. Most current textbooks list URLs of sites related to the subject area of the book.

I'm concerned about publishing students' photographs or work on the Internet. Do I need parental permission?

Most school districts have now set policies regarding publishing on the Internet. Some require parents to sign permission slips, others publish photos but leave off the student's name, while some do not allow any publishing of photographs. Find out the school and district policy.

Do I have to use the Internet in my classroom?

No. The Internet is a tool. If it is appropriate, you should use it in your classroom. There are many resources in your school and local library that you can use to build your Internet skills and many experts you can invite into your classroom personally or electronically to help your students.

I am afraid my students will abuse the acceptable use policy for the school. What can I do?

Someone once said rules were made to be broken, and, as former students, we tend to agree. You should discuss the policy with your students before they use the Internet and then again at various intervals. The students should understand that Internet access is a privilege, not a right. They must demonstrate that they are responsible citizens if they want continued access. Then be prepared for problems. Ask other teachers how they have dealt with problems and then develop a plan of action. We have found that successful teachers handle problems quietly. One teacher described an instance in which a student created a PowerPoint presentation of sexually explicit images at home. The presentation was then circulated among some of her friends. When the teacher discovered the problem, the computers were confiscated. Each student who participated attended a conference with his or her parents, the teacher, and the principal. The student then showed the presentation to his or her parents.

The school revoked the students' access to the Internet. We assume that the parents imposed additional constraints on the students.

Another approach is to have students and parents sign an agreement that they have read and understand the acceptable use policy. Some districts have a simplified version for students to make sure they understand the policy and consequences for violating it.

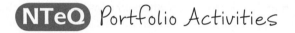

Technology Integration Activities

Integrating the Internet into your lesson plans requires planning and evaluation of materials. Select at least two of the following and evaluate at least three resources for implementing each in your classroom. Determine which best meets your needs.

1. Email for your students
2. Blog for your students
3. Wiki for your students
4. Professional development site for yourself
5. Content management software
6. Video streaming/webcasting or repository

NTeQ Portfolio Activities

Please complete the following activities as part of your NTeQ Portfolio on classroom implementation.

Reflections

The Getting Ready portion of this chapter posed three Reflecting on What I Know questions that teachers might commonly ask. In this portion of your journal, reflection activities have been added to help you reflect on each question. Please use information from this chapter to answer the questions.

❶ Now that I have access to the Web, how can I use it effectively?

Reflection Activity: Create a two-column table and list the tools we have described in this chapter in the left column. In the second column, list function(s) and various objective verbs for the tool. For example, if you listed search engines or Google in the left column, then you might list the function as *searching* and the verbs as *finding* and *locating.*

❷ How do I manage students' use of the Web in my class?

Reflection Activity: Thinking back on the chapter and on your experiences, identify three instances where you saw the Web being used in a class and identify a potential problem. Then describe how you would manage that problem in your classroom.

❸ Which features of the Web do I use?

Reflection Activity: Create a two-column table and list the tools we have described in this chapter in the left column. In the second column, brainstorm ideas on how you might use each tool in your classroom.

Lesson Plan

As a final demonstration of your understanding of how to use the World Wide Web as a tool to enhance learning, select an appropriate topic from the content area that you teach or will teach and follow the NTeQ Lesson Plan Template to create a web-enhanced lesson. Make sure to create a sample of the product that students would be expected to submit at the conclusion of the lesson.

Additional Activities

1. Using either your school's acceptable use policy (AUP), a model policy, or one that you have found on the Web, create a handout appropriate for your students that explains the AUP.
2. Develop an action plan for students and teacher to follow if students receive inappropriate email or visit an inappropriate website.
3. Develop a permission slip for parents that will allow you to post a student's project on your school-approved website. Describe what school, classroom, and student information will be included on the website.
4. Develop a letter that you might send on behalf of your students asking for your mayor's participation in a video conference on recycling in the community.

 **NTeQ** Lesson Plan

Rather than a lesson plan for this chapter, we have created a chart (p. 171) that recommends different Internet strategies for the NTeQ problem-solving model presented in Chapter 5.

NTeQ Student Problem-Solving Steps	Internet Strategies
Define the problem	Searching with search engines Blog or wiki for posting information to synthesize and define problem Conference call or video conference with expert or remote team
Identify what is known about the problem	Blog, wiki, or web page to post known information; can be created by individuals or teams
Identify what needs to be known to solve the problem	Blog or wiki to identify what needs to be known; can be created by individuals or teams
Identify data that needs to be collected to solve the problem	Conduct web-based research to locate relevant information Blog or wiki to generate list of what data to collect Conference call or video conference with expert or remote team
Determine how the data needs to be manipulated to solve the problem	Blog or wiki to list ideas from each student or team Conference call or video conference with expert or remote team
Generate possible solutions	Blog or wiki for brainstorming and refinement of solutions
Determine how to evaluate each solution	Blog or wiki to list ideas from each student or team Conference call or video conference with expert or remote team
Select the best solution	Blog or wiki to list ideas from each student or team
Present findings	Web page for posting documents or media presentations Streaming video/webcast for presentations

Word Processing

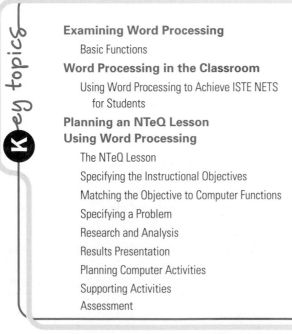

Getting Started

As students increasingly rely on text messaging to communicate with each other, word processing is a "natural" extension of the knowledge and skills it takes to use digital text to share information and express thoughts. Students will need to transition from using text messaging terms, such as *UR* for "you are" and *GR8* for "great," to use of traditional language. This chapter examines word processing and the many ways that students can use this application as a tool to enhance and improve learning. The chapter ends with a detailed description of how to create lesson plans that integrate the use of word processing.

Reflecting on What I Know

1. Doesn't word processing make the writing process too easy?

2. How can word processing be used to engage students in higher-level thinking?

3. In what ways are the individual needs of students met when their work is completed with a word processor?

Classroom

SNAPSHOT

A Classroom without Computers

Maria was happy about going to school today because the class was going to write their first "friendly letter" to someone special. Maria chose her grandmother in Mexico. Her teacher explained how to write the letter and emphasized that the draft copy was to be done in pencil to make it easier to correct mistakes. Maria wrote, erased, and rewrote the draft copy multiple times before taking it to her teacher. Upon approval to make the final copy, Maria took out a clean sheet of white notebook paper and a new ballpoint pen and began using her best handwriting to copy the letter. She very carefully added the date, address, greeting, and first paragraph; then, as her teacher recommended, she reviewed what she had done so far. She found a misspelled word in the second line, so had to get out another sheet of notebook paper. Maria took a deep breath and used her best handwriting to write the second copy of her letter. She was almost finished with the second copy, which was looking great, when Bobby "accidentally" bumped her arm. Her pen slashed across the letter, ruining it. After yelling at Bobby, she pulled out another clean sheet of notebook paper and began again. Although she didn't like having to start over, the writing went a little faster because she had most of the letter memorized.

Then her teacher reminded the class to once again proofread the letters. Maria was sure hers would be perfect because she had been so careful. But to her dismay, she realized that a complete sentence had been left out, so the last paragraph did not make any sense. She reluctantly pulled out yet another clean sheet of notebook paper. All of the elation was gone. In fact, she was beginning to dislike writing.

Classroom

SNAPSHOT

A Classroom with Computers

Maria was happy about going to school today because the class was going to write their first "friendly letter" to someone special. Maria chose her grandmother in Mexico. Her teacher explained how to write the letter and emphasized that a draft outline was to be done in pencil to make it easier to correct mistakes. Maria wrote, erased, and rewrote her outline copy a *couple* of times before taking it to the teacher. Upon approval to make the final copy, Maria went to the computer to "write" her letter. Because her class had finished keyboarding lessons, she quickly used word processing to enter her draft, making sure to frequently save her work. Using the outline as a guide, she carefully wrote each part of her letter to make sure it would make sense to her grandmother. She felt confident in her ability to write a good letter because she could easily correct errors and make changes with the copy, cut, and paste tools. She also changed the font to a larger size to make it easier for her grandmother to read. And, finally, she used the class digital camera to add a recent photo of herself with her teacher. She really enjoyed writing the letter and asked the teacher if she could write another letter to her cousin in New York.

Examining Word Processing

As seen in the Classroom Snapshot, not only did Maria's use of word processing increase her interest and engagement in writing, it also provided the tools that enabled her to enhance her letter beyond what was possible with just paper and pencil. The following section presents an overview of the basic word processing functions and how they can be used to enhance learning (see Figure 7.1).

Basic Functions

Word processing has three key functions that can be used to enhance student learning: (1) entering and editing text, (2) organizing information with tables and graphic organizers, and (3) inserting objects and hyperlinks.

Entering and Editing Text.   One of the most important functions of a word processing application is the ability to edit and change what has been entered. In addition to checking spelling and grammar, the editing process involves four basic functions that begin by either highlighting the text to be edited or inserting the cursor where changes are needed:

- *Delete* a word, sentence, or paragraph
- *Rewrite* a word, sentence, or paragraph
- *Add* a word, sentence, or paragraph
- *Copy* a word, sentence, or paragraph to *paste* in a new position in the document

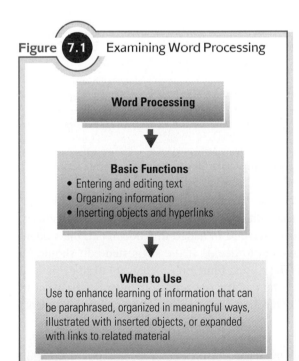

Figure 7.1   Examining Word Processing

Word Processing

Basic Functions
- Entering and editing text
- Organizing information
- Inserting objects and hyperlinks

When to Use
Use to enhance learning of information that can be paraphrased, organized in meaningful ways, illustrated with inserted objects, or expanded with links to related material

Some word processing software applications have revision tools that *track* changes made to the original document. Editing changes that are tracked include the addition of new text, the deletion of text, and changes to the format—e.g., going from single- to double-spaced lines, changing the font style, or adding bullets. The changes are typically noted in two ways, inline or in balloons. Inline edits are "tracked" in the original document by changing the color of the font, using strikethrough fonts for deletions, and adding lines in the margin to note the location of changes. Balloon edits are noted in an extended margin with "call-out" balloons that show the location of the edit. Details about each edit can be seen when the cursor is placed over the change—referred to as a "mouse-over." These details often include who made the change, when it was made, and what was changed. Examples of inline and balloon editing are shown in Figure 7.2.

Figure 7.2 Examples of Inline and Balloon Tracked Changes

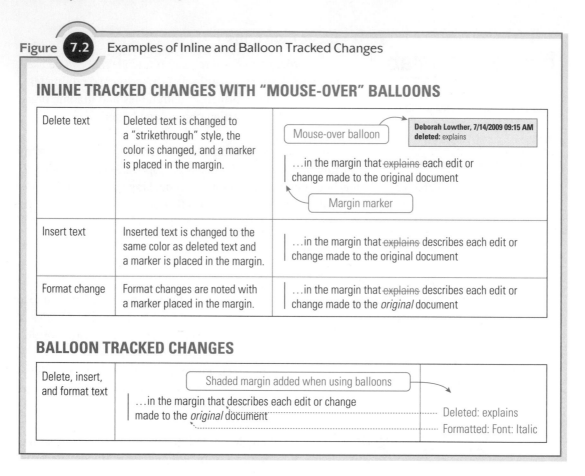

If more than one student is working on a document at separate computers the edits of each one are displayed in a different color text and the "mouse-over" feature will indicate who added the edits. Teachers or students can also add typed comments to help explain a suggested edit or to provide other feedback in handwritten comments. Once tracked changes have been added to a document, the student uses the "Accept" or "Reject" function to decide if the suggested edit should be included in the revised document. The editing function is beneficial to students who wish to rewrite a paper to improve the quality, to groups of students who want to collaboratively write a paper, and to teachers who want to suggest edits for students in revising their papers.

Organizing Information. When students are engaged in organizing information to show how new ideas relate to previously learned information, deeper and more meaningful learning occurs (Jonassen, Howland, Marra, & Crismond, 2008). Many word processing applications provide two functions that assist students with organizing information: tables and graphic organizers. Chapter 10 provides an in-depth examination of graphic organizers.

Tables.   Tables are a very common addition to textbooks, newspaper articles, reports, and advertisements because they readily display connections between related ideas, concepts, and information. These relationships are shown in the table through a series of connected rows and columns that typically begin with headers that explain the contents of the corresponding cells. Students can easily include tables in their word-processed documents with the use of "built-in" tools. For example, one option in MS Word is for students to insert a table by selecting the number of rows and columns from a grid that creates the table in their document. When using Mac's iWork, students use a drop-down menu to insert the number of rows and columns needed in a table. Within each cell, text automatically wraps to fit the cell margins and expands to hold text as it is entered. Tables can be modified with color fills and borders and cells can also accommodate graphics, charts, and hyperlinks, which are discussed in the next section. At any point, students can insert or delete rows and columns as they learn more about the content they are gathering. These features enable students to better concentrate on identifying the main concepts and ideas and using the table to demonstrate relationships between them rather than on the logistics of formatting the information.

Graphic Organizers.   Some word processing applications incorporate special graphic organizer tools that provide a variety of options for visually organizing information. In MS Word, SmartArt tools enable students to easily create graphic organizers to depict such formats as a list, process, cycle, hierarchy, relationship, matrix, or pyramid (see Figure 7.3). Each organizer component accepts text and some are programmed for graphics. Once the content is entered, students have a variety of choices for adding or deleting parts and formatting color and special effects like 3-D shaping and perspective. Student creation of graphic organizers involves numerous decisions that require higher-order thinking about the new information to be learned (IARE, 2003). For example, they need to determine which type of graphic organizer best represents what they want to convey, what information should be included, and the order in which the information should be presented.

Inserting Objects and Hyperlinks.   There are a variety of "Insert" options for word processing. These include inserting pages and page breaks, tables, illustrations or objects, links, headers and footers, and specialized text features such as date and

Figure 7.3 SmartArt Graphic Organizers

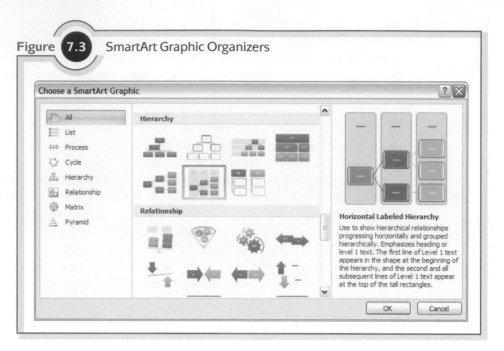

time, symbols, and text boxes. The two that are of importance as tools for student use during NTeQ lessons are inserting objects and hyperlinks.

Inserting Objects. Inserting objects such as pictures, clip art, shapes, and charts is one of the most exciting features of word processing because it enhances students' ability to be creative and allows for the personalization of student work. There are two primary ways to insert objects into a document. The first involves using the "Insert" function of your word processing software, which frequently has menu icons for clip art, pictures, charts, shapes, and so on. When selected, the icon leads to a file menu to locate the desired object from the Internet, hard drive, or CD and insert it into the document. Once inserted, the object can be selected and formatted for text wrapping, size, rotation, and other enhancements. The second way to insert an object is to copy and paste it directly into your word processing document. The object can be, for example, a picture created with a drawing program, a spreadsheet chart, a database report, or a concept map. Begin by selecting the object by clicking on it with the mouse ("handles" appear at the corners) or selecting the area with the "object" selection tool. Copy the item and then move to your word processing document and paste the picture where you want it to be located. As mentioned, you may need to reformat the image once it is placed into the document, based on the desired

Figure **7.4**   Hyperlink Screen from MS Word

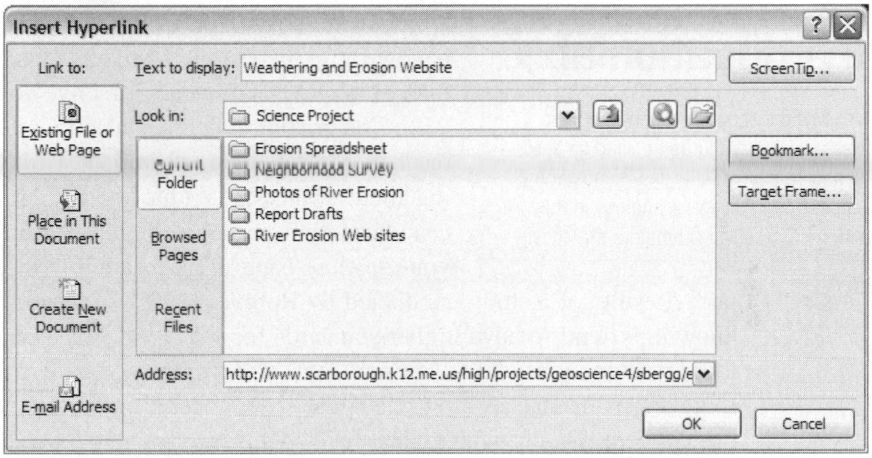

effect of the graphic in the final product. These functions are performed from the Format menu when the object is selected.

Inserting Hyperlinks.   Word processing documents can be much more than a paper "typed" on the computer. Through the use of hyperlinks, the "paper" becomes an interactive product that links to a variety of resources to support and enhance the content. For example, students can insert hyperlinks to Internet sites, email addresses, or other digital files. As seen in Figure 7.4, the MS Word Insert Hyperlink menu provides options for adding "Text to display" for the links. In other words, instead of having a report that shows a really long URL address, the student can use a title that describes the website content.

Word Processing in the Classroom

After examining the main functions of word processing, it is clear that the application provides much more than the name implies. In other words, the software doesn't just "process words," but rather provides a variety of tools to create and enhance reports, letters, newspaper articles, brochures, books, posters, and anything else that contains text, objects, and hyperlinks. Understandably, word processing is one of the most commonly used software applications in business as well as in the classroom (Becker, 2000; Ross, Smith, Alberg, & Lowther, 2004). A key benefit of word processing is that it allows students to concentrate more on *what* they write rather than their handwriting; therefore, all students have an equal opportunity to create legible and attractive documents.

The grading process is also more equitable because teachers can actually read student work rather than guessing about what a student has written. However, if students can choose to use the computer or write papers by hand, you must use caution when grading the two types of papers. Results of a study conducted by Roblyer (1997) indicated that teachers unknowingly tend to have higher standards for word-processed papers compared to those written by hand. One reason is that word-processed papers take up much less room on a page than a handwritten paper, thus appearing shorter. One way to address this concern is to consider giving word counts, such as a 500-word essay, rather than giving the number of required pages for assignments.

Another benefit was revealed when students regularly used word processing in a one-to-one laptop environment that implemented the NTeQ learning approach. The laptop students improved their writing skills significantly more than students who used computers for drill and practice (Lowther, Ross, & Morrison, 2003). Because of these and other reasons, the National Education Technology Standards (NETS) for Students suggests that students in all grades (K–12) use digital tools such as word processing to demonstrate creativity and learning, research and information fluency, and critical thinking, problem solving, and decision making (ISTE, 2007).

Using Word Processing to Achieve ISTE NETS for Students

When students use word processing software to communicate their understanding of new knowledge as it relates to previously learned subject-area content as defined by curriculum standards, four of the six NETS for Students are directly addressed: (1) Creativity and Innovation; (3) Research and Information Fluency; (4) Critical Thinking, Problem Solving, and Decision Making; and (6) Technology Operations and Concepts. Details are provided below.

1. Creativity and Innovation: Students demonstrate creative thinking, construct knowledge, and develop innovative products and processes using technology. As mentioned previously, most word processing applications have a wide variety of formatting choices for students to use when creating their work on the computer. Students can choose numerous fonts and change the appearance of those fonts by us-

---

PEARSON
myeducationlab
The Power of Classroom Practice

Go to MyEducationLab, select the topic "Language Arts Integration," and go to the Building Teaching Skills and Dispositions section. Open "Using Technology in the Writing Process" and complete the activity.

Production of a quality final product takes time and careful planning.

ing different sizes and styles such as bold, italic, or adding a shadow. The font colors can follow a set theme or be designed by the students. Students can personalize their work by including borders, drawings, charts, or pictures that they have created or downloaded. Another way to customize student work is to use the "columns" feature of word processing and add graphics to create products that resemble a newspaper, magazine article, or informative handout (see Figure 7.5). When creating a new document, students have the option of using a template of predesigned handouts, brochures, posters, and reports to provide a professional look for student documents while saving time. These functions help students demonstrate their creativity and innovation.

3. Research and Information Fluency: Students apply digital tools to gather, evaluate, and use information. Word processing documents begin as a "blank slate" that requires students to gather information from what they read in the textbook, on-line, in periodicals, or other sources. With guidance, practice, and criteria specific to the task, students learn to evaluate and use information that "answers the questions" that are posed for the lesson.

4. Critical Thinking, Problem Solving, and Decision Making: Students use critical thinking skills to plan and conduct research, manage projects, solve problems, and make informed decisions using appropriate digital tools and resources. When

Figure **7.5**   A Word-Processed Handout

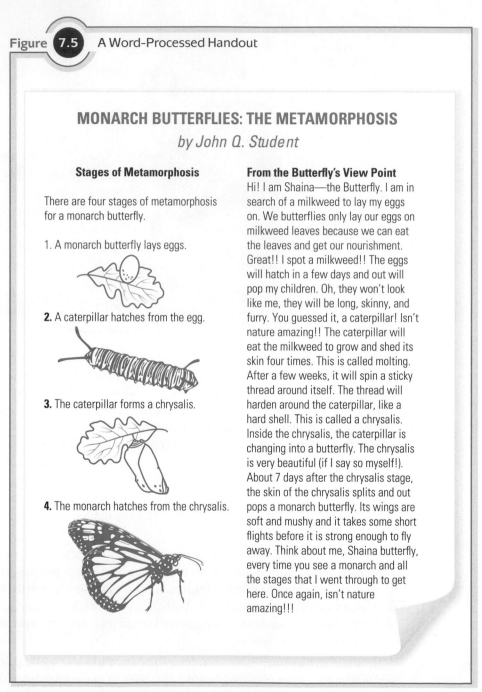

MONARCH BUTTERFLIES: THE METAMORPHOSIS
by *John Q. Student*

Stages of Metamorphosis

There are four stages of metamorphosis for a monarch butterfly.

1. A monarch butterfly lays eggs.

2. A caterpillar hatches from the egg.

3. The caterpillar forms a chrysalis.

4. The monarch hatches from the chrysalis.

From the Butterfly's View Point

Hi! I am Shaina—the Butterfly. I am in search of a milkweed to lay my eggs on. We butterflies only lay our eggs on milkweed leaves because we can eat the leaves and get our nourishment. Great!! I spot a milkweed!! The eggs will hatch in a few days and out will pop my children. Oh, they won't look like me, they will be long, skinny, and furry. You guessed it, a caterpillar! Isn't nature amazing!! The caterpillar will eat the milkweed to grow and shed its skin four times. This is called molting. After a few weeks, it will spin a sticky thread around itself. The thread will harden around the caterpillar, like a hard shell. This is called a chrysalis. Inside the chrysalis, the caterpillar is changing into a butterfly. The chrysalis is very beautiful (if I say so myself!). About 7 days after the chrysalis stage, the skin of the chrysalis splits and out pops a monarch butterfly. Its wings are soft and mushy and it takes some short flights before it is strong enough to fly away. Think about me, Shaina butterfly, every time you see a monarch and all the stages that I went through to get here. Once again, isn't nature amazing!!!

Source: Created by Mindy Morris.

the NTeQ model is used to develop problem-based lessons, students are required to use digital tools to reach solutions and make decisions based on the solutions. In word processing, this involves student use of tables to categorize and organize information, critical selection or creation of graphics to demonstrate concepts, insertion of charts to support arguments, use of hyperlinks to extend descriptions, and use of tracked changes editing tools. All of these activities require students to engage in generative learning strategies, which, as described in Chapter 2, are a basis for engaging students in higher order critical thinking.

6. Technology Operations and Concepts: Students demonstrate a sound understanding of technology concepts, systems, and operations. Word processing functions are basic to numerous software applications. For example, almost all programs use basic text formatting tools, cut and paste, spacing, tabs, alignment and margin rules, and so on. As a result, student use of word processing helps students to gain foundational information on technology operations and concepts.

The Teacher's Diary

Of all the computer applications, I use word processing the most in my classroom. The students use the computer for all of their writing activities—everything from creating lists to writing paragraphs and reports. Although many students have used word processing, they often lack basic keyboarding skills, which I teach during the first six weeks of school. The students catch on quickly and develop some word processing speed.

I guess what I really like about word processing is that I am able to create one word processing activity that can combine several curriculum areas and learning objectives. For example, the students created books on exercise for the culminating activity of a thematic unit. The book writing activity incorporated different types of exercises from the health curriculum, sequencing and identifying the parts of a book from the reading curriculum, identifying and using action verbs from the language

arts curriculum, and creating a flow chart from the social studies curriculum.

Before the students began writing these books, they looked at examples of fiction and nonfiction books. They then created computer-generated Venn diagrams to compare and contrast the parts of a fiction and nonfiction book. Student groups then brainstormed to make a list of physical exercises. Each student picked one exercise and created a flow chart of the exercise steps. The students then exchanged flow charts and tried to do the exercises based solely on the flow chart, without input from the student who created it. It was a great learning experience for the students. They realized that their directions had to be very specific and that the steps to follow must be in sequential order.

At this point, the students were ready to begin writing their exercise books. As a class, they helped me develop the rubric that would be used to assess their exercise books. They decided that each book had to have an illustrated cover, a title page, a copyright page, a table of contents, and ten exercise pages with illustrations.

It was interesting to watch them work independently. They decided to split up the tasks so that each student would be responsible for two exercise pages and an additional page. While working on their rough drafts, they always worked with a partner. One partner wrote and edited the directions as the other demonstrated the exercise. They also exchanged pages among themselves for an informal peer review.

By the time their rough drafts were completed, there was little that needed to be corrected. They took turns using the word processing program and usually worked in pairs. While one pair worked on the text, the other pair worked on the book cover or illustrations. Before the books were bound, they exchanged books among groups and tried out each other's exercises to make final edits and recheck for spelling and grammatical errors. The use of the word processing application made this task easy and quick. Their books were fantastic! Each book was different. The students were proud of their accomplishments and their final products. These books were placed in the classroom library and were used quite often that year when the students could not go outside because of the weather conditions.

Fran Clark
Third-Grade Teacher

Planning an NTeQ Lesson Using Word Processing

The ultimate goal of any technology integration lesson is improved student learning and achievement of the objectives (curriculum and technology standards). When using the NTeQ model to create problem-solving lesson plans that integrate student use of word processing, the nature of the activities require students to use higher-order thinking. For word processing this means students will be involved in activities such as creating compare and contrast tables, finding graphics to illustrate ideas and concepts, and working with a fellow student to create a document that collectively "solves" the lesson problem. Students in grades pre-K through high school across all subject areas can use word processing at age-appropriate levels. To get you started, Table 7.1 on pages 186–187 provides grade-level and core subject-area example problem statements and student word processing products created during lessons that address national curriculum and technology standards (NETS-S).

The NTeQ Lesson

The basic components of the ten-step NTeQ model for developing technology integration lessons were first presented in Chapter 2. This section elaborates further on

Incorporating technology into instruction requires careful planning to make sure the focus of the lesson is on the key functions of the technology in order to help students fully process information.

the NTeQ components, with an emphasis on creating lesson plans that have students use word processing as a learning tool (see Figure 7.6, p. 188).

Specifying the Instructional Objectives

Lesson planning should always begin with specifying the instructional objectives or stating what you want your students to know and do after they finish the lesson. These objectives are written in ways that measure student attainment of local, state, or national standards. Once you have identified the objective(s) for your lesson, you can then determine whether the use of word processing will help students with the learning process. Start by examining the functions of word processing and determining if they align with what the students are to learn. The following section describes this process.

Matching the Objective to Computer Functions

If you look through the menu or ribbon of a word processing program, you will see that numerous fun and exciting functions are available. For teachers, however, it is important to focus on key functions that help students process information at a deeper, long-term level. As seen in Figure 7.3, the word processing functions that fit these criteria are editing text, organizing information with tables and graphic organizers, and inserting objects and hyperlinks.

Table 7.1	Using Word Processing and Problem Solving to Meet Curriculum and Technology Standards	
Standards	**Example Problem**	**Example Student Product**
Elementary		
Language Arts/English		
NCTE Curriculum Standard 3: Students will use specified criteria to evaluate written material. *NETS-S: 3.b. Research and Information Fluency:* locate, organize, analyze, evaluate, synthesize, and ethically use information from a variety of sources and media.	Because many book reviews are written by adults, our class is going to create an online review site for children's book reviews. What criteria should we use to evaluate the books?	Each group member will write a book review and then work together to create a summary review to post on the Web.
Mathematics		
NCTM Communication Standard 1: Organize and consolidate their mathematical thinking through communication. *NETS-S: 3.b. Research and Information Fluency:* locate, organize, analyze, evaluate, synthesize, and ethically use information from a variety of sources and media.	Can you write the secret code to solve a math mystery?	Students use a table to write step-by-step directions to solve a math problem, which is the secret code for accessing the sunken treasure game.
Science		
NSES Life Science Standard C (K–4): Students should develop an understanding of life cycles of organisms. *NETS-S: 3.b. Research and Information Fluency:* locate, organize, analyze, evaluate, synthesize, and ethically use information from a variety of sources and media.	How many genetic traits do you share with your family?	Each student produces a table with columns showing the student's genetic traits and family members' traits.
Social Studies/History		
NCHS Curriculum Standard 1-B: Students will compare and contrast New Year's celebrations between countries. *NETS-S: 3.b. Research and Information Fluency:* locate, organize, analyze, evaluate, synthesize, and ethically use information from a variety of sources and media.	If you were a child living in Israel, how would your celebration of New Year's be different from a celebration in the United States?	Students create an illustrated story from the viewpoint of a child living in Israel.

Table 7.1   *Continued*

Standards	Example Problem	Example Student Product

Middle/High School

Language Arts/English

NCTE Curriculum Standard 7: Students conduct research on issues and interests. . . . They gather, evaluate, and synthesize data from a variety of sources. . . . *NETS-S: 3.b. Research and Information Fluency:* locate, organize, analyze, evaluate, synthesize, and ethically use information from a variety of sources and media.	Our society has several issues that directly affect teenagers, yet their opinions are often not heard. What issue do you think should be shared with the members of our community?	Each team investigates an issue of choice and writes a letter to the editor of the local newspaper.

Mathematics

NCTM Geometry Standard: In grades 9–12 all students should use visualization, spatial reasoning, and geometric modeling to solve problems. *NETS-S: 1.c. Creativity and Innovation:* Students use models and simulations to explore complex systems and issues.	What geometric properties may contribute to the collapse of bridges during earthquakes?	Students create an illustrated report proposing geometric properties that may have contributed to the collapse of an actual bridge during an earthquake.

Science

NSES Earth Science Standard D (5–8): Students should develop an understanding of the structure of the earth system. *NETS-S: 3.b. Research and Information Fluency:* locate, organize, analyze, evaluate, synthesize, and ethically use information from a variety of sources and media.	If plate tectonics or movement of the Earth's crust continues, how will the Earth's continents be configured in the year 7000?	Student teams create a travel brochure that includes descriptions and illustrations of the Earth's continents in the year 7000.

Social Studies/History

NCHS US History Standard: Era 10 Contemporary (1968 to present)—Standard 2A: Evaluate how scientific advances and technological changes such as robotics and the computer revolution affect the . . . nature of work. *NETS-S: 3.b. Research and Information Fluency:* locate, organize, analyze, evaluate, synthesize, and ethically use information from a variety of sources and media.	How has technology changed the summer jobs that high school students had when your grandparents were teenagers as compared to the summer jobs of today?	Students create a compare/contrast table of popular student jobs when their grandparents were teenagers versus today to show how technology has changed (e.g., use of manual cash registers as compared to digital touchscreen registers).

Figure 7.6 NTeQ Components Unique to Technology Integration Lessons

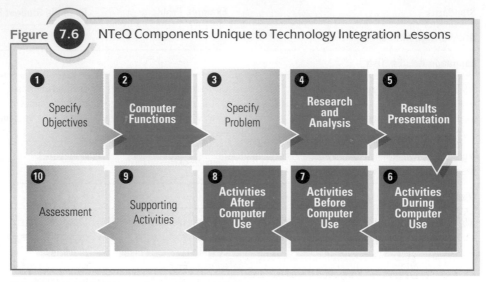

Note: Components relevant to word processing are shaded.

To match a computer function to an objective, compare the learning tasks required by the objective with the functions of the computer, in this case, word processing. It is important to emphasize the "action" portion of the objective when aligning it with the computer. For example, action words in the elementary mathematics standard in Table 7.1 include *organize* and *consolidate,* both of which can be achieved with the use of a table. The middle/high school language arts/English standard lists *gather, evaluate,* and *synthesize* as action verbs. These tasks match with the combined overall functions of word processing. As you learn about additional software programs, you will be better able to match your objectives with computer functions. Of course, there will also be some lessons for which computer use does not align with the objectives, so the NTeQ model would not be needed.

Specifying a Problem

When you have specified the lesson objectives and determined that the use of word processing can be integrated effectively, the next step involves creating a problem for the students to solve. When possible, involve students in the NTeQ problem-solving process, as presented in Chapter 5. As you guide students in identifying a problem, keep the instructional objective in mind, because the objectives should be achieved as students proceed through the problem-solving process. The problem does not have to be elaborate, but it needs to be interesting enough to keep students engaged as they work toward a solution.

The sample problems in Table 7.1 demonstrate problem statements for different age levels that create interest through personalization and intrigue. Personalization in the elementary problem for math is achieved by having students collect and analyze data about the genetic traits of their family members, and the social studies problem has students adopt the role of a child from Israel. Intrigue is sparked by asking high school students to predict what the world will look like in the year 7000, to investigate why a bridge collapsed, and to let their voices be heard by writing letters to the editor. These problems go beyond traditional teaching that often depends on textbook content and computer drill and practice. With practice, time, and perhaps help from fellow teachers, you will be able to generate problems for your technology integration lessons as a natural part of your lesson-planning routine.

Research and Analysis

Once the problem is specified, you can then plan strategies for how students will research and analyze information needed to solve the problem. Student research activities will typically take place prior to use of word processing, although the gathered information will afterward be word processed with the various functions available to students. The overall emphasis of the research and analysis phase is for students to become engaged with the content and to use the targeted skills in order to achieve the learning objectives for this lesson. When using a word processing program, students can be easily engaged in the three types of generative strategies (see Chapter 2): integration, organization, and elaboration. Example activities are seen in Table 7.1. For integration, students can analyze information by writing questions, generating examples, or paraphrasing. For example, students paraphrase when writing book reviews for a specified set of criteria.

Organizational strategies require students to analyze information they are learning. These activities are demonstrated by elementary students creating a table to show their genetic traits and those of family members or the step-by-step process to solve a math problem. Organization is also seen when middle/high school students create compare/contrast tables of technologies used for typical summer jobs when their grandparents were teenagers versus those used today. You can also have students analyze the information they are learning by elaboration. The examples of elaboration in Table 7.1 are the student story of what it would be like to celebrate New Year's as a child living in Israel and students creating a travel brochure for world travel in the year 7000.

Results Presentation

How students present their results or solutions to the problems they are solving will be used to assess the degree to which each student has achieved the stated objectives.

Because of this chapter's focus, the presentation of results will include some form of word-processed material. This could be a traditional report including a description of the problem, hypothesis, procedures, results, and conclusion. The report could be enhanced by including spreadsheet charts (Chapter 8) or information from the Internet (Chapter 6). Students may also create a book, display, or handout that supports an oral presentation. Each of these methods requires the students to interpret their results and determine how to share the findings with others. In other words, students are engaged in synthesizing information learned from the research and analysis to demonstrate their learning.

If students are to prepare a report as part of an NTeQ lesson or any lesson they must identify or locate specific information. If students are using library materials, they have a tendency to *copy* information from one or two sources. If they have access to the Internet or electronic encyclopedias, students often have a tendency to simply copy and paste a lot of information. Rather than requiring the students to prepare an informational report that basically consists of restating facts, we recommend that they prepare an *analysis* paper. The benefit of preparing an analysis paper is that students go beyond the facts by providing their interpretation of the information rather than simply copying and pasting. Be sure to have the students help identify what should go in the analysis paper. The list of criteria can then be used to create the grading rubric for the assignment. It is also imperative that students follow all copyright regulations and include citations for all references used in the results presentation.

Planning Computer Activities

When you plan computer activities, you not only plan what the students will do but also how they will be grouped and what resources they will need. Students need to be actively engaged in processing the information to be learned, and collaborative group work that includes student discussions, decision making, and problem solving should reinforce knowledge and skill attainment (Jonassen et al., 2008).

When deciding which resources are needed for your activities, keep in mind that students can learn a great deal from finding their own resources. For instance, if students were to create the compare/contrast table of summer jobs today versus when their grandparents were teenagers, they could brainstorm ideas about where to obtain accurate and appropriate information. Their list would probably include interviewing parents or grandparents, reviewing periodicals and reference materials in the library, and conducting Internet searches. As students examine each of these resources, they actively process the information and determine if it will help solve the problem. In other words, rather than provide students with specific resources that "solve" the problem, let them engage in the resource-gathering process.

Begin planning the computer activities by deciding what the students will do during computer use—in this case, using word processing software. To assist with this process, we recommend that you create a sample student product to make sure your directions are clear, the planned resources are suitable, and the time allotted is adequate. This sample can then be used as a model for the students. After planning what the students will do at the computer, you decide what they need to do before they go to the computer and then after they finish their computer work. Descriptions of how to plan these activities are given in the following sections.

During Computer Use.   As you plan the word processing activities that students will do at the computer, realize that a lesson may involve more than one use of the computer. For example, consider another lesson from Table 7.1: "How many genetic traits do you share with your family?" For this lesson, students could use the computer three times. During the first visit, students would use word processing and their textbooks to generate a table that includes a brief description of key genetic traits and a column for personal data and other columns for each family member. The second visit would occur after students have gathered the data on family and personal genetic traits. At the computer the students enter "Yes" or "No" for each genetic trait. If students have access to digital cameras, photos of each family member can be added to the table. The final visit to the computer would be used for writing reports describing the key family genetic traits and answering the question, "How many genetic traits do you share with your family?" The resources needed for this activity include word processing software, science textbooks, digital cameras (if used), and a printer.

Another example of a lesson that would use word processing to assist students in achieving the instructional objective is "How will the Earth's continents be configured in the year 7000?" As mentioned earlier, this lesson involves elaboration because students must first know about plate tectonics and the rate of continent movement in order to predict drift over the next 5000 years. The students choose to create a travel brochure to describe and illustrate the continents in 7000. Students could use word processing for several portions of this lesson. The first visit could involve creating a team-planning document that lists strategies for learning the background information and designing the brochure. The next visit could be used to write an outline of the travel brochure content, including suggested graphics for each section and selecting a brochure template (see Figure 7.7). Several computer sessions would then be used to write and edit each version of the brochure, remembering to rotate computer tasks among team members.

Figure 7.7 Selecting a Travel Brochure Template from MS Word New Document Window

Before Computer Use. After you have identified the types of word processing activities your students will do at the computer, you need to plan the activities that will prepare them for the computer work. This preparation can involve from one to several activities. These activities can include brainstorming sessions to clarify the problem they will be solving, listing information sources needed to reach the solution, or sketching out the basic design of a booklet. Once the information sources are obtained, students can take handwritten notes on relevant information. These notes will be the basis for a draft outline of the final product, which is often written by hand and then entered into the computer.

As mentioned, the lesson on family genetic traits involves three trips to the computer. The following example shows a sequential list of activities that would be completed before each trip to the computer:

- Before the first computer visit, students must do some research to generate a brief description of key genetic traits. Since these traits are well-established scientific information, students can use their science textbooks. However, it is critical that students paraphrase the descriptions rather than copying directly from the text. These handwritten description drafts will be taken to the computer to create the final descriptions used in the table. Students will also generate a list of family members that will be included in the table.

- Students prepare for the second computer visit by interviewing family members to collect genetic trait data. Students record the data on a printed copy of the table created in the first computer activity. If a digital camera is available, students also take photos of each member during the interview.
- Preparation for the final visit to the computer involves reviewing the collected genetic data and writing a draft report that describes the key genetic traits of the student's family and how many of the traits the student shares with his or her family members.

Following is an example of the before and during computer activities for the lesson on movement of the earth's continents (see Table 7.2). This lesson requires the students to visit the computer several times.

After Computer Use.   It is a common classroom practice to finish lessons similar to those listed in Table 7.1 by simply having students turn in their completed work to the teacher. The teacher grades each assignment and gives it back to the student or a group of students, who glance at the grade and teacher comments and then file the work in a portfolio, the desk, or the trash can.

Table 7.2	Activities before and during Computer Use: Movement of the Earth's Continents
Before Computer Use	**During Computer Use**

• Brainstorm ideas:
  Plan of action for the project
  Format for the brochure
	Students create a team-planning document that lists strategies for learning the background information about plate tectonics and designing the brochure.

• Review various resources containing information about plate tectonics or movement of the Earth's crust • Take notes on items that may be included in the content • Create a handwritten draft outline of the brochure with notes for types of graphics to include	Students write an outline of the travel brochure content, which includes suggested graphics for each section, and select a brochure template (see Figure 7.7).
• Write first draft of the brochure content by hand • After draft is entered in the computer and printed, the team engages in "read and discuss" sessions to revise and edit the content until it meets the criteria established in the plan of action	Students return to computers for several sessions to write and edit each version of the brochure.

An alternative to this approach is to engage the students in culminating activities after they have completed the computer assignments. As mentioned in Chapter 5, a Think Sheet is a critical component of this final activity. The Think Sheet questions should guide critical thinking about the information the students worked with and have students predict what might happen if circumstances were different. Think Sheets also create links across disciplines. For example, the high school geometry activity on collapsed bridges could include science by having students investigate the most frequent locations of earthquakes. Or you could move to social studies by having students learn about the societal impacts of disasters, such as a bridge collapsing (e.g., traffic being cut off from a hospital, loss of life from the collapse, or pollution from debris). A sample Think Sheet for the movement of the Earth's continents is provided in Figure 7.8. After students finish their computer work, they can individually complete the Think Sheet questions and then form small groups to discuss their responses and determine which ones they would like to share during the whole-class lesson summary.

Student journals are another way students can reflect on what has been learned. Before students write entries in their journals, you can facilitate a summary and review session with the whole class. During the session, you can clarify any misconceptions and also reemphasize the key objectives and why it is important for the students to have the identified knowledge and skills.

Supporting Activities

A wide variety of supporting activities can be used for NTeQ lessons that use word processing. In referring back to the lessons provided in Table 7.1, supporting activities for the elementary mathematics "secret code" problem could involve students completing practice math problems that are needed to write directions to solve the math problem. A supporting activity that would help prepare students to write a story about being a child celebrating New Year's in Israel could include watching a video about family life in Israel. Middle or high school students could read editorials in local and national newspapers and magazines to better understand how editorials are written and to learn about topics of interest to teenagers. High school mathematics students could use hands-on manipulatives to conduct experiments to test the use of different geometric shapes in the construction of model bridges. In summary, the supporting activities are used to engage students in hands-on or minds-on activities to strengthen and expand the learning experiences provided in the NTeQ lesson.

Assessment

When planning assessment strategies for lessons that integrate student use of word processing, the rubrics will probably have increased emphasis on the written com-

Figure 7.8   Sample Think Sheet

MOVEMENT OF THE EARTH'S CONTINENTS
Think Sheet

Directions
Using information from your research and the brochure you created, please complete these items.

1. Describe your impression of how the continental shift predicted to occur by 7000 will impact the following:

Global Warming ....

Democracy ....

Population Growth ....

Economics ....

2. What do you think would be the greatest benefit of the continental shift?
....

3. What concerns you most about the continental shift?
....

4. Do you think the world's nations should be preparing for the continental shift?
❏ Yes ❏ No   Explain your answer below.

....
....
....

ponents of each product. For example, criteria for this aspect of performance could include some of the following:

- Scope of description
- Consistency

- Clarity of expression
- Accuracy of information
- Sufficiency of detail
- Relevance of information
- Logic in organization

Summary

Word processing is a commonly used application that is easily learned by students of all ages. It basically assists students with writing and thus can be integrated into almost any lesson. It also has functions that go beyond the basics of writing to support critical-thinking activities. These functions include being able to easily cut, paste, move, and add to what has been written, thus fostering student ability to create documents that reflect their best work. Word processing also enables students to track edits or examine information in a table to see patterns and groupings of concepts. Students can express their creativity by changing the fonts, sizes, and styles of text and adding graphics, diagrams, and color to further illustrate thoughts. When students work collaboratively to create a word-processed document, ideas can easily be intermingled, changed, and expanded. Plus, discrimination based on poor handwriting is eliminated because *all* students can produce a professional-looking final product.

Teacher Technology FAQ

If my students use the spellcheck tool in word processing, will their ability to spell on their own be limited?

Let's imagine that your class has just completed a unit on Egypt. For one of your culminating activities, your students are required to write with pen and paper a paragraph describing an Egyptian pyramid. The completed papers are turned in to you for grading. You begin reading each paper and circle the misspelled words as they are encountered. You also write in the correct spelling above each word. For other assignments, you require the students to look up the misspelled words in the dictionary and turn in a list of correctly spelled words. Both of these methods require extra time on your part, but more importantly, the students receive delayed feedback. When students run a spellcheck on their papers, they receive immediate feedback on questionable words. In most cases, the spellchecker will suggest more than one word, so students must still think about their error and select the correct spelling. They are also better able to see possible patterns of misspelling and how to correct them. Proofreading, however, is still necessary because spellcheckers only identify misspelled words, not words out of context. For example, the spellcheck will not catch the misspelling of *pen* in the following example: "The author used a quill *pin* to write the letter." You might also want to turn off any options to correct/check spelling as the learner types. For example, some word processors will automatically correct a misspelling such as "teh" as it is typed. By turning off this option, the learner must then proofread the paper for *all* mistakes. Similarly, depending on your objectives, you may want to turn on or off an option that highlights misspelled words with an underscore or squiggly line.

My students easily send text messages using just their thumbs. How can they switch to using a keyboard?

Teachers can approach keyboarding by either providing some form of instruction or allowing students to develop their own approach. When students use their own approaches to enter information with a word processor, it takes about twice as long as when they write a paper by hand (Peacock, 1993; Wetzel, 1990). However, the students who wrote their papers using a word processing program tended to write longer papers that were of slightly higher quality than those written in pencil (Peacock, 1993).

Technology Integration Activities

The following activities provide an opportunity for you to explore the options for using word processing as described in this chapter.

1. Create one NTeQ lesson plan for each basic word processing function: editing, organizing information, and inserting objects and hyperlinks.
2. Create a lesson that involves providing feedback on student word processing assignments with tracked changes and inserted comments of needed revisions.

Lesson Bytes for Word Processing

The following list contains suggestions for word processing that can be created by elementary, middle, or high school students and a sample problem statement for each.

Rewrite

Elementary Students
- Rewrite the "Ugly Duckling" story about a different animal that would have a similar story to tell.

- Some students find the descriptions of pictures in our history book hard to understand. Your team is to rewrite or simplify the picture descriptions for your assigned chapter.

Middle and High School Students
- The U.S. Constitution can be difficult for middle school students to understand. Your group is to use the online thesaurus to rewrite or simplify Amendments 1 to 10 of the Bill of Rights.
- Rewrite a short version of *Robin Hood* so you are the hero and the story takes place in your hometown.

Create "How-To" Descriptions

Elementary Students
- Your new friend wants to come over to your home after going to the library, but doesn't know how to get there. You need to create a step-by-step guide that her mother can use to drive her from the library to your home.
- Which group can create the most concise list of steps needed to multiply two numbers?

Middle and High School Students
- The science lab just received new digital scales that people do not know how to operate. Your team is to create a step-by-step guide that explains how to use the scales.
- You are going to be given an "unknown" chemical to identify. List the steps you will follow to reach a solution.

Compose a Description

Elementary Students
- The zoo is creating a new exhibit for its reptiles and would like to add student descriptions for each animal. Use your observation notes to write a one-paragraph description of your assigned reptile. Make sure to use the thesaurus to include a variety of descriptive words.
- Think about yesterday's history lesson and write a one-page description of a typical day for a Native American boy living in New Mexico.

Middle and High School Students
- Imagine that you are a tornado. Write a description of your life from beginning to end.
- Describe the components of an expertly written persuasive letter.

Generate Examples and Nonexamples

Elementary Students
- Create a table using a word processing program that provides an example and nonexample for basic shapes. For example: A cookie is an example of a circle, but a sheet of paper is not an example of a circle because it is a rectangle.
- Create a plant classification table that has digital pictures and descriptions of local plants and downloaded photographs and descriptions of plants that could not be grown locally.

Middle and High School Students
- Use a table created using a word processing program to demonstrate examples and nonexamples of democratic governments.
- Create a document that displays examples of art created in the same year and describe how they are or are not typical pieces from that time period.

Generate Compare and Contrast Charts

Elementary Students
- Use tables created using a word processing program and clip art to show how animal cells and plant cells are similar and how they are different.
- Spanish is the primary language spoken in Spain and Mexico; demonstrate in a chart that there are other similarities and differences between the two countries.

Middle and High School Students
- If you had to choose the East or West Coast of the United States as your future home, which would you choose and why? Write a three-page response that includes a chart demonstrating the comparisons.
- Shakespeare and Hemingway are well-known authors. Are there any key traits that are similar between the two? What are their greatest differences?

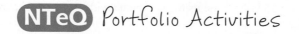 **NTeQ** Portfolio Activities

Please complete the following activities as part of the word processing section of your NTeQ Portfolio.

Reflections

The Getting Started portion of this chapter posed three Reflecting on What I Know questions that teachers might commonly ask. In this portion of your journal, reflection activities have been added to help you reflect on each question. Please use information from this chapter to answer the questions.

1 **Doesn't word processing make the writing process too easy?**

Reflection Activity: Review the chapter and create a position paper that lists the benefits of having students use word processing software for writing projects as opposed to writing papers with pen and paper.

2 **How can word processing be used to engage students in higher-level thinking?**

Reflection Activity: List several examples of student activities that have students use word processing for higher-level learning.

3 **In what ways are the individual needs of students met when their work is completed with a word processor?**

Reflection Activity: Teachers often have classes of students with a wide range of abilities and needs. List ways that student use of word processing increases opportunities for equity in learning.

Lesson Ideas

Create a list of ten word processing activities that would be meaningful for your students to create. You can use the Lesson Bytes (pp. 197–199) or your curriculum standards to help you generate ideas. Expand five of those word processing ideas by creating brief outlines, column and row titles when using a table, or a brief description of the final products.

Lesson Plan

The next step is to create a lesson plan that has students use word processing as a tool to enhance learning. The easiest way to do this is to select a favorite topic that is appropriate for integrating word processing and then complete an NTeQ lesson plan template. While you are developing the lesson plan or afterward, create sample word processing documents that are the same as those your students will create. By making the sample(s), you will be able to catch any areas of difficulty and make corrections. The sample product also can be shown to your students to give them an idea of what is expected.

 **NTeQ** Lesson Plan

Lesson Title: **Remembering the Civil Rights Movement**

Subject Area: **Social Studies**

Grade Level: **6 to 8**

Learning Objective

The students will list and describe key events of the Civil Rights Movement.

Computer Functions

Word processing will be used to list and describe the key events of the Civil Rights Movement.

Specify Problem

In honor of Martin Luther King Jr. Day, our class has been asked to create memorial booklets for the library. Each booklet is to focus on three key events in the Civil Rights Movement. What three events of the Civil Rights Movement will your group choose as a focus for your booklet and why were they chosen?

Research and Analysis

Word processing will be used to edit and revise the information to be included in the final booklets.

Results Presentation

The final product will be the memorial booklets, which will be created with a word processing program and include graphics.

Planning Computer Activities

Divide students into teams of three and have them follow the guidelines listed in the sections that follow.

Before Computer Use

- Present the problem to students and, as a whole group, complete the first two sections of a KWL (what you Know, what you Want to learn, what you Learned) chart that lists what the students know about the problem and what they want to learn.
- Divide students into teams of three and have them complete the remainder of the NTeQ problem-solving process (Chapter 4), which is embedded in the following activities.
- Create a draft plan of action that includes the following:
  - where to obtain the best resources
  - how to choose three key events
  - how to format the booklets
- Create a list of search terms for the Internet and CD-ROM encyclopedia.
- Generate a list of questions for an email interview.
- Collect resources from library and classroom.
- Review collected resources containing information about the Civil Rights Movement.
- Select three key events for the booklet.
- Take notes on items that may be included in the content.
- Create a draft copy of the outline to be written on the computer.
- As a team, write the first draft on paper. Then engage in "read and discuss" sessions with each printout to revise and edit the content.

- Determine which graphics would best support the content and identify search terms for finding the images.

During Computer Use

- Enter the draft plan of action.
- Conduct Internet and CD-ROM encyclopedia searches.
- Use email to correspond with either a civil rights expert or participant.
- Enter outline of the booklet content.
- Enter and revise the content drafts.
- Create final copy that contains the graphics.
- Print final copy on a color printer.

After Computer Use

Answer the following Think Sheet questions:

1. What was the most startling fact or idea you learned? Why was this surprising?
2. How does the Civil Rights Movement affect what is happening today?
3. What still needs to be done?

The teacher facilitates a summary and review session with the whole class by discussing the Think Sheet responses. During the discussion, clarify any misconceptions that arise and reemphasize the key learning objectives and why it is important for the students to have an understanding of the Civil Rights Movement.

Supporting Activities

- Play "Can You Guess?" Create a set of note cards that list the name of a Civil Rights Movement event or person on one side and descriptive details on the other side. Selected students randomly draw a card. Other students try to identify the person or event by asking questions that can only be answered with a yes or no reply. The student who correctly guesses the answer draws the next card.
- View videotapes of events related to the Civil Rights Movement.

Assessment

Create a rubric with items similar to the following for assessing the memorial booklets:

- The three events selected by the students represent key occurrences.
- Each event is presented with clarity.
- Appropriate graphics are included.
- The booklet is formatted in an appealing manner.
- The work is free of errors.

Spreadsheets

Getting Started

Much of the early success of both mainframe and personal computers is attributed to the ability of these machines to manipulate numbers quickly. The first personal computers such as the Apple II and the IBM PC allowed people to change numbers quickly and easily on a spreadsheet to portray a variety of scenarios. Thus, it became easier to determine the effects of giving everyone in a company a 3 percent raise or having the company absorb a 5 percent increase in medical insurance cost. As we have gained experience with productivity suites like Microsoft Office and AppleWorks, educators have recognized that spreadsheets are powerful instructional tools with applications beyond the business environment. Spreadsheets can be used to solve time and distance problems or predict the weather based on wind data. In this chapter, we will explore the basic functions of spreadsheets and how and when students can enhance learning by using them to manipulate and analyze data.

Reflecting on What I Know

1 Can you identify two types of data your students could collect as part of a lesson?

2 How could your students manipulate the data to discover relationships or trends?

3 Can you identify three graphs or charts your students could make that would help them develop a better understanding of the content?

4 Is it possible to create an interactive simulation or model with a spreadsheet?

Classroom SNAPSHOT

Susie teaches sixth-grade science in a school near Lake Superior and is struggling with the unit on friction. Although her students understand the basic concept, they are not able to apply the concept or principles to a real-world application. Last year, Susie obtained a 12-foot water test tank with a pump causing the water to flow so that students can test various boat designs. She also purchased a ramp that was used for model car races at a garage sale. Students placed various types of flooring at the bottom of the ramp, ranging from vinyl flooring to low- to high-nap carpeting, and measured how far the cars would travel. The students' excitement about friction increased as they tested their cars and boats, but their scores on the statewide achievement testing in scientific reasoning did not increase.

This year, Susie's classroom received 15 laptop computers that caused her to rethink how she was teaching the unit on friction. Susie began by showing the students a series of pictures and videotapes of cars on a highway, race track, beach, gravel road, snow, and rain-soaked highway and even in a highway median. She asked the class about riding their bicycles and skateboards in each of these conditions and the benefits or hazards. Having piqued the students' interests, Susie began to ask why some surfaces are better than others.

The discussion evolved into the design of an experiment. Groups of students would select a vehicle and collect data for three trials as they measured distance on several pieces of flooring placed at the bottom of the ramp. Each group would then calculate the mean for each piece of flooring and graph the results. Then Susie suggested that they run additional tests outside using a concrete walkway, blacktop, grass, and packed dirt. First, she had the students examine the characteristics of each surface. Second, she had them predict how far the vehicles would travel based on their existing data. Third, the students collected their data and graphed their results. Fourth, they interpreted their data and explained how friction affected the results. Fifth, they generated several ideas and scenarios on how they could use friction to control the speed of cars around their school to make it safer.

Susie is still waiting for the results of the state achievement test, but her own observations suggested the students were improving their scientific reasoning skills throughout the year.

Examining Spreadsheets

For those of us who use computers primarily for word processing or creating drawings, the spreadsheet may seem foreign. Spreadsheets are very powerful tools, and an examination of all the features is beyond the scope of this book. However, we will examine the basic features so that you can explore and begin to use the functions of a spreadsheet. Let's begin by examining the basic components (see Figure 8.1).

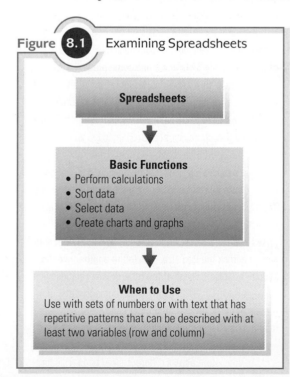

Figure 8.1   Examining Spreadsheets

Spreadsheets

Basic Functions
- Perform calculations
- Sort data
- Select data
- Create charts and graphs

When to Use
Use with sets of numbers or with text that has repetitive patterns that can be described with at least two variables (row and column)

Basic Functions

If you have used a spreadsheet, then you might think of it as a tool for entering and manipulating numerical data. Spreadsheets, however, are very versatile tools. Besides entering simple numbers into a spreadsheet, we can also enter numbers in various formats, including currency ($1.50), date (March 1, 08 or 3/1/08), time (2:30 P.M. or 14:30), percentages (26%), fractions (4/5), and scientific notation (3.14E+00), to name a few of the more common types. However, we are not limited to numbers but can also enter text (maple, hardwood, deciduous). A spreadsheet, though, is more than a series of columns and rows for manipulating numbers. At the heart of every database is a table, and if we examine this table we will find that it is actually a spreadsheet! Thus, we can use a spreadsheet to manipulate numbers, but we can also use it for some database functions that allow us to select, filter, and sort data. For example, the phone book on your cell phone is a database. Each entry is a record. Within each record, you might have a field for cell phone number, another for email address, and another for the home address. Each row of a spreadsheet is a record and the cells in a column comprise the fields of the database.

The Teacher's Diary

The spreadsheet was the one application that I did not use in the early years of my computer experience. I associated the spreadsheet with numbers, and math was not one of my favorite subjects in school. Not until I had to develop a lesson plan that incorporated a spreadsheet did I discover that the spreadsheet could be a useful tool. I learned that it could be used for creating simulations, analyzing data, and exploring number concepts and mathematical relationships.

Deciding that I would give the spreadsheet a try, I adapted the AIMS M&Ms lesson to include the use of a spreadsheet. The students sorted and counted M&Ms by color. Instead of the students entering this data on a mimeographed sheet as we had done in the past, they entered it into a spreadsheet. I was able to teach them how to enter the data and how to calculate the total number of M&Ms in a bag by entering a simple addition formula. They even created a bar graph from this data. They loved this lesson because it was totally hands-on!

This experience gave me the confidence that I needed. I extended this lesson the next day by having the students analyze the percentage of each color in a bag. My students did not have the math skills to determine percentage, but this lack of skill did not stop us. I entered a formula in their spreadsheets that would determine the percentage of each color for them. The students made another bar graph showing the results for each color of M&Ms in their snack-size bags. They could visually analyze this numerical data. The students wondered if the percentages of each color would be similar in other sizes of packages of M&Ms and made some predictions.

I was able to extend this lesson again. I purchased various sizes of bags of M&Ms. The students sorted and counted the M&Ms by color. The students entered this data in another spreadsheet and repeated the process that was followed with the snack-size bags. I entered this new data into a master spreadsheet that included the percentages of color for each size of bag and created a bar graph. The students were easily able to analyze the percentages of each color in different-sized packages. They were surprised to discover the percentages of color were not consistent across the bag size. This led to another question. Would this also be true of the other M&M candies such as peanut M&Ms? This led to more spreadsheets, more graphs, more analyzing, and more candy. But they were learning and using those higher-order thinking skills!

They discovered that the percentages of colors were still not consistent across different-sized bags. This finding led to the next question. Was this result due to something in the M&M manufacturing process? We discussed what might cause this to happen. I got on the Internet and found the website for M&Ms. The students were able to take a virtual tour of the factory to see how these candies were made. We discussed what we saw and whether there was anything in the process that could explain why the percentages of colors were not consistent. With a little bit of questioning, they soon discovered that the bags were filled according to weight, not percentage of each color, and that the M&M colors are already mixed in huge containers before they are poured into the bags.

You can probably guess what the next question was. Would this also be true of other candies such as Skittles? We did not pursue this one in class, but we did come back to it later when we did a group science fair project. What started out as an hour lesson turned into a week's lesson! They entered data into a spreadsheet. They performed calculations. They created and interpreted graphs. They solved a problem. They learned a lot!

Fran Clark
Third-Grade Teacher

Performing Calculations.   The most common function of a spreadsheet is to perform calculations. You can either enter a calculation or you can use one of the built-in formulas to manipulate your numbers. For simple calculations you can add (+), subtract (−), multiply (*), and divide (/) numbers by entering a calculation in a cell.

You can also create a calculation that uses numbers entered into each cell. Thus, rather than dividing $3.99 by 24 ounces to determine the price per ounce for the loaf of bread, we can divide the cells by entering the formula "=C2/B2" in cell D2 (see Figure 8.2). If we need to calculate the price per loaf for several loaves

Figure 8.2   Entering a Formula into a Cell

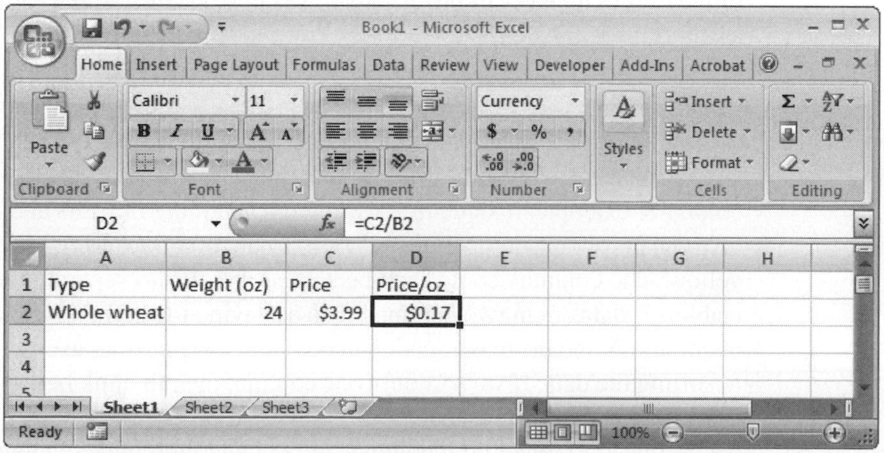

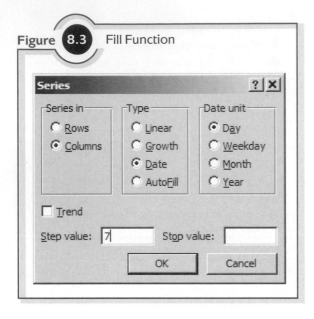

Figure 8.3   Fill Function

of bread, we use the fill function to copy the formula into several cells. The spreadsheet will automatically adjust the cell references (e.g., C3/B3) to make the correct calculation.

Spreadsheets can do a number of calculations including dates. For example, you might want to create a list of hall monitors for a week, month, grading period, or the semester. You know the week or day each student will start, but having to enter the dates for each additional student is time consuming. Fortunately, a spreadsheet can calculate dates. In Figure 8.3, we want Jill to serve as hall monitor for the week of January 12th. Rather than entering the date of the next assignment, we can use the fill function. By selecting Date as the type and entering 7 as the Step Value, we can fill a column with the dates of Mondays. The fill function offers several methods for manipulating numbers.

The last option for manipulating numbers is to use a predefined formula. We could easily enter a formula for calculating the average of a column of numbers, but it is more efficient to use an existing formula or function. Of course, there might be times in a mathematics class when you want the students to enter their own formula. In Figure 8.4, we have inserted a formula to calculate the average price per ounce of the different loaves of bread. When we click on cell D7, the formula is displayed in the Data Entry area.

Sorting Data.   You can sort data in a spreadsheet column several ways. The most common approach is to highlight the cells and sort the data alphabetically or numerically from high to low or low to high. We can also sort the cells based on font or cell color. For example, if students have entered a number of fruits and vegetables into a column, they could color code the cells so that vegetables were green and fruits were yellow. The columns could then be sorted by color to separate the fruits and vegetables. If data are in two columns such as having the name of the vegetable or fruit in column A and the classification in column B, we need to use a different approach to sorting the data. If we sort only one column, then the link between column A and B will be lost and apples could be reclassified as vegetables. To sort two columns, we will need to select both columns of data and then indicate how we want to sort

Figure **8.4**   Insert a Function

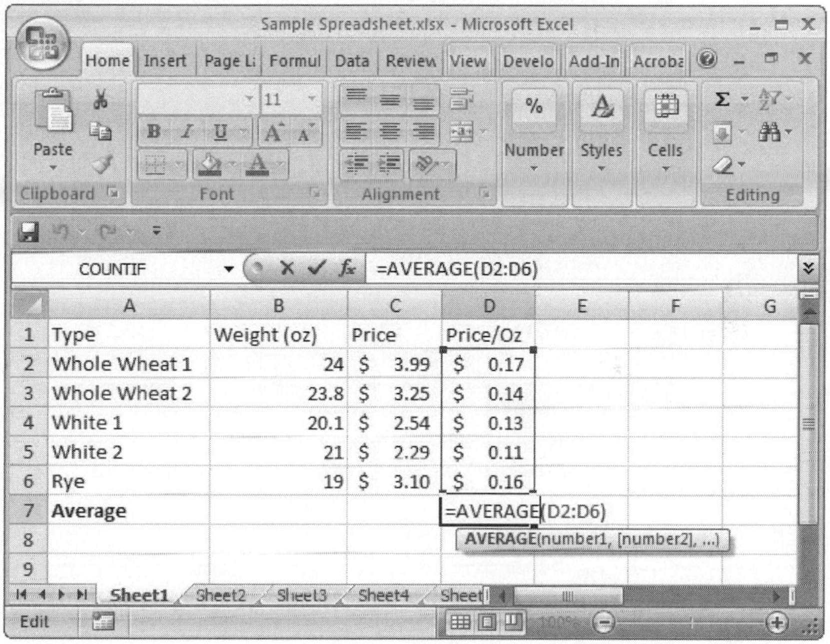

the data (see Figure 8.5). Sorting data can help the student find specific information and identify groups of common items.

Selecting Data.   While you can sort a column of data to group similar items, there may be times when you want to select rows with specific information. Specific information is selected by using a filter. Filters determine the values of items in a column and then let you select one or more to display. Values that are not selected are hidden from view (see Figure 8.6). Using the filter function, you can use the spreadsheet in place of a database to select specific information. You can then perform additional manipulations of this information.

Creating Graphs and Charts.   The last function of a spreadsheet is to create charts and graphs. Spreadsheets provide a wide variety of ways to display your data ranging from traditional bar, line, and pie graphs to several other variations. Creating a graph is simply a process of selecting the data, selecting a graph type, and then entering the titles (see Figure 8.7, p. 211). You can change the color scheme of a chart

Figure 8.5 Sorting Multiple Columns of Data

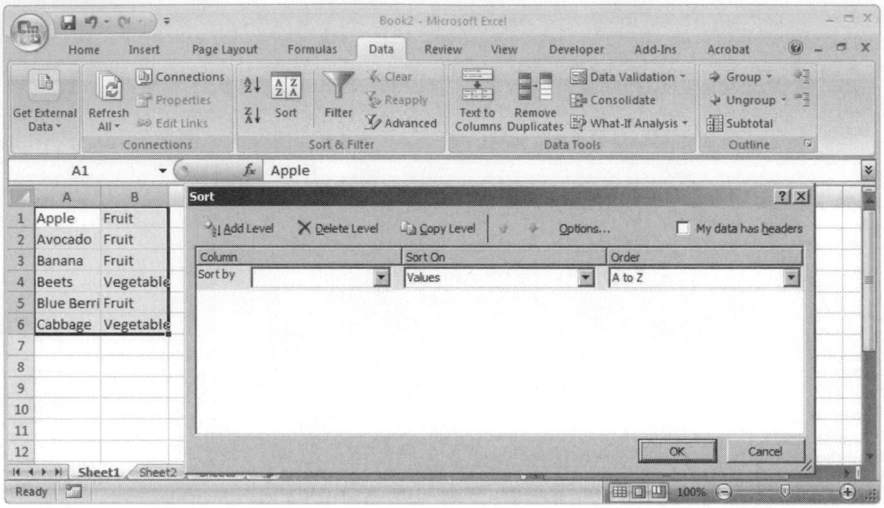

Figure 8.6 Filtering Data

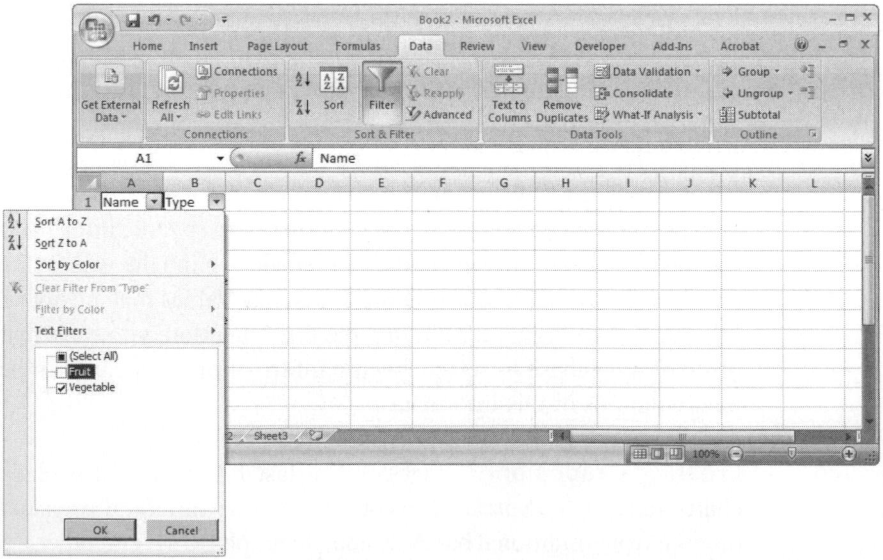

and even change the chart type after selecting your data. Charts are also interactive in that they are updated when you make changes to the data.

You can also use spreadsheets to create interactive graphs. For example, an algebra class studying the slope of a line can vary the values in the equation $f(x) = 3x - 6$ by substituting both whole numbers and fractions for the values of 3 and 6. A plot of the points illustrates how the line changes as the numbers are changed (see Figure 8.8).

Summary of Spreadsheet Functions

As seen, spreadsheet software goes beyond traditional "number-crunching," providing a variety of additional functions. Table 8.1 gives a summary with brief examples of the four basic spreadsheet functions: perform calculations, sort data, select data, and create charts and graphs.

Figure 8.7   Creating a Chart from Data

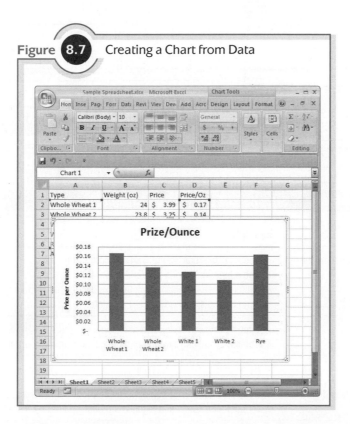

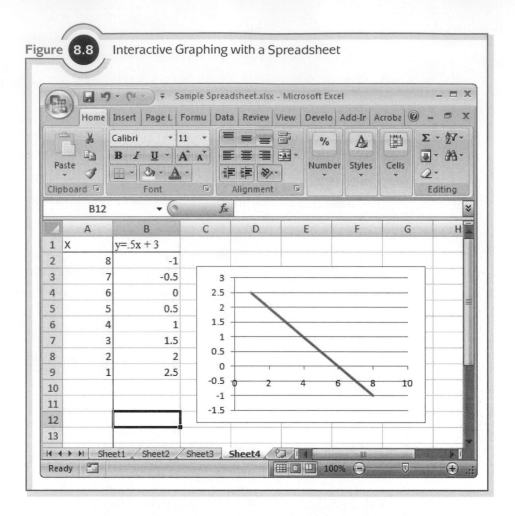

Figure 8.8 Interactive Graphing with a Spreadsheet

| Table 8.1 | Summary of Basic Spreadsheet Functions |

Function	Example
Perform calculations	• Enter calculations (=8+16, =C4+D4) into a cell • Use a built-in function [=AVERAGE(D2:D6)] • Fill function can perform simple tasks as well as create a series using various step sizes for numbers and dates
Sort data	• Simple sorts can be applied to a single column • Complex sorts can sort one or more columns in different orders
Select data	• Filtering is used to select one or more values from a column to display
Create charts and graphs	• Columns and rows of numbers can be plotted on different chart and graph formats, and labels and legends are easily edited

Spreadsheets in the Classroom

How many teachers have used one of the green-ruled worksheets we associate with accountants? Many teachers avoid spreadsheet applications on the premise that they have no need to work accounting problems. They have not yet learned how teachers, professors, and information specialists use spreadsheets for a variety of tasks besides tracking finances. Spreadsheets have been identified as the *most* important tool for students to master prior to seeking a job (Galbraith & Haines, 2001). Spreadsheets can also enhance the students' conceptual development in mathematics (Drier, 2001). Similarly, a teacher can use spreadsheets to create scaffolding needed to understand mathematical concepts (Neiss, 2005). In the following section we will describe examples of how students can use spreadsheets as an instructional tool.

PEARSON
myeducationlab
The Power of Classroom Practice

Go to MyEducationLab, select the topic "Math Integration," and go to the Activities and Applications section. Access the video "Technology in Classrooms" and consider how one teacher encourages higher-order thinking with her second-graders. Complete the activity that follows.

Using Spreadsheets to Achieve ISTE NETS for Students

NETS

When spreadsheets are used a tool in the classroom, four of the six NETS for Students are directly addressed: (1) Creativity and Innovation; (3) Research and

Student pairs can help each other enter data into a spreadsheet.

Information Fluency; (4) Critical Thinking, Problem Solving, and Decision Making; and (6) Technology Operations and Concepts (ISTE, 2007). The following paragraphs describe the details.

1. Creativity and Innovation: Students demonstrate creative thinking, construct knowledge, and develop innovative products and processes using technology. Spreadsheets provide a means for students to apply their existing knowledge to test ideas. For example, Figure 8.8 illustrates how students can apply their existing knowledge of algebraic equations to generate new ideas about the behavior of the slope of a line. Similarly, students can use spreadsheets to test or create models and simulations of the real world. Creative layout of data as well as the use of graphs and charts generated in a spreadsheet allow for individual and group expression of ideas.

3. Research and Information Fluency: Students apply digital tools to gather, evaluate, and use information. Spreadsheets are an excellent tool for processing data and then generating charts and graphs to report results. Students can enter their own data from an experiment or survey and then analyze it in different ways. This analysis and interpretation helps them synthesize the information so that they can present the results to others.

4. Critical Thinking, Problem Solving, and Decision Making: Students use critical-thinking skills to plan and conduct research, manage projects, solve problems, and make informed decisions using appropriate digital tools and resources. An NTeQ lesson places the student in the role of researcher in solving problems and making decisions based on the data collected. Spreadsheets provide students with a tool for analyzing their data, which is then used to make appropriate conclusions and informed decisions. Tables as well as charts and graphs created with a spreadsheet can be copied and pasted into a word processing, publishing, or web page document to create a report.

6. Technology Operations and Concepts: Students demonstrate a sound understanding of technology concepts, systems, and operations. Spreadsheets are considered the essential tool for a work environment (Galbraith & Haines, 2001). As students use spreadsheets, they develop an understanding of technology concepts as well as mathematics and other disciplines. By manipulating their data, students can develop a deeper conceptual understanding of math operations as well as the functioning of various social, political, biological, and other types of systems.

Using Spreadsheets for Learning

As demonstrated, spreadsheets are useful for more than accounting. They are a useful tool for creating simulations, analyzing data, and exploring number concepts

PEARSON
myeducationlab

The Power of Classroom Practice

Go to MyEducationLab, select the topic "Software," and access the practical tutorials for "Excel for PC, Basics," "Incorporating Excel into a Lesson: Elementary," and "Incorporating Excel into a Lesson: Middle/Secondary." Use the tutorials to learn the basic skills of using and creating lessons with Excel.

and mathematical relationships as well as understanding principles in other disciplines, such as friction and migration patterns. Spreadsheets are well suited for addressing standards and benchmarks on collecting and analyzing data, identifying relationships, and using mathematics in inquiry. The following paragraphs explain some of these applications of spreadsheets in the classroom.

Creating Simulations. Simulation software often conjures up images of expensive, complex software that is beyond the budgets of many public schools. Teachers and students can create a simulation that demonstrates manipulation of one or more variables using a spreadsheet. These simulations are much simpler than a typical microworld, simulation, or model that would include animation. However, they do allow the student to manipulate a variable and see the resulting numerical change or change in a graph.

Did you study the solar system and gravity in one of your science classes? A common illustration depicts a man on Earth weighing 160 pounds and the same man on our Earth's moon and other planets with the different weights. To a student who weighs only 60 pounds, the thought of weighing more than twice as much might be difficult to imagine. So the instructional task simply involved memorizing on which planet a person weighed the most and on which the least, without developing an understanding of the effects of gravity. Using a spreadsheet, however, a teacher can create realistic examples using students' weights or weights of common objects with problems to help students understand and apply the concept of gravity.

For example, when students enter the classroom, they can weigh themselves and then enter their weights in a spreadsheet. Formulas in the spreadsheet then calculate the weights on the moon and other planets. Similarly, they can enter the weight of other objects such as a bag of sugar, a pair of boots, or a bicycle. Students can then use the graph function to determine where they or an object would weigh the most and the least in the solar system. In a math class, students could calculate how much a bag of sugar would cost on each planet based on a price per pound. Advanced students could use these weights to determine how much force a space shuttle would need to leave a planet's gravitational field. Using a spreadsheet, they can make adjustments in their supplies and personnel to achieve the desired load. Another use of spreadsheets is having students observe change over a period of time by graphing the results of mathematical models they have constructed of a real-world problem (Walsh, 1996). Students can change different variables in the model to observe the effect on change. Similarly, students can use spreadsheets to model events such as population growth (Carter, 1999).

Creating Discovery Spreadsheets. You can also create a spreadsheet simulation that allows students to manipulate variables and discover rules and laws. A chemistry teacher could design a spreadsheet to simulate the results of an experiment. For example, students could recreate the discovery of Charles' Law—a fixed quantity of gas at a constant pressure will increase linearly with temperature. Students enter various temperatures and the spreadsheet calculates the corresponding volume. After entering the data, the student can create a graph and then determine the relationship between temperature and volume (see Figure 8.9). This type of spreadsheet also can be used to teach students how to make predictions based on the rules or laws they have discovered. For example, they can predict the results of an election based on demographic and historical voting data or use data from an NOAA website (www.ncdc.noaa.gov/oa/ncdc.html) to predict the weather. Students can collect data on seismic activity from various sites on the Internet and make predictions concerning possible earthquakes. The students can then monitor the activity over several weeks to determine the accuracy of their predictions. These examples can be extended to the foreign language classroom by having the students enter the labels in the foreign language.

Figure 8.9 Using a Spreadsheet for Charles' Law Simulations

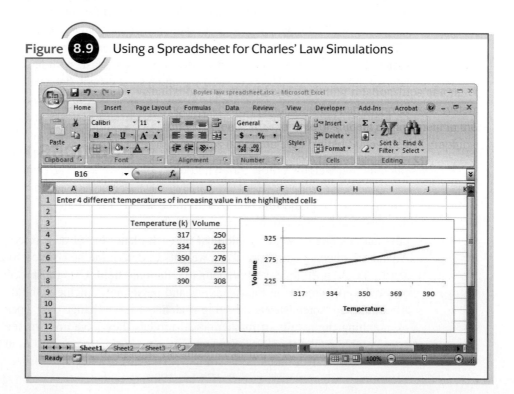

Exploring Math Concepts and Rules.   Another example of spreadsheet use is to let students explore mathematical relationships. Either the student or teacher can create a spreadsheet to both calculate and plot the relationship between an unknown (x) and its coefficient and constants. As students change the values, the equation is solved for x, and the relationships among the coefficient, constants, and x are displayed in a graph that is automatically updated with each change. Spreadsheets are useful for teaching math concepts such as surface area and volume. Teachers can use spreadsheets to teach math concepts in classes such as economics and personal finance. Spreadsheets also can be used to illustrate graphically the solving of simple and complex equations. Another example is using a spreadsheet to explore probability problems such as the probability of two people in the room having the same birthday or to collect and analyze data on penny tossing. We can use spreadsheets to track nutritional information, voting trends, population trends, and word or phrase usage. The use of spreadsheets is not limited to mathematics classes; they can be used in many disciplines in which students analyze data to identify trends and solve problems.

Solving Problems.   Our last example requires students to use a spreadsheet to solve a specific problem. For example, the class has collected $47.83 for a party. They have decided that they want to serve candy at the party. The problem, then, is what type of candy they can purchase so that they get the most for their money. The class can list all the various types of candy they might purchase and enter these items in a spreadsheet. After completing their list, individuals check the weights and prices of the various items. The price and weight of each are then entered into the spreadsheet, and the price per ounce is calculated. Students can create a chart from the data to identify the most expensive and least expensive candies. For advanced students, you might ask them to determine a mix of "good" and "average" tasting candy based on the price per ounce. A more complex problem is one of planning a pizza party that requires the students to calculate the area of various cheese pizzas and then determine the price per square inch.

Spreadsheets can play an important role in solving real-world problems such as studying the quality of river or lake water or redistricting a school district. Students in a language arts class can track types of novels they have read and produce graphs to help them determine which genre they prefer. Students in a communications or social studies class can compare the column inches in newspapers or the minutes a television or radio station devotes to a story to study patterns of news coverage. Students can conduct a contextual analysis of essays, political speeches, short stories, or

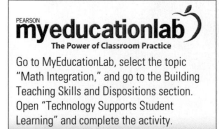

Go to MyEducationLab, select the topic "Math Integration," and go to the Building Teaching Skills and Dispositions section. Open "Technology Supports Student Learning" and complete the activity.

books by analyzing the use of imagery, appeal to ethos, appeal to logos, appeal to pathos, or verb tense and other grammatical structures. Once the data are collected, they are entered into a spreadsheet and analyzed to identify differences and trends.

Spreadsheets are excellent tools for students to use for problem solving, inquiry, and discovery learning. In each of the previous examples, students manipulated data to find an answer. They manipulated the data and constructed new charts and graphs or sorted the data to identify patterns. These opportunities to explore numerical relationships provide a laboratory for problem solving and inquiry. Students make discoveries through active learning as opposed to passively reading a text or listening to a lecture. For example, rather than reading that they will weigh less on the moon and Mars and more on Jupiter, students can enter their weight and graph it. Then they can calculate the weights of common objects such as a bag of sugar or a bottle of cola. Students can try various options and obtain an answer as quickly as they can press the Return key. This immediacy of response provides more motivation to explore different possibilities. Spreadsheets can remove the burden of completing tedious calculations by hand or calculator and allow the learner to focus on analyzing the patterns and results. This use of the spreadsheet as a tool not only enhances learning but also improves the likelihood of the learner transferring the use of the tool to other situations (Salomon, 1993).

Spreadsheets are excellent tools for students to use for problem solving, inquiry, and discovery learning.

Planning an NTeQ Lesson for Spreadsheets

Spreadsheets are an excellent tool teachers can use to integrate computer technology into the classroom. The NTeQ model provides a process for developing an integrated lesson plan or to develop inquiry units that encourage the development of higher-level thinking skills. Spreadsheets are used to enter, arrange, sort, select, and perform calculations on data. You can use spreadsheets at all levels pre-K through high school as well as all disciplines because spreadsheets can handle both numerical and text entries (see Table 8.2 on pp. 220–221). In the next section, we will describe how to use the NTeQ model to develop an integrated lesson plan using a spreadsheet.

The NTeQ Lesson

This section describes the key components of the NTeQ model, shaded in Figure 8.10 (p. 222), that a teacher specifically needs to address when creating lesson plans with spreadsheets as a learning tool. The remaining NTeQ components, already discussed in Chapter 2, remain consistent across all lessons.

Matching the Objective to Computer Functions

If there is a match between the objective(s) and the functions of a spreadsheet, you can plan to integrate the spreadsheet activity into the lesson. If there is not a match between the objective(s) and the spreadsheet's functions, you should consider another strategy rather than the spreadsheet. Let's examine the relationship between the functions of a spreadsheet and instructional objectives.

We can categorize the functions of a spreadsheet into four broad categories: manipulation of numbers or data, creation of charts and graphs, sorting and filtering, and discrimination and interpretation. The first, manipulation of numbers, includes the capabilities to add, subtract, multiply, divide, sum, sort, convert, find the highest and lowest numbers, and calculate the average, to name a few. Spreadsheets can do a number of mathematical calculations ranging from simple addition to geometric calculations to financial calculations. The second grouping of functions is the creation of charts and graphs. Once students have entered their data, they can create a variety of charts and graphs to display the data visually. The third category is sorting and filtering information, which can be used with both numerical and text data. Students can use these functions to organize and analyze data. The fourth category is discrimination and interpretation, which includes inferring, discriminating, interpreting, and generalizing. Students can analyze the results of a sort, selection, calculation, or chart to make inferences, predictions, generalizations, or interpretations of data to make decisions.

Table 8.2	Using Spreadsheets to Meet Curriculum and Technology Standards	
Standards	**Example Problem**	**Example Student Product**
Elementary		
Language Arts/English		
NCTE Curriculum Standard 9: Students develop an understanding of and respect for diversity in language use, patterns, and dialects across cultures, ethnic groups, geographic regions, and social roles. *NETS-S: 3.b. Research and Information Fluency:* locate, organize, analyze, evaluate, synthesize, and ethically use information from a variety of sources and media.	With the increased use of text messaging, students are using a greater number of abbreviations. How do these shortened forms of communication differ across geographic regions?	Students gather examples of abbreviations and sayings that they share with a class in Ireland and New Zealand. A database is created with the phrases from each geographic location and the translation. Students identify examples where "translations" differ.
Mathematics		
NCTM Data Analysis: Formulate questions that can be addressed with data and collect, organize, and display relevant data to answer them. *NETS-S: 4.c. Critical Thinking:* collect and analyze data to identify solutions and/or make informed decisions.	Determine the most common type of tree in the area surrounding the school.	Students create a spreadsheet with the different types of trees and their frequencies. A bar chart is created.
Science		
NSES Physical Science Standards (K–4): Light, heat, electricity, and magnetism. *NETS-S: 4.c. Critical Thinking:* collect and analyze data to identify solutions and/or make informed decisions.	What materials reflect the most light?	Students measure light reflected from different types of material and record the results in a spreadsheet.
Social Studies/History		
NCHS Curriculum Standard Theme III: Social studies programs should include experiences that provide for the study of the ways human beings view themselves in and over time. *NETS-S: 4.c. Critical Thinking:* collect and analyze data to identify solutions and/or make informed decisions.	How has our community changed in the last 50 years?	Students enter data in a spreadsheet for square miles of the city and population for each ten-year period. A line graph is created to illustrate population change.
Middle/High School		
Language Arts/English		
NCTE Curriculum Standard 6: Students apply knowledge of language structure, language conventions (e.g., spelling and punctuation), media techniques, figurative language, and genre to create, critique, and discuss print and nonprint texts.	How do advertisers use different conventions to persuade buyers?	Students create a spreadsheet listing different words advertisers use. They do an analysis of the frequency of keywords.

Table 8.2	*Continued*

Standards	Example Problem	Example Student Product
Middle/High School *(continued)*		
Language Arts/English *(continued)*		
NETS-S: 3.b. Research and Information Fluency: locate, organize, analyze, evaluate, synthesize, and ethically use information from a variety of sources and media.		
Mathematics		
NCTM Measurement Standard I: Apply appropriate techniques, tools, and formulas to determine measurements. *NETS-S: 4.c. Critical Thinking:* collect and analyze data to identify solutions and/or make informed decisions.	How accurate are our measurements?	Students measure and weigh solids and liquids and enter information into a spreadsheet. Data are analyzed for accuracy of measurements between individuals and groups.
Science		
NSES Motions and Forces (9–12): Gravitation is a universal force that each mass exerts on any other mass. *NETS-S: 4.c. Critical Thinking:* collect and analyze data to identify solutions and/or make informed decisions.	How does gravity affect the speed of a vehicle?	Students measure the time it takes different weighted models to race down a ramp. Data are analyzed in a spreadsheet.
Social Studies/History		
NCHS Curriculum Standard People, Places and Environment: The study of people, places, and human–environment interactions assists learners as they develop their spatial views and perspectives of the world. *NETS-S: 4.c. Critical Thinking:* collect and analyze data to identify solutions and/or make informed decisions.	How do changes in the meaning, use, and distribution of resources in this nation and others affect people's lives?	Students collect data on the types of products shipped by railroads and where they are shipped. The data are entered into a spreadsheet and then a graph created to show relationships.

Source: National Council of Teachers of English (NCTE). *Standards for the English Language Arts,* by the International Reading Association and the National Council of Teachers of English. Copyright 1996 by the International Reading Association and the National Council of Teachers of English. Reprinted with permission. Complete set of standards can be found at www.ncte.org/standards; National Council of Teachers of Mathematics (NCTM). *Principles and Standards for School Mathematics,* by National Council of Teachers of Mathematics Staff. Copyright 2000 by National Council of Teachers of Mathematics. Reproduced with permission of National Council of Teachers of Mathematics via Copyright Clearance Center. http://standards.nctm.org/document/appendix/numb .htm; National Science Education Standards (NSES). Reprinted with permission from *National Science Education Standards: Observe, Interact, Change, Learn,* by the National Academy of Sciences. Courtesy of the National Academies Press, Washington, DC. www.nsta.org/publications/nses.aspx; National Center for History in Schools (NCHS). Courtesy of http://nchs.ucla.edu; *National Education Technology Standards for Students,* Second Edition, © 2007, ISTE® International Society for Technology in Education, www.iste.org. All rights reserved.

Figure 8.10 NTeQ Components Unique to Technology Integration Lessons

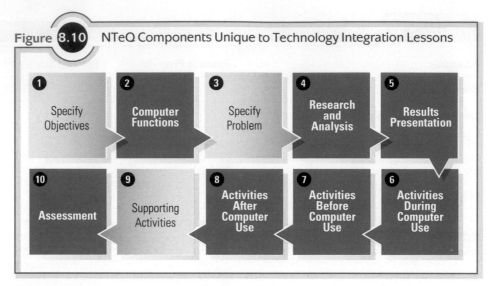

Note: Components relevant to spreadsheets are shaded.

There is a very close relationship between objectives and functions. Both use verbs (e.g., *sort, add*) and both are observable actions. For example, an objective might state that the learner will determine the average number of people in the five largest cities of Ohio. One of the functions of a spreadsheet (actually a built-in function) is the capability of averaging a row or column of numbers. Thus, there is a match between the objective and a spreadsheet function. Similarly, an objective in a nutrition unit might require students to interpret the results of a taste test using a bar chart. Again, there is a match between the objective (*interpret*) and the charting function of a spreadsheet. Some objectives related to spreadsheet functions are listed in Table 8.3. Although this is not a complete list, it provides several examples related to manipulation of numbers (e.g., *alter, convert, combine*), charting and graphing (e.g., *chart, graph*), and discrimination and interpretation of numbers (*assess, discriminate, differentiate, infer*). (See the Appendix for a more complete listing of objectives and tool functions.)

Research and Analysis

The research and analysis component needs to be based on problem statements that focus on issues students feel are relevant and worthy of solving. The problem context should be anchored in a realistic setting that has meaning for the students and motivates them (Bottge, Heinrichs, & Mehta, 2004; Cognition and Technology Group at Vanderbilt, 1990; Gagnon & Bottge, 2006). For example, a math or psychology unit might focus on frequency distributions and measures of central tendency. One approach is to define a problem in the context of a scientist collecting data in a lab. A

Table 8.3	Spreadsheet Functions, Learning Tasks, and Example Student Activities	

Primary Spreadsheet Function(s)	Learning Task	Example
Perform calculations	Add, Divide, Multiply, Subtract, Sum, Average	Enter a formula to calculate the temperature range on the hottest and coldest days of the year.
	Alter, Change, Vary	Determine the effect on profit if the fixed price increases.
	Deduce, Infer, Generalize, Estimate, Predict, Formulate	Calculate how much the force on a billboard will increase if the wind speed goes from 12 mph to 20 mph.
Sort data	Analyze	Determine which city had the greatest rainfall in June.
	Compare, Contrast, Differentiate, Discriminate, Relate, Assess	Compare the voting records of young voters in rural and urban environments.
Chart/graph	Interpret, Interpolate, Extend	Which region of the country has the most rain per year?
	Solve, Determine	Based on the per capita income for the surrounding counties, which would be the best location for a midvalue car dealership?

more realistic setting would cast the student as a researcher hired by a local grocery store to conduct a taste test of five new brands of crackers. Although both contexts allow for developing a data-collection strategy, the grocery store context provides a realistic setting that students could use to collect data in their school.

Once you have identified the problem, you need to identify the data the students will use to solve the problem. Will they collect all or part of the data or use data you provide? If the students are collecting the data, you will need to plan for the collection process. For example, if they are doing an experiment, they will need equipment and materials. If the students are working on designing a new size of can for a soup company, they will need at least one appropriate can to calculate the needed volume, or you will need to provide the volume data. Similarly, if the students are searching for information on a CD or the Internet, you will need to develop guidelines to help their search. If you are providing the data, you will need to organize the data and prepare either handouts or files with data. Giving careful consideration to the data the students will use can help solve problems as the students work on the unit.

After the data and collection methods are identified, you need to plan the specific data manipulation. The alignment of spreadsheet functions with the learning objectives was completed in Step 2. Now you need to describe specifically how the students are to manipulate the data. Do students need to multiply the area of the face by the height, find the best interest rate, or determine the rate of growth? Do students need to see the data displayed to help them understand the calculations? If yes, which charts or graphs are best? It is often helpful to create a sample spreadsheet with data similar to what the students will use to ensure it works and to find shortcuts that may make the task easier.

Results Presentation

After the students have solved the problem, they will need to present their work and solution. Their results can take the form of numerical answers on the spreadsheet or a chart or graph generated by the spreadsheet application. For most reports, the students may want to include parts of either the spreadsheet or graphs in their written report or oral presentation. You will need to determine some basic guidelines and expectations for the report before the students start the lesson. For example, will they make a slide show, a multimedia presentation, a poster presentation, a written report, or some combination of these? Will the students organize all the papers and produce a magazine, book, or newsletter?

Planning Computer Activities

Planning for active use of computers in the classrooms requires careful consideration. While the number of computers per student in a classroom can vary from one computer for six students to one computer per student, proper use of computer technology should be efficient to allow students to focus on tasks related to the objectives. For example, it is easy to enter a term such as "greenhouse gases" into a search engine and generate pages and pages of decreasingly relevant links. A better approach would involve careful planning to ensure that proper search terms are entered to generate fewer irrelevant links. The following three steps will help you plan for efficient use of computer technology in your classroom.

During Computer Use.   What will the students do when they work at the computer? For example, if they are entering information, will they use a template you have created or will they create their own? If they are doing calculations, will they use your formulas or must they create their own? You can create spreadsheet templates that include the formulas and the students need only enter their data. Students also can use a spreadsheet template that already has the data; they just add the formulas and calculations to answer questions and solve problems. Another alternative is to allow the students to create the complete spreadsheet using data they have gathered and then create the necessary calculations. For example, a project of designing a new soup can might have students in a lower grade enter various heights and radii to calculate volumes, whereas a high school class might create the formula for the calculation. Proper planning for the computer activities will help you determine the materials and instructions that you must provide for efficient computer time. After you have identified what the students are going to do with the data, you can design any necessary spreadsheets and lock or protect the cells. If the students are unfamiliar with the computer task, you may need to develop a step-by-step instruction sheet for creating and using a spreadsheet.

Before Computer Use.   As you plan the lesson, consider how you can make each student's time at the computer efficient and effective. For example, if students are searching the Internet for information, they could generate a list of keywords or terms to use *before* they start searching. Similarly, if students are entering data they have collected from observations, experiments, or other research, they can organize the data before they begin entering the data. Thus, if students must enter their own formula for calculating the volume of a can, they should have instructions to determine the formula *before* using the computer. If they must also create the spreadsheet, they can plan for the labels, columns, and rows. Careful planning of these activities will help students adequately proceed even with a limited number of computers to complete their work. When planning these activities, you may need to complete each step of the process yourself to identify what the students must do. Working through these steps can help you identify organizational and planning concerns that are not readily apparent.

After Computer Use.   Once the students have manipulated the data in a spreadsheet, what should they do with the information? As a teacher, you may need to help them interpret the data or charts so that they can solve the problem. Guidance for exploring the spreadsheet data or charts can take different forms. For example, if your chemistry class has entered data from a series of experiments, you might prepare a Think Sheet (Chapter 5) with questions that will focus the students' attention on the salient points. In their quest to find an appropriately sized can, you might have them create models from construction paper and collect data from others as to which can is most appealing. They might also determine which can appears to hold the most and why. A Think Sheet might ask questions such as the following:

- How many of each can design can you place on a grocery shelf that is 24 inches wide by 18 inches deep and 13 inches high?
- Which can is most likely to tip over? Which is least likely to tip over? Why?
- Which can design is most appealing to a buyer and which to a grocer? Why?
- How many different can designs can you find that hold the same amount?
- Does a change in diameter or height have a greater effect on the volume?

As each group works through their analysis and interpretation, you can facilitate their efforts by asking questions and modeling the behaviors you are teaching. Once the students understand the process for analyzing and interpreting the data, they will need less and less direction from you.

Assessment

The assessment for an integrated lesson using a spreadsheet will focus on several objectives. An assessment will include spreadsheet skills such as entering data, producing formulas, and creating graphs. Another aspect of the assessment will probably focus on the results presentation. The results presentation might include assessment of a report but, more importantly, it should also focus on the higher-level thinking skills involved in interpreting and applying the results generated from the analysis of the data. Criteria to include in a rubric might include the following:

- Ability to enter data
- Ability to enter a formula
- Presentation of data
- Selection of appropriate chart
- Explanation of results
- Appropriate conclusions

When students are working in collaborative groups, it is important to explain your expectations for each student. For example, if you are requiring the students to enter or develop a formula for a calculation, must only one person on the team know how to do it? Or must each team member demonstrate how to create a formula?

Summary

Spreadsheets are a versatile application that you can easily adapt as a tool for learning at most grade levels. First, spreadsheets are excellent for demonstrating and testing "what if?" scenarios. You can create a template with formulas and graphs that allow students to simply input data and see the results. After entering several data points, they can analyze the results and begin to discover relationships. The results are displayed immediately as numerical values and changes to a graph or chart. Second, students can create their own spreadsheets to analyze and display results based on their data collection. This approach allows the students to focus not only on the results but also on the mathematical operations needed to solve the problem. Third, spreadsheets can also perform simple database functions. All three approaches address NETS for Students to use technology tools for processing data and reporting results, problem solving, and decision making.

Teacher Technology FAQ

My students are having trouble using a spreadsheet. What can I do?

One approach is to prepare a template complete with instructions. For example, you can include the instructions and spreadsheet in a single document. You can take screenshots, or screen captures, of parts of a spreadsheet and include them in a document along with simple step-by-step instructions. We have found that several short instruction sheets explaining a single task are better than longer sheets that address several different tasks.

My students have a tendency to lose, modify, or erase the formulas that I include. Is there any way to keep them from modifying my spreadsheet?

There are two solutions. First, you can save your spreadsheet as a stationary or template file. When they try to open it, the spreadsheet application will open an exact copy of your original spreadsheet. Second, you can select the cells with your data and formulas and lock or protect them. Students will not be able to change the cell. By protecting selected cells of the spreadsheets, you can keep students from modifying or deleting critical information or formulas. You can thus limit their data input into specific cells and reduce the chances that they will have to start all over with a new copy of the template.

How can I tell if my students are old enough to use a spreadsheet?

We have seen first-graders use spreadsheets to enter data and copy calculations. Younger students often need more hands-on directions, as do other inexperienced learners. A spreadsheet provides a virtual playground for the inquisitive student who is interested in discovering mathematical concepts and relationships. As a teacher, you must keep in mind both the students' developmental readiness and their computer skills.

What can I do if my students do not know the formula for calculating the needed information?

Let's consider two scenarios. First, consider the problem of redesigning a soup can. For younger students, you might create a spreadsheet where they enter the diameter and height of their proposed can. The spreadsheet would then calculate the volume. Second, consider a unit in which students are exploring the relation between the sides of a rectangle and the area. Again, you could create a template where students enter the length of each side and the area is calculated. In both instances, the students can explore the relationship between the numbers by graphing their data. Then, when they understand the relationships, you can introduce the formula and repeat the exercise as they do the complete calculation.

How can I get my students to examine a spreadsheet to discover new information?

Suppose you are teaching the concept of a prime number. You might create a spreadsheet that has the numbers 1 to 15 in the first column. In the next columns you label and display the results of the number divided by 1, 2, 3, and by itself (format so only two decimal places show). Each of the columns is color-coded by selecting a background color for the columns. You can then turn the task into a game. Students are directed to examine the columns and describe the differences among the numbers. If they need help, they can ask you for a hint card that directs their attention to specific information. However, for each hint card they lose 5 points or 15 seconds are added to their problem-solving time. The winners are all rewarded with a Nobel Prize in mathematics for discovering a new math concept.

Technology Integration Activities

The following activities provide an opportunity for you to explore the use of spreadsheets in your classroom.

1. Create a lesson plan to analyze numerical data students collect.
2. Create a list of "Lesson Byte" ideas for using spreadsheets as a database for the grade level and subject area(s) that you teach or plan to teach.

Lesson Bytes for Spreadsheets

Following are different spreadsheets that can be created by elementary, middle, and high school students and a sample problem statement for each.

Elementary Students

Growth of Bacteria
- In which conditions do bacteria grow the fastest?

Amount Read
- Who reads more paragraphs per week—boys or girls?
- Athletes or nonathletes?

Genetic Trait Tendencies
- Do girls tend to have different observable genetic traits than boys (e.g., curling tongue, attached ear lobe)?

Counting and Measuring
- Do bigger pumpkins have more seeds or just bigger seeds?
- Which foods affect your heart rate?
- How many more steps would it take for the shortest person in your class to walk the length of the hallway compared to the tallest person in your class?

- Can the height of a person be predicted by knowing his or her arm span?

Calculating Food Costs
- Which pizza place has the best price per square inch of pizza?
- Find three examples of a larger item being more economical than a smaller item; then find the reverse where the smaller items cost less per unit.

Middle School and High School Students
Change in Motion
- Which factor has the greatest impact on how high a ball will bounce?

Determining Mileage
- Determine the shortest route from your school to the state capital and the fastest route if driving a car.
- Does the distance flown by North American migratory birds differ based on where they reside?

Plant Growth
- Demonstrate how the chemical balance of soil affects plant growth.

Voting Patterns
- How have the voting patterns for your state changed over the past 50 years?

Recycling
- Based on a sample of your home's recycling, how much glass, paper, and metal does your community recycle each year?
- Determine how many trees can be saved each year in your community by the amount of paper recycled.

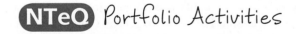

NTeQ Portfolio Activities

The following activities are designed to help you build your NTeQ Portfolio with regard to students using spreadsheets as a tool to foster deeper learning.

Reflections
The Getting Started section of this chapter posed four Reflecting on What I Know questions that are often asked about spreadsheets. In this portion of your journal, reflection activities have been added to address how you would answer each question. Please use information from this chapter to answer the questions.

❶ **Can you identify two types of data your students could collect as part of a lesson?**

Reflection Activity: Users can enter two types of data into a spreadsheet cell—numbers and text. In addition, numbers can be entered into a variety of formats. Create a two-column table in your word processor and list the various data formats available in a spreadsheet in the left column. In the right column, generate a list of ways you might use each format in a lesson plan.

❷ **How could your students manipulate the data to discover relationships or trends?**

Reflection Activity: When we think of manipulating data, we almost always think of numbers. In a spreadsheet, we can also manipulate text by sorting, selecting, and so on. Add another column to the right of your table from Reflection Activity 1 and list ways you could manipulate the data.

❸ **Can you identify three graphs or charts your students could make that would help them develop a better understanding of the content?**

Reflection Activity: Spreadsheets allow the user to create a variety of charts and graphs. Select three different graphs or charts and describe the type of data, giving an example, that each is best suited to display.

❹ **Is it possible to create an interactive simulation or model with a spreadsheet?**

Reflection Activity: If you have a problem that is math-based, such as converting temperatures between Celsius and Fahrenheit, you can create a simulation. Can you describe a simulation that you could create with a spreadsheet for your classroom?

Lesson Ideas

For this activity, we want you to identify five potential lesson plans that you can create or modify as an integrated lesson. There are two general sources for ideas. First, you can review benchmarks or standards for a source of ideas. These standards can come from a national organization (e.g., NCTM) or from your state or local school districts. You can find many of these standards on the Internet (see www.NTeQ.com). Second, you can modify existing lesson plans to create an integrated lesson. The lesson plans can come from your own resources, or you can search the Internet for existing lesson plans. For each lesson idea, create a three- to five-sentence description of the lesson including the problem for your NTeQ Portfolio.

Lesson Plan

The last step is to create an integrated lesson plan that uses a spreadsheet as the tool. Your lesson plan can be for a single discipline, or it can span two or more disciplines. Add the lesson plan to your NTeQ Portfolio.

 **NTeQ** Lesson Plan

Lesson Title: **Product Testing Lab**

Subject Area: **Math**

Grade Level: **5 to 8**

Learning Objective

By the end of this lesson, students will collect and use data to complete a compare and contrast analysis of a product (e.g., paper towels).

Computer Functions

- Spreadsheets will be used to calculate strength and absorbency.
- Word processing will be used to write a report for the school newsletter.

Specify Problem

We have all seen the various television advertisements for paper towels showing their strength and absorbency. But which is really the best when tested in our lab?

Research and Analysis

- Students will use a spreadsheet to determine the average weight a paper towel can hold.
- Students will use a spreadsheet to determine how much water a paper towel can absorb in 15 seconds.
- Students will use word processing to edit and revise a report on the results of the tests.

Results Presentation

The final product will be a word-processed report that contains graphs supporting the final recommendation for the best paper towel.

Planning Computer Activities

Small groups of students complete the following activities.

During Computer Use

The following computer tasks are divided among group members:

- Create spreadsheet columns and rows.
- Enter formulas.
- Enter testing data.
- Create a graph that effectively depicts the results of each test.

Before Computer Use

- Decide on a plan of action for solving the problem.

- Conduct three trials of each product to test the strength by securing a stretched piece of paper towel over a coffee can with a rubber band. Add weights (e.g., pennies) until the towel breaks.
- Conduct three trials of each product to test the absorbency. Place a paper towel in a container with 6 ounces of water for 15 seconds. Remove the towel and measure the amount of water remaining in the container.
- Determine how to set up the spreadsheet (i.e., column and row names, formulas for calculating the average weight held and for calculating the average amount of water collected).

After Computer Use

Answer the following Think Sheet questions:

1. List the supporting reasons for the final selection.
2. Which product holds the most weight? Which product absorbed the most liquid? Please explain why.
3. How did you select the best product?
4. What was the most difficult aspect of this lesson?
   - As a large group, have the reporters from each group share their findings.
   - Facilitate a summary and review session with the whole class by discussing the Think Sheet responses. During the discussion, clarify any misconceptions that arise and reemphasize the key learning objectives.
   - Prepare a report describing the results and select the best product.

Supporting Activities

- Study how paper is made.
- Investigate how paper is recycled.
- Look for ways paper is used and how it is made stronger.

Assessment

Create a rubric for assessing the following:

Spreadsheet

- Columns and rows named appropriately.
- Data entered accurately.
- Formulas are accurate.
- Manipulation of data is evident.

Graph

- Depicts the final selection.
- Displays information in easy-to-read manner.
- Appropriate graph is used.

Report

- Supporting arguments are reasonable.
- Format is appropriate.
- Report is free of errors.

Integrating Multimedia as a Tool

Getting Started

Over the past 200 years, we have seen significant changes in the ways students communicate and how they submit their assignments. About 200 years ago when paper was scarce, students completed their homework using chalk to write on a piece of slate. As paper became available, students could use paper and pencil or pen to complete their assignments. This paper-and-pen approach remained the norm until the 1980s, when students used a word processor and dot-matrix printer. In the last 10 to 15 years, the variety of formats for submitting assignments has greatly expanded. Students can easily create a word processing document with pictures and charts, and they can produce the same type of document for the Web. Student presentations using tools such as PowerPoint can include audio, pictures, animations, and video to create attractive as well as unattractive reports and presentations. While multimedia can be a powerful tool for students and teachers, it can also be hindrance to learning and communicating when it is rich on bells and whistles and short on information.

Reflecting on What I Know

1 How can my students use multimedia for their projects?

2 What applications are available for creating a multimedia presentation?

3 Should I place limits on how my students use multimedia?

Classroom SNAPSHOT

Mr. Asel's ninth-grade language arts class was a flurry of activity; even more surprising were the number of adults in the room who were working with small groups of students. The students were completing a multidisciplinary ecology unit. The unit problem was to determine the effect of neighborhood growth on the environment around the school. For the past few weeks, they had conducted a study of their school property and the small wooded lot next door. They counted birds and small animals at the feeders they had purchased or constructed. They gathered weather data, including rainfall and temperatures. A survey was made to count the types of trees and plants on the schoolground as well as in the wooded lot. They also worked with a surveyor to measure the total area as well as the area of the buildings and paved playground and parking lots. Now was the time to prepare their final reports.

Ms. Ritter was working with a small group of students as they wrote about the number of trees and plants. Ms. Ritter, an information systems specialist with a local company, was one of the adult volunteers. She was busy helping the students ask and answer relevant questions about their data and charts. Mr. Roberts is a retired photojournalist and was helping another group edit their digital photographs for use in a PowerPoint presentation. A third group was coached by Ms.

Washington, who is a graphic designer at the local newspaper. She was helping the group create the layout for web pages. One group was working outside the building as Mr. Miller, a video producer from the television station, helped them tape a segment for the class's news program. As a group finished one aspect of their project, they would work with a different adult volunteer to finish the next step. While each group was producing a different piece of media, the focus was always on their writing skills, whether captions for photographs or the script for the videotape or the other ecology-related content.

Examining Multimedia

Advances in computer technology and connectivity provide students, teachers, and adults a variety of ways to communicate. For example, today's cell phones have more capabilities for communication, ranging from texting to displaying video, than early desktop computers. The term *multimedia* is often used to describe these different forms of communication; however, the meaning continues to evolve as new technologies are introduced. One definition of *multimedia* is communication that involves more than one format (Mayer, Moreno, Boire, & Vagge, 1999). For example, an animation with narration is considered multimedia, as is a PowerPoint presentation with text, graphics, and perhaps a speaker. In this chapter, we will examine the use of PowerPoint presentations and digital video, both commonly used in today's classrooms and work settings. Let's begin by examining the basic components (see Figure 9.1).

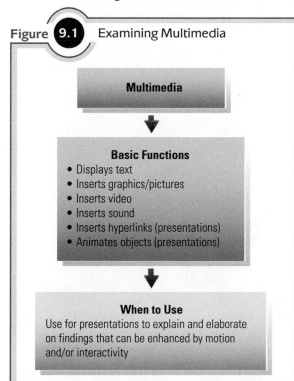

Figure 9.1 Examining Multimedia

Multimedia

Basic Functions
- Displays text
- Inserts graphics/pictures
- Inserts video
- Inserts sound
- Inserts hyperlinks (presentations)
- Animates objects (presentations)

When to Use
Use for presentations to explain and elaborate on findings that can be enhanced by motion and/or interactivity

Basic Functions

Multimedia can incorporate text, graphics, pictures and photographs, video, sound, hyperlinks, and animated objects. With tools like Apple's iMovie, Windows Movie Maker, PowerPoint, and more sophisticated applications like Adobe's Flash, your students can easily incorporate a variety of media into a single presentation. While the technology makes it very easy for the student to create an elaborate project, we need to help our students maintain their focus on the goal of communicating the knowledge and skills stated in the objectives.

Creating Digital Video.   Digital video presentations can utilize existing movies that you can find on the Internet, or students can produce their own movies. Production always starts with a script and storyboard (see Figure 9.2), whether using existing video or having students create their own video.

Figure 9.2   Script and Storyboard

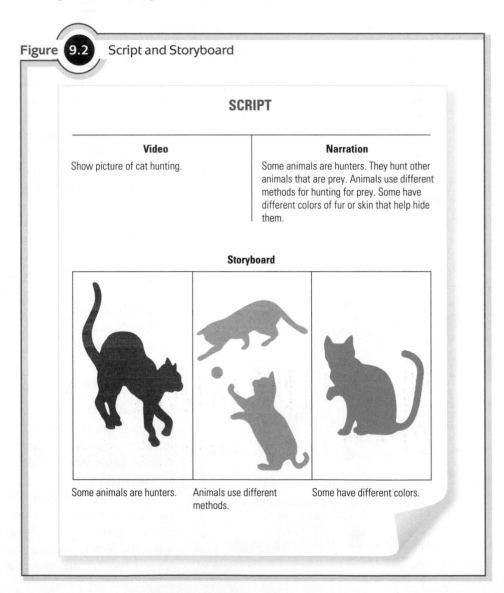

SCRIPT

Video	Narration
Show picture of cat hunting.	Some animals are hunters. They hunt other animals that are prey. Animals use different methods for hunting for prey. Some have different colors of fur or skin that help hide them.

Storyboard

Some animals are hunters.   Animals use different methods.   Some have different colors.

Movies require a sequence that builds a story; in fact, movie making is a type of storytelling. The script and storyboard can help us plan our story so that our movie will have continuity. Using our script, we can move to the next step of recording or locating video that that will tell the story in the preplanned sequence.

Once we have the video needed for the presentation, we can start to create the movie using iMovie or Windows Movie Maker. The first step is to add the title and credits at the beginning of the movie (see Figure 9.3). In Windows Movie Maker, we click the link under Edit Movie to Make Titles or Credits. There are options to select different fonts and colors as well as ways to animate the text that affect how the title and credits will appear on the screen.

After the credits, we can start to assemble our movie. First, we will need to import all the video segments into the application. If all your clips are located in one folder, you will find it much quicker to import them. You can also import any additional audio clips such as narration, music, or sound effects. Second, you can drag and drop your video clips and audio clips into the correct sequence (see Figure 9.4). Third, you can edit your movie by adding transitions and adjusting the lengths of individual segments.

Figure 9.3 Adding Titles and Credits

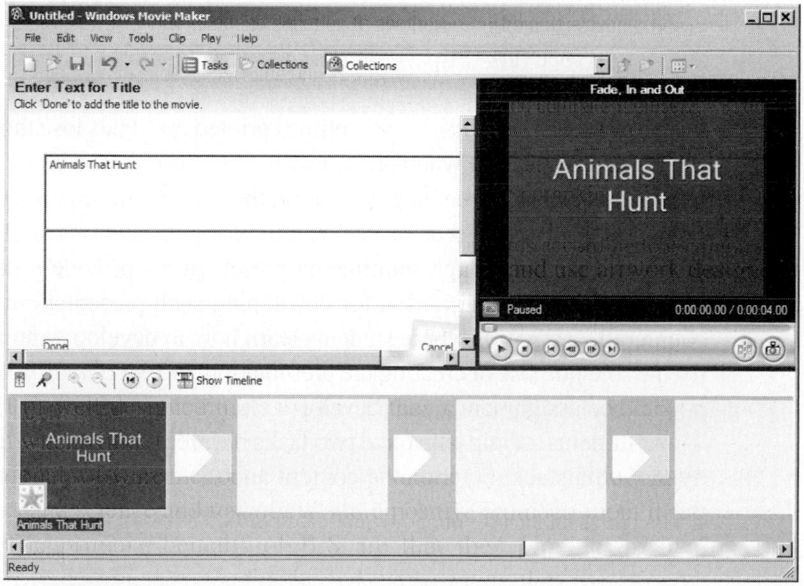

Figure 9.4   Editing a Movie

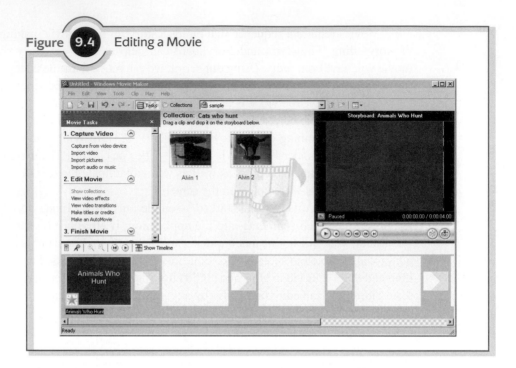

You can find detailed instructions for creating movies using Windows Movie Maker on the Microsoft website (www.microsoft.com) and for iMovie on Apple's website (www.apple.com). Additional information on scripting and editing is available on EdTechTalk (http://delicious.com/edtechtalk/movie).

Creating Presentations.   Sometimes printed materials lose their impact when used for presentations, even when printed with a color printer. An alternative to printed communication is a multimedia presentation that can incorporate sound, graphics, animation, video, and text. Students can create these presentations as electronic slide shows or hypermedia. Although multimedia presentations provide a number of "bells and whistles," consider the reason for developing such presentations. We have often encountered classrooms where students learn how to develop a multimedia presentation for the sole purpose of creating the presentation. We encourage you to consider the purpose of the assignment and to develop a clear rationale for including such a project.

Students should complete two tasks before creating an electronic slide show or hypermedia stack: (1) plan the content and (2) create a storyboard. When planning the content of the presentation, the students need to address the following:

- Who is the intended audience?
- What is the presentation topic?

- What information will this presentation share?
- What is the actual purpose or goal of this presentation?

Next, students need to create a storyboard of the project. Storyboards are sketches of each card or slide in the presentation. Students can draw storyboards on a piece of notebook paper divided into four sections or use note cards. Drawing only one card per page makes it very easy to reorder the cards. Careful planning before going to the computer results in less student frustration and more meaningful presentations (McBride & Luntz, 1996).

There are several applications for creating electronic slide shows or multimedia presentations. Some, including PowerPoint, are designed specifically for creating electronic presentations. One advantage to using PowerPoint is the ability to save the presentation as a movie or web page, as well as to print a variety of handouts and presentation notes.

Creating a PowerPoint Presentation.   Once you have completed the planning, you can start to develop your presentation. There are three approaches for creating the presentation. First, you can create an outline in Word. The first level (headings 1, 2, 3 or I, II, III) starts a new slide. Information in lower-level headings (headings 2, 3, and 4 or A, B, 1, 2, a, b) are on the same slide as the first-level headings. You should not include graphics or pictures in the outline, as they will not import into PowerPoint. The second method for creating a presentation is to work in the outline view of PowerPoint (see Figure 9.5). Start by typing a title for the slide. As you start, think of a style you want to use consistently—for example, do you capitalize each word, or only the first word? For the title slide, we capitalized the first letter of each word and then only the first word of the title for each of the subsequent slides. To enter subpoints for each slide, press the tab key at the start of a new line. To move to a different level, such as a level 3 subpoint, press the tab key. To move up a level, such as from level 3 to level 2 or from level 2 to level 1 to create a new slide, press Shift+Tab. As you type in outline mode, you will see the formatting of the slide in the right window. The third option for creating a presentation is to type on the slide (see Figure 9.6). You will need to type the slide title in the top text box, then tab to enter additional information. Tab and Shift+Tab are used to change the level of the information.

PEARSON
myeducationlab
The Power of Classroom Practice

Go to MyEducationLab, select the topic "Software," and go to the Activities and Applications section. Access the video "PowerPoint Guides and Prompts Teaching" and consider various ways PowerPoint can be used in the classroom. Complete the activity that follows.

As you enter information in any mode, you can change the appearance of the text by changing the font, size, style, color, and spacing between characters to expand or contract a word. In addition, special effects such as shadows or reflections

Figure **9.5**   Creating a Presentation in Outline View

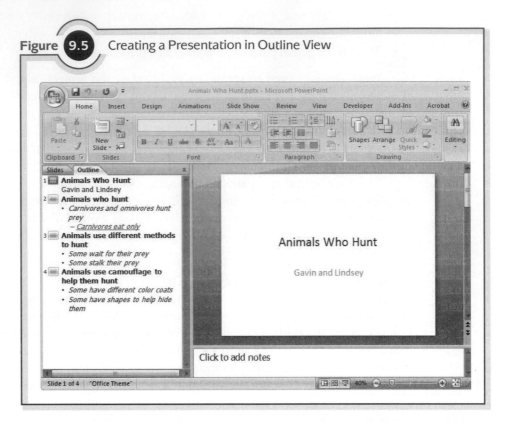

Figure **9.6**   Creating the Slide

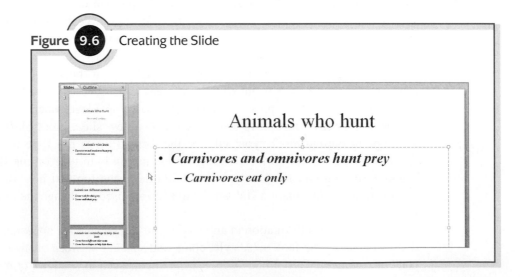

Figure 9.7   Layout Options

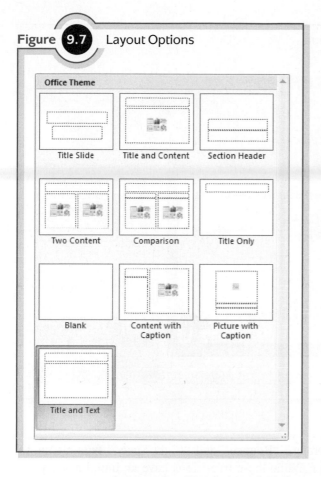

can be added. The background, color, and font style can also be changed by selecting one of the themes or templates. Additional templates and themes are available for downloading from the Internet.

The layout for individual slides is easily changed (see Figure 9.7) by using one of the preformatted Slide Layout options. For example, layouts are provided for title slides as well as different content layouts and comparisons. These formats make it easier to organize certain types of information. For example, the Comparison layout provides an easy way to create two columns of information with a heading for each column.

Adding Media. The steps you have completed thus far have focused on entering text information. It is now time to add pictures, sounds, music, and digital video to make a true multimedia presentation. The Insert tab in PowerPoint provides a means to insert pictures, clip art, SmartArt, and charts onto individual slides. You can select a picture that you have created, a photograph, clip art, or a chart that you created with Excel. SmartArt layouts for diagrams, charts, and lists add new design possibilities to your slides.

The last option is to add video clips and sound to your presentation. You can select video and audio clips from the PowerPoint library or you can add a clip that you have created, such as the digital video in the previous section. You can also select the option to record your own narration directly into PowerPoint.

Animating Objects and Slide Transitions.   Animation can be used to attract attention and to explain ideas. You can use PowerPoint to animate an object so that it moves across the slide using a variety of shaped paths (see Figure 9.8). You can select from straight lines or you can create your own random animation path. The last option is create a transition between slides. Basic transitions include simple movements such as "Wipes" that move the new slide over the old slide from a corner, top, bottom, or side. More complex or "exciting" transitions use

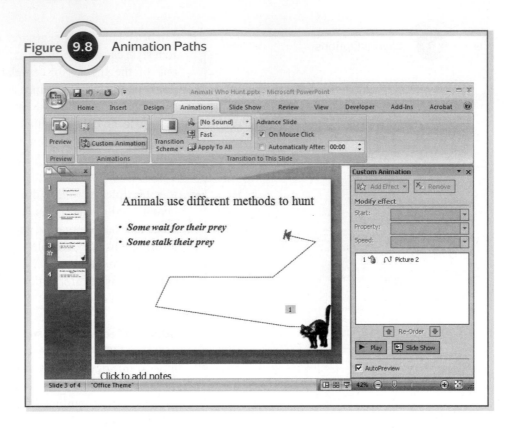

Figure 9.8   Animation Paths

movements such as "Boomerang," "Bounce," and "Light Speed" type effects to reveal the new slide or object. While these transitions have an initial novelty effect, the viewers soon tire of the transitions and may even lose interest in your message.

Adding Hyperlinks.   Most PowerPoint presentations are displayed in a linear manner by clicking the mouse or pressing the right arrow key. With hyperlinks, you can jump to any slide in the presentation, another document such as an Excel file, or a specific website. To jump to a slide in the presentation, start by selecting a word, a phrase, or a picture. Then click on the Insert ribbon and select Hyperlink (see Figure 9.9). When the dialog appears, click on Place in this Document and select the slide. If you want to jump to a web page, you select Existing File or Web Page and browse to the file or enter the URL. When you show the presentation, you can click on the hyperlink and the link will appear. Similar Hyperlink functions can be added by using the Action Settings located in PowerPoint's Slide Show options.

Figure 9.9   Adding Hyperlinks

Insert Hyperlink   ? X

Link to: Text to display: Carnivores   ScreenTip...

[Existing File or Web Page]

Select a place in this document: Slide preview:

- First Slide   Animals use camouflage to help them
- Last Slide   hunt
- Next Slide
- Previous Slide   • Some have different color coats
- Slide Titles   • Some have shapes to help hide them
  - 1. Animals Who Hunt
  - 2. Animals who hunt
  - 3. Animals use different methods to
  - 4. Animals use camouflage to help
- Custom Shows

[Place in This Document]

[Create New Document]

☐ Show and return

[E-mail Address]

            OK   Cancel

Summary

While multimedia presentations in the classroom are often limited to PowerPoint presentations or digital video due to limitation of equipment or software, there are endless possibilities for creating interesting presentations. But just as with a paper, a multimedia presentation requires careful and thoughtful planning. Overuse of animations, color, and transitions can diminish a good presentation. However, proper and creative use of these tools results in powerful presentations that are captivating and informative.

The Teacher's

As a high school English teacher, I strive to utilize a variety of computer applications each school year. I have incorporated word processing, Internet scavenger hunts, wikis, podcasting, PowerPoint, and multimedia projects. Media literacy is a component of my curriculum and a testing category on the standardized state test for my grade level and subject area. I feel that a great way to

enable students to understand that media messages are carefully constructed by their producers to elicit specific responses from the viewers is to have students create their own multimedia productions.

Although I usually anchor their projects to a novel or theme we are studying, I encourage the students to make it their own by allowing them to pursue their unique strategies for creating and producing their multimedia project. We use iMovie in conjunction with images gathered from books, magazines, and Internet sources in addition to images and video clips taken by the students using digital cameras and video cameras. The importance of soundtracks and sound effects is also addressed.

Students have to conduct research on their topics, create storyboards for their movies, reach group consensus about the scripts, and edit the materials they have gathered and created on their own into a sophisticated movie. I am not an expert on iMovie and I don't have to be one. One member of each production team is responsible for becoming an iMovie guru. I help the teams to stay on schedule and on track where meeting the objectives of the projects are concerned. I meet with each team every day and assess their progress. I provide feedback on their information, organization, and execution of their projects. When students are stumped by a computer issue, I provide guidance in searching for the solution if I don't know how to troubleshoot the problem myself.

Although these projects take a great deal of classroom time, I am able to address multiple standards with one activity. Students have to create storyboards and scripts wherein we focus on writing and grammar skills as well as standards related to developing media applications for a variety of audiences. We discuss the plot, character, themes, and symbols contained in their movies. Students have to select, evaluate, and adapt resource material in order to create, display, and explain the information they have gathered. We also learn technology skills; producing an iMovie usually requires students to master multiple computer skills most have never before encountered. They learn to use computers as tools to achieve specific goals in a flexible and creative way. They have to take risks and discover that making mistakes can lead to better solutions.

The most exciting part of the process for all of us is the day that they "show off" to each other what they have accomplished. They are really proud of what they have put together and very impressed with each other's work. When we watch the completed movies, they don't even realize all of the new knowledge and skills they have developed. They think they just had fun!

Julie Forbess
Tenth-Grade English
Teacher

Multimedia in the Classroom

If your students have completed an integrated computer lesson, they have learned new content, solved problems, and maybe discovered new relationships among ideas that you had not anticipated. A final step in an integrated lesson is for the results to be presented by each student or team. This publishing process can help students synthesize ideas as they work through their data and determine what they want to tell others (Brookes, 1988; Corbine, 1995; Johannessen & Kahn, 1991) and to become active and involved in the learning (Keys, 1999). Similarly, the process of creating a presentation encourages students to reflect on what they have done (Wang, Kedem, & Hertzog, 2004). For example, students working on an oral history project (Huerta & Flemmer, 2000) could prepare a PowerPoint presentation as part of their organization and archival process. The process of writing or elaborating on ideas can help students discover new ideas and relationships (Corbine, 1995)

PEARSON
myeducationlab
The Power of Classroom Practice

Go to MyEducationLab, select the topic "Instructional Strategies," and go to the Activities and Applications section. Access the video "Presentation Software in Literature" and consider how integrating games into instruction can enhance student learning. Complete the activity that follows.

from their data analysis. Students can also respond to provocative questions from the teacher and their peers, which helps focus their writing and improve their understanding of the content (Brookes, 1988).

Preparing a report of a study conducted in a science, social studies, math, or language arts class provides the students with an opportunity to generate meaning for the lesson concepts (Wittrock, 1974, 1990). Writing allows the students to expand their ideas in a report. This expansion can include defining or explaining an idea (elaboration), making a new connection between two ideas (extension), and supporting or qualifying an idea with additional information (enhancement) (Halliday, 1985). In the following section we will describe examples of how students can use multimedia as an instructional tool.

Using Multimedia to Achieve ISTE NETS for Students

When multimedia are used a tool in the classroom, three of the six NETS for Students are directly addressed: (1) Creativity and Innovation; (3) Research and Information Fluency; and (6) Technology Operations and Concepts (ISTE, 2007). The following paragraphs describe the details.

1. Creativity and Innovation: Students demonstrate creative thinking, construct knowledge, and develop innovative products and processes using technology. Multimedia presentations provide an opportunity for students to reflect on their research or project (Wang et al., 2004). As they create a presentation, they must organize their information and then plan how to best communicate the knowledge and skills gained during the problem-solving process. The possibilities of digital media presentations allow the student to prepare an innovative approach to communicating their information. They can integrate information from word processing, spreadsheets, graphic software, and digital movies and audio to illustrate their ideas.

3. Research and Information Fluency: Students apply digital tools to gather, evaluate, and use information. Multimedia provides an excellent tool for students to use to report their results. Students can build their communication skills by creating presentations that best use text, graphics, charts, audio, animations, and/or digital video to relay the intended message.

6. Technology Operations and Concepts: Students demonstrate a sound understanding of technology concepts, systems, and operations. Creating multimedia presentations requires students to use presentation technology to communicate their ideas. As they create presentations, students will develop a variety of skills, learn new concepts related to technology use, and gain an understanding of operations involved in using both hardware and applications. For example, developing a digital video or audio file may require the students to understand the operation of a microphone, video camera, recording software, and editing software. As they produce their product, they may also gain an understanding of ambient noise and lighting.

Planning an NTeQ Lesson for Multimedia

As the students complete their projects, multimedia presentations are one method they can use to present their results. However, presentations are not the only use of multimedia. Students can use audio and video as part of their research as well as to provide archives. For example, they might tape a student, a dog, and a duck and then study the motion of how each walks. Similarly, they might use digital audio to record the oral history of their school, community, or larger event such as World War II. You can use multimedia with pre-K through high school students across all disciplines (see Table 9.1). In the next section, we will describe how to use the NTeQ model to develop an integrated lesson plan using multimedia.

Multimedia programs make it possible for students to tap into their audiovisual literacy skills.

Table 9.1	Using Multimedia to Meet Curriculum and Technology Standards	

Standards	Example Problem	Example Student Product
Elementary		
Language Arts/English		
NCTE Curriculum Standard 4: Students adjust their use of spoken, written, and visual language (e.g., conventions, style, vocabulary) to communicate effectively with a variety of audiences and for different purposes. *NETS-S: 1.b. Research and Information Fluency:* create original works as a means of personal or group expression.	With the increased use of text messaging, students are using a greater number of abbreviations. How do these shortened forms of communication differ across geographic regions?	Students create a table in PowerPoint to show differences. Hyperlinks are provided for each phrase to a slide with an interpretation.
Mathematics		
NCTM Data Analysis: use multiple models to develop initial understandings of place value and the base-ten number system. *NETS-S: 2.a. Communication and Collaboration:* interact, collaborate, and publish with peers, experts, or others employing a variety of digital environments and media.	How many does each number represent?	Using a template, student teams will create number lines and other illustrations of base-ten numbers.
Science		
NSES Science and Technology (K–4): abilities to distinguish between natural objects and objects made by humans. *NETS-S: 4.c. Critical Thinking:* collect and analyze data to identify solutions and/or make informed decisions.	How do man-made objects differ from natural objects?	Students create a multimedia presentation with pictures of various objects.
Social Studies/History		
NCHS Curriculum Standard Theme 4.1. Scarcity: The opportunity cost of a choice is the value of the best alternative given up. *NETS-S: 4.c. Critical Thinking:* collect and analyze data to identify solutions and/or make informed decisions.	What is opportunity cost?	Students create a multimedia presentation showing selected choices and the alternative (opportunity cost).

(continued)

Table 9.1 *Continued*

Standards	Example Problem	Example Student Product
Middle/High School		
Language Arts/English		
NCTE Curriculum Standard 6: Students apply knowledge of language structure, language conventions (e.g., spelling and punctuation), media techniques, figurative language, and genre to create, critique, and discuss print and nonprint texts. *NETS-S: 3.b. Research and Information Fluency:* locate, organize, analyze, evaluate, synthesize, and ethically use information from a variety of sources and media.	How do advertisers use different conventions to persuade buyers?	Students create a multimedia presentation that incorporates newspaper, radio, television, and Internet advertising.
Mathematics		
NCTM Computer Fluency: develop and analyze algorithms for computing with fractions, decimals, and integers and develop fluency in their use. *NETS-S: 2.a. Communication and Collaboration:* interact, collaborate, and publish with peers, experts, or others employing a variety of digital environments and media.	How can you divide with whole numbers?	Groups of students will work together to illustrate various algorithms for division.
Science		
NSES Life Science (9–12): Molecular basis of heredity *NETS-S: 4.c. Critical Thinking:* collect and analyze data to identify solutions and/or make informed decisions.	Is the gene for tongue curling a sex-linked gene?	Students create a pedigree chart with hyperlinks for each individual that provides more detail.
Social Studies/History		
NCHS Curriculum Standard Civic Life, Politics and Government. 9–12.1: What are the essential characteristics of limited and unlimited government? *NETS-S: 4.c. Critical Thinking:* collect and analyze data to identify solutions and/or make informed decisions.	How do governments differ?	Students create a presentation that shows comparisons between the U.S. government and foreign governments.

Source: National Council of Teachers of English (NCTE). *Standards for the English Language Arts,* by the International Reading Association and the National Council of Teachers of English. Copyright 1996 by the International Reading Association and the National Council of Teachers of English. Reprinted with permission. Complete set of standards can be found at www.ncte.org/standards; National Council of Teachers of Mathematics (NCTM). *Principles and Standards for School Mathematics,* by National Council of Teachers of Mathematics Staff. Copyright 2000 by National Council of Teachers of Mathematics. Reproduced with permission of National Council of Teachers of Mathematics via Copyright Clearance Center. http://standards.nctm.org/document/appendix/numb.htm; National Science Education Standards (NSES). Reprinted with permission from *National Science Education Standards: Observe, Interact, Change, Learn,* by the National Academy of Sciences. Courtesy of the National Academies Press, Washington, DC. www.nsta.org/publications/nses.aspx; National Center for History in Schools (NCHS). Courtesy of http://nchs.ucla.edu; *National Education Technology Standards for Students*, Second Edition, © 2007, ISTE® International Society for Technology in Education, www.iste.org. All rights reserved.

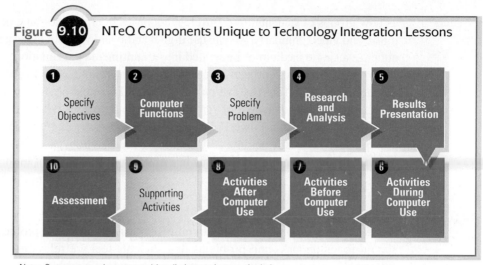

Figure **9.10**   NTeQ Components Unique to Technology Integration Lessons

Note: Components relevant to multimedia integration are shaded.

The NTeQ Lesson

This section describes the key components of the NTeQ model, shaded in Figure 9.10, that a teacher specifically needs to address when creating lesson plans that have students use multimedia as a learning tool. The remaining NTeQ components, which are discussed in Chapter 2, remain consistent across all lessons.

Matching the Objective to Computer Functions.   Multimedia tools are used when there is a match between multimedia functions and your objectives. If there is no match, you might consider using a more traditional method, such as a printed report rather than a multimedia presentation. Let's examine the relationship between the functions of multimedia and instructional objectives.

The multimedia functions listed in Figure 9.1 can be grouped into three primary categories used to match with objectives: organization, illustration, and selection of digital media. The first, organization, is the planning, design, and layout of the presentation. To communicate effectively, students must give thought to not only the message (e.g., content) they wish to convey but also the sequencing, design, and layout. Feature-rich software such as PowerPoint can often misconstrue the original message due to all the bells and whistles. An effective presenter quickly learns how to use these features intelligently to enhance the communication rather than detract from it. The second function is illustration of ideas. Adding photographs, drawings, charts, and graphs can help communicate your point. Showing a bar graph helps the learner see a trend in numbers that is not always visible from a list of numbers. Proper selection of digital media is the third function of multimedia presentations. Digital media are useful both as research tools and as presentation tools. Video and audio recordings can document events such as the movement of clouds as well as examine concepts such as how groups of students from different countries interpret the same poem through music and video. Similarly, we can use digital audio and video to make a presentation either as a single medium or integrated into a multimedia presentation.

The verbs in your objectives need to match the functions performed by a multimedia presentation for effective use of the tool. The most obvious match between objective and function is that of "creating a presentation." If we consider the different layouts available in PowerPoint, then we can also see that objectives requiring comparisons are easily achieved by creating a presentation. Similarly, an objective requiring students to sequence items is a match with PowerPoint in that individual slides are easily moved into different sequences. Thus, students might sequence the events in a story or pictures of a task.

Research and Analysis. As with all NTeQ lesson plans, the problem statement should focus on tasks and problems that students feel are relevant and worthy of solving. Thus, a multimedia presentation can be part of a problem unit in which students have collected data and need to present the data. Presentations can incorporate charts and graphs to illustrate the results as well as digital photos of the experiment or data collection. The multimedia can also be a means of collecting data. Digital audio and video are useful tools for conducting interviews and documenting a process, such as how different students solve a math problem or plan to write a story.

After you have identified a problem, you need to identify the data the students will use to solve the problem. If you want the students to sequence a story or task, you might provide them with a presentation that has the individual steps, but in the incorrect order. If your students are collecting data such as interviews, then you might need to make arrangements for them to interview specific individuals. After identifying the data collection method, you will need to specify how the students will manipulate the data. For example, if they have interviewed someone you might have them write a summary of the interview. They could also identify the key points and then edit the interview (i.e., audio or video) to convey just a few of the key points and shorten a lengthy recording to just a few minutes. Finally, the manipulation of data also includes the creation of an effective presentation using data students have collected and manipulated with other tools.

Results Presentation. The results presentation for a multimedia presentation is a natural extension of the data manipulation step. For the results presentation, the process may simply be a refinement of the manipulated data, or it might require the process of including the results (e.g., finished digital audio or media sequence) into a PowerPoint presentation. For this step, you will need to provide some guidelines to the students regarding expectations for the final product. This can be accomplished by providing or having students assist in the development of a rubric for the results presentation product(s).

Planning Computer Activities. Multimedia projects are computer intensive by their very nature. Thus, it is critical to plan for the use of computers if you have either a limited number or limited access. Even when your students have almost total access to computers, it still important to carefully plan the computer activities to make the most efficient use of time and to keep the students on task. The following three steps will help you plan for efficient use of computer technology in your classroom during multimedia production.

During Computer Use. Start your planning by determining what the students will do when they are working with a computer. Are they searching for information or graphics on the Internet? If they are editing audio or video, will they use their own material or material that you provide? Or will they use finished digital media in their project and thus eliminate the need for editing? When students are creating a PowerPoint presentation, can they choose any design, template, and layout, or will you impose certain limitations? Once you have defined what the students will do while working with a computer, you can prepare the materials they will need. If the task is new or one with which they have had limited experience, then you may need to prepare step-by-step instructions they can use individually.

Before Computer Use. Now that you have defined what the students will do while working with a computer, you can plan what they must do *before* they have access to a computer. For example, if the students are creating a presentation you can have them create an outline or storyboards of their presentation. If students have recorded video or audio, they might watch it on an iPod or mp3 player to determine how they will edit the presentation. Sometimes, it is helpful if you actually complete each step of the process to help you identify additional activities or information that may be needed.

After Computer Use. If the students have created a multimedia presentation, then the *after* computer activities generally involve reviewing and proofing their production. For a PowerPoint presentation, they can check spelling, grammar, and the sequencing of slides. If they have produced a digital media presentation, they can review it to see if the final product includes the information they intended and determine if it flows smoothly.

Assessment. Assessment of a multimedia project can focus on the subject-matter knowledge and skills, as well as various technology-related aspects. Depending on your objectives, you might assess the media production by the quality of audio, images, and flow if it is a digital video production. Similarly, you can assess the quality of the layout, legibility of text, appropriateness of graphics and animation, and sequencing of a PowerPoint presentation. If your objectives focus on the student presentation, you can assess how well the student(s) presented the material, their effective use of the multimedia presentation, and the appropriateness of the presentation. If the project was a collaboration of several students, it is important that you explain your expectations for each student early in the process.

Summary

Multimedia presentations and projects provide a variety of formats for students to express their individual ideas at any grade level. Students learn to combine text, graphics, audio, and video to effectively communicate their ideas. In addition, digital media are excellent research tools that students can use to collect data through recordings that they can then analyze and share with others.

Teacher Technology FAQ

My students are more interested in using the bells and whistles of PowerPoint than focusing on their message. What can I do?

We must admit that the first time we saw PowerPoint we wanted to try everything and include everything in our presentations. It was only after sitting through a "supercharged" presentation that we realized how distracting the various features were to the presentation. There are two approaches to addressing this problem. First, let the students experiment and see what they can craft. Then have them explain how the "supercharging" helps communicate their ideas rather than get in the way. The second approach is to limit the presentation to a rather plain background and design as they create their presentation. Once the students are finished crafting their message, you can give them 10 minutes to add enhancements that support their message.

How do I help my class produce a digital video?

The process is surprisingly easy. There are several tutorials on the Internet including ones on both the Microsoft and Apple websites. In addition, you can find some excellent guidance at www.edtechtalk.com. We have often found that students in the classroom are excellent resources for either helping others or discovering how to do something new.

Technology Integration Activities

The following activities provide an opportunity for you to explore the use of multimedia in your classroom.

1. Create two columns on a piece of paper and label one "Paper Report" and the other "Multimedia Report." Now list the advantages and disadvantages of using each in your classroom.
2. Next, list verbs from objectives that you teach and show how they match with use of multimedia.

3. Create a list of "Lesson Byte" ideas to use multimedia for the grade level and subject area(s) that you teach or plan to teach.

Lesson Bytes for Multimedia

Following are different multimedia ideas that can be created by elementary and middle/high school students and a sample problem statement for each.

Elementary Students

Digital Video

- *Language Arts.* Create an "In My Own Words" book review video that has a story summary provided by five students.
- *Mathematics.* Use video and narration to illustrate how form fits function.
- *Science.* Create a "Plants at Our School" documentary.
- *Social Studies.* Videotape a relative talking about the history of the oldest thing they own.

PowerPoint

- *Language Arts.* Which group can create the shortest narrated and illustrated story that incorporates all of the vocabulary words for the week?
- *Mathematics.* Use photos you take with a digital camera to create a ten-slide presentation that has a title slide followed by a slide with a photo of one object, then a slide with a photo of two objects, and so on. The last slide should have a photo with ten items.
- *Science.* In what ways do spiders and insects differ and in what ways are they alike?
- *Social Studies.* How have shoes worn by elementary school students changed over the past 25 years?

Middle School and High School Students

Digital Video

- *English.* Produce a "Charlie Rose"–type interview with a famous author, with members of your team assuming the various talent and production team roles.
- *Mathematics.* Work with your team members to create an algebra video tutorial that will result in more eighth-grade students passing an algebra test compared to tutorials created by other teams.
- *Science.* Produce a 30-second TV advertisement for reducing carbon footprints.
- *Social Studies.* Use archived videos to demonstrate common themes in State of the Union addresses over the past 50 years.

PowerPoint

- *English.* How would you use music and images to depict the meaning of a poem?
- *History.* What components would be included in an interactive model that depicts the growth of women's rights in the United States?
- *Mathematics.* Create a narrated presentation that shows the basic mathematics strategies needed to solve algebraic equations.

- *Science.* Use Custom Animation and Action Settings to illustrate erosion of a river.

NTeQ Portfolio Activities

The following activities are designed to help you build your NTeQ Portfolio with regard to students using multimedia as a tool to foster deeper learning.

Reflections

The Getting Started section posed three Reflecting on What I Know questions that are often asked about multimedia. In this portion of your journal, reflection activities have been added to help you reflect on each question. Please use the information from this chapter to answer the questions.

1 **How can my students use multimedia for their projects?**

Reflection Activity: Consider lessons that you currently use in your classroom. Describe three lessons where your students could either produce a presentation or use multimedia as a tool for gathering data.

2 **What applications are available for creating a multimedia presentation?**

Reflection Activity: You can answer this question by yourself or with a school technology specialist. List the various multimedia applications available on your computer and on the school's computers.

3 **Should I place limits on how my students use multimedia?**

Reflection Activity: The Teacher Technology FAQ addresses how to help your students effectively use multimedia. Using one of the examples from the first question, describe what problems you might encounter and how you will solve them.

Lesson Plan

The last step is to create an integrated lesson plan that uses some type of multimedia as the tool. Your lesson plan can be for a single discipline or it can go across two or more disciplines. Add the lesson plan to your NTeQ Portfolio.

NTeQ Lesson Plan

Lesson Title: **Animals That Hunt**
Subject Area: **Science**
Grade Level: **5 to 8**

Learning Objective

By the end of this lesson, students will identify characteristics (e.g., camouflage, individual vs. group, and prey) of animals that hunt.

Computer Functions

- Spreadsheets will be used to record the data.
- PowerPoint will be used to create a presentation.

Specify Problem

Animals in the wild have to hunt for their food. What makes some animals better hunters than others?

Research and Analysis

- Students will use a spreadsheet to enter their information about the animal, hunting method, and prey.
- Students will create a PowerPoint presentation incorporating pictures and/or digital movies to communicate their findings.

Results Presentation

The final product will be a multimedia presentation that demonstrates why some animals are better hunters than other animals.

Planning Computer Activities

Small groups of students complete the following activities.

During Computer Use

The following computer tasks are divided among group members:

- Search for information on selected animals.
- Gather data required in spreadsheet.
- Find pictures or digital movies of animal.
- Create a PowerPoint presentation.

Before Computer Use

- Identify a list of five animals that hunt.
- Enter known information into spreadsheet.
- List information needed from Internet search.
- Plan PowerPoint presentation.

After Computer Use

- Organize information and determine if any information is missing.
- Review presentation and check for errors.

Supporting Activities

- Study how the environment affects animals' hunting habits.
- Study carnivores on the endangered species list.

Assessment

Create a rubric for assessing the following:

- Rationale and support for explaining why some animals are better hunters
- PowerPoint production.
- Student presentation

Graphic Organizers

Getting Started

This chapter guides you through the key components of a graphic organizer and how to develop lesson plans in which your students use them as learning tools. More specifically, we will look at how students can use graphic organizers to build models that visually represent their understanding of concepts and ideas while expanding their knowledge by sharing and learning from others. Graphic organizers assist students to find meaningful ways to visualize their knowledge and organize information into new and meaningful patterns that lead to a greater depth of understanding.

Reflecting on What I Know

1 How do you know that students understand a concept?

2 How can you depict student misconceptions of key information?

3 How can students capture and transfer brainstorming ideas into written thoughts?

Classroom

SNAPSHOT

Mr. O'Malley is one of ten elementary teachers in his district selected to receive a classroom set of wireless laptops for his fourth-grade students. The district equipped the MacBooks with a variety of applications, including Inspiration, a graphic organizer tool. This is exciting to Mr. O'Malley, because he recently completed training for Inspiration, but hasn't had the opportunity for his students to use the application. He decides to make Inspiration the first application students will use with the new laptops and to begin with his favorite lesson that addresses civic ideals and practices. The specific social studies standard for the lesson is:

a. Identify key ideals of the United States' democratic republican form of government, such as individual human dignity, liberty, justice, equality, and the rule of law, and discuss their application in specific situations. (NCHS, 1996)

Mr. O'Malley begins the lesson with an overview and active discussion about the topic, and then asks students to work in teams of four to jot down ideas for each of the main topics (e.g., human dignity, liberty, justice) before going to the computers. When at the computers, Mr. O'Malley asks students to create a model that represents each key ideal with a labeled image and a brief definition (in their own words) of the ideal (see Figure 10.1). After each student creates a model, the class engages in a "Share and Learn" session in which they randomly visit the laptops of six students to review their models. As students visit each laptop, they take notes of what is most different and most similar compared to their own model, and they leave a note for each student to share what they like best about the model. The last activity involves students returning to their own laptops and viewing the previously created model in an outline format and exporting it to a word processing application to summarize their learning in a report.

Mr. O'Malley realizes that there are multiple benefits of using graphic organizers for this lesson. They reinforce and build on students' understanding of the lesson's content (1) each time they examine a graphic for use in the model, (2) when they explain each component in their own words, and (3) when they review others' interpretations of the same concepts. This activity engages students in higher-order thinking, yet is fun and engaging because it encourages creativity and individual expression while requiring students to focus on the content of the lesson.

Examining Graphic Organizers

As seen in the example from Mr. O'Malley's class, graphic organizers provide tools to create visual displays that depict relationships among and between various elements. Example elements might include ideas, facts, interactions, terms, and images. Common names for graphic organizers are concept maps, mind maps, advance organizers, and mental models. As seen in Figure 10.1, they typically consist of labeled icons or graphics that are linked to show relationships.

Figure 10.1 "United States Ideals" Graphic Organizer

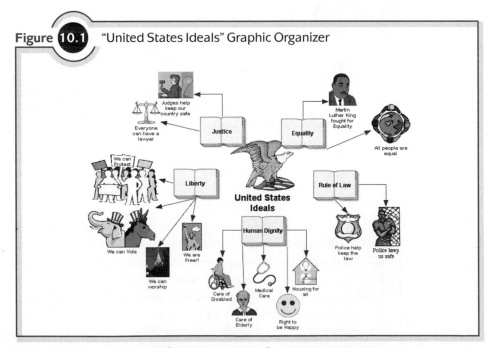

Source: Example created in Inspiration® by Inspiration Software®, Inc. Reprinted by permission.

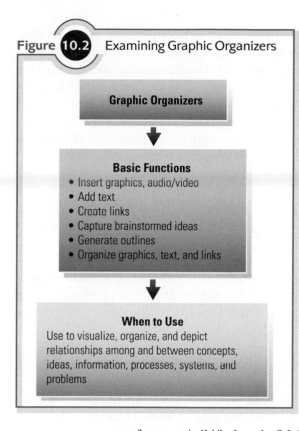

Figure 10.2 Examining Graphic Organizers

Graphic Organizers

Basic Functions
- Insert graphics, audio/video
- Add text
- Create links
- Capture brainstormed ideas
- Generate outlines
- Organize graphics, text, and links

When to Use
Use to visualize, organize, and depict relationships among and between concepts, ideas, information, processes, systems, and problems

Nondigital versions of graphic organizers have long been used as educational aids. Most textbooks include several graphic organizers, and teachers often use them to support their lectures. For example, most of us have used textbooks with diagrams of different cycles, a history timeline, or a labeled drawing indicating the key components of different systems. Most of us have also created some form of paper-based graphic organizer as part of a classroom assignment, such as a labeled drawing of a volcano, or an insect, or a map showing major cities in our state. While the idea of creating graphic organizers is important, the tediousness of drawing, coloring, and labeling the images combined with the inability to easily make changes inhibits rather than enhances learning when creating paper-based models. On the other hand, the use of digital graphic organizers such as Inspiration, SmartDraw, or free web versions like FreeMind (http://freemind .sourceforge.net/wiki/index.php/Main_Page), View your Mind (http://sourceforge .net/projects/vym) or Cmap Tools (http://cmap.ihmc.us) overcome these barriers by providing an environment that supports instantaneous creativity through a variety of functions (see Figure 10.2).

Basic Functions

Most graphic organizers have the following functions: insert graphics; add text; create links; insert/record sounds and narrations; generate outlines; and organize graphics, text, and links. Descriptions and examples of these functions follow.

Insert Graphics, Audio/Video. One of the key features of a graphic organizer is the ability to insert graphics and audio or video clips to represent components of a model. The application provides online and embedded collections of searchable clip art, photos, icons, and shapes that can easily be added to the model with a few clicks of the mouse. Graphics from other sources or student-generated images can also be easily inserted into the model.

Graphic organizers can also be personalized by inserting audio and video files. Audio files can be prerecorded sounds from the application, downloaded from the Web, an oral reading tool, or recorded files created by the students. Younger students may enhance their models by adding the sounds of animals included on a model about life on a farm. Middle school students can add oral narration of a model describing traits of the leading characters in a recently read novel. High school students can add narration that explains their reasoning for the placement of links in a model that predicts negative outcomes of overpopulation in major U.S. cities.

Similar guidelines apply when adding video to a model. The video files can be digital files from the Web, CD, or a digital video recording produced by the students. An autobiography of a student could include an interview with Aunt Aila from Finland, whereas a visual model of ancient Egyptian ruins could include video clips of legendary sites.

Add Text.   Most graphic organizers have the ability to add text to the images or links or as separate elements in the model. For clip art, photos, and intricate shapes, students can add text as a label or description adjacent to the image, whereas icons and basic shapes can serve as text boxes that contain information.

Create Links.   Relationships are expressed by creating links between and among the elements and images. Again, students can add text to a link to explain or label a relationship. The students select the link options that best represent the concepts, processes, and ideas they have visualized. The options include straight, right angle, or curved lines that can have arrowheads added to one or both ends.

Capture Brainstormed Ideas.   Many graphic organizers offer a brainstorming tool that lets the recorder type in an idea of one student and then instantly create a link and new icon ready for the next idea with a press of the Enter/Return key. This feature easily captures student thoughts as they are expressed and encourages students to add their ideas to those of others. After the brainstorming session, students can review the ideas, modifying and rearranging them into meaningful groups, without having to re-enter the information, as would be the case if a whiteboard or flip chart were used.

Generate Outlines.   Another key function of a graphic organizer is the ability to generate outlines. This function allows users to instantly move back and forth between a graphic representation or diagram view of the model and an outline of the model content (see Figure 10.3). Students can add additional information "notes" to the outline. The notes can be programmed to not appear in the diagram view. Students can export the outlines to a word processing application for further development into a report.

Figure **10.3** Graphic Organizers Easily Transition between an Outline and Diagram View

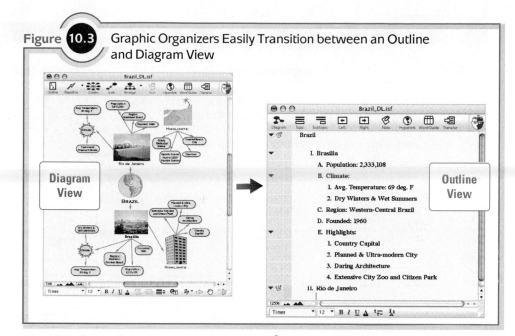

Source: Example created in Inspiration® by Inspiration Software®, Inc. Reprinted with permission.

Organize Graphics, Text, and Links. An important factor in portraying the message of the visual model is the approach used to organize graphics, text, and links. For example, students can show the passage of time in a linear model, whereas interrelationships are shown in a Venn diagram, web, or spider diagram. Table 10.1 presents a variety of organizational patterns commonly used with graphic organizers and how students can use them to increase understanding of the concepts. Tools are provided to automatically arrange the model components into the chosen format. However, it is easy to modify these prearranged formats by moving items, changing links, or adding text to create a final model that represents the desired outcomes. The links between the model components remain as they are being rearranged; however, the links are redirected or deleted as needed.

Graphic Organizers in the Classroom

Graphic organizers like Inspiration and Kidspiration are fast becoming a favorite software tool used in today's classrooms. They are very easy to use, which means that student training time is minimal. Plus, they are fun and engaging for students of all ages. To get started with a lesson, you need to know the basic functions of graphic organizers and how students can use the functions to achieve the

Table 10.1   Graphic Organizers by Type and Purpose, with Examples

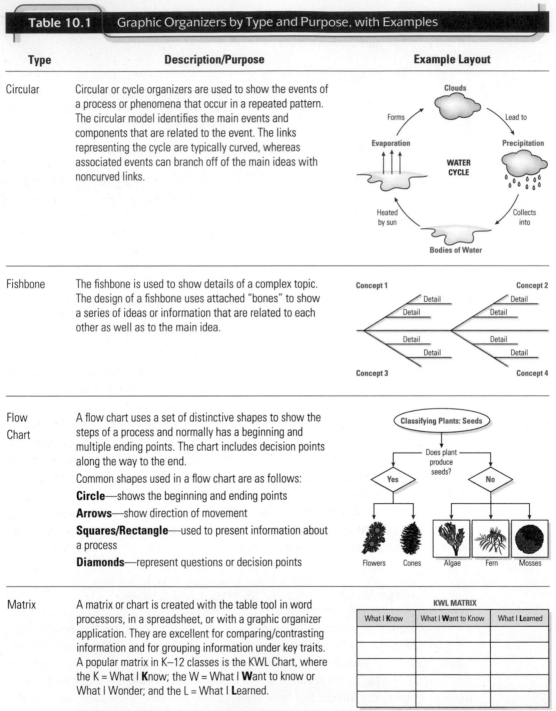

Type	Description/Purpose	Example Layout
Circular	Circular or cycle organizers are used to show the events of a process or phenomena that occur in a repeated pattern. The circular model identifies the main events and components that are related to the event. The links representing the cycle are typically curved, whereas associated events can branch off of the main ideas with noncurved links.	
Fishbone	The fishbone is used to show details of a complex topic. The design of a fishbone uses attached "bones" to show a series of ideas or information that are related to each other as well as to the main idea.	
Flow Chart	A flow chart uses a set of distinctive shapes to show the steps of a process and normally has a beginning and multiple ending points. The chart includes decision points along the way to the end. Common shapes used in a flow chart are as follows: **Circle**—shows the beginning and ending points **Arrows**—show direction of movement **Squares/Rectangle**—used to present information about a process **Diamonds**—represent questions or decision points	
Matrix	A matrix or chart is created with the table tool in word processors, in a spreadsheet, or with a graphic organizer application. They are excellent for comparing/contrasting information and for grouping information under key traits. A popular matrix in K–12 classes is the KWL Chart, where the K = What I **K**now; the W = What I **W**ant to know or What I Wonder; and the L = What I **L**earned.	

Table 10.1 *Continued*

Series	Series or chain models show the steps, stages, or sequence of events. They are different from the cycle model because they represent a linear rather than a cyclical process.	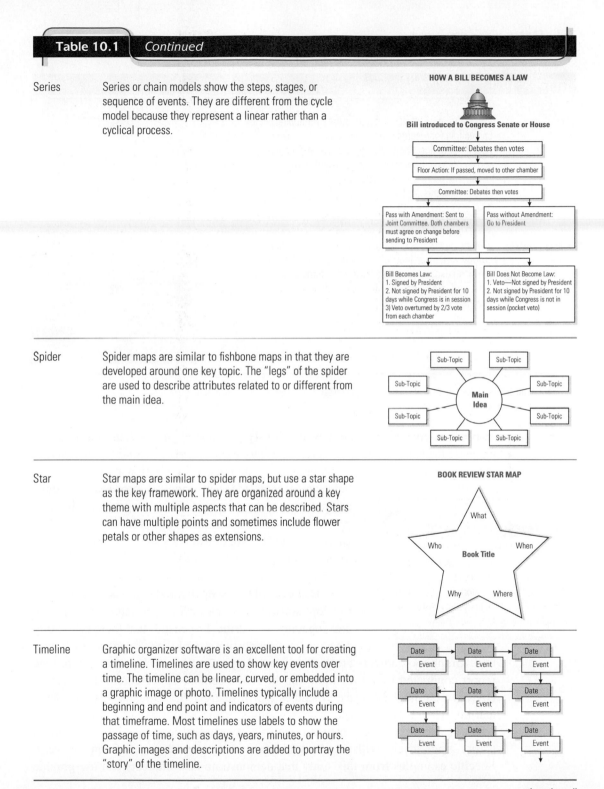
Spider	Spider maps are similar to fishbone maps in that they are developed around one key topic. The "legs" of the spider are used to describe attributes related to or different from the main idea.	
Star	Star maps are similar to spider maps, but use a star shape as the key framework. They are organized around a key theme with multiple aspects that can be described. Stars can have multiple points and sometimes include flower petals or other shapes as extensions.	
Timeline	Graphic organizer software is an excellent tool for creating a timeline. Timelines are used to show key events over time. The timeline can be linear, curved, or embedded into a graphic image or photo. Timelines typically include a beginning and end point and indicators of events during that timeframe. Most timelines use labels to show the passage of time, such as days, years, minutes, or hours. Graphic images and descriptions are added to portray the "story" of the timeline.	

(continued)

Table 10.1	*Continued*

Venn	Venn diagrams consist of two or more overlapping circles. Each circle represents a set, such as ideas, concepts, people, or things. The overlapping areas of the circles show commonalities or interrelationships between and among the representative sets in the circles. John Venn (1880), a mathematician from London, created the Venn diagram in the late 1800s.	
Web or Cluster	Web or cluster designs are nonlinear models used to portray various aspects of one or more central topics. They are often used to record student brainstorming sessions. Cluster diagrams can also be used to depict a hierarchy and compare/contrast models.	

Source: Interactive Bird Web/Cluster model reprinted by permission of the Florida Institute of Human and Machine Cognition (http://cmap.ihmc.us/conceptmap.html).

learning outcomes for a lesson. As previously shown in Figure 10.2, graphic organizers yield the best results when integrated into lessons for which student understanding is enhanced by visualizing, organizing, and depicting relationships among and between concepts, ideas, information, processes, systems, and problems. An example of student engagement in these processes is seen in the "United States Ideals" graphic organizer created by Mr. O'Malley's students. Since deeper-level learning is a goal for all students, you can integrate graphic organizers into many of your lessons.

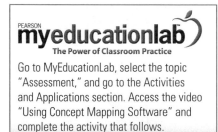

Go to MyEducationLab, select the topic "Assessment," and go to the Activities and Applications section. Access the video "Using Concept Mapping Software" and complete the activity that follows.

However, please keep in mind that it is important not to adopt software applications just because they are fun and engaging. It is critical to ensure that there is a strong research base supporting use of the software as a learning tool. Graphic organizers are well supported by scientifically based research. One report conducted by the Institute for the Advancement of Research in Education (IARE) examined 29 research studies that investigated various aspects of visual learning (IARE, 2003). The overall findings of the study revealed evidence that effective use of graphic organizers can improve student learning and performance across grade levels, with diverse students, and in a broad range of content areas. Specific examples from this study that demonstrate how students can use graphic

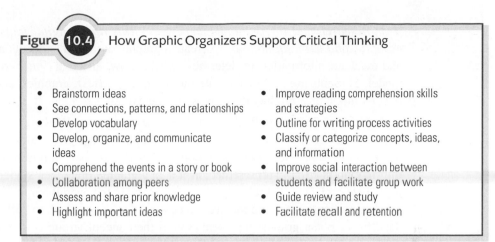

Figure **10.4** How Graphic Organizers Support Critical Thinking

- Brainstorm ideas
- See connections, patterns, and relationships
- Develop vocabulary
- Develop, organize, and communicate ideas
- Comprehend the events in a story or book
- Collaboration among peers
- Assess and share prior knowledge
- Highlight important ideas

- Improve reading comprehension skills and strategies
- Outline for writing process activities
- Classify or categorize concepts, ideas, and information
- Improve social interaction between students and facilitate group work
- Guide review and study
- Facilitate recall and retention

Source: Institute for the Advancement of Research in Education. (2003). *Graphic organizers: A review of scientifically based research* (p. 38). Charleston, WV: Appalachian Educational Lab.

organizers to achieve greater understanding and retention of concepts, processes, and information are seen in Figure 10.4.

As noted, the important factor in achieving improved student learning, achievement, and greater student attention and motivation is to implement effective lessons that have students use graphic organizers in the ways mentioned above and according to the International Society for Technology in Education (ISTE) National Educational Technology Standards for Students (NETS-S) (ISTE, 2007) as described in the next section.

Using Graphic Organizers to Achieve ISTE NETS for Students

When students engage in the development and use of graphic organizers to more closely examine and learn subject-area content as defined by curriculum standards, four of the six NETS for Students are directly addressed: (1) Creativity and Innovation; (3) Research and Information Fluency; (4) Critical Thinking, Problem Solving, and Decision Making; and (6) Technology Operations and Concepts. Details are provided below.

1. Creativity and Innovation: Students demonstrate creative thinking, construct knowledge, and develop innovative products and processes using technology. The very nature of graphic organizer software enables students to engage in creative and innovative learning activities. The use of easy-to-use tools that allow students to find just the right image to represent a concept by using a "built-in" search engine and the click of a mouse engages the learner in creative and innovative strategies. Ideas are visualized with color, text, video, and audio and arranged into patterns that explain relationships. Each product represents individual or group thinking and results in a uniquely different perspective on the targeted outcomes.

3. Research and Information Fluency: Students apply digital tools to gather, evaluate, and use information. To create a graphic organizer, students must gather and evaluate information to determine where, how, and if it "fits" on the visual model. Students use and manipulate the information (text, graphics, audio, video) to construct a final product that represents the overall goal.

4. Critical Thinking, Problem Solving, and Decision Making: Students use critical-thinking skills to plan and conduct research, manage projects, solve problems, and make informed decisions using appropriate digital tools and resources. When information is visually represented, as it is in a graphic organizer, students are able to analyze each item as it relates to other items and to the overall purpose. During the process, students often find the need to conduct further research to "fill in" missing data, find a better graphic representation of the concept, group common items together, or use a color scheme or a different arrangement to better depict the concepts and ideas and reach a solution.

6. Technology Operations and Concepts: Students demonstrate a sound understanding of technology concepts, systems, and operations. Common technology operations and associated concepts such as word processing, graphics/drawing, audio/video, search techniques, and export to other applications are embedded within a graphic organizer application. For example, when students create a graphic organizer, they use basic word processing formatting and outlining tools. The graphics and draw skills include inserting, resizing, coloring, grouping, and layering graphic images. Many graphic organizers include tools to create audio or import audio and video files. Search engines are often included with graphic image collections to enable students to use keyword searches to locate specific images. The final graphic organizer diagram or outline can be exported to word processing or presentation software.

Planning an NTeQ Lesson for Graphic Organizers

When using the NTeQ model to create lesson plans that integrate student use of graphic organizers, it is critical to ensure that use of the software will enhance achievement of the stated objectives/curriculum standards and achievement of ISTE NETS for Students. Since graphic organizer software is very adaptable for use with students in grades pre-K through high school as well as across all subject areas, you will find it easy to integrate these tools into many lesson plans. The computer activities can be planned for individual, small-group, or even whole-class creation of visual models to represent learning, as seen in the grade level and core subject-area examples in Table 10.2.

Table 10.2	Using Graphic Organizers and Problem Solving to Meet Curriculum and Technology Standards

Standards	Example Problem	Example Student Product
Elementary		
Language Arts/English		
NCTE Curriculum Standard 3: Students apply a wide range of strategies to comprehend, interpret, evaluate, and appreciate texts. *NETS-S: 1.a. Creativity and Innovation:* Students apply existing knowledge to generate new ideas, products, or processes.	When people read the same book, is their understanding of the story the same?	Each student creates a concept map depicting the key events of a story and compares it with those created by other students.
Mathematics		
NCTM Curriculum Standard (pre-K–2): Students connect number words and numerals to the quantities they represent, using various physical models and representations. *NETS-S: 1.a. Creativity and Innovation:* Students apply existing knowledge to generate new ideas, products, or processes.	Today you are going on an animal safari to see if you can discover photos of animals that are in groups of two, three, four, five, and six, as well as photos showing just one animal.	Students create a graphic organizer that has clusters for the numbers 1 through 6. Each cluster will include the numeral, number word, and at least one animal photo representing the number.
Science		
NSES Curriculum Standard Elementary (K–4): Life Science: Organisms and environments. *NETS-S: 1.c. Creativity and Innovation:* Students use models and simulations to explore complex systems and issues.	In what ways do the feet of birds differ based on the environments in which they live?	Students create a concept map that shows how bird feet are adapted to their environment through the use of photos and video.
Social Studies/History		
NCHS Curriculum Standard 2A: The student examines local architecture and landscape to compare changes in function and appearance over time. *NETS-S: 3.b. Research and Information Fluency:* Locate, organize, analyze, evaluate, synthesize, and ethically use information from a variety of sources and media.	What is different about the buildings in our town center today as compared to the buildings that were there 100 years ago?	Students create a compare/contrast map that shows "Then" and "Now" photos of a bank, grocery store, post office, drug store, and doctor's office with descriptions of what is different.

(continued)

Table 10.2	Continued

Standards	Example Problem	Example Student Product
Middle/High School		
Language Arts/English		
NCTE Curriculum Standard 9: Students develop an understanding of and respect for diversity in language use, patterns, and dialects across cultures, ethnic groups, geographic regions, and social roles. *NETS-S: 1.c. Creativity and Innovation:* Students use models and simulations to explore complex systems and issues.	How does the structure of sentences differ across cultures?	Students create a concept map that depicts basic structure for a sentence written in English as compared to Spanish, French, German, and Greek.
Mathematics		
NCTM Curriculum Standard: In grades 6–8 all students should develop, analyze, and explain methods for solving problems involving proportions. *NETS-S: 1.c. Creativity and Innovation:* Students use models and simulations to explore complex systems and issues.	What decisions are made to solve a problem involving proportions?	Students create a decision tree that includes audio descriptions for each step required to solve a problem involving proportions.
Science		
NSES Curriculum Standard (9–12): Physical Science Standards: Chemical Reactions. *NETS-S: 4.d. Critical Thinking, Problem-Solving & Decision-Making:* students use multiple processes and diverse perspectives to explore alternative solutions.	Create a map that shows the similarities and differences between an organic and an inorganic chemical reaction.	Students create a map that depicts an organic reaction and an inorganic reaction and shows how they are similar and how they are different.
Social Studies/History		
NCHS Curriculum Standard: Era 2 Colonization and Settlement (1585–1763)—Standard 2: How political, religious, and social institutions emerged in the English colonies. *NETS-S: 1.a. Creativity and Innovation:* Students apply existing knowledge to generate new ideas, products, or processes.	How did the political structure of the English colonies change over time?	Students create a timeline with graphics, photos, and audio descriptions that depict the changes in the political structure of the English colonies between 1585 and 1763.

Source: National Council of Teachers of English (NCTE). *Standards for the English Language Arts,* by the International Reading Association and the National Council of Teachers of English. Copyright 1996 by the International Reading Association and the National Council of Teachers of English. Reprinted with permission. Complete set of standards can be found at www.ncte.org/standards; National Council of Teachers of Mathematics (NCTM). *Principles and Standards for School Mathematics,* by National Council of Teachers of Mathematics Staff. Copyright 2000 by National Council of Teachers of Mathematics. Reproduced with permission of National Council of Teachers of Mathematics via Copyright Clearance Center. http://standards.nctm.org/document/appendix/numb.htm; National Science Education Standards (NSES). Reprinted with permission from *National Science Education Standards: Observe, Interact, Change, Learn,* by the National Academy of Sciences. Courtesy of the National Academies Press, Washington, DC. www.nsta.org/publications/nses.aspx; National Center for History in Schools (NCHS). Courtesy of http://nchs.ucla.edu; *National Education Technology Standards for Students,* Second Edition, © 2007, ISTE® International Society for Technology in Education, www.iste.org. All rights reserved.

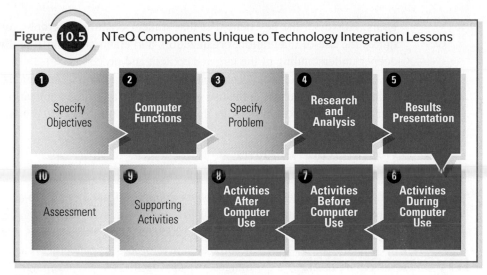

Figure **10.5**   NTeQ Components Unique to Technology Integration Lessons

1 Specify Objectives   **2** Computer Functions   **3** Specify Problem   **4** Research and Analysis   **5** Results Presentation

10 Assessment   **9** Supporting Activities   **8** Activities After Computer Use   **7** Activities Before Computer Use   **6** Activities During Computer Use

Note: Components relevant to graphic organizers are shaded.

The NTeQ Lesson

This section describes the key components of the NTeQ model, shaded in Figure 10.5, that a teacher specifically needs to address when creating lesson plans in which students use graphic organizers as a learning tool. The remaining NTeQ components, already discussed in Chapter 2, remain consistent across all lessons.

Computer Functions

When you examine a graphic organizer to determine its primary functions, the following capabilities would emerge:

- Insert graphics, audio, and/or video
- Add text
- Create links
- Capture brainstormed ideas
- Generate outlines
- Organize graphics, text, and links

The next step is to determine if any of the graphic organizer functions can be used to support the achievement of the specified objectives. As seen in Table 10.2, graphic organizers can be used to support pre-K–12 learner achievement in language arts/English, mathematics, science, and social studies. When examining the example elementary student products as opposed to the middle/high school products, it is clear that the number of functions used and the degree of complexity of the final products varies on the basis of the grade level of the students and the academic goals. However, the key benefit is that student creation of graphic organizers requires the use of integration, organization, and elaboration skills and will result in deeper understanding of the targeted content and processes.

When you use specialized applications, such as a graphic organizer, it is common to engage students in the use of all or nearly all of the application's functions. This is seen when examining the different student products listed in Table 10.2.

Research and Analysis

There are several considerations when planning the Research and Analysis component of your NTeQ lesson for graphic organizers. First, in order to achieve the benefits of using a multimedia approach to learning, such as graphic organizers, Moreno and Mayer (2000) suggest that students need to engage in three cognitive processes: selecting relevant words and images, organizing the words and images into a logical model, and integrating related components into a verbal and visual model. Thus, as students create a graphic organizer, they are engaged in all of these critical-thinking processes. For example, in order to generate a model, students must *analyze* the relevance of each model component, *synthesize* new information as the components are grouped and organized, and *evaluate* the groupings to determine if the model is illustrating what they had in mind.

Go to MyEducationLab, select the topic "Language Arts Integration," and go to the Activities and Applications section. Access the video "An Interactive Writing Project" and consider how technology is used to enhance students' writing. Complete the activity that follows.

In addition, Jonassen (2006) advocates that the important learning benefits derived from the creation of models are that model building requires students to "express and externalize their thinking, and visualize and test components of their theories" (p. 13). Thus, as you plan for student use of graphic organizers, ensure that they are engaged in all of these critical-thinking processes.

Results Presentation

The problem-solving process ends with students generating results that are used to answer or explain a solution to the problem. When using graphic organizers, the end results may or may not include a product that students generated with the graphic organizer software. Graphic organizers are often used during the preliminary stages of the problem-solving process rather than representing the final solution. For example, when students create a map of brainstormed ideas, the product is typically used to guide further research. Or when a student uses a concept map as a planning tool for a research report, the graphic organizer is a tool to help generate the final product instead of being the final product.

In contrast, graphic organizers are also excellent tools for presenting the results of problem-based lessons. The middle/high school social studies students in the example in Table 10.2 could use a graphic organizer to present their results. Specifically, the student-created timeline of changes in the political structure of the English colonies between 1585 and 1763 will allow the teacher to assess and determine student understanding and achievement of the objectives. A similar example is seen for elementary children in Table 10.2. The graphic organizer for this lesson would represent student understanding of the numerals 1 to 6, the associated number words, and the ability of students to choose an animal photo that represents the number. In other words, the final product presents the student's "Animal Safari" results. When the graphic organizer is the final product, it is beneficial to also include a brief written or digital audio recording of the student's explanation of how the product presents a solution to the lesson problem. This extension will enable you to identify any misconceptions that may not be evident in the results that are presented.

Planning Computer Activities

Please remember that the following steps are for *planning* the lesson rather than for implementing the lesson. Therefore, you begin by planning During Computer Use activities in order to develop the Before Computer Use activities. The following sections provide suggestions for planning activities in which students use graphic organizers.

Careful planning of student tasks prior to computer use can ensure successful results.

During Computer Use. At this point in the development of your NTeQ lesson plan for graphic organizers, you already know the product students will create and the graphic organizer functions they will use. So this portion of the lesson involves specifically detailing what students will do while using the computer. This planning will help you arrange for needed resources as well as inform students of the activity details.

The key considerations when planning for students to create graphic organizers are access to relevant information, graphics, and setting clear expectations for the final product. Begin with your objectives/standards to identify the scope and possible sources of relevant information students will use when creating the graphic organizers. Setting the scope of the information will help students to focus their work on the targeted content. Referring back to Table 10.2, elementary students investigating the "then" and "now" of buildings in their town center only include bank, grocery store, post office, drug store, and doctor's office. Also, parameters need to be determined for what is meant by "then"—which years qualify? Another consideration is deciding the sources students will use for the "then" and "now" photos. Availability and online security will drive the final decisions. If the library has a good collection of local history books, you may plan for students to scan photos they want to include in their products. In contrast, you may find a wide variety of archived photos available online at government and historical society websites. Your planning will help you discover the best resources for your class and your specific computer access to scanners or digital cameras to capture current photos and digitize existing photos.

One of the best ways to plan for student creation of a graphic organizer is to actually develop a sample student product. Using the identified resources will enable you to determine compatibility issues with regard to using scanned, digital camera, or downloaded images. It will also allow you to determine the appropriateness of the product scope—does it require too much information, not enough information, or information that doesn't align well with the objectives? During development of the sample product, you can also generate questions for the Think Sheet to help guide student thinking during the lesson.

This prototype can serve as a guide when showing the students how to build their own graphic organizers. Please emphasize that their graphic organizers should not look exactly like the teacher example but should reflect their creativity and expression while satisfying all of the listed criteria. In addition, although the students may possibly reach different solutions than the teacher expected, their engagement with the information will still help them achieve the lesson objectives (Resnick & Klopfer, 1987).

Once a workable prototype of the graphic organizer is developed, the teacher needs to decide how to group the students at the computer. Will individual students go to the computer and complete various activities, or is it more beneficial to have students working collaboratively? In developing a graphic organizer, it is sometimes helpful to have two or three students involved during the creation of the product because it causes the students to verbalize their thinking as well as explain visually oriented concepts. The synergism created from these small-group activities can increase the amount of meaningful learning that takes place (Jonassen, 2006).

To promote equity among student opportunities, you must estimate the number of computer tasks and then divide them among the students. This strategy gives all students opportunities for keyboarding and other computer experiences. You may need to monitor student groups to ensure that the more computer-literate students are not doing most of the computer work to avoid the struggles of less proficient members.

Before Computer Use.   After the computer activities are planned, the next step is to determine what students need to do as preparation for their computer time. These preparations can include whole-class, small-group, or individual activities depending on the learning objectives and the instructional approach used. When graphic organizers are used as a planning or brainstorming tool, students will need less time preparing for computer use but will still benefit from activities that help prepare their minds for learning. Example activities could include students creating an individual list of brainstormed ideas to be shared with the group or class when the graphic organizer is being created. Students could also sketch out a couple of layouts that show possible placement of key components to guide the computer-based process.

When students are creating graphic organizers as final products, the activities before computer use require more extensive planning. However, it is often helpful to begin precomputer work with students jotting down a list of ideas and possible graphics that might work in the final product. You may want to use one of many online paper-based graphic organizer templates to help guide the initial thinking process. Once students have a basic plan in place, they then collect data needed to create the graphic organizer. For instance, elementary students given the problem of showing how the feet of birds differ according to their habitat could use science textbooks and library books to obtain information or take notes while watching a video on adaptations of birds. Preparation can also involve Internet research, which you would plan as a separate computer activity that has its own during, before, and after components.

After Computer Use.   Once the graphic organizers are generated, students then use their Think Sheets for guidance in analyzing the information and solving the driving question or problem. During this time, students often go back and forth between their group area and their assigned computer. This activity is very engaging because students begin to discover or synthesize new information as they closely examine the graphic organizer created during the computer activity. This discovery process often leads to the development of new questions, further analysis, modifications of the final product, and a need for additional research.

It is important for students to participate in some type of culminating activity that requires them to reflect on their learning. This culminating activity can involve writing a group report that includes a copy of the final and modified graphic organizers and explanations for the changes. It could also end with a discussion of key differences that emerged in the group or individual products or ways that students would approach the problem differently, if given another opportunity. Again, all of these activities actively engage the students in multiple generative learning strategies.

Assessment

When planning assessment strategies for lessons that integrate student use of graphic organizers, the rubrics will probably have increased emphasis on organization, connections, and visual representation. For example, criteria for this aspect of performance could include some of the following:

- Relevance of key components
- Meaningful connections
- Relevant graphics
- Logical organization
- Creativity that strengthens understanding

Summary

In this chapter, we've shown how students can individually or collaboratively use graphic organizers to not only visually represent their understanding of concepts and ideas, but to also expand their knowledge by sharing and learning from others. You can integrate graphic organizers into numerous lesson plans since their functions emulate many learning objectives that focus on developing critical-thinking skills. When students create a graphic organizer, they are actively engaged in reading, analyzing, categorizing, organizing, and paraphrasing. These processes help students organize information into new and meaningful patterns that lead to a greater depth of understanding.

Teacher Technology FAQ

I've successfully used paper-based graphic organizers for years; why should I bother to switch to using computers for the same activity?

Although paper-based graphic organizers are excellent tools to engage students in higher-order thinking, they are somewhat limiting because students cannot easily change ideas and the patterns are not flexible. When students use a digital application, they can easily change text descriptions, but they can also search multiple graphic images to find the one that best represents their thinking, add and change colors, move icons, and change links. They can also look at the overall product in multiple layouts to find the best fit to display the overall idea.

Creating and using a graphic organizer seems to be a pretty complicated process. How can younger students do this?

One approach is to use an application specifically designed for younger children, such as Kidspiration. It includes brighter colors, simpler graphics, and offers a feature that reads all of the menu options aloud to assist early readers.

Technology Integration Activities

The following activities provide an opportunity for you to explore the options for using graphic organizers as described in this chapter.

1. Create one lesson for each of the ten types of graphic organizers.
2. Conduct an Internet search to locate graphic organizers for your content area. Develop a lesson plan that uses the graphic organizer as a starting place for student groups to create their own model.

Lesson Bytes for Graphic Organizers

The following list contains suggestions for graphic organizers that can be created by elementary and middle/high school students.

Elementary Students

Language Arts
- Create a story timeline for a book.
- Plan the contents of a newsletter about fairy tales.
- Show the steps to create a perfect paragraph.
- Create a concept map showing the most common spelling mistakes.

Mathematics
- Create a "shapes in nature" model to show naturally occurring shapes.
- Demonstrate fractions with photos of food.
- Create a decision tree for subtraction.
- Compare and contrast geometric shapes.

Science
- Compare the digestive systems of insects, reptiles, birds, and mammals.
- Depict cell division with images other than cells.
- Demonstrate the most common genetic traits of your classmates.
- Plot the "life" of a plastic bottle.

Social Studies
- Show differences in the homes of Native Americans living in different regions during the 1800s.
- Create a timeline of a vote.
- Show the population diversity of your county.
- Develop the "history of" a modern technology (e.g., phone, car).

Middle and High School Students
English
- Create a model showing factors that may have influenced the style of writing used by an American author.
- Use graphics to depict the traits of the main characters of a book.
- Create a concept web showing the key features of different genres.
- Develop a step-by-step model for writing an effective literature review.

Mathematics
- Create a graphic model of a word problem.
- Diagram the key functions in calculus.
- Use shapes to represent an algebraic problem.
- Create a tessellation.

Science
- Demonstrate negative impacts of global warming on plants.
- Create a graphic model that depicts DNA functions.
- Show examples of Newton's laws in a motorcycle.
- Compare and contrast types of volcanoes.

History
- Compare the similarities and differences of Kennedy and Lincoln.
- Show three landmarks that should be added as national historical landmarks.
- Brainstorm ideas that describe a "perfect" U.S. president.
- Create a timeline of key Civil War events.

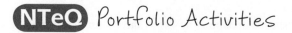

NTeQ Portfolio Activities

Please complete the following activities as part of the graphic organizer section of your NTeQ Portfolio.

Reflections

The Getting Ready section of this chapter posed three Reflecting on What I Know questions that teachers might commonly ask. In this portion of your journal, reflection activities have been added to address how you would answer each question. Please use information from this chapter to answer the questions.

1 **How do you know that students understand a concept?**

Reflection Activity: Provide an example of how use of a graphic organizer can help a student go beyond memorization to deeper understanding and learning.

2 **How can you depict student misconceptions of key information?**

Reflection Activity: Discuss how a student-generated graphic organizer can assist you in identifying student misconceptions of key content, concepts, and processes. Expand this to show how a student can also use graphic organizers to identify his or her misconceptions.

3 **How can students capture and transfer brainstorming ideas into written thoughts?**

Reflection Activity: Describe how you would prepare a brainstorming activity that engages all students while reinforcing the lesson's objectives.

Lesson Bytes

Create a list of ten graphic organizers that would be meaningful for your students to create. You can use the Lesson Bytes from this chapter or your curriculum standards to help you generate ideas. Expand five of the ideas by actually creating examples. Then write a problem statement that could be used to direct the focus of a lesson in which students created each graphic organizer.

Lesson Plan

As a final demonstration of your understanding of how to have students use graphic organizers as a tool to enhance learning, select an appropriate topic and follow the NTeQ Lesson Plan Template to create a graphic organizer lesson. Make sure to create a sample graphic organizer that students would submit with or as their final product.

 **NTeQ** Lesson Plan

Lesson Title: **Moving to South America!**

Subject Area: **Social Studies**

Grade Level: **8**

Learning Objectives

Given access to the Internet and a graphic organizer application, the students will create a product that compares the population, climate, landmarks, points of interest, and cultures of two major cities in South America.

Computer Functions

1. In this lesson, students will use a graphic organizer to

   - create a written outline
   - search for graphics
   - insert text, graphic symbols, images, and arrows
   - format text, graphics, symbols, images, and arrows to create the desired model
   - arrange components to create the desired model

2. They will use the Internet to locate information and graphics.

Specify Problem

The executive director of the international company for which you work has asked that you transfer to your choice of seven offices located in different Brazilian cities. You've narrowed the decision to two cities but need assistance in making the final choice. Your current supervisor has asked that you create a visual representation of the pros and cons of both locations to help in the decision-making process.

Research and Analysis

- The students will use keyword searches to locate information and graphics associated with the selected cities.
- The students will create a written outline comparing the two cities of choice on population, climate, landmarks, points of interest, and culture.
- The students will use graphics and descriptions to illustrate the differences between both cities by creating one concept map that illustrates the differences and highlights the similarities.

Results Presentation

Each student is required to create a concept map that compares and contrasts the required facts and any "fun facts" for both cities (see Figure 10.6).

Planning Computer Activities

Before Computer Use

- Teacher introduces the problem and guides the class through the beginning problem-solving steps.
- Students review textbooks and library books to identify cities of choice.
- Students create checklist for specific facts required and ideas for "fun" facts.

Figure **10.6** Graphic Organizer Comparing Two Brazilian Cities

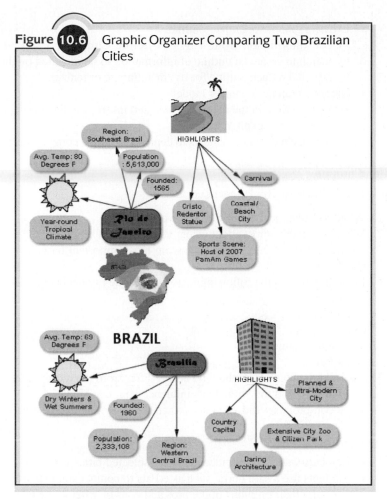

Source: Example created in Inspiration® by Inspiration Software®, Inc. Reprinted with permission.

- Students plan computer tasks:
  - Create rough draft of graphic organizer outline.
  - Sketch out possible model to display information.
  - List ideas for images to represent ideas.

During Computer Use

Students engage in the following tasks:

- Conduct an Internet search.
  - Paraphrase and obtain citation information for text-based information.
  - Download and obtain citation information for graphic images.

- Create a graphic organizer outline.
  - Use information from activities Before Computer Use and the Internet search to create an outline of information to be included on the model.
  - Edit and reduce outline for use in a graphic organizer.
- Create a graphic organizer model.
  - View outline in the diagram mode and insert graphics to support text.
  - Insert text to explain links.
  - Arrange model components to depict the desired comparison between cities.

After Computer Use

Answer the following Think Sheet questions:

1. What do I like most about where I live now?
2. What do I dislike most about where I live now?
3. Of the required facts, which ones seem most important based on my answers to Questions 1 and 2?
4. In what ways did the following factors influence my decision:
   a. Population
   b. Climate
   c. Landmarks
   d. Points of interest
   e. Culture
5. How did the "fun" facts that you added differ from the required facts?
6. In what ways did the "fun" facts influence your decision?
7. What compromises did you make when selecting the final destination?

Supporting Activities

- Students watch travel videos for their selected cities.
- Students use a safe portal such as e-Pals to contact students living in the cities to obtain their opinions of the pros and cons of where they live.

Assessment

Create a rubric for assessing the following components of the final product:

Content

- Association of information and graphics to the selected cities
- Meaningfulness of the city comparisons

Graphic organizer

- Layout support of overall purpose
- Appropriate use of arrows
- Appropriate use of graphic features, such as color, size, line weight, and pattern

Source: Adapted from a lesson developed by Michael Tucker and John Marquart; used with permission.

Chapter 11

Integrating Problem-Solving and Educational Software

Getting Started

This chapter extends information provided in Chapter 4, Computer Software in Today's Classrooms, by providing more detailed information on how to integrate problem-solving and educational software into lessons and the benefits of doing so. The chapter discusses ways to evaluate the software and presents guidelines to develop NTeQ lessons that integrate meaningful student use of problem-solving and educational software.

Reflecting on What I Know

1 What are the benefits of using problem-solving or educational software?

2 How do I choose the correct software?

3 When I integrate problem-solving or educational software into a lesson, what changes will be needed?

Classroom SNAPSHOT

First let's go to High Marks Elementary School, the technology showcase of the district. Every classroom has three to five computers and the library has numerous software programs in all content areas. Ms. New-Trend, the principal, enthusiastically encourages all teachers to integrate technology into their lessons. To gain the attention of the principal, the lead fifth-grade teacher, Mr. Try-It-All, regularly goes to the library to select just the right software for each lesson. This week, he begins by scanning titles in the social studies section to find something about U.S. agriculture. A box covered with brightly colored vegetables and fruit, titled "Farmland," catches his attention. After quickly reading the software box to see if it will be fun for the students, he decides that Farmland is his computer integration activity for this week. He writes Farmland in the "technology integration" section of his weekly lesson plan, loads the software on Computer 2, and adds time to the weekly schedule for pairs of students to "use" the software during a 20-minute rotation plan. As Mr. Try-It-All introduces the lesson on U.S. agriculture, he indicates that students will "use" the Farmland software on Computer 2 for this week's computer activity. He tells students to begin by clicking on the ear of corn and spend 20 minutes exploring the various aspects of the program, while they "think about" U.S. agriculture.

Next, let's visit Meaningful Learning Middle School, the district's top-achieving school. The principal, Ms. High Standards, also enthusiastically encourages all teachers to integrate technology; however, the computer activities must be standards-based and well supported with classroom activities. In an effort to enhance student learning and meet the high criteria for technology integration set by the principal, the lead seventh-grade language arts teacher, Ms. Commendable, regularly goes to the library to select the most appropriate software for each lesson. This week, she begins by reviewing the curriculum standards for each lesson, then scanning software titles in the language arts section to find specific lessons to help her students achieve the targeted standards. She locates three software programs that we'll call Programs 1, 2, and 3 that seem appropriate for her lesson. Programs 1 and 2 have district labels indicating that the software has been evaluated by district teachers. She asks the librarian to see the evaluations, which reveal that Program 2 is rated highly and well aligned to her lesson goals, while Program 1 lacks sufficient student feedback to support learning. She decides to check out Programs 2 and 3, the newer one that lacked an evaluation.

Ms. Commendable selects two lessons from each program to review. She goes through each lesson as if she were a seventh-grade student to check ease of navigation, reading level, and how well each provides practice and feedback for the targeted standards. She agrees with the positive evaluation for Program 2 and finds that it is very well aligned with the lesson goals. She decides to complete the district software evaluation form for Program 3 and finds that although it is based on a newer multimedia gaming approach targeted to raise student attention, the underlying support for improving student learning is minimal. Therefore, the two lessons from Program 2 are integrated into her week's lessons as a student rotation activity to be completed on Computers 1, 2, and 3. She begins with an overview of the key concepts for the week, emphasizing those to be learned during computer time. There are three activities related to use of the educational software. The first is to be completed before using the computer to assist with recall of prerequisite skills needed for the software activities. The second involves students completing the two designated lessons. And the final activity involves students applying their newly practiced skills after the computer lessons have been completed.

The strategies for integrating educational software portrayed by our Ms. Commendable character reflect the key ideas and approaches of the NTeQ model. This chapter provides you with the information and tools to integrate problem-solving and educational software into your instruction in a meaningful way.

Choosing the Right Software

Producers of educational software are taking advantage of the increased availability of computers in today's classrooms and homes by creating vast varieties of educational software. This never-ending supply of games, simulations, and drill-and-practice packages "guarantee" to teach children everything from basic math skills to advanced physics. And of course, no "guarantee" would be complete without a knowledgeable vendor to convince you of the software's credibility and value. When you combine the sheer number of available educational software programs with the skillful tactics of salespersons, it is obvious that educators need some basic guidelines to assist them in making wise purchase decisions. This section discusses the benefits of problem-solving and educational software, criteria

The Power of Classroom Practice

Go to MyEducationLab, select the topic "Assessment," and go to the Activities and Applications section. Access the video "Drill and Practice" and complete the activity that follows.

for assessing software, types of software reviews, and two approaches to software evaluation. The following section provides guidance for integrating problem-solving and educational software into NTeQ lessons.

Benefits of Problem-Solving Software

Problem-solving software seen in today's classrooms increasingly includes games and simulations. The benefits of well-designed games and simulations go beyond increased student attention and motivation; "game players exercise a skill set closely matching the thinking, planning, learning, and technical skills increasingly demanded by employers in a wide range of industries" (Federation of Scientists, 2006, p. 2).

A key benefit of well-designed educational games is that they are structured to require application of content knowledge and skills in order to "win" the game, which results in students wanting to learn the information rather than learning it to pass a test. In other words, "games offer second-by-second decision making that takes players over and over through the loop of decision, action, feedback, and reflection that is the basis for all learning" (Prensky, 2007, p. 1). The benefits of games are further demonstrated by Oblinger (2004, p. 7), who delineates how the use of games supports selected principles of effective pedagogy (Table 11.1).

Similar benefits are found for student use of simulations. In a study examining the effects of simulation and higher-order software on the mathematics achievement of over 13,000 middle school students, improved performance was demonstrated for those who used the software (Wenglinsky, 1998). Features of computer simulation software that contribute to increased student learning include the ability of students to manipulate components of a simulated environment. Example manipulations include viewing multiple angles of a bridge, zooming in for a macro view of DNA, or conducting experiments to compare nuclear chain reactions. The software provides the tools and environment to support and actively engage students in critical-thinking activities that require real-world application of knowledge and skills.

Benefits of Educational Software

Over the years, numerous studies have examined the learning benefits of using educational software such as drill and practice, tutorials, and integrated learning systems (ILS). Meta-analyses of this research indicate that student achievement in basic skills does improve if the software is regularly used according to suggested implementation guidelines (Kulik, 1994, 2003; Mann, Shakeshaft, Becker, & Kottkamp, 1999; Sivin-Kachala, 1998). One of the key benefits of drill-and-practice software is the opportunity for students to engage in interactive basic skills practice that provides immediate

Table 11.1	Principles of Effective Pedagogy Applied in Educational Games	
Principle	**Description**	**Application in Games**
Individualization	Learning is tailored to the needs of the individual	Games adapt to the level of the individual
Feedback	Immediate and contextual feedback improves learning and reduces uncertainty	Games provide immediate and contextualized feedback
Active learning	Learning should engage the learner in active discovery and construction of new knowledge	Games provide an active environment which leads to discovery
Motivation	Students are motivated when presented with meaningful and rewarding activities	Games engage users for hours of engagement in pursuit of a goal
Social	Learning is a social and participatory process	Games can be played with others (e.g., multiplayer games) or involve communities of users interested in the same game
Scaffolding	Learners are gradually challenged with greater levels of difficulty in a progression that allows them to be successful in incremental steps	Games are built with multiple levels; players cannot move to a higher level until competence is displayed at the current level
Transfer	Learners develop the ability to transfer learning from one situation to another	Games allow users to transfer information from an existing context to a novel one
Assessment	Individuals have the opportunity to assess their own learning and/or compare it to that of others	Games allow users to evaluate their skill and compare themselves to others

individual performance feedback. Most are colorful and use artwork designed for the target grade level. Some use a game format that is competitive and motivational.

Most of today's tutorial software uses a multimedia combination of animation, video, and interactivity to teach students new information and basic skills. The major benefit of well-designed tutorials is that they can produce favorable results. For example, when Kulik (2002) examined the results of 36 studies investigating the use of educational software, he found that use of tutorials increased student learning in mathematics and science and resulted in more positive attitudes about these subject areas.

The primary benefits of ILS are that they provide instructional content, mastery-type practice, feedback, and assessments that are aligned to state standards of the purchaser and tracked by individual students. Although ILS programs

With careful planning, NTeQ lessons can be enhanced by integrating appropriate educational software.

have a long history of increasing student performance in mathematics, their success is less evident for other subjects such as reading (Kulik, 2003). Suggestions for improving the effectiveness of ILS use include increasing student time using the product and integrating and supporting ILS in regular classroom instruction (Kulik, 2003).

Software Evaluation

Since there is such a wide variety of software available to teachers, it is critical to evaluate the educational soundness of the software, preferably before purchasing the product. Begin by determining why you want your students to use the software and how you will know if use of the software helped students achieve the learning objectives. Do this by identifying criteria to judge software effectiveness and then deciding how to use the criteria as a basis for using software reviews or conducting software evaluations.

Software Evaluation Criteria

When examining criteria commonly used to evaluate educational software, the following are consistently recommended: content accuracy, research-based instructional strategies, alignment with instructional objectives, assessment of learning, and ease of use (ESPG, 2007; Gill, Dick, Reiser, & Zahner, 1992; Hubbard, 1992; Wrench, 2001). Other items of interest that may be evaluated are teacher support materials, technology system requirements, and software features not addressed in the list below (e.g., providing student tools such as a calculator, glossary, or journal).

It is important to keep the following criteria in mind when examining software reviews or choosing an evaluation format when selecting software to use with your students (see Figure 11.1):

1. Content accuracy (information is correct, current, and consistent)
2. Research-based instructional strategies
   a. Learner control of program features (sound, pace, sequence, etc.)
   b. Variety of appropriate feedback
   c. Motivational and interesting
3. Effectively meets instructional objectives
   a. Content is aligned to objectives
   b. Practice and feedback are aligned to objectives
4. Assessment of learning (student attainment of objectives is assessed)
5. Ease of use
   a. Technical quality
   b. Precise and consistent directions
   c. Appropriate reading level for target audience

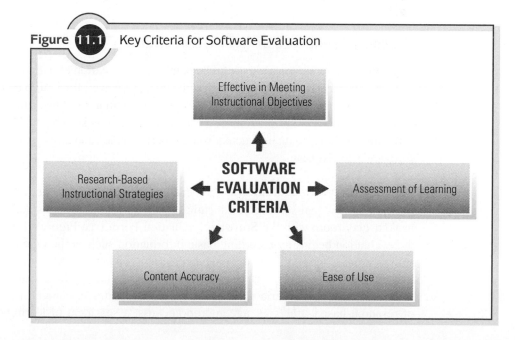

Figure 11.1 Key Criteria for Software Evaluation

Software Reviews

If you examine the online Educational Software Preview Guide (ESPG) hosted by the Education Office of Fermi National Accelerator Laboratory, you will find the titles of over 1000 software programs that have received "favorable" reviews for use in pre-K–12 classrooms (ESPG, 2007). Other popular sites that include software reviews by educators are SuperKids (www.superkids.com), Discovery Education (http://school.discoveryeducation.com), Learning Village (www.learningvillage .com/html/guide.html), Teachers Evaluating Educational Multimedia (TEEM) (www.teem.org.uk), and Children's Technology Review (www.childrenssoftware .com/default.html).

With so many software review options, making a decision on which one to use can become confusing. We suggest the following guidelines for using software reviews. First, read potential reviews to determine the degree to which the software evaluation criteria (p. 287) are addressed. Second, determine if the review addresses other items related to the particular needs of your students, such as provision for modifications for learners needing special accommodations. The next decision is to determine whether the reviewer will provide the most useful information for your situation. Reviews can be conducted by a variety of people, including teachers, parents, children, university faculty, graduate students, and professional reviewers (Gill et al., 1992; Rickenberg, 1996; Wong, 2006). It is often helpful to examine reviews completed by a variety of reviewers to obtain a more comprehensive perspective.

Teacher-Conducted Software Evaluation

Software reviews can provide useful background information about a piece of educational software and its perceived effectiveness. However, for you to be confident that the software will meet the needs of your particular students, you may want to conduct your own evaluation. The evaluation can consist of your review of the software and can also include actual student performance and attitude data to verify software effectiveness.

Teacher Software Evaluation. You can use your own experience and expertise to evaluate problem-solving or educational software you are considering for use in your classroom with the Software Evaluation Form (see Figure 11.2). As seen, the evaluation begins by recording basic information such as the type of software, subject area, grade level, and the intended learning objectives. After these items are identified, you rate several aspects of the software, including those that address the software evaluation criteria noted previously—for example, content accuracy, use of research-based strategies, age appropriateness, assessment of learning, ease of

Figure 11.2 Teacher-Conducted Software Evaluation

Software Evaluation Form

Title: _____

Type of Software: ❑ Drill and Practice   ❑ Tutorial
                       ❑ Game   ❑ Simulation   ❑ Other _____

Grade Level _____ Subject Area _____ Specific Topic _____

Key Instructional Objectives:

_____

_____

_____

Rating
Use the scale below to rate the following aspects of the software.

	Yes	Somewhat	No
Content is accurate	❑	❑	❑
Content is appropriate for specified age group	❑	❑	❑
Instructional strategies are research-based "best practices"	❑	❑	❑
The software will maintain student interest	❑	❑	❑
Instructional objectives are thoroughly addressed	❑	❑	❑
Learners control various features (e.g., sound, pace, sequence)	❑	❑	❑
Assessment of learning is appropriate	❑	❑	❑
A variety of appropriate feedback is provided	❑	❑	❑
Software is easy to use	❑	❑	❑
Technical quality is high	❑	❑	❑
Software is appropriate for your students	❑*	❑	❑

*If yes, what activities would be most useful for your students?

_____   _____

_____   _____

_____   _____

Describe how you would integrate the software into your instruction. _____

_____

_____

_____

NOTES: _____

_____

_____

use, and suitability of the software for your students. If it is appropriate, space is provided to list activities that would be most useful for your students, to describe how the software would be integrated into your instruction, and to add any notes that may help when the software is used.

Software Evaluation with Student Performance and Attitudes. Another well-established approach proposed by Reiser and Dick (1990) determines whether or not students actually learn from the software and what they like and do not like about using it. This approach takes more time and teacher involvement than completing an evaluation form. However, the benefits of collecting student performance and attitude data outweigh the effort when considering the purchase of an expensive educational software package to integrate into your curriculum. Before conducting this level of evaluation, it is important to begin with software that has received posi-

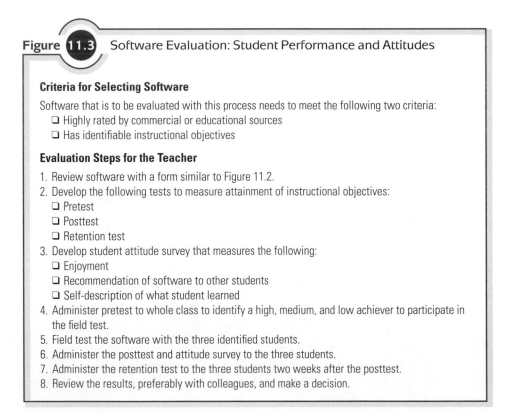

Figure 11.3 Software Evaluation: Student Performance and Attitudes

Criteria for Selecting Software

Software that is to be evaluated with this process needs to meet the following two criteria:
- ❏ Highly rated by commercial or educational sources
- ❏ Has identifiable instructional objectives

Evaluation Steps for the Teacher

1. Review software with a form similar to Figure 11.2.
2. Develop the following tests to measure attainment of instructional objectives:
   - ❏ Pretest
   - ❏ Posttest
   - ❏ Retention test
3. Develop student attitude survey that measures the following:
   - ❏ Enjoyment
   - ❏ Recommendation of software to other students
   - ❏ Self-description of what student learned
4. Administer pretest to whole class to identify a high, medium, and low achiever to participate in the field test.
5. Field test the software with the three identified students.
6. Administer the posttest and attitude survey to the three students.
7. Administer the retention test to the three students two weeks after the posttest.
8. Review the results, preferably with colleagues, and make a decision.

Source: Adapted from R. A. Reiser & W. Dick, Evaluating instructional software, *Educational Technology Research and Development, 38*(3), 43–50, 1990.

tive ratings from commercial or educational software reviewers and that is structured on identifiable objectives. In other words, you want to ensure that the software has promising potential before you determine whether it is actually effective in improving student learning. Software companies often provide a review copy that can be used for prepurchase evaluations. The criteria for software selection and the evaluation steps for this approach can be seen in Figure 11.3.

Planning an NTeQ Lesson for Problem-Solving and Educational Software

The process for integrating problem-solving and educational software into your instruction is similar to integrating other types of computer use into a lesson, except that, as seen in the previous section, the software should be evaluated or selected from trusted software reviews before considering it for inclusion in lessons. The following section describes how to use the NTeQ model to meaningfully integrate problem-solving and educational software into your curriculum.

It is important for teachers to carefully evaluate educational software before having students use it during a lesson.

Six Key Components

All ten components of the NTeQ lesson plan (see Figure 11.4) are addressed when integrating *problem-solving* or *educational software* into a lesson, but only six differ from an NTeQ lesson plan that does not integrate these applications. These six will be discussed in the section below:

> Computer Functions
>
> Research and Analysis
>
> Results Presentation
>
> Activities During Computer Use
>
> Activities Before Computer Use
>
> Activities After Computer Use

Computer Functions

To determine if use of problem-solving or educational software will enhance student ability to achieve objectives, identify the basic functions of the problem-solving or educational software to see whether they align with the objectives (see the Appendix). Although the level of interactivity may vary greatly between problem-solving games and simulations as compared to drill and practice or tutorials, the basic func-

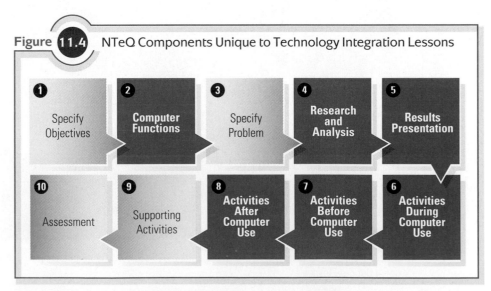

Figure 11.4 NTeQ Components Unique to Technology Integration Lessons

1. Specify Objectives
2. Computer Functions
3. Specify Problem
4. Research and Analysis
5. Results Presentation
10. Assessment
9. Supporting Activities
8. Activities After Computer Use
7. Activities Before Computer Use
6. Activities During Computer Use

Note: Components relevant to educational or problem-solving software are shaded.

Go to MyEducationLab, select the topic "Software," and go to the Building Teaching Skills and Dispositions section. Open "Supporting Instruction with Technology" and complete the activity.

tions of both types of software primarily fall into three main categories: providing content, providing practice and feedback, and providing process tools.

Providing Content. The function of providing content includes such formats as descriptions, definitions, examples and nonexamples, diagrams, photographs, images, animations, maps, or any type of information to be learned by the students. One way to think about this information is to group it by facts, concepts, principles and rules, procedures, interpersonal skills, and attitudes (Morrison, Ross, & Kemp, 2006). For example, the content area of a software program could be 18th-century British literature, basic shapes, or the water cycle. The content can be provided in any combination of text to be read by the student or computer features, such as interactive animations or static graphics videos, or as narration that does not have the script provided on the screen.

Providing Practice and Feedback. The next main function of problem-solving or educational software is the provision of practice and feedback. This is the most unique aspect of the software because it creates a learning environment that is *interactive*. The software can be programmed to provide "individualized" feedback based on student input into the program. Within games and simulations, the feedback is given in response to student manipulation of various components. For example, students using the OnScreen Particle Physics software can manipulate subatomic particle decay with tools provided with the simulated detection chamber (see Figure 11.5).

For drill and practice and tutorials, the feedback is available in several forms (Morrison, Ross, Gopalakrishnan, & Casey, 1995):

Correctness of response (right or wrong)

Answer until correct

Review of material if wrong answer is given

Branching to next material based on performance

    Advancement

    Reinforcement

    Remediation

The practice and feedback function is what separates educational software from digitized reference materials, such as CD-ROM encyclopedias, that primarily provide content. Although some of the newer reference materials have added some interactivity into the programs, it typically involves learner choice to hear an audio file, view a video, or activate an animation of a concept or process.

Figure 11.5 Screenshot of Interactive Tools Used to Manipulate Subatomic Particles

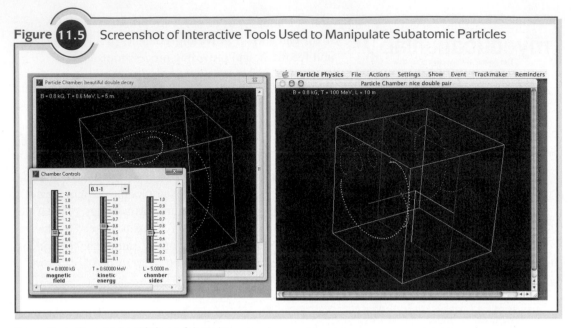

Source: Used with permission of OnScreen Science, Inc.

Providing Process Tools. The final primary function of educational software is providing process tools. The tools can include prompts or they can be stand-alone tools. The tools that provide prompts are different from basic application tools in that the learner is given tips or guidance at varying stages of the process that is being learned. For example, if students are using educational software that provides them with tools that help with the writing process, they might receive prompts similar to the following when learning to write a book review:

- Write a sentence that describes the main character.
- Choose the drawing that best shows how the main character felt at the beginning of the story, and then write one sentence to describe the feeling.
- Choose a drawing that shows how the main character felt at the end of the story and write two sentences to describe the feeling.

Process tools that do not include prompts include those used to create calendars or timelines, graph information, create shapes, and so on. Most of these software programs have underlying preformatted templates that still allow for creativity but offer less freedom than basic application tools. The key advantage is that the preprogramming of process tools allows students to concentrate on and learn the concepts or processes rather than worry about computer skills. For example, Geometer's Sketchpad provides dynamic tools that enable students to construct and

Figure **11.6**   Interactive Tools to Manipulate Objects in Geometer's Sketchpad

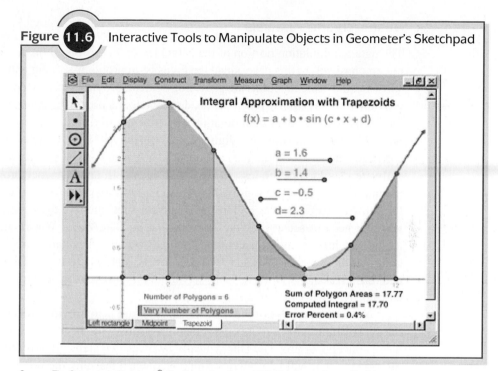

Source: The Geometer's Sketchpad®. Key Curriculum Press, 1150 65th Street, Emeryville, CA 94608, 1-800-995-MATH, www.keypress.com. Reprinted by permission.

change objects by dragging points and lines with the mouse while examining the associated mathematical relationships (see Figure 11.6).

Software Selection.   Once you have determined that integrating one or more of the functions of problem-solving or educational software will enhance student attainment of the lesson objectives, you then select the appropriate software. If the functions that align with your objectives are to provide content and practice with feedback, then you will need to consider the content area, grade level, and the quality and appropriateness of the activities. If the function that aligns with your objectives involves process tools, you will need to match the type of needed process skills with those provided by the software.

Much of the information needed to select software is provided by software reviews or product descriptions. For example, the Educational Software Preview Guide (ESPG, 2007) has the following information for each reviewed program: title, publisher, subject area, grade level, instructional mode (e.g., drill and practice, problem solving, simulation, tutorial), and hardware (platform/operating system); it also has the ability to search by any of the descriptors.

Research and Analysis

The data manipulation portion of the NTeQ lesson varies based on the function being emphasized. In this case, since the focus is on problem-solving and educational software, the basic functions are providing content, providing practice/feedback, and providing process tools. When the needed function is providing content or practice/ feedback, then the data manipulation involves identifying the specific sections or portions of the software that align with the objectives. For example, language arts software may have 15 practice lessons for identifying parts of speech, social studies software may include ten lessons about World War II, and a science program could include three sections that provide tools to build various portions of DNA. Unless the entire software package addresses student achievement of the lesson objectives, you will need to select only the portions that do. The World War II software may include the history and impact of the conflict, as well as key battles and other lesson topics. If the primary lesson objective is for the students to understand the history and impact, assign only these sections. Students can cover the remaining sections as enhancement activities, if time permits.

When the purpose of the educational software is to provide process tools, then the data manipulation will involve students working with the tools to learn the designated concepts or process. This typically involves two steps: identifying the data or information that will be used or manipulated when learning the process and selecting the specific process tool(s). For example, software that teaches and supports the writing process may have lessons on several different types of writing projects—for example, book reviews, friendly letters, or persuasive arguments. If your lesson is to have students learn how to write friendly letters, in order to plan the research and analysis you will need to determine the recipient and the content of the letters (even if just "free choice" of the students). The second step is choosing the friendly letter lesson from the writing process software.

Results Presentation

The results presentation portion of the NTeQ lesson may or may not be applicable based on the function being emphasized: providing content, providing practice/ feedback, or providing process tools. Final products are not created when students use software to learn and explore new content, such as examining the structure of a bridge or learning the differences between adjectives and adverbs. Some software may allow students to print out the results of practice activities or products created when using process tools; however, the format and structure of the products typically are predetermined by the software. As you plan for the use of problem-based or educational software, examine the program to determine if any student products or progress reports can be generated.

The Teacher's
Diary

One of the most memorable events this year was watching my students working together on a project I put together about Martin Luther King, Jr. I researched to find several excellent Internet sites about MLK, obtained the Timeliner software, and then put together some project ideas.

The groups began by creating a timeline of key events in the life of Martin Luther King, Jr. Students then worked in groups of two, and I assigned them a project topic. Some topics were much more advanced than others, so I assigned the more difficult topics to students who had demonstrated the ability to handle higher-level thinking tasks.

Most of the assignment topics were given to two groups of students. The class became deeply involved in research and discussion. I wandered around the classroom, stopping to answer questions and to monitor the progress of each group. Watching the groups do their work and noting the direction that each group intended to go made me feel thankful to be a part of these young people's lives. Even groups assigned to the same topic were attacking the project in different ways, which I always encourage.

Two groups were given the task of finding a movement similar to the Civil Rights Movement that exists today. Both groups were frustrated at first. "Help us, Mrs. Shoemaker. We have no idea how to even research this!" I hinted to both groups to think of issues that we've been discussing in social studies class, but didn't say more. The frustra-

tion continued for about 15 minutes, as these two groups watched other groups around them, feeling like they were way behind the progress of other groups. However, both groups came to me when they thought of the direction they intended to go with the project. One group decided to research the events that happened in Kosovo. The other group decided to focus on women's rights. Both groups were so proud of themselves for coming up with the project idea on their own. The discussion that I overheard was fascinating. The students became more and more involved as they became more aware of other injustices in the world. One of the students became so involved in the study of women's rights that I've told her since that I believe she will be the first woman to be President.

What was so enjoyable to me was seeing how involved the students were. The projects turned out so much better than I ever imagined, and they all looked very different. I believe that every one of my students now has a whole new outlook about the significance of Martin Luther King, Jr., and what he did for our country. These projects were meaningful to each and every one of my students, and the computers made this possible.

Pam Shoemaker
Sixth-Grade Teacher

Planning Computer Activities

When planning NTeQ lessons, begin with the activities *during* computer use in order to know what you are preparing students for in the activities *before* computer use.

During Computer Use.   Planning what students do at the computer while using the selected software is pretty well designated by the time you reach this portion of the lesson planning. When students use application tools, you must plan for students to set up the format, enter data, and complete a variety of manipulations. Problem-solving or educational software requires minimal planning because the software is already programmed. To plan the computer time, you will need to determine how many computers will have the software, how you will let students know exactly which sections or lessons they will be completing, and whether they will work alone or with other students. It might be helpful to "cue up" the software before each student comes to the computer if the designated lesson is not easily accessible.

Before Computer Use.   Activities to get students ready to use educational software will again vary based on the functions that are being emphasized. If the software will be providing new content or practice and feedback, students may need to complete activities that will provide reinforcement of prerequisite knowledge and skills required to complete the assigned lessons. This might involve reviewing designated sections of the textbook, reading a library book or periodical, completing workbook activities, or watching a video. If the lesson is primarily practice and feedback for remediation, it is useful to have students review the rules and procedures for skills that are to be practiced. If students are learning or reinforcing a process skill, such as concept mapping or writing, then students will need to prepare or collect ideas and information that will be used at the computer.

After Computer Use.   When the use of problem-solving or educational software is to provide content and practice/feedback, students typically do not have products to work with when they finish their computer time. You could, however, plan time for students to discuss or write about what they learned or even draw diagrams to represent new learning. Students often have final products when they use educational software that provides process tools. If each student or small group of students produces a product, students can complete a compare/contrast activity to determine similarities and differences in how the process was completed. For example, if students used a tool to create a timeline of events leading up to the Civil War, they can compare the timeline entries and descriptions from each team. Students can discuss what changes would be needed if two groups combined their timelines into one.

Meaningful Integration of Educational Software

Games and drill and practice are too often the emphasis of technology integration in today's classrooms. It is not that educational software, in and of itself, does not provide effective instruction, but rather that teachers often do not plan for its meaningful use. It is easy to think that a software program is complete and self-explanatory and that if students just begin with lesson one and go through all lessons, the software will show what is important and guide their learning activities as they progress through each level. In reality, the only difference between educational software and books is the degree of interactivity. Teachers typically carefully review material students will be covering in the textbook. They typically even choose which chapter questions should be answered or which map should be copied. Yet these same teachers may not carefully review software and determine which portions best support the learning objectives.

To meaningfully integrate educational software into a lesson, teachers need to review the content and activities carefully to select the appropriate portions to support the intended learning. Teachers should also provide support activities that reinforce material and skills being taught with the software. The fact that computer-based programs may appear sophisticated and professionally produced does not mean that your careful judgment and planning are not needed. You, their teacher, are still the best judge of what your students need to achieve successful learning.

Summary

Educational and to a lesser degree problem-solving software are the most prevalent types of software used in today's classrooms. Numerous packages are available for every grade level and subject area and most are very easy to use. However, this vast array of choices makes it challenging for teachers to know which type of software to choose (e.g., tutorials, drill and practice, learning games, simulations) and how to determine whether the software is of high quality. This chapter recommends that teachers solicit credible software reviews or conduct their own evaluations. These evaluations need to examine the software's accuracy of content, use of effective instructional strategies for attainment of the targeted objectives, and ease of use. Software packages meeting these standards can with careful planning, as seen in the NTeQ model, be meaningfully integrated into classroom instruction.

Teacher Technology FAQ

Because there are so many software programs to choose from, I do not have the time to review each one. Is there a quicker way to see if the software will work with my students?

There are a couple of approaches you can take. You could start by working with other teachers in your school to divide up the software programs that seem interesting and then share your reviews. Another approach is to join an online teachers' discussion board or blog and ask for comments and suggestions about a particular software package that you are considering or ask for recommended software for topics of interest.

We have quite a large selection of software in our school and I have reviewed several packages but am finding it difficult to keep track of the information. Is there a way to make this information easier to use?

It would be helpful to keep a database of information you have collected about the software collection. This could include software title, subject area, specific skills being taught, alignment with district performance standards, number of copies available, sections to use, and so on. If a server is available at your school or a common computer is available in the library, the database could be used and updated by more than one teacher.

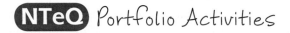

Technology Integration Activities

The following activities provide an opportunity for you to explore options for using problem-solving and educational software as described in this chapter.

1. Meet with your library media specialist to identify problem-solving and educational software that supports your curriculum. Use the software evaluation tools to evaluate the software packages.
2. Create NTeQ lesson plans integrating student use of software that received the most positive evaluations in the previous activity.

NTeQ Portfolio Activities

Please complete the following activities as part of the problem-solving and educational software section of your NTeQ Portfolio.

Reflections

The Getting Started section of this chapter posed three Reflecting on What I Know questions that teachers might commonly ask. In this portion of your journal, reflection activities have been added to address how you would answer each question. Please use information from this chapter to answer the questions.

❶ What are the benefits of using problem-solving or educational software?

Reflection Activity: Select a problem-solving software and an educational software appropriate for the subject and grade level you teach or plan to teach and write a description of the benefits of using each program.

❷ How do I choose the correct software?

Reflection Activity: Create a compare and contrast chart of the provided software review sites (listed below) and select one that you best meets your needs. Write a brief rationale for your choice.

- Educational Software Preview Guide (ESPG)
- SuperKids
- Discovery Education
- Learning Village
- Teachers Evaluating Educational Multimedia (TEEM)
- Children's Technology Review

❸ When I integrate problem-solving or educational software into a lesson, what changes will be needed?

Reflection Activity: For the software package selected in the first question, complete the following six NTeQ lesson components to show how you will adapt the lesson: Computer Functions, Research and Analysis, Results Presentation, and Activities During, Before, and After Computer Use.

Select two previously developed lessons that you have taught or found on the Internet. Modify one lesson by integrating student use of problem-solving software into the lesson. Modify the second lesson by integrating student use of educational software.

Teacher, Technology, and the Classroom

Getting Started

As evidenced throughout this text, there is a critical need for our students to learn and participate in collaborative environments that equip them to be successful in careers requiring the application of 21st-century skills. This need is evidenced in the 2008 decision to add assessment of 21st-century technology skills to the National Assessment of Educational Progress starting in 2012 (Electronic Education Report, 2008). If our students are to emerge from high school with these technological competencies, our educational systems must take necessary measures to ensure that our teachers are prepared to meet these challenges. This chapter provides guidelines to help teachers meet these goals.

Reflecting on What I Know

1 What can I do to "get ready" for a lesson in which my students use computers?

2 Where does the "computer part" come when I am teaching a lesson?

3 How do you ensure equal access for all students with only three computers?

Classroom

SNAPSHOT

Teacher Journal: My First NTeQ Lesson

Wednesday, October 15

I'm very excited because I have my first NTeQ lesson developed and am going to use it next Wednesday! The lesson problem is: Do states get bigger when moving from the East to the West Coast? The students are going to do Internet research, create a spreadsheet with information from the Internet, and then create a final PowerPoint presentation to share the results. I need to make samples of the student products and make sure to find some Internet sites to help make the searching easier.

Thursday, October 16

I reserved the laptop cart today. It has 14 computers, so I plan to have two children per computer. It has a wireless connection to the Internet, so I only need to worry about keeping the batteries charged. The cart comes with a printer and a digital projector, so the students can show their presentations to the whole class.

Friday, October 17

Today, I used my planning period to find Internet sites that would be appropriate for the students to use. I had a word processing document open during the search so I could copy and paste the URL for the sites chosen for the lesson. I saved the list of URLs to the school server so students can access it for the lesson. I'm glad I did the Internet search because it took me a long time to find just the right sites.

Monday, October 20

Only 2 days left till the lesson. I am very excited. I made a sample spreadsheet to make sure it would work, then printed a copy of the final chart so students can see what their spreadsheet should look like. Tomorrow I am going to make a PowerPoint presentation—the final thing.

Tuesday, October 21

I made the sample PowerPoint presentation today. It was so much fun. I added graphics and sounds to enhance the content. The students will love doing this. I printed the slides on a handout with six slides per page to save paper. I had 14 copies made of the spreadsheet and presentation to share with the student pairs.

Wednesday, October 22

What a disaster! I had no idea that so many things could go wrong. I started out by presenting the problem to the students. They were very interested in finding the answer. I put students into pairs and gave out the laptops and the handouts with the completed spreadsheet and presentation. I then wrote directions for getting the list of URLs from the server on the whiteboard and told students to collect information and then create a spreadsheet and a presentation of the results using the handouts as a guide.

All of the students knew how to use the laptops from lessons completed in the lab, so they quickly opened the computers and started to work. However, in a short amount of time the students began asking a million questions: Can you tell me the problem again? Why are we doing this lesson? How do we create a spreadsheet chart? Do our slides have to look just like yours? Can we add animation? Where do we save our work? What do we call the documents? How can we find the presentation we started before lunch? Is this good enough to get a good grade? Why don't some of the URLs work? What do we do when we get to the Internet site? Why is Hector doing all the computer work? What formulas do we use in the spreadsheets? How do we choose the best solution? Our laptop's battery is dead—what do we do now?

Thursday, October 23

I know there has to be a better way to implement a technology lesson. Where can I find some tips and guidelines that will make the process easier?

The Technologically Competent Teacher

The description of the NTeQ model in Chapter 1 clearly indicates that technologically competent teachers are a critical and foundational component of the model. Specifically, teachers need to personally experience using the computer as a tool to learn new information and to understand the relationship between basic computer functions and student learning. Teachers need to use their knowledge of student learning and technology to design, manage, and facilitate a student-centered learning environment. These competencies are fully aligned with the ISTE National Educational Technology Standards for Teachers (NETS-T), which present the knowledge, skills, and experiences that enable teachers to become and remain technologically competent (ISTE, 2008).

National Educational Technology Standards for Teachers (NETS-T)

Teachers in today's classrooms must ensure that students not only meet rigorous curriculum standards but also fulfill the National Educational Technology Standards for Students (NETS-S). As shown in Figure 12.1, teachers must facilitate, inspire, design, develop, model, promote, and engage in activities that yield technologically competent performances (ISTE, 2008). As seen in the NETS-T performance indicators, teachers build upon their classroom experiences, subject-matter knowledge, and knowledge of how students learn to effectively integrate student use of computers into their instruction (see Table 12.1). However, the expectations extend beyond the classroom in that teachers are encouraged to use technology as a tool for professional growth and leadership. Today's teachers must stay active contributors and consumers of online courses, tutorials, and resources. Our educators can no

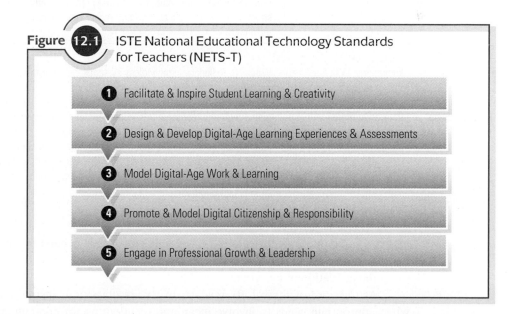

Figure 12.1 ISTE National Educational Technology Standards for Teachers (NETS-T)

1. Facilitate & Inspire Student Learning & Creativity
2. Design & Develop Digital-Age Learning Experiences & Assessments
3. Model Digital-Age Work & Learning
4. Promote & Model Digital Citizenship & Responsibility
5. Engage in Professional Growth & Leadership

Table 12.1	ISTE NETS and Performance Indicators for Teachers

1. Facilitate and Inspire Student Learning and Creativity	Teachers use their knowledge of subject matter, teaching and learning, and technology to facilitate experiences that advance student learning, creativity, and innovation in both face-to-face and virtual environments.	Teachers: a) promote, support, and model creative and innovative thinking and inventiveness. b) engage students in exploring real-world issues and solving authentic problems using digital tools and resources. c) promote student reflection using collaborative tools to reveal and clarify students' conceptual understanding and thinking, planning, and creative processes. d) model collaborative knowledge construction by engaging in learning with students, colleagues, and others in face-to-face and virtual environments.
2. Design and Develop Digital-Age Learning Experiences and Assessments	Teachers design, develop, and evaluate authentic learning experiences and assessment incorporating contemporary tools and resources to maximize content learning in context and to develop the knowledge, skills, and attitudes identified in the NETS-S.	Teachers: a) design or adapt relevant learning experiences that incorporate digital tools and resources to promote student learning and creativity. b) develop technology-enriched learning environments that enable all students to pursue their individual curiosities and become active participants in setting their own educational goals, managing their own learning, and assessing their own progress. c) customize and personalize learning activities to address students' diverse learning styles, working strategies, and abilities using digital tools and resources. d) provide students with multiple and varied formative and summative assessments aligned with content and technology standards and use resulting data to inform learning and teaching.
3. Model Digital-Age Work and Learning	Teachers exhibit knowledge, skills, and work processes representative of an innovative professional in a global and digital society.	Teachers: a) demonstrate fluency in technology systems and the transfer of current knowledge to new technologies and situations. b) collaborate with students, peers, parents, and community members using digital tools and resources to support student success and innovation. c) communicate relevant information and ideas effectively to students, parents, and peers using a variety of digital-age media and formats. d) model and facilitate effective use of current and emerging digital tools to locate, analyze, evaluate, and use information resources to support research and learning.

longer remain the "sole provider" of knowledge and skills needed by our students, but rather need to actively participate in global communities connected by an interest in the education of our youth.

At the core of these lofty goals is everyday classroom instruction—which when appropriate needs to involve meaningful student use of computers. The fol-

Table 12.1	Continued

| 4. Promote and Model Digital Citizenship and Responsibility | Teachers understand local and global societal issues and responsibilities in an evolving digital culture and exhibit legal and ethical behavior in their professional practices. | Teachers:
a) advocate, model, and teach safe, legal, and ethical use of digital information and technology, including respect for copyright, intellectual property, and the appropriate documentation of sources.
b) address the diverse needs of all learners by using learner-centered strategies providing equitable access to appropriate digital tools and resources.
c) promote and model digital etiquette and responsible social interactions related to the use of technology and information.
d) develop and model cultural understanding and global awareness by engaging with colleagues and students of other cultures using digital-age communication and collaboration tools. |
| 5. Engage in Professional Growth and Leadership | Teachers continuously improve their professional practice, model lifelong learning, and exhibit leadership in their school and professional community by promoting and demonstrating the effective use of digital tools and resources. | Teachers:
a) participate in local and global learning communities to explore creative applications of technology to improve student learning.
b) exhibit leadership by demonstrating a vision of technology infusion, participating in shared decision making and community building, and developing the leadership and technology skills of others.
c) evaluate and reflect on current research and professional practice on a regular basis to make effective use of existing and emerging digital tools and resources in support of student learning.
d) contribute to the effectiveness, vitality, and self-renewal of the teaching profession and of their school and community. |

Source: National Education Technology Standards for Teachers, Second Edition, © 2008, ISTE® International Society for Technology in Education, www.iste.org. All rights reserved.

lowing sections provide practical guidelines for preparing to implement and manage students during a technology integration lesson.

Preparing to Implement Technology Integration Lessons

As mentioned in Chapter 2, the ten-step NTeQ model is a *planning* model that guides you through the development of problem-based lessons that integrate student use of computers. Developing a well-thought-out lesson plan is a critical component to achieving effective instruction. However, additional preparation is necessary to go from a lesson plan to successful implementation in the classroom. This section discusses the preparation needed to implement a technology lesson.

Go to MyEducationLab, select the topic "Instructional Planning," and go to the Activities and Applications section. Access the video "Technology Manages Flow of Activities" and consider how one teacher uses technology to manage instruction. Complete the activity that follows.

Preparing a lesson that integrates student use of computers, use of multiple resources, and a variety of activities requires more time compared to preparing a more traditional lesson—such as reading a chapter and completing worksheets. The amount of time required, however, decreases as you and your students become more experienced using technology in a classroom setting. Appropriate preparations before implementing your NTeQ lesson include the following:

Preparing Handouts

- Technical step-by-step guides
- Resource guides
- Assessment tools

Preparing Technology

- Create digital folders
- Design templates
- Load specialized software
- Bookmark Internet sites
- Turn on computers and open applications

The Teacher's Diary

A fifth-grade teacher was having her students create a timeline on World War II. She wanted them to include at least ten events. I encouraged her to integrate technology into the project by allowing her students to use Kidspiration to create and organize their timeline. I even suggested that we could create a template with five event boxes to get the kids started. Then, during the lesson, we could show the kids how to add the other five event boxes that they needed. Knowing that she was limited on time, she thought the template was a great way to get the students started.

Before the lesson, the teacher had her students research important events from World War II. We worked together to compile a list of Internet sites that the students could use. We posted the sites to a web page so that the students could access them easily. By doing this, we knew that the students were going to age-appropriate sites with reliable information. Students were allowed to research their own sites at home if they wanted to, but while at school, they could only visit the sites on the list.

On the day of the lesson, the students had their events ready. Once laptops were passed out, they followed along with the teacher as she showed them how to open the timeline template in Kidspiration and create five more event boxes on their timeline. Once they had all their event boxes ready, they typed in their dates and events, added clip art, and printed their work. The completed timelines looked great and the students really enjoyed creating them.

Amy Overby
Curriculum Technology
Trainer

Preparing Handouts

As with most lessons, students will need information and instructions to guide them through the various activities. Handouts have proven to be a very successful means of transmitting this information to students. As mentioned in Chapter 5, Think Sheets will probably be used with most NTeQ lessons. In addition to Think Sheets, technology lessons may also use one or more of the following handouts: technical step-by-step guides, resource guides, and assessment tools such as task lists and rubrics.

Technical Step-by-Step Guides. If students are doing a computer task that is new or fairly new, it may be worth your time to create or use previously developed step-by-step job aids to assist students. For example, generic guides could be made for inserting and formatting tables, creating spreadsheet charts, inserting hyperlinks to a graphic organizer, or adding custom animation to a presentation. These guides will better enable your students to work through the lesson independently without needing extra assistance from you or others. Step-by-step guides can be presented on the Think Sheet, on a separate handout, or on a laminated sheet that is accessed when students need assistance. At times it is also useful to create lesson-specific guides, such as how to enter spreadsheet formulas to calculate population growth, how to create the layout of a scientific newsletter, or how to use Track Changes to edit a group-written story.

Resource Guides. When a lesson requires students to use multiple resources, it may be useful to create a resource guide to assist students in using their time wisely.

Students soon learn to use task lists and rubrics to help improve performance.

The amount of information needed on the guides will decrease as students become more familiar with using resources. A sample resource guide for a social studies lesson on U.S. landmarks is shown in Table 12.2.

Assessment Tools. Other handouts that can be prepared before a computer lesson include assessment tools, such as a task list or rubric. These tools can be used to guide student learning during the instructional process and to ascertain the degree to which students applied the specified knowledge and skills. A task list is basically a check sheet that students use to guide them while working on a project. The list goes beyond being a tally, though, in that students not only mark off each step, but also assess the quality of what is produced. In Figure 12.2, you can see that students circle the face that shows how they feel about each item they complete.

Table 12.2	Sample Resource Guide for a Coast-to-Coast Excursion

Problem: You want to plan the trip of a lifetime that will allow you to visit the biggest and best that America has to offer (tallest mountain, tallest building, most populated city, most visited park, etc.). You live in New York City and want to travel from the Atlantic to the Pacific coast, but only have two weeks' vacation. You can fly home, so the two weeks can be spent traveling from coast to coast. Create a travel brochure that would convince people that this would be the trip of a lifetime.

Resource	Type	Where Located	Information Provided
eGo Travel Guide	Website: www.ego.net/us/textnav.htm	Computer 1	Siteseeing guides
TripSpot	Website: www.tripspot.com	Computer 1	Siteseeing guides
Compton's	CD Encyclopedia	Computer 2	Basic information on U.S.
World Atlas	CD Reference	Computer 3	Distances between cities
Worldbook	Encyclopedia	Resource Bookshelf	Basic information on U.S.
Our Exciting Country	Book	Resource Table	Basic information on U.S.
Fun U.S. Vacations	AAA Magazine	Resource Table	Basic information on U.S.
World Atlas	Book	Resource Table	Distances between cities
Traveling the Northwest	Travel Brochure	Resource Table	Ideas for designing a brochure
Rocky Mountain Hiking	Travel Brochure	Resource Table	Ideas for designing a brochure

Figure **12.2**   Sample Task List

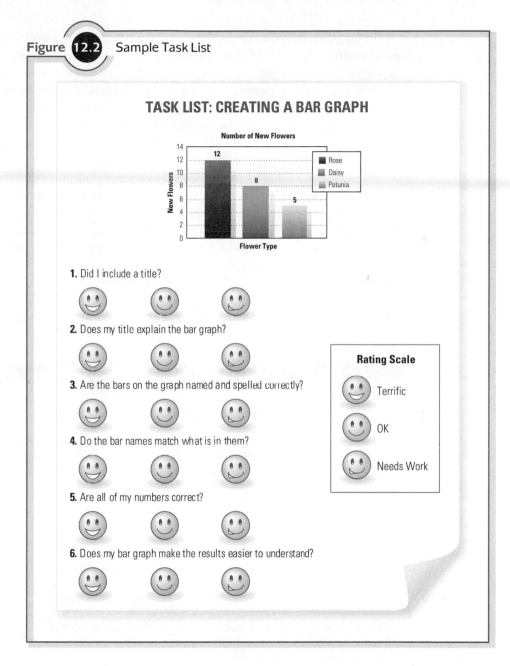

The task list, in and of itself, is a great tool and would improve the completion and quality of student work if it were used consistently. But as most teachers know, a student product can have all of the components and still not represent a high level of understanding and achievement. The overall product may lack cohesiveness. The overall findings may lack sufficient support for the conclusions reported. The presentation of ideas may be concise and complete, but the overall flow of the material may not create a relevant or interesting depiction of the content. These aspects of student work comprise what is often described by a teacher as being "right"—or that vague knowledge possessed only by the teacher. As seen in Table 12.3, a rubric defines what is meant by being "right" in a clear and understandable manner. It takes all the pieces and places them into descriptions of different levels of final student products.

Even though it is highly recommended to involve students in the development of rubrics, it is advisable to create a sample rubric to help you determine critical components of the lesson that need to be reflected in the final products. Your sample rubric more than likely will be altered as students provide input, but this rubric will enable you to guide student thinking and ensure the critical aspects are incorporated into the instrument. You may want to develop a template for the lesson that includes a place for the lesson title, the objectives or performance, and a blank grid for the levels of performance and rating scale. Students would then complete the rubric during the brainstorming session and use as it a guide when proceeding through

Table 12.3	Sample Rubric for Newspaper Article on Seat Belt Safety				
Objective or Performance	**Beginning 1**	**Developing 2**	**Accomplished 3**	**Exemplary 4**	**Score**
1. Students will write a persuasive article on why drivers should wear seat belts.	Persuasive arguments are not clear or concise and had very poor references made to supporting graphics.	Persuasive arguments are fairly clear and concise. References made to graphics provide limited support.	Persuasive arguments are clear, concise, and articulate. References made to supporting graphics are useful.	Persuasive arguments are very clear, concise, and articulate. Excellent references made to supporting graphics.	
2. Students will generate spreadsheet charts that demonstrate a trend.	The charts show very little about seat belt use. The title, labels, and legend are missing or incomplete.	The charts show limited aspects of seat belt use. The title, labels, legend, and type of chart provide incomplete support.	The charts demonstrate trends in seat belt use. The title, labels, legend, and type of chart support understanding.	The charts clearly demonstrate trends in seat belt use. Excellent choice of title, labels, legend, and type of chart.	

Figure 12.3 Rubric Template

Objective or Performance	Beginning 1	Developing 2	Accomplished 3	Exemplary 4	Score
				Overall Score	

the lesson (see Figure 12.3). Rubistar (www.rubistar.com) is a free online teacher resource with multitudes of subject-specific and generic rubrics that can easily be adapted to meet your specific needs and saved for future use.

Preparing Technology

Student use of technology, as wonderful as it is, does take careful planning and extra time to ensure smoother integration into a lesson. The following section describes how you can create digital folders for student work, generate digital templates, load software, add bookmarks, and get the computers up and running before class to increase the amount of learning time available to students.

Create Digital Folders.   When students work on a computer, it is critical that they frequently back up their work to a hard drive, network drive, or USB flash drive. If ample hard drive space is available, you or your computer support person can create class or student folders for saving files. It is important to use meaningful and easy to locate folder names such as "Grade 5 Science" or "Ms. Smith Grade 6 Science" rather than names such as "Sec003" and "Sec004." If more than one group of students uses the same computer, title folders with names that distinguish the difference, for example, "Group 2 folders." More information on digital folders is found in the Managing the Resources section (p. 327).

Design Templates. If students are working with a spreadsheet, presentation, word processing, or other type of document that may require detailed setup and initial formatting, design a template to save time and help avoid frustration. This process might involve entering the row and column names and formulas in a spreadsheet or setting up a word processing outline for a student report (see Figure 12.4). These documents are saved as templates, identified in MS Word as files with ".dotm" rather than ".docx" as the extension. The use of templates also shows students how to properly format different documents. When introducing the template to students, make sure to point out specific features in the template format, for example, "Notice that every other row of the table is shaded to make it easier to read the numbers in each category."

Load Specialized Software. Another task that can be completed before implementing the lesson is to install any specialized software on the student computers. For example, if students are going to use a world atlas, writing, tessellation, or math software, these can be installed on the computers (if your school has the necessary license agreement). If you only have a single copy of the software or CD, install it on one computer and then indicate with a sign what is installed—for example, "World Atlas"—to direct student traffic to the correct computer.

Bookmark Internet Sites. It is very helpful to provide guidance to students as they search for information on the Web. One way to accomplish this is to create bookmarks or favorites (within the browser) for websites that contain information relevant to your lesson. These can be sites with very specific information or more general sites that may have multiple links to related sites. For example, if you are doing a unit on weather, you can bookmark www.nws.noaa.gov and have your students stay within that site by clicking on the site navigation keys along with using the Back function. Or if you want your students to use a broader yet still controlled search, you can bookmark a site designed for student research, such as "Ask Kids," www.askkids.com, which provides links to pages that are age appropriate and specifically written for children. If the automatically assigned bookmark names will not be meaningful to your students, most browsers offer the capability to change the name. More information about the Internet can be found in Chapter 6, Exploring the World Wide Web in the Classroom.

Turn On Computers and Open Applications. One last task that can help prepare for class implementation is to turn on the computers and open applications

Figure 12.4   Report Template

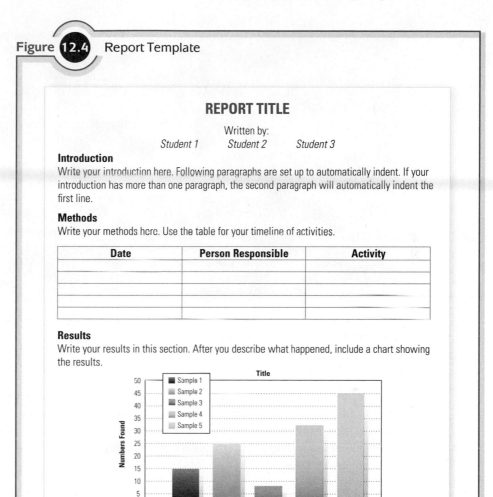

before the lesson is to begin. This step is especially helpful when using older computers that have a longer boot-up time than newer computers. The same can be true for the time it takes to open a software application. Some of the Internet browsers

The amount and type of materials that teachers manage changes when computers are part of daily classroom usage and instruction.

or large applications can take several minutes to open and be ready for student use. It is also helpful to have students leave applications open when finished with their work to avoid start-up time for the next student. When student time at the computers is limited because only a few computers are available, it is important to save even a few minutes of time.

Managing Student Use of Computers

Managing a classroom that uses an innovative approach (such as the NTeQ model) involves much more than just keeping the students quiet, in their seats, and working. To effectively manage a classroom that is integrating computers in a *meaningful* way, the teacher must create an environment that is conducive to learning. In this environment, she must manage the movement of students to and from various activities, manage students while they are engaged in the activities, and oversee the management of extra resources that are used in these activities. If Internet access is available, the teacher must also manage student use of these web-based resources. All of these managerial responsibilities may seem overwhelming at first, but with careful planning and practice they will, over time, become part of everyday routines.

The Teacher's Diary

I had been in the public school classroom for 20 years when I received my computers. I had seen a lot of innovations come and go. I felt like technology was going to be around for a long time and that it was time for me to become more technologically competent. When I got the computers, I felt excited, but also overwhelmed. How was I ever going to learn how to use the equipment and remember how to create a spreadsheet or a database? There was so much to learn! I spent many hours just learning how to operate the equipment and how to use the basic computer applications. By the end of that first year, I had become comfortable with the computer and had discovered that it was going to be a useful tool for me. I could see how it was making my job easier.

When school started the next year, I was ready for a change. I had mastered the computer, so to speak, and I wanted my students to master it too. I began to look at education from a more constructivist point of view and wanted my classroom to become child centered. One of the first things I learned was that my role as a teacher had to change. I had to become a facilitator of learning, not a director. Once I accepted that role, I began to look at how I had been teaching and realized that I was going to have to make some significant changes in how I approached learning and classroom management. I had many frustrations that year as I began to make those changes! It took me more time to plan my lessons. I had peers question what I was doing. I had to develop alternative assessments. I had to learn that a noisy classroom was OK. I had to let go and allow my students to have some input into what and how they were going to learn. There were days when I questioned what I had gotten myself into. Sometimes, I wondered if my students were really learning.

When working on thematic unit projects about trains, I grouped the students into pairs to work on different topics related to trains. Some were working at desks, some were working at the computers, and some were working on the floor. The room was noisy because the students were talking as they worked together on their projects. There was a lot of movement to and from the computers. I was on the floor helping some students work on a model of a freight train. I was so engrossed in what they were doing that I did not realize a supervisor from the central office had come into the room until she was standing over me. She had come to visit. She said she'd only be able to stay for a few minutes and that she would just walk around the room to see what was going on. She told me to continue what I was doing. So, I got back on the floor and continued helping. I wondered what she was thinking as the room was noisy and no one was at their own seat working!

I continued to watch her as I worked with other groups, and I noticed that she was moving from group to group talking to the students about their projects and what they had learned. Her "few minutes" visit turned into the rest of the afternoon. I apologized for the noise level and what appeared to be "organized" chaos. I thought that she might be disappointed because I was not "teaching" a lesson. She wasn't disappointed. Instead, she thanked me for letting her spend the afternoon with my students. She told me that I needed to remember that learning is not always going to be neat and tidy! She said that noise and "organized" chaos were sometimes part of an effective learning environment. She said she could tell that my students were learning and that was what was really important.

Fran Clark
Third-Grade Teacher

Managing the Classroom Environment

It is clear by now that the NTeQ model emphasizes a student-centered environment. The students are actively engaged in the learning process and assume the roles of researchers. To engage them in this manner, the teacher must work with the students to create an atmosphere or culture that fosters and supports a high level of student involvement, not only with the information they are learning, but also with each other. Early suggestions for creating a "computer learning culture" are still applicable in today's classrooms (Ryba & Anderson, 1993, p. 5):

- Helping one another solve problems
- Openly sharing information and ideas
- Reinforcing each other for making progress
- [Effectively] working in physically close proximity to one another
- Collectively supporting anyone who has a personal "crisis"
- Extending the effective working relationships beyond the computer environment

Additional classroom management strategies for lessons that integrate student use of computers are below:

- Create a checklist and proposed timeline of computer tasks to be completed
- Frequently model effective and appropriate use of computers
- Grade student computer work in stages (outline, rough draft, final draft) to keep students on task
- Give points/grade for productive lab time
- Define and communicate inappropriate use, and enforce loss of computer privileges as a consequence (Intel Education Initiative, 2004)

Managing the Rotation

There are several factors to consider when planning student rotation through multiple activities. Your plan will vary according to computer access. For example, will your students use computers in the classroom, in the lab, or in both places? If you have computers in your classroom, then you need to consider the room layout and how the students will rotate through the available computers, as discussed below.

Working with What You Have.   As you develop your NTeQ lessons, it is important to build them around the resources that you have available. The types of computer access can be categorized into four typical groups:

- *One computer.* One to two computers per classroom
- *Small group.* Three to six computers per classroom
- *Computer lab.* Room of computers with one to two students per computer
- *One-to-one laptop access.* Laptops for each student during class time

One-Computer Class.   If you only have one computer in your classroom, lessons should require minimal computer access for students. Activities are typically focused toward creating a "class" product that is produced from group or individual student work. For example, student groups can collect and enter data for designated sections of a class database; each group could collect and enter information for one state from each region, five presidents, endangered species from one country, or real-world examples of a particular shape. Student groups could also enter data similar to the following into a class spreadsheet: weather data from different TV stations, science experiment results (e.g., how high Ping-Pong balls bounce when dropped from different heights), or social observation (e.g., the number of people wearing seat belts at different times of day). Individual students can contribute to a classroom computer product by, for example, adding an original poem in a class book of spring poems, writing a "Correct Grammar" example, adding a brief biographical sketch of a famous mathematician, or adding a paragraph to an original class story.

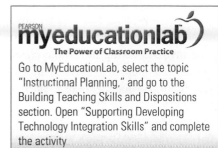

Go to MyEducationLab, select the topic "Instructional Planning," and go to the Building Teaching Skills and Dispositions section. Open "Supporting Developing Technology Integration Skills" and complete the activity

Anderson (2005) suggests student time at the computer will be enhanced with the use of a projector or large monitor to provide a preview of web pages students will use during computer time. He also suggests the use of small groups, matching task to the resource (e.g., using AlphaSmarts for data entry), and perhaps offering alternative access time before or after school.

Small Group.   When a classroom has three to six computers, student use of technology can be routinely included in the lessons. Students can be involved in the same types of activities listed for the single-computer classroom; however, the assignments would be *group* projects rather than *class* projects. In fact, cooperative learning is effective for student learning even in a setting with more computers (Johnson & Johnson, 2004).

Computer Labs.   Computer use also can be routinely included in lessons if teachers regularly have access to a lab. The number of computers in the lab may require that students work together or each student may work at an individual computer. It is important to encourage students to share ideas and provide assistance to one another in a lab setting to ensure that the "computer-learning culture" is maintained.

One-to-One Laptop Access.   Access to laptop computers ranges from laptop carts that teachers can reserve, classroom sets that provide one computer for each student, or 24/7 access to computers that students bring to each class and take home.

A one-to-one environment offers both challenges and opportunities. You can easily plan integrated lessons that make extensive use of the computers. Students can work individually or in small groups. Managing the classroom, however, often becomes a challenge because you must now keep an eye on more than twenty computers rather than four or five. Even when students have laptop computers, we encourage teachers to design their lessons for small groups to encourage collaborative learning.

Group or Independent Rotation.   Once you know where your students will use the computers, you can determine the best layout and plan for student movement to and from the computers. Moving to a computer lab involves taking the whole class; thus, we will focus on rotation schedules for classroom computers. You can plan lessons around two primary types of schedules: group rotation or independent rotation.

Group Rotation.   Small groups of students stay together as they move from one lesson activity center to another in a group rotation format (see Figure 12.5). To manage this type of rotation, the teacher needs to determine approximately how

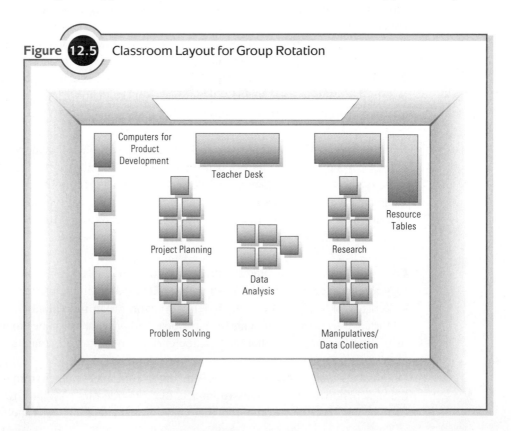

Figure **12.5**   Classroom Layout for Group Rotation

long the activity at each station or center will take. If possible, each center should take about the same amount of time for completion. This scheduling helps students rotate through the centers at regular intervals.

Another consideration is to have more than one center for activities that take longer. For example, if students are collecting information about several different categories from a variety of travel brochures, the research activity may take longer than setting up the database and entering the collected information. In this case, you may want to set up two research centers so students can spend twice as long on this activity. One center could be for researching historical sites, and the other could be for researching weather patterns. The rotation can be managed by having students move through the stations in a clockwise or other predetermined pattern. You can use a kitchen timer to alert students when it is time to move. If the timer is set for two minutes before they need to move, the students will have time to finish the task at hand and straighten the area. When group rotations are used, the student-to-computer ratio in the computer center is often one to one, which ensures equal computer access.

Independent Rotation.   Although still in small cooperative groups, the groups of students do not rotate to each activity in an established pattern when using independent rotation (see Figure 12.6). Rather, in this setup, students can access all the resources needed to solve the problem designated in the lesson, thus allowing the students to use the resources on an as-needed basis. With independent rotation, each group is assigned a computer. If more than one group is assigned to a computer, you will need to establish a schedule for computer use. The teacher can create a schedule, or the student groups who are sharing the computer can establish their own schedule. It is probably wise to have the teacher create the first schedule so students can experience well-planned routines. After students have been involved with several integration lessons, they will become more adept at planning their own rotation schedules. In either situation, however, computer tasks must be divided equally among group members.

When planning for the layout of computers in the classroom, if at all possible, arrange the computers with enough room to accommodate from two to three chairs to better facilitate group work. Position grouped desks in locations where you are able to see all students at all times and students can see classroom presentations (Cataldo, 2008). These accommodations will better facilitate student computer activities.

Managing Student Activities

Once students are using the computers, the teacher must facilitate student learning and manage three primary types of student activities: assisting students who need help with computer skills, dealing with any technical problems, and keeping

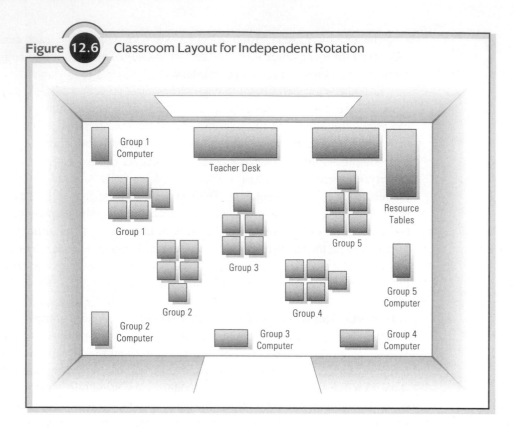

Figure 12.6   Classroom Layout for Independent Rotation

students on task. Management suggestions for these activities are described in the following paragraphs.

Assisting Students with Computer Skills.   When computers are added to a classroom, many teachers are faced not only with teaching subject-matter content but also with teaching computer skills. There are several ways to help students acquire and use new computer skills. We will discuss the four methods listed below:

- Teacher modeling/demonstration
- Peer modeling and assistance
- Technology posters or job aids
- Student handouts

Teacher Modeling/Demonstration.   Students can learn new computer skills by observing the teacher modeling the desired task. The teacher gives verbal cues as the new technology skill is demonstrated with the aid of a digital projector. Students take notes and ask questions during the demonstration. Student groups then rotate to the computers to practice what they have learned.

Peer Modeling and Assistance.   Another method involves training a corps of students to help their peers and teachers learn new computer skills and assist with technology problems. An excellent example is Kentucky's Student Technology Leadership Program (STLP), which is a statewide initiative open to students in all grade levels. The STL students are trained by teachers or community members to design strategies that address technology issues and concerns in their school and community. The STL students emerge from the program with increased confidence, improved teaming ability, and marketable knowledge and skills needed for careers in the 21st century (KY STLP, 2008).

One simple classroom strategy to use when students need help with a computer task is an "I'm in trouble" signal. An example signal is a paper cup placed on each monitor. If the paper cup is upside down, the students are OK; if it is turned upright, the students need assistance. This type of system, or another type of signal, avoids students waving their arms and causing distractions to get attention.

Technology Posters or Job Aids.   Students can also learn computer skills by using technology posters or job aids for frequently used tasks. Technology posters consist of very brief step-by-step instructions for common computer tasks such as saving to a flash drive, opening an application, or printing a document. The posters are displayed by the computers so students can easily refer to them when needed (see Figure 12.7). Job aids also provide easy step-by-step instructions for commonly used computer functions and applications. They typically include more information than a poster can display, however, and are often kept in folders, in notebooks, or on note cards. The job aids are not put on display because they are created for tasks that are not completed every day. For example, job aids might be made for creating a simple spreadsheet, working with word processing tables, or adding animation to a presentation.

Student Handouts.   You can also assist with computer skills by including step-by-step instructions with the handouts used for a lesson, as mentioned earlier. This method automatically integrates the content with the technology guidelines. Many times the teacher can create one handout that serves several purposes. The handout can include the problem statement, general instructions for the lesson, step-by-step guidelines for using the computer as a tool to solve the problem, and the Think Sheet questions (Chapter 5). Mary Kemp, a middle school teacher, uses the student handout shown in Figure 12.8 (p. 325) for a lesson she created on vertebrates.

Assisting with Technical Problems.   Since the early introduction of classroom computers, the risk of technical problems has been a frequent teacher concern

Figure 12.7 Job Aid for Saving MS Office Files to a USB Drive

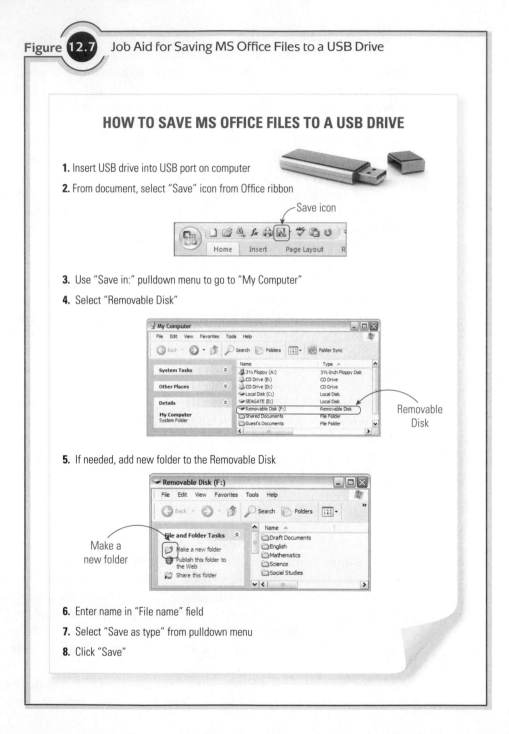

HOW TO SAVE MS OFFICE FILES TO A USB DRIVE

1. Insert USB drive into USB port on computer

2. From document, select "Save" icon from Office ribbon

3. Use "Save in:" pulldown menu to go to "My Computer"

4. Select "Removable Disk"

5. If needed, add new folder to the Removable Disk

6. Enter name in "File name" field

7. Select "Save as type" from pulldown menu

8. Click "Save"

Figure **12.8**   Lesson Handout with Technology Guidelines

Vertebrate Unit

Problem Statement

Do all vertebrates lay eggs? If not, which groups do not? Are there any exceptions?

Directions:

To answer these questions, you will go to the computer assigned to your group and use the vertebrate database compiled by the class. Follow the directions below and work cooperatively with your group to sort the data by different fields, analyze the data to answer some questions, and complete a word processing document (using the format previously taught in class) that answers the questions. You will have the entire class period to complete the assignment. Turn in the word processing document and the printouts of your database sorts by the end of the class.

Step-by-Step:

1. Open the vertebrate database and select Layout 2 under Layout on the menu bar.
2. Select Sort under Organize on the menu bar.
3. Select Vertebrate Group under the Field List, and click the Move button to move it to the Sort Order box. Click the Ascending Order button and then click OK. Print your sorted list.
4. Following the directions above, select the fields listed below from the Field List, one at a time, and Move them to the Sort Order box. Be sure to Move the previous field from the Sort Order box before clicking OK. Print each sorted list before choosing the next field.

Sort by the following fields and print your sorted lists:

- Body Temperature
- Body Covering
- Method of Fertilization
- Method of Birth

5. Review your sorted lists and work together to answer the questions listed below.
6. Use word processing to answer the questions. Be sure to type each question and then a short paragraph answering it.

Think Sheet Questions:

I. Do all vertebrates lay eggs? If not, which groups do not? Are there any exceptions?
II. What is the main body covering for each vertebrate group? Compare body temperature to body covering. How would you explain the major differences in body covering for cold-blooded versus warm-blooded vertebrates?
III. Compare body temperature to method of fertilization. Which groups are alike? Which group is different from the others?
IV. Compare method of fertilization to method of birth. What is the main difference between vertebrates with external fertilization versus those with internal fertilization? How do you explain this?
V. What are the major subgroups for each vertebrate group?

(Casson et al., 1997; Sandholtz & Reilly, 2004). When computer technicians are not readily available, teachers often rely on methods such as the following for support:

- Advice from teachers who regularly use computers
- Advice from "expert" students
- Troubleshooting handbooks or hotlines
- Adult volunteers (parents, college staff, business or government employees) willing to assist teachers and students with technological concerns
- Participation in seminars and workshops to learn technical troubleshooting

The Power of Classroom Practice

Go to MyEducationLab, select the topic "Ethical, Legal, and Social Issues," and go to the Activities and Applications section. Access the video "Technology Improves Teaching Skills" and consider how you could enhance your technology skills and learn new skills. Complete the activity that follows.

Keeping Students on Task. Keeping students on task is often more challenging when students are working at computers. Computers are equipped with many fascinating features that beckon to inquisitive student minds. There are intriguing screensavers that can be modified, games to be played, and, of course, little mischievous pranks to be pulled. Students quickly learn that they can easily change the names of folders, (e.g., "Susie" to "Skinny Susie") or hide a student's file in an obscure folder somewhere on the hard drive. However, many of these student diversions occur because the required computer tasks are not relevant, interesting, or challenging. The following guidelines will help to keep students on task:

- Implement the NTeQ model.
- Present students with interesting problems that use real-world information and data that they collect.
- Use collaborative learning groups.
- Involve students in decision making.
- Monitor student activities (Churchward, 1997):
  - Pass through an area about two minutes after students have started a new assignment. This delay allows the teacher to determine if the students understand what is required.
  - Provide individual assistance to students as it is needed.
  - Make general announcements only if several students are experiencing the same problem.
- Make it a habit to check the Internet sites the students have visited while conducting a search (e.g., use the "history" feature).
- Involve students in establishing class rules for using the computer. These rules could include the following:
  - Only use the computer for the assigned lesson unless special permission is obtained. Special permission might be given for students who have completed their assignments and want to create a customized screensaver, con-

duct an Internet search for an upcoming vacation, check on their favorite football team, or find the admission requirements for a college.

- Never open or alter another student's computer files or any computer files other than your own.

Managing the Resources

Computers require more "stuff" to make them work than other learning tools, such as calculators or DVD players. Computers need software, CDs, a printer, ink cartridges, and storage devices like flash drives. Besides the computer needing more resources, the desktop files also need to be managed, and the computer itself needs to be maintained. This section provides some practical guidelines for managing these components.

Student Storage Devices.   Each student should have at least one USB storage device and, if possible, a server-based folder to save digital files. If students are going to create multimedia projects, such as PowerPoint presentations or iMovies, they will need large-capacity storage. Some teachers keep the student flash drives in a centralized location rather than have the students keep track of their own drives. In a self-contained class, the teacher can have one storage box with divided drawers that holds the labeled student drives in alphabetical order by the student's last name. In a departmentalized setting, the teacher can have one disk storage box or drawer for each period. The storage boxes should be kept in a dry location without temperature extremes or direct sunlight. It is also important to keep them away from magnetic fields such as TVs, computer monitors, or speakers.

The Teacher's Diary

"I can't find where I saved it."

"I deleted it."

"I can't open the file."

"I have a virus!"

"I copied my friend's work."

"I copied my work and gave it to my friend."

"I can't connect to the Internet."

"I dropped my computer."

"I was playing a game when I should have been doing my work."

"I didn't back up my files and my computer crashed."

"My sister changed the settings on my computer."

"I know I wasn't supposed to be at that Internet site."

"Somebody took my power cord."

"I left my computer on the bus."

"I lost my USB drive."

"I don't have my computer today. It's getting fixed."

Welcome to my world. Managing a computer classroom involves many unique problem-solving situations, and new problems appear all the time. I've learned a lot over the course of the year and know that I have more to learn.

My students think that having a computer is really cool. One thing that students learn very quickly is how fun and easy it is to change their computer settings. Some enjoy doing this so much that they spend their class time looking at screensavers when they should be doing their work. Students have learned how to have their work open while fiddling with the computer settings. They do this so that when I come by, all they need to do is exit out with a simple click of the mouse, and I'll never know what they were doing. Something that I have found that helps me monitor the computer use is to turn the students around so that their backs face my desk. This makes their computer screens visible to me from my desk (or other places in the room), and they don't know when they are being monitored.

Using a filtered email service to transmit files has been a tremendous time-saver. Students can no longer say, "I didn't get the file." My response to them now is "You must have deleted it. Look in your recycle bin." Having a filter is helpful to prevent inappropriate picture files or messages from being passed around the classroom.

Something that I did not do this year, but intend to do next year, is to have a labeled USB flash drive kept in the classroom for each student that is only for backing up files from "My Documents." Once a day I will give students 5 minutes to back up documents.

I think that setting up guidelines and expectations regarding computer use at the beginning of the year is very important. The majority of students will be responsible and trustworthy. However, inappropriate use of the computer by even one student can affect the integrity of the entire program. It is wise to prevent problems before they occur whenever possible.

Pam Shoemaker
Sixth-Grade Teacher

Software.   Computers need software applications to be useful. Many computers come equipped with applications already installed; however, most people want to enhance their computers by adding new applications. This new software normally comes with a CD-ROM containing the actual application and sometimes the user's guide. The CD is used to install the application on the hard drive. After the installation, the teacher needs to find a safe location to store the CD and the user's manual, if supplied. Some software includes a "key" or code to activate the software. We have found it useful to record the code on the CD storage case and on the inside cover of the manual. You will need this code if you ever reinstall or upgrade the software. If you are using software that is licensed by your school or district, you can probably obtain the key from your support group. The manuals need to be kept in a place that is easily accessible for quick reference. The CDs can be stored in a box marked as "Master Software Disks." There are strict copyright laws regarding software applications; therefore, it is very important to always have the original software for all applications on each computer.

Printing Supplies.   For printers to function, they need paper and some form of cartridge, both of which can become costly if a monitoring system for student printing is not used. The cost of printer cartridges can be reduced by purchasing recycled ones or refilling them with ink when using an inkjet printer.

The amount of printing can be minimized by having students complete the majority of their editing and reading on the computer. When students are conducting searches from the Internet or a CD-ROM, have them use the Preview function of the Print dialog box to determine how many pages the document contains. They can then print only the pages they actually need. Web pages can also be bookmarked for future reference or the content can be transferred to an organization software such as MS OneNote to be read from the computer rather than being printed. Another option to save ink is to set the printer default to Draft format, which in most cases produces products appropriate for classroom use. Teachers often recycle paper by printing on the back of previously used paper that isn't bent or crumpled. As we collectively strive to save our environment, the goal is to move toward a *paperless* classroom.

File Management.   There are multiple ways to manage the files stored on a computer, whether a classroom computer, district or school server, or on portable storage devices such as a USB drive. Departmentalized high school or middle school teachers will need a folder for each class that they teach. Within the class folders, each student should be given an individual folder that is titled with the student's last name and first initial (see Figure 12.9). Elementary teachers with self-contained classrooms have the option of setting up individual folders for each student that contain subfolders for the main content areas or creating subject-area folders that contain individual student folders in each one. Other tips for managing digital files include the following ideas:

- Use concise, easy-to-understand names.
- Use color coding when appropriate.
- Use folders within folders to increase organization.
- Add numbers before file names to keep them sequential, making sure to add a "0" to single-digit numbers (e.g., 01, 02, 03).

Computer Care

Not only do the computer resources and computer file systems need to be managed, but the computers themselves need to be maintained and managed, as shown by these simple guidelines for computer management:

- Do not allow students to have any food, drinks, or gum when using computers.
- Avoid touching the computer monitor with fingers.
- Use screensaver software to protect the monitor.
- Secure cords and cables away from traffic.
- If using a mechanical mouse, clean tracking ball and contact points with alcohol on a regular basis.
- Use virus protection software.

Figure 12.9   High School Teacher File Management Example

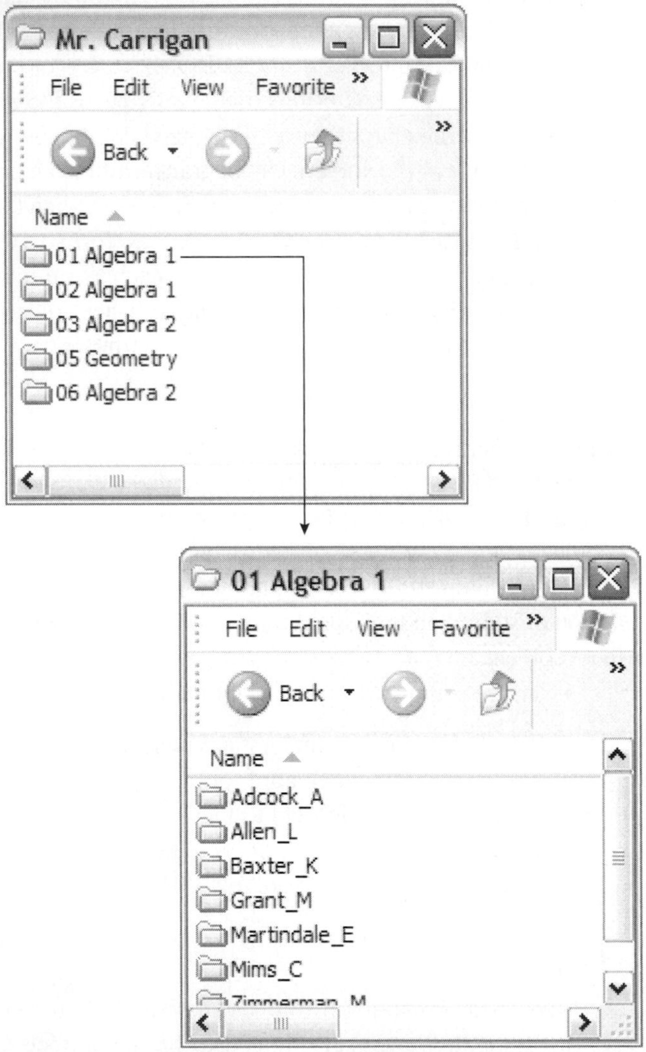

Summary

As seen in this chapter and throughout this text, teachers are the critical component for achieving effective integration of computer technology into the classroom. Teaching in today's classrooms requires that teachers go beyond computer literacy to achieve technological competence. The NETS for Teachers clearly defines the standards and performance indicators of the 21st-century teacher. Specifically, teachers must facilitate and inspire, design and develop, model, promote, and engage in activities that yield technologically competent performance to prepare our children for successful careers.

At the classroom level, teachers must give careful thought and planning to effectively implement inquiry-based lessons that incorporate student use of technology. Before the lesson, teachers make support documents that will help guide student learning. These include Think Sheets, technical step-by-step guides, resource guides, task lists, and rubrics. This is also the time to prepare the computers for the lesson. Preparation activities can include creating folders for student computer work, creating templates for students to use when producing their computer projects, installing any specialized software, and bookmarking key Internet sites.

This chapter also emphasizes that it takes time and careful planning to achieve a well-managed student-centered classroom in which students use computers. When establishing your management plan it is important to implement and follow basic guidelines that help your students to achieve within a computer learning culture. Your assignments will vary based on the number of computers available to the students and the rotation plan chosen (group or independent rotation). As you manage student activities, you will need to assist students with learning computer skills, keep students who are using the computer on task, and solve technical problems. A final aspect of managing classroom use of computers is taking care of extra resources, managing the computer desktops, and maintaining the equipment.

Teacher Technology FAQ

How can I teach my children 21st-century skills when I don't have these skills yet?

Keeping up with the latest technology is a daunting task, especially for teachers who were not born in the age of technology. However, a key concept underlying the new approaches presented in the NTeQ model emphasizes the need to start slow, begin with what you are most familiar, and gain trust to use student expertise for technology tasks that you are learning. It is impossible to know how to use all of the available technologies, but you can have an open attitude to learn how to use the functions that will assist your student in achieving greater understanding and learning of core content as well as greater ability to think and problem-solve.

It sounds good to have a corps of students who are trained as computer assistants, but how do we get these students trained?

Students can become knowledgeable about computers in several different ways. One approach is to include a group of students when the teachers receive technology training. Another way is to have tech-savvy teachers offer minilessons before or after school or at lunch. If a school has a computer lab staffed with a computer teacher, he or she may offer specialized training to future student technology assistants. Business or university personnel or parents can also volunteer to train students in basic computer troubleshooting or operations.

Technology Integration Activities

The following activities provide an opportunity for you to expand your professional growth through digital networks.

1. Participate in an online learning community of teachers such as Tapped In (http://tappedin.org/tappedin) who regularly use technology to support and improve student learning.
2. Explore online resources to create a classroom management plan for student use of computers.

NTeQ Portfolio Activities

Please complete the following activities as part of the teacher, technology, and classroom section of your NTeQ Portfolio.

Reflections

The Getting Started section of this chapter posed three Reflecting on What I Know questions that teachers might commonly ask. In this portion of your journal, reflection questions have been added to address how you would answer each question. Please use information from this chapter to answer the questions.

❶ What can I do to "get ready" for a lesson in which my students use computers?

Reflection Activity: What would you include on a step-by-step sheet that you and other teachers could use when planning the implementation portion of an NTeQ lesson?

❷ Where does the "computer part" come when I am teaching a lesson?

Reflection Activity: Imagine that you are describing the NTeQ lesson plan to your best friend. How would you describe the "During Computer Use" section?

❸ How do you ensure equal access for all students with only three computers?

Reflection Activity: Choose an NTeQ lesson you developed for an earlier chapter. What arrangements would you need to make in the rotation schedule to ensure that all of your students had equal access to a computer during the lesson?

Create a poster that displays the rules your students will follow when using computers in your classroom.

Choose a previously developed lesson and include student computer tasks that may be unfamiliar to them. Create a step-by-step job aid for this lesson.

Appendix

Learning Tasks and Computer Functions

Learning Task	Computer Function Examples
Alter, Change, Convert, Modify, Vary	Use a spreadsheet to alter the data to produce a different graph. Convert a picture to create a different perspective, meaning, etc. Modify a sentence to create an opposite meaning.
Analyze	Use a spreadsheet to determine the smallest, largest, middle, etc. Use a database to find the most or least common characteristics. Use a spreadsheet to make a graph or chart.
Appraise	Use a graph to determine the solution to problem. Use a spreadsheet to evaluate.
Arrange	Use a database to arrange the states by their order of entry into the Union. Use a spreadsheet to arrange the cells from smallest to largest. Use the draw program to arrange pictures in correct sequence.
Assemble, Produce	Produce a drawing of how you would assemble the equipment for this experiment.
Assess	Use a digital camera to compare and contrast. Use word processing to write an evaluation. Use word processing to create a survey or record data on a spreadsheet or database.
Calculate	Create a formula to calculate the area of rectangles. Determine the average weight of five pumpkins.
Choose, Select, Categorize	Use a database to sort or match records according to common characteristics. Use the database of the presidents and select all who served two terms. Categorize the states by their electoral vote in the last three elections.
Classify, Identify, Isolate, List, Recognize	Identify the plants in the database that have particular characteristics. Use a word processing program to keep a list of your new words.
Collaborate, Cooperate, Contribute	Use email to collaborate with other students at a distant location. Use a word processing program to share ideas and conclusions with others.

(continued)

Learning Task	Computer Function Examples
Collect, Observe, Gather	Enter your data from the observation into the database. Observe how the line changes as you change the first variable. Use the Internet to gather information and data.
Combine, Match, Tabulate, Sequence	Use a spreadsheet to determine the most preferred drink and snack from your taste test. Determine how many perennials and annuals you have observed. Sequence the states according to their joining the Union.
Compare, Contrast, Differentiate, Discriminate, Relate	Compare last year's cookie sales to this year's cookie sales. Draw two pictures to help you differentiate between rotation and revolution. Use a spreadsheet with charts to show similarities and differences. Use a database to find common/uncommon characteristics. Use word processing to communicate similarities and differences. Use draw and copy functions to compare geometric shapes.
Deduce, Infer, Generalize	Use a database to analyze information to support generalizations. Based on the graph of the cookie sales for the last two years, how many will this class sell this year? Based on plants with similar characteristics in the database, how would you classify this example?
Describe, Outline, Paraphrase, Reconstruct, Rephrase	Use a word processor to outline the chapter. Paraphrase the information you found in the CD-ROM encyclopedia. Based on your research, write a story to reconstruct the events leading to the railroad strike.
Design, Plan	Create a drawing showing your plan for the house of tomorrow. Use the draw program to create a safe playground. Make a map of your neighborhood.
Diagram, Draw, Graph, Illustrate, Plot	Use a spreadsheet to make a chart. Use the digital camera to illustrate safety in the classroom. Use clip art/draw program to illustrate your newsletter.
Edit, Punctuate, Report, Write	Allow students to print their first drafts and then exchange with other students to proofread. Create a worksheet. Use spell check to correct spelling errors. Type a story and have members of the group proofread, make suggestions to clarify ideas, and edit the final copy. Gather information on a given topic and write a report.
Estimate, Formulate, Predict,	Use a spreadsheet to manipulate data for estimations and predictions with graphs. Use a database to sort, categorize, and support predictions. Use a database to predict the basketball scores for the teams in the NBA. On a spreadsheet, write formulas for students to multiply, subtract, add, and divide the NBA scores. Use the Internet to have the students estimate how much they would spend at three different stores.

Learning Task	Computer Function Examples
Interpolate, Interpret Extend	Analyze data collected on the spreadsheet and determine which planet will show your lowest and highest weight. Determine how many years it will take to arrive at a planet going a designated speed and record that on a database and spreadsheet. Then calculate your age upon arrival. Use the digital camera to take pictures of an experiment in various stages. Use the pictures and presentations in class.
Judge	Use a CD-ROM encyclopedia to review periods of history such as the World Wars and decide or judge which had the greater impact on modern life.
Judge, Evaluate	Make a judgment based on data collected from CD-ROM encyclopedias, the Internet, books, and *National Geographic* animal software as to which animal should be adopted as a pet. Use word processing to prepare a written report justifying your position. Use charts to make comparisons for evaluations.
Plan	Write a letter about opening your own business. Draw a floor plan in the draw program. Use a spreadsheet to plan your daily expenditures.
Solve, Determine	Use a spreadsheet to determine the classroom with the most square feet. Use a spreadsheet and database to solve word problems. Use the spellcheck to check spelling. Determine the mean, mode, and median scores from a basketball game. Determine which graph will best show the results.
Synthesize	Write a report using word processing, a spreadsheet, and a database.
Verify	Use a spellchecker to check your spelling words. Estimate math problems and then use a spreadsheet to verify the exact answers. Use databases to verify predictions.

This chart was prepared as part of a class exercise by teachers who participated in Project SMART summer training at the University of Memphis.

References

Dear Teacher

Casner-Lotto, J., & Barrington, L. (2006). *Are they really ready to work: Employers' perspectives on the knowledge and applied skills of new entrants to the 21st century U.S. workforce.* The Conference Board, Inc., the Partnership for 21st Century Skills, Corporate Voices for Working Families, and the Society for Human Resource Management. Retrieved January 21, 2009, from http://www.21stcenturyskills.org/index.php?option=com_content&task=view&id=82&Itemid=40.

Newman, H. (2002, February 26). Computers used more to learn than teach. *Detroit Free Press.* Retrieved June 7, 2007, from http://www.freepress.com/news/education/newman 26_20020226.htm.

Ross, S. M., Smith, L., Alberg, M., & Lowther, D. (2004). Using classroom observations as a research and formative evaluation tool in educational reform: The school observation measure. In S. Hilberg and H. Waxman (Eds.), *New directions for observational research in culturally and linguistically diverse classrooms* (pp. 144–173). Santa Cruz, CA: Center for Research on Education, Diversity, & Excellence.

U.S. Department of Commerce, Economics and Statistics Administration (ESA). (2003). *Digital Economy 2003.* Washington, DC: Author. Retrieved January 17, 2009, from http://www.esa.doc.gov/reports/DE-Chap4.pdf.

U.S. Department of Education (DOE). (2003). Federal funding for educational technology and how it is used in the classroom: A summary of findings from the Integrated Studies of Educational Technology. Washington, DC: Office of the Under Secretary, Policy and Program Studies Service. Retrieved January 24, 2009, from http://www.ed.gov/about/offices/list/os/technology/evaluation.html.

Chapter 1

Albanese, M. A., & Mitchell, S. (1993). Problem-based learning: A review of the literature on its outcomes and implementation issues. *Academic Medicine, 68,* 52–81.

Barrows, H. S. (1985). *How to design a problem-based curriculum for the preclinical years.* New York: Springer.

Blumenfeld, P. C., Soloway, E., Marx, R., Krajcik, J. S., Guzdial, M., & Palincsar, A. (1991). Motivating project-based learning: Sustaining the doing, supporting the learning. *Educational Psychologist, 26*(3 & 4), 369–398.

Bork, A. (1987). *Learning with personal computers.* New York: Harper & Row.

Brooks, J. G., & Brooks, M. G. (1993). *In search of understanding: The case for constructivist classrooms.* Alexandria, VA: Association for Supervision and Curriculum Development.

Brown, J. S., Collins, A., & Duguid, P. (1989). Situated cognition and the culture of learning. *Educational Researcher, 18,* 32–42.

Bruner, J. S. (1960). *The process of education.* Cambridge, MA: Harvard University Press.

Casner-Lotto, J., & Barrington, L. (2006). *Are they really ready to work: Employers' perspectives on the knowledge and applied skills of new entrants to the 21st century U.S. workforce.* The Conference Board, Inc., the Partnership for 21st Century Skills, Corporate Voices for Working Families, and the Society for Human Resource Management. Retrieved January

21, 2009, from http://www.21stcenturyskills.org/index.php?option=com_content&task=view&id=82&Itemid=40.

Dewey, J. (1916). *Democracy and education.* New York: MacMillan Company.

Festinger, L. (1957). *A theory of cognitive dissonance.* Stanford, CA: Stanford University Press.

Gardner, H. (1991). *The unschooled mind: How children think and how schools should teach.* New York: Basic Books.

Herrington, J., & Oliver, R. (2000). An instructional design framework for authentic learning environments. *Educational Technology Research and Development, 48,* 23–48.

International Society for Technology in Education. (2007). *National educational technology standards.* Eugene, OR: Author.

Johnson, D. W., Johnson, R. T., & Smith, K. A. (1991). *Active learning: Cooperation in the college classroom.* Edina, MN: Interaction Book Company.

Jonassen, D. (1997). Instructional design models for well-structured and ill-structured problem-solving learning outcomes. *Educational Technology Research and Development, 45*(1), 65–95.

Jonassen, D., Howland, J., Marra, R., & Crismond, D. (2008). *Meaningful learning with technology.* Upper Saddle River, NJ: Pearson/Merrill Prentice Hall.

Land, S. M., & Hannafin, M. J. (1997). Patterns of understanding with open-ended learning environments: A qualitative study. *Educational Technology Research and Development, 45*(2), 47–73.

Lowther, D. L., Inan, F. A., Strahl, J. D., & Ross, S. M. (2008). Does technology integration "work" when key barriers are removed? *Educational Media International, 45*(3), 189–206.

Lowther, D. L., Ross, S. M., & Morrison, G. R. (2003). The laptop classroom: The effect on instruction and achievement. *Educational Technology Research and Development, 51,* 23–44.

Means, B. (1994). Introduction: Using technology to advance educational goals. In B. Means (Ed.), *Technology and educational reform* (pp. 1–21). San Francisco: Jossey-Bass.

National Commission on Excellence in Education. (1983). *A nation at risk: The imperative for educational reform.* Washington, DC: Decision Resources Corporation.

Newmann, F. M., Bryk, A. S., & Nagaoka, J. K. (2001). *Authentic intellectual work and standardized tests: Conflict or coexistence?* Consortium on Chicago School Research. [Online]. Available at www.consortium-chicago.org/publications/pdfs/p0a02.pdf.

Norman, D. A. (1993). *Things that make us smart: Defending human attributes in the age of the machine.* Cambridge, MA: Perseus Books.

Partnership for 21st Century Skills. (2008). *21st century skills, education, & competitiveness: A resource and policy guide.* Retrieved January 7, 2008, from http://www.21stcenturyskills.org/documents/21st_century_skills_education_and_competitiveness_guide.pdf.

Ross, S. M., Smith, L. J., Alberg, M., & Lowther, D. L. (2004). Using classroom observations as a research and formative evaluation tool in educational reform: The school observation measure. In S. Hilberg & H. Waxman (Eds.), *New directions for observational research in culturally and linguistically diverse classrooms* (pp. 144–173). Santa Cruz, CA: Center for Research on Education, Diversity, & Excellence.

Savery, J. R. (2006). Overview of problem-based learning: Definitions and distinctions. *The Interdisciplinary Journal of Problem-Based Learning, 1*(1), 9–20.

Savery, J. R., & Duffy, T. M. (1995). Problem-based learning: An instructional model and its constructivist framework. *Educational Technology, 45,* 31–38.

21st Century Education System Task Force. (2007). *Maximizing the impact: The pivotal role of technology in a 21st century education system.* International Society for Technology in Education, Partnership for 21st Century Skills, and State Education Technology Directors Association. Retrieved January 27, 2008, from http://www.setda.org/web/guest/maximizingimpactreport.

U.S. Department of Commerce, Economics and Statistics Administration (ESA). (2003). *Digital economy 2003*. Washington, DC: Author. Retrieved January 17, 2008, from https://www.esa.doc.gov/reports/DE-Chap4.pdf.

U.S. Department of Education (DOE). (2001). *No Child Left Behind Act of 2001: Enhancing education through technology* (II-D-1&2). Retrieved August 2, 2007, from http://www.ed.gov/admins/lead/account/nclbreference/page_pg28.html#iid1.

Vygotsky, L. (1978). *Mind in society*. Cambridge, MA: Harvard University Press.

Chapter 2

Bloom, B. S., Englehart, M. D., Furst, E. J., Hill, W. H., & Krathwohl, D. R. (Eds.). (1956). *Taxonomy of educational objectives: The classification of education goals. Handbook I: Cognitive domain*. New York: David McKay.

Bransford, J. D., Brown, A. L., & Cocking, R. R. (1999). *How people learn: Brain, mind, experience, and school*. Washington, DC: National Academy Press.

Bransford, J. D., Sherwood, R. D., Hasselbring, T. S., Kinzer, C. K., & Williams, S. M. (1990). Anchored instruction: Why we need it and how technology can help. In D. Nix & R. J. Spiro (Eds.), *Cognition, education, and multimedia: Exploring ideas in high technology* (pp. 115–142). Hillsdale, NJ: Erlbaum.

Bruner, J. S. (1960). *The process of education*. Cambridge, MA: Harvard University Press.

Bruner, J. S. (1996). *The culture of education*. Cambridge, MA: Harvard University Press.

Campbell, D. (2000). Authentic assessment and authentic standards. *Phi Delta Kappan, 81*, 405–407.

Christensen, R., Overall, T., & Knezek, G. (2006). Personal educational tools (PETs) for type II learning. *Computers in the Schools, 23*(1–2), 173–189.

Clark, R. E. (1983). Reconsidering research on learning from media. *Review of Educational Research, 53*, 445–459.

Collins, A., & Stevens, A. L. (1983). A cognitive theory of inquiry teaching. In C. M. Reigeluth (Ed.), *Instructional design theories and models: An overview of their status* (pp. 247–278). Hillsdale, NJ: Erlbaum.

Danielson, C. (1997). *A collection of performance tasks and rubrics: Middle school mathematics*. Larchmont, NY: Eye on Education.

Deal, D., & Sterling, D. (1997). Kids ask the best questions. *Educational Leadership, 54*, 61–63.

Deming, J. C., & Cracolice, M. S. (2004). Learning to think. *Science Education, 71*(3), 42–47.

DiMartino, J., & Castaneda, A. (2007). Assessing applied skills. *Educational Leadership, 64*(7), 38–42.

Gandal, M. (1995). Not all standards are created equal. *Educational Leadership, 52*, 16–21.

Grambs, L. H., & Starr, I. S. (1976). *Modern methods in secondary education* (5th ed.). Fort Worth, TX: Holt, Rinehart and Winston.

Gronlund, N. E. (1985). *Stating behavioral objectives for classroom instruction*. New York: Macmillan.

Gronlund, N. E. (1995). *How to write and use instructional objectives* (5th ed.). New York: Prentice Hall.

Gronlund, N. E. (2004). *Writing instructional objectives for teaching and assessment* (7th ed.). New York: Prentice Hall.

Hancock, C., Kaput, J. J., & Goldsmith, L. T. (1992). Authentic inquiry with data: Critical barriers to classroom interpretation. *Educational Psychologist, 27,* 337–364.

Jonassen, D., Howland, J., Marra, R., & Crismond, D. (2008). *Meaningful learning with technology* (3rd ed.). Upper Saddle River, NJ: Pearson/Merrill Prentice Hall.

Latourelle, S. M., & Elwess, N. L. (2006). Inquiry, observation and expression: Be creative but stay genuine! *American Biology Teacher, 68*(5), 54–60.

Mager, R. F. (1984). *Preparing instructional objectives* (2nd ed.). Belmont, CA: Pitman.

Marcoulides, G. A., & Heck, R. H. (1994). The changing role of educational assessment in the 1990s. *Education and Urban Society, 26*(4), 332–337.

Mayer, R. (1987). *Educational psychology: A cognitive approach.* Boston: Little Brown and Co.

McCain, T. (2005). *Teaching for tomorrow: Teaching content and problem-solving.* Thousand Oaks, CA: Corwin Press.

Merrill, M. D. (2007). A task-centered instructional strategy. *Journal of Research on Technology in Education, 40*(1), 33–50.

Moursund, D. G. (2007). Introduction to problem solving in the Information Age. Eugene, OR: Information Age Education. Retrieved September 20, 2008, from http://darkwing.uoregon.edu/~moursund/Books/IAE-PS/PS-in-IA.pdf.

Petraglia, J. (1998). The real world on a short leash: The (mis)application of constructivism to the design of educational technology. *Educational Technology Research and Development, 46*(3), 54–65.

Sharma, S. (2007). From chaos to clarity: Using the research portfolio to teach and assess information literacy skills. *Journal of Academic Librarianship, 33*(1), 127–135.

Spandel, V. (2006). In defense of rubrics. *English Journal, 96*(1), 19–22.

Winne, P. H., & Hadwin, A. F. (1998). Studying as self-regulated learning. In D. J. Hacker, J. Dunlosky, & A. C. Graesser (Eds.), *Metacognition in educational theory and practice.* Mahwah, NJ: Lawrence Erlbaum.

Wolf, S., & Fraser, B. J. (2008). Learning environment, attitudes and achievement among middle-school science students using inquiry-based laboratory activities. *Research in Science Education, 38*(3), 321–341.

Yoshina, J. M., & Harada, V. H. (2007). Involving students in learning through rubrics. *Library Media Connection, 25*(5), 10–14.

Chapter 3

Apple. (2008). Apple reports first quarter results: Best quarterly revenue & earnings in Apple history. Retrieved June 7, 2008, from www.apple.com/pr/library/2008/01/22results.html.

DiCamillo, K. (2000). *Because of Winn-Dixie.* Somerville, MA: Candlewick Press.

Electronista. (2008). Zune reaches 2m sales flat versus iPod. Retrieved June 7, 2008, from http://www.electronista.com/articles/08/05/09/ms.sells.2m.zunes.

Ellington, A. J. (2003). A meta-analysis of the effects of calculators on students' achievement and attitude levels in precollege mathematics classes. *Journal for Research in Mathematics Education, 34*(5), 433–463.

Flavelle, C. (2008, May). The Tom Sawyer of innovation. *Newsweek International Edition, 151*(20), online. Retrieved June 16, 2008, from www.newsweek.com/id/136381.

International Society for Technology in Education (ISTE). (2007). National educational technology standards for students (NETS-S). Eugene, OR: Author.

Khoju, M., Jaciw, A., & Miller, G. I. (2005). *Effectiveness of graphing calculators in K–12 mathematics achievement: A systematic review.* Palo Alto, CA: Empirical Education.

Leath, A. (2007). *STEM education a hot topic on Capitol Hill.* American Institute of Physics. Retrieved June 21, 2008, from http://www.aip.org/fyi/2007/041.html.

Moss, L. (2006). GPS for schools: How to use satellite technology [in and] out of the classroom. Retrieved June 8, 2008, from http://www.btinternet.com/~laurencemoss/pdf/GPS.pdf.

National Center for Education Statistics (NCES). (2001). *The nation's report card: Mathematics 2000.* (No. NCES 2001-571). Washington, DC: U.S. Department of Education.

National Council of Teachers of Mathematics (NCTM). (2000). *Principles and standards for school mathematics.* Reston, VA: Author.

Natsu, J. (2008, May). eSN special report: Virtual desktops: How virtual desktops will revolutionize personal computing. *eSchool News, 21,* 22–27.

Nielsen, J. H., & Furst, C. (2007, September). Toward more-compact digital microphones. *Analog Dialogue, 41*(9), 1–3.

Pellerin, C. (2006). United States updates global positioning system technology. Retrieved June 8, 2008, from http://www.america.gov/st/washfile-english/2006/February/20060203125928lcnirellep0.5061609.html.

Prensky, M. (2008). Turning on the lights. *Educational Leadership, 65*(6), 40–45.

Schrock, K. (2007). *Power in the palm of your hand.* Retrieved June 14, 2008, from http://kathy schrock.net/power.

Thornton, C. (2008). *Palm pocket PC.* Retrieved June 15, 2008, from http://pcworld.about.com/magazine/1904p092id41466.htm.

Wichary, M. (2004). *Macintosh: Twenty years later.* Retrieved June 7, 2008, from http://www.digibarn.com/collections/ads/apple-mac/index.htm.

Chapter 4

Federation of American Scientists. (2006). *Harnessing the power of educational games.* Retrieved November 10, 2006, from http://fas.org/gamesummit/Resources/Summit%20on%20Educational%20Games.pdf.

Institute of Education Sciences (IES). (2008). *What works clearinghouse.* U.S. Department of Education. Retrieved February 8, 2009, from http://ies.ed.gov/ncee/wwc/reports/beginning_reading/arrr.

International Society for Technology in Education (ISTE). (2007). National educational technology standards for students (NETS-S). Eugene, OR: Author.

Lowther, D. L., Ross, S. M., & Morrison, G. R. (2003). When each one has one: The influences on teaching strategies and student achievement of using laptops in the classroom. *Educational Technology Research and Development, 51*(3), 23–44.

Prensky, M. (2007, March). Sims vs. games: The difference defined. *Edutopia Magazine.* Retrieved September 24, 2008, from http://www.edutopia.org/sims-vs-games.

Technorati. (2007, April). *Blog potato.* Retrieved April 21, 2007, from http://www.blogpotato.com/blogging/technorati.

U.S. Department of Education (DOE). (2001). *No Child Left Behind Act of 2001.* Retrieved April 21, 2007, from http://www.ed.gov/admins/lead/account/nclbreference/page_pg28.html.

Chapter 5

Ames, C. (1992). Achievement goals and the classroom motivational climate. In D. H. Schunk & J. L. Meece (Eds.), *Student perceptions in the classroom* (pp. 327–348). Mahwah, NJ: Erlbaum.

Berthold, K., Nückles, M., & Renkl, A. (2007). Do learning protocols support learning strategies and outcomes? The role of cognitive and metacognitive prompts. *Learning and Instruction, 17,* 564–577.

Darling-Hammond, L., Barron, B., Pearson, P. D., Schoenfeld, A. H., Stage, E. K., Zimmerman, T. D., Cervetti, G. N., & Tilson, J. L. (2008). *Powerful learning: What we know about teaching for understanding.* San Francisco: Jossey-Bass.

Dunbar, K. (2000). How scientists think the real world: Implications for science education. *Journal of Applied Developmental Psychology, 21*(1), 49–58.

Durkin, D. (1979). What classroom observations reveal about reading comprehension instruction. *Reading Research Quarterly, 15,* 481–533.

Jonassen, D. H. (1988). Integrating learning strategies into courseware to facilitate deeper processing. In D. H. Jonassen (Ed.), *Instructional designs for microcomputer courseware* (pp. 151–181). Hillsdale, NJ: Lawrence Erlbaum.

Ogle, D. S. (1986). K-W-L group instructional strategy. In A. S. Palincsar, D. S. Ogle, B. F. Jones, & E. G. Carr (Eds.), *Teaching reading as thinking* (Teleconference Resource Guide, pp. 11–17). Alexandria, VA: Association for Supervision and Curriculum Development.

Pressley, M., El-Dinary, P. B., Wharton-McDonald, R., & Brown, R. (1998). Transactional instruction of comprehension strategies in the elementary grades. In D. H. Schunk & B. J. Zimmerman (Eds.), *Self-regulated learning: From teaching to self-reflective practice* (pp. 42–56). New York: Guilford Press.

Rigney, J. W. (1978). Learning strategies: A theoretical perspective. In H. F. O'Neil, Jr. (Ed.), *Learning strategies* (pp. 165–205). New York: Academic Press.

Schraw, G., Crippen, K. J., & Hartley, K. (2006). Promoting self-regulation in science education: Metacognition as part of a broader perspective on learning. *Research in Science Education, 36,* 111–139.

Wittrock, M. C. (1974). Learning as a generative process. *Educational Psychologist, 11*(2), 87–95.

Wittrock, M. C. (1990). Generative processes of comprehension. *Educational Psychologist, 24*(4), 345–376.

Wittrock, M.C. (1991). Generative teaching of comprehension. *Elementary School Journal, 92,* 167–182.

Wittrock, M. C. (1992). Generative teaching: An enhancement strategy for the learning of economics in cooperative groups. *American Educational Research Journal, 29*(4), 861–876.

Zimmerman, B. (1998). Developing self-fulfilling cycles of academic regulation: An analysis of exemplary instructional models. In D. H. Schunk & B. J. Zimmerman (Eds.), *Self-regulated learning: From teaching to self-reflective practice* (pp. 1–19). New York: Guilford Press.

Zimmerman, B. (2008). Regulation and motivation: Historical background, methodological developments, and future prospects. *American Educational Research Journal, 45*(1), 166–183.

Zimmerman B., & Tsikalas, K. E. (2005). Can computer-based learning environments (CBLEs) be used as self-regulatory tools to enhance learning? *Educational Psychologist, 40*(4), 267–271.

Chapter 6

Alpert, J., & Hajaj, N. (2008, July). *We knew the web was big . . .* The Official Google Blog. Retrieved November 17, 2008, from http://googleblog.blogspot.com/2008/07/we-knew-web-was-big.html.

Barry, E. S. (2006). Can paraphrasing practice help students define plagiarism? *College Student Journal, 40*(2), 377–384.

Bauerlein, M. (2008, November). *The dumbest generation: How the digital age stupefies young Americans.* Education Week presentation at Old Dominion University, Norfolk, VA.

comScore Press Release. (2008, July 18). comScore releases June 2008 U.S. search engine rankings. Retrieved November 17, 2008, from www.comscore.com/press/release.asp?press=2337.

Crawford, T. (1993). *Legal guide for the visual artist.* New York: Allworth Press.

Creative Commons. (n.d.). *Choosing a license: Creative common licenses.* Retrieved November 20, 2008, from http://creativecommons.org/about/licenses/meet-the-licenses.

Google Guide. (2008, September 8). *GoogleGuide: Making searching even easier.* Retrieved November 18, 2008, from http://www.googleguide.com/advanced_operators_reference.html.

Molnar, J. P. (1969). Picturephone service—A new way of communicating. *Bell Laboratories Record, 47,* 134–135. Retrieved February 18, 2009, from http://www.porticus.org/bell/pdf/picturephone.pdf.

Parsad, B., & Jones, J. (2005). *Internet access in U.S. public schools and classrooms: 1994–2003* (NCES 2005-015). U.S. Department of Education. Washington, DC: National Center for Education Statistics.

Chapter 7

Becker, H. J. (2000). Internet use by teachers. *The Jossey-Bass Reader on Technology and Learning.* San Francisco: Jossey-Bass.

Institute for the Advancement of Research in Education (IARE). (2003, July). *Graphic organizers: A review of scientifically based research.* Charleston, WV: Appalachian Educational Lab (AEL).

International Society for Technology in Education (ISTE). (2007). National educational technology standards (NETS) for students. Retrieved October 20, 2007, from http://cnets.iste.org/students/index.html.

Jonassen, D., Howland, J., Marra, R., & Crismond, D. (2008). *Meaningful learning with technology* (3rd ed.). Upper Saddle River, NJ: Pearson/Merrill Prentice Hall.

Lowther, D. L., Ross, S. M., & Morrison, G. R. (2003). When each one has one: The influences on teaching strategies and student achievement of using laptops in the classroom. *Educational Technology Research & Development, 51*(3), 23–44.

Peacock, G. (1993). Word-processors and collaborative writing. In J. Beynon & H. Mackay (Eds.), *Computers into classrooms: More questions than answers* (pp. 92–97). Washington, DC: Falmer Press.

Roblyer, M. D. (1997). Technology and the oops! effect: Finding a bias against word processing. *Learning and Leading with Technology, 24*(7), 14–16.

Ross, S. M., Smith, L. J., Alberg, M., & Lowther, D. L. (2004). Using classroom observations as a research and formative evaluation tool in educational reform: The school observation measure. In S. Hilberg & H. Waxman (Eds.), *New directions for observational research in culturally and linguistically diverse classrooms* (pp. 144–173). Santa Cruz, CA: Center for Research in Education, Diversity, & Excellence.

Wetzel, K. (1990). Keyboarding. In S. Franklin (Ed.), *The best of the writing notebook* (pp. 46–48). Eugene, OR: The Writing Notebook.

Chapter 8

Bottge, B. A., Heinrichs, M., & Mehta, Z. D. (2004). Teaching mathematical problem solving to middle school students in math, technology education, and special education classrooms. *RMLE Online: Research in Middle Level Education, 27,* 1–17.

Carter, A. (1999). Using spreadsheets to model population growth, competition, and predation in nature. *American Biology Teacher, 61,* 294–296.

Cognition and Technology Group at Vanderbilt. (1990). Anchored instruction and its relationship to situated cognition. *Educational Researcher, 19,* 2–10.

Drier, H. S. (2001). Teaching and learning mathematics with interactive spreadsheets. *School Science and Mathematics, 101*(4), 170–179.

Gagnon, J. C., & Bottge, B. A. (2006). Mathematics instruction in secondary interim, short- and long-term alternative school placements. *Preventing School Failure, 51,* 39–47.

Galbraith, P., & Haines, C. (2001). The key skills agenda: Exploring implications for mathematics. *International Journal of Math, Science, and Technology, 32*(3), 337–354.

International Society for Technology in Education (ISTE). (2007). National educational technology standards for students (NETS). Retrieved October 20, 2007, from http://cnets.iste.org/students/index.html.

Neiss, M. L. (2005). Scaffolding math learning with spreadsheets. *Learning & Leading with Technology, 32*(5), 24–25, 48.

Salomon, G. (1993). On the nature of pedagogic computer tools: The case of the writing partner. In S. P. LaJoie & S. J. Derry (Eds.), *Computers as cognitive tools*. Mahwah, NJ: Lawrence Erlbaum.

Walsh, T. P. (1996). Exploring difference equations with spreadsheets. *Learning and Leading with Technology, 24*(1), 28–32.

Chapter 9

Brookes, G. (1988). Exploring the world through reading and writing. *Language Arts, 65*(3), 245–253.

Corbine, M. (1995). The effective use of student journal writing. *ERIC Digest*. Bloomington, IN: ERIC/REC [ED378 587].

Halliday, M. A. (1985). *An introduction to functional grammar*. Baltimore: Edward Arnold.

Huerta, G. C., & Flemmer, L. A. (2000). *Using student-generated oral history research in the secondary classroom. Clearing House, 74*(2), 105–111.

International Society for Technology in Education (ISTE). (2007). National Educational Technology Standards (NETS) for Students. Retrieved October 20, 2007, from http://cnets.iste.org/students/index.html.

Johannessen, L. R., & Kahn, E. A. (1991). *Writing across the curriculum*. Paper presented at the Teachers' Institute, Summit, IL.

Keys, C. W. (1999). Language as an indicator of meaning generation: An analysis of middle school students' written discourse about scientific investigations. *Journal of Research in Science Teaching, 36,* 1044–1061.

Mayer, R. E., Moreno, R., Boire, M., & Vagge, S. (1999). Maximizing constructivist learning from multimedia communication by minimizing cognitive load. *Journal of Educational Psychology, 91,* 639–643.

McBride, K. H., & Luntz, E. D. (1996). *Help, I have HyperStudio® . . . now what do I do?* Glendora, CA: McB Media.

Wang, X. C., Kedem, Y., & Hertzog, N. (2004). Scaffolding young children's reflections with student-created PowerPoint presentations. *Journal of Research in Childhood Education, 19*(2), 159–175.

Wittrock, M. C. (1974). Learning as a generative process. *Educational Psychologist, 11*(2), 87–95.

Wittrock, M. C. (1990). Generative processes of comprehension. *Educational Psychologist, 24*(4), 345–376.

Chapter 10

Institute for the Advancement of Research in Education (IARE). (2003, July). *Graphic organizers: A review of scientifically based research*. Charleston, WV: Appalachian Educational Lab (AEL).

International Society for Technology in Education (ISTE). (2007). National educational technology standards for students. Retrieved October 20, 2007, from http://cnets.iste.org/students/index.html.

Jonassen, D. H. (2006). *Modeling with technology: Mindtools for conception change* (3rd ed.). Upper Saddle River, NJ: Pearson/Merrill Prentice Hall.

Moreno, R., & Mayer, R. (2000). *A learner-centered approach to multimedia explanations: Deriving instructional design principles from cognitive theory.* Retrieved June 16, 2007, from http://imej.wfu.edu/articles/2000/2/05/index.asp.

National Center for History in Schools (NCHS). (1996). *National standards for history.* Retrieved July 14, 2008, from http://nchs.ucla.edu.

Resnick, L. B., & Klopfer, L. E. (1987). Toward the thinking curriculum: An overview. In L. B. Resnick & L. E. Klopfer (Eds.), *Toward the thinking curriculum: Current cognitive research.* Alexandria, VA: ASCD.

Venn, J. (1880). On the diagrammatic and mechanical representation of propositions and reasonings, *The London, Edinburgh, and Dublin Philosophical Magazine and Journal of Science, 9,* 1–18.

Chapter 11

Educational Software Preview Guide (ESPG). (2007). *Educational software preview guide.* Retrieved January 6, 2008, from http://ed.fnal.gov/espg.

Federation of American Scientists. (2006). *Harnessing the power of educational games.* Retrieved January 11, 2008, from http://www.fas.org/gamesummit.

Gill, B. J., Dick, W., Reiser, R. A., & Zahner, J. E. (1992). A new model for evaluating instructional software. *Educational Technology, 32*(3), 39–44.

Hubbard, P. (1992). *Software evaluation guide* [Online]. Retrieved February 11, 2009, from www.athel.com/eval.html.

Kulik, J. A. (1994). Meta-analytic studies of findings on computer-based instruction. In E. L. Baker & H. F. O'Neil, Jr. (Eds.), *Technology assessment in education and training.* Mahwah, NJ: Lawrence.

Kulik, J. (2002). *School mathematics and science programs benefit from instructional technology.* National Science Foundation: Science Resource Statistics, NSF 03-301. Retrieved March 16, 2008, from http://www.nsf.gov/sbe/srs/infbrief/nsf03301/start.htm.

Kulik, J. (2003). *Effects of using instructional technology in elementary and secondary schools: What controlled evaluation studies say.* Arlington, VA: SRI International. Retrieved March 16, 2008, from http://www.sri.com/policy/csted/reports/sandt/it/Kulik_ITinK-12_Main_Report.pdf.

Mann, D., Shakeshaft, C., Becker, J., & Kottkamp, R. (1999). *West Virginia's basic skills/computer education program: An analysis of student achievement.* Santa Monica, CA: Milken Family Foundation.

Morrison, G. R., Ross, S. M., Gopalakrishnan, M., & Casey, J. (1995). The effects of feedback and incentives on achievement in computer-based instruction. *Contemporary Educational Psychology, 20,* 32–50.

Morrison, G. R., Ross, S. M., & Kemp, J. E. (2006). *Designing effective instruction: Applications of instructional design* (5th ed.). New York: Wiley.

Oblinger, D. (2004). The next generation of educational engagement. *Journal of Interactive Media in Education, 8,* 1–18.

Prensky, M. (2007). Sims vs. games, *Edutopia Magazine.* Retrieved January 10, 2007, from www.edutopia.org/sims-vs-games#comment-16941.

Reiser, R. A., & Dick, W. (1990). Evaluating instructional software. *Educational Technology Research and Development, 38*(3), 43–50.

Sivin-Kachala, J. (1998). *Report of effectiveness of technology in schools, 1990–1997.* Washington, DC: Software Publishers Association.

Wenglinsky, H. (1998, September). *Does it compute? The relationship between educational technology and student achievement in mathematics.* Princeton, NJ: Educational Testing Service Policy Information Center.

Wong, Y. K. (2006). *Modern software review: Techniques and technologies.* Hershey, PA: IGI Global.

Wrench, J. S. (2001). Educational software evaluation form: Towards a new evaluation of educational software. *The Source: A Journal of Education, 3,* 34–46.

Chapter 12

Anderson, W. (2005). *That's not a drinking fountain or how to survive in a one computer classroom.* North Central Regional Technology in Education Consortium. Retrieved December 22, 2008, from www.ncrtec.org/tl/digi/onecomp.

Casson, L., Bauman, J., Fisher, E., Sumpter, J., & Tornatzky, L. G. (1997). *Making technology happen: Best practices and policies from exemplary K–12 schools.* Report. Southern Technology Council. Research Triangle Park, NC: Southern Growth Publications.

Cataldo, J. (2008). *Arranging your classroom: Part 1.* Bright Hub. Retrieved December 22, 2008, from http://www.brighthub.com/education/k-12/articles/4959.aspx.

Churchward, B. (1997, September 11). *The honor level system: Discipline by design—11 techniques for better classroom discipline.* [Online]. Available at http://members.aol.com/churchward/hls/techniques.html.

Electronic Education Report. (2008). NAEP will include technology literacy in 2012. *Electronic Education Report, 14*(20), 1. Retrieved December 22, 2008, from www.learning.com/press/pdf/SIMBA-Bill-Kelly-article.pdf.

Intel Education Initiative. (2004). *Managing computer use: Challenges and solutions.* Retrieved December 21, 2008, from www.intel.com/education/newtotech/managing.htm.

International Society for Technology in Education. (2008). *National educational technology standards for teachers.* Eugene, OR: Author.

Johnson, D. W., & Johnson, R. T. (2004). Cooperation and the use of technology. In D. H. Jonassen (Ed.), *Handbook of research on educational communications and technology* (pp. 785–811). Mahwah, NJ: Erlbaum.

Kentucky Student Technology Leadership Program (KY STLP). (2008). *Kentucky Department of Education student technology leadership program.* Retrieved December 22, 2008, from www.education.ky.gov/KDE/Instructional+Resources/Technology/Student+Initiatives/STLP+Student+Technology+Leadership+Program.

Ryba, K., & Anderson, B. (1993). *Learning with computers: Effective teaching strategies.* Eugene, OR: International Society for Technology in Education.

Sandholtz, J. H., & Reilly, B. (2004). Teachers, not technicians: Rethinking technical expectations for teachers. *Teachers College Press, 106*(3), 487–512.

Credits

ISTE National Educational Technology Standards and Performance Indicators for Teachers

1. Facilitate and Inspire Student Learning and Creativity

Teachers use their knowledge of subject matter, teaching and learning, and technology to facilitate experiences that advance student learning, creativity, and innovation in both face-to-face and virtual environments. Teachers:

a. promote, support, and model creative and innovative thinking and inventiveness.
b. engage students in exploring real-world issues and solving authentic problems using digital tools and resources.
c. promote student reflection using collaborative tools to reveal and clarify students' conceptual understanding and thinking, planning, and creative processes.
d. model collaborative knowledge construction by engaging in learning with students, colleagues, and others in face-to-face and virtual environments.

2. Design and Develop Digital-Age Learning Experiences and Assessments

Teachers design, develop, and evaluate authentic learning experiences and assessment incorporating contemporary tools and resources to maximize content learning in context and to develop the knowledge, skills, and attitudes identified in the NETS·S. Teachers:

a. design or adapt relevant learning experiences that incorporate digital tools and resources to promote student learning and creativity.
b. develop technology-enriched learning environments that enable all students to pursue their individual curiosities and become active participants in setting their own educational goals, managing their own learning, and assessing their own progress.
c. customize and personalize learning activities to address students' diverse learning styles, working strategies, and abilities using digital tools and resources.
d. provide students with multiple and varied formative and summative assessments aligned with content and technology standards and use resulting data to inform learning and teaching.

3. Model Digital-Age Work and Learning

Teachers exhibit knowledge, skills, and work processes representative of an innovative professional in a global and digital society. Teachers:

a. demonstrate fluency in technology systems and the transfer of current knowledge to new technologies and situations.
b. collaborate with students, peers, parents, and community members using digital tools and resources to support student success and innovation.
c. communicate relevant information and ideas effectively to students, parents, and peers using a variety of digital-age media and formats.
d. model and facilitate effective use of current and emerging digital tools to locate, analyze, evaluate, and use information resources to support research and learning.

4. Promote and Model Digital Citizenship and Responsibility

Teachers understand local and global societal issues and responsibilities in an evolving digital culture and exhibit legal and ethical behavior in their professional practices. Teachers:

a. advocate, model, and teach safe, legal, and ethical use of digital information and technology, including respect for copyright, intellectual property, and the appropriate documentation of sources.
b. address the diverse needs of all learners by using learner-centered strategies providing equitable access to appropriate digital tools and resources.
c. promote and model digital etiquette and responsible social interactions related to the use of technology and information.
d. develop and model cultural understanding and global awareness by engaging with colleagues and students of other cultures using digital-age communication and collaboration tools.

5. Engage in Professional Growth and Leadership

Teachers continuously improve their professional practice, model lifelong learning, and exhibit leadership in their school and professional community by promoting and demonstrating the effective use of digital tools and resources. Teachers:

a. participate in local and global learning communities to explore creative applications of technology to improve student learning.
b. exhibit leadership by demonstrating a vision of technology infusion, participating in shared decision making and community building, and developing the leadership and technology skills of others.
c. evaluate and reflect on current research and professional practice on a regular basis to make effective use of existing and emerging digital tools and resources in support of student learning.
d. contribute to the effectiveness, vitality, and self-renewal of the teaching profession and of their school and community.

National Educational Technology Standards for Teachers, Second Edition, © 2008, ISTE® (International Society for Technology in Education, www.iste.org. All rights reserved.